P94 = Dōlōn Sln ...
    — Jrsh Hymc ...
  dsltn — Dc. 15 ...
P95 — Dhanaras
P4R — Jrsh Unta

Dramatists Sourcebook

1996–97 EDITION

Dramatists Sourcebook

1996-97 Edition

Complete opportunities for playwrights, translators, composers, lyricists and librettists

**EDITED BY
Kathy Sova
Wendy Weiner**

Theatre Communications Group • New York

Published by Theatre Communications Group, Inc.
355 Lexington Ave., New York, NY 10017-0217

Manufactured in the United States of America

ISSN 0733-1606
ISBN 1-55936-120-4

Contents

Preface

When planning this edition of the *Dramatists Sourcebook*, we were a bit nervous. How would the near collapse of federal and state arts funding affect the listings provided here? With great spirit and dedication, we set out to find new organizations that produce and support the work of playwrights, and to discover those that might have slipped through our fingers in past editions. We were able to add 90 new entries this year, expanding the *1996–97 Sourcebook* to more than 900 listings, more entries than ever before. Theatre is a resilient muscle. And though government funding has reduced, arts agencies and organizations have adapted and continue to offer programs and support to playwrights and the theatre community.

Each year, we work very hard to ensure that this guide is up-to-date and accurate. We contact every listing. Those we are unable to reach, we don't list. We want to make sure that we list only those organizations ready and able to assist you who write for the stage. Almost all entries are modified in some way, so please always work with the most recent *Sourcebook*. This year, we added E-mail and Web site addresses for those listings currently on-line. We also added "solo pieces" to our list of "types of material."

Select those listings your work is best suited for and follow the guidelines meticulously. The Special Interests Index is helpful in finding those listings that may be suited to your type of work. When instructed to write for guidelines, do so. Familiarize yourself with this guide and its many sections; each contains pertinent submission tips. Most important is ALWAYS to enclose an SASE with every mailed script, if you'd like it returned (unless the entry specifies that scripts will not be returned). If a listing accepts scripts, it is assumed that an SASE must be sent along; this is not stated in every listing.

Study—or restudy—Tony Kushner's guide to script submission. It's logical, current and filled with good advice.

You should know that throughout this book, "full-length play" means just that—a full-length, original work for adult audiences, without a score or libretto. One-acts, musicals, adaptations, translations, plays for young audiences, solo pieces and screenplays are listed separately. "Young audiences" refers to audiences age 18 or younger, "young playwrights" refers to playwrights age 18 or younger, "students" refers to college students or students in an affiliated writing program. Always assume the deadline dates in this book refer to the day materials should arrive, not the postmark date.

Entries are alphabetized by first word (excluding "the") even if the title starts with a proper name. So, for example, the Mark Taper Forum is listed under M. In the index, you will also find this theatre cross-listed under T. Regardless of the way "theatre" is spelled in an organization's title, we still alphabetize it as if it were spelled "re," not "er."

We are always trying to improve the *Sourcebook*, including new information in an easy-to-use format. And we'd like to hear from you. Is this book meeting your needs or are there any ways we can improve? Change the organization of material, clarify the language, add or delete information? In a way, we're like long-distance relatives who send you a graduation gift but never learn if it was what you wanted. Please E-mail to Sova@tcg.org or write to Kathy Sova at TCG, 355 Lexington Ave, New York, NY 10017. The experience of seeing a good new work performed in a theatre is unequaled and brings insurmountable joy. We wish you success and happiness and luck.

Many thanks to expert editor, Wendy Weiner, the grande dame of DSB and all its computer finery. Much gratitude to Robin Spaulding who as intern for the *Sourcebook* got quite an education. Thanks to all of you. Write!

Kathy Sova
July 1996

Prologue

A Simple Working Guide for Playwrights
by Tony Kushner

A) *Format:* Most playwrights use a format in which character headings are placed centered above the line and capitalized:

<u>LIONEL</u>

I don't possess a mansion, a car, or a string of polo ponies...

Lines should be one-and-a-half spaced. Stage directions should be indented and single-spaced. If a character's line is interrupted at the end of the page, its continuance on the following page should be marked as such:

<u>LIONEL</u> (cont'd)

or a string of polo ponies...

There are denser, and thus more economical, formats; since Xeroxing is expensive, and heavy scripts cost more to ship, you may be tempted to use these, but a generously spaced format is much easier to read, and in these matters it doesn't pay to be parsimonious.

B) *Typing and reproducing:* Scripts should be typed neatly and reproduced clearly. Remember that everyone who reads your script will be reading many others additionally, and it will work to your serious disadvantage if the copy's sloppy, faded, or otherwise unappealing. If you use a computer printer, eschew old-fashioned dot-matrix and other robotic kinds of print. Also, I think it's best to avoid using incredibly fancy word-processing printing programs with eight different typefaces and decorative borders. Simple typescript, carefully done, is best. Check for typos. A playwright's punctuation may be idiosyncratic for purposes of expressiveness, but not too idiosyncratic, and spelling should be correct.

C) *Sending the script:*

1) The script should have a title page with the title, your name, address and phone number, or that of your agent or representative. Scripts are now automatically copyrighted at the moment of creation, but simply writing © and the date on the title page can serve as a kind of scarecrow for thievish magpies.

2) Never, never send an unbound script. Loose pages held together by a rubber band don't qualify as bound, nor do pages clamped together with a mega-paperclip. A heavy paper cover will protect the script as it passes from hand to hand.

3) Always, always enclose a self-addressed stamped envelope (SASE) or you will never see your script again. You may enclose a note telling the theatre to dispose of the copy instead of returning it; but you must have the ultimate fate of the script planned for in the eventuality of its not being selected for production. Don't leave this up to the theatre! If you want receipt of the script acknowledged, include a self-addressed, stamped postcard (SASP).

D) *Letter of inquiry and synopsis:* If a theatre states, in its entry in the *Sourcebook*, that it does not accept unsolicited scripts, believe it. Don't call and ask if there are exceptions; there aren't. A well-written and concise letter of inquiry, however, accompanied by a synopsis possessed of similar virtues *can* get you an invitation to submit your play. It's prudent, then, to spend time on both letter and synopsis. It is, admittedly, very hard for a writer to sum up his or her work in less than a page, but this kind of boiling-down can be of value beyond its necessity as a tool for marketing; use it to help clarify for yourself what's central and essential about your play. A good synopsis should *briefly* summarize the basic features of the plot without going into excessive detail; it should evoke both the style and the thematic substance of the play without recourse to clichéd description ("This play is about what happens when people lose their dreams..."); and it should convey essential information, such as cast size, gender breakdown, period, location, or anything else a literary manager deciding whether to send for the play might want to know. Make reference to other productions in your letter, but don't send thick packets of reviews and photos. And don't offer your opinion of the play's worth, which will be inferred as being positive from the fact that you are its parent.

E) *Waiting:* Theatres almost always take a long time to respond to playwrights about a specific play, frequently far in excess of the time given in their listings in the *Sourcebook*. This is due neither to spite nor indolence. Literary departments are usually understaffed and their workload is fearsome. Then, too, the process of selection invariably involves a host of people and considerations of all kinds. In my opinion you do yourself no good by repeatedly calling after the status of your script; you will become identified as a pest. It's terribly expensive to copy and mail scripts, but you must be prepared to shoulder the expense and keep making copies if they don't get returned. If, after a certain length of time past the deadline, you haven't heard from a theatre, send a letter inquiring politely about the play, reminding the appropriate people that you'd sent an SASE with the script; and then forget about it. In most cases, you will get a response and the script returned eventually.

One way to cut down on the expenses involved is to be selective about venues for submission. Reading *Sourcebook* entries and scrutinizing a copy of *Theatre Profiles* (see Useful Publications) will help you select the theatres most compatible with your work. If you've written a musical celebration of the life of Phyllis Schlafly, for example, you won't want to send it to theatres with an interest in radical feminist dramas. Or you won't necessarily want to send your play about the history of Western imperialism to a theatre that produces an annual season of musical comedy.

F) *Produce yourself!* In *Endgame*, Clov asks Hamm, "Do you believe in the life to come?" and Hamm responds, "Mine was always that." The condition of endless deferment is one that modern American playwrights share with Beckett's characters and other denizens of the postmodern world. Don't spend your life waiting. You may not be an actor, but that doesn't mean that action is forbidden you. Playwrights can, with very little expense, mount readings of their work; they can band together with other playwrights for readings and discussions; and they can, if they want to, produce their work themselves. Growth as a writer for the stage depends on seeing your work on stage, and if no one else will put it there, the job is up to you. At the very least, and above all else, while waiting, waiting, waiting for responses and offers, keep reading, thinking and writing.

Tony Kushner's plays include *Angels in America, A Gay Fantasia on National Themes, Part One: Millennium Approaches* and *Part Two: Perestroika; A Bright Room Called Day; The Illusion*, freely adapted from Corneille's *L'Illusion Comique, Slavs!* (*Thinking About the Longstanding Problems of Virtue and Happiness*); and adaptations of Goethe's *Stella*, Brecht's *The Good Person of Setzuan* and Ansky's *The Dybbuk*. His work has been produced by theatres throughout the United States, including Mark Taper Forum, Public Theater/New York Shakespeare Festival, New York Theatre Workshop, Hartford Stage Company, Berkeley Repertory Theatre and Los Angeles Theatre Center, as well as other theatres around the country and abroad. *Angels in America* has been produced in over 30 countries. Mr. Kushner is the recipient of numerous awards, including the 1993 Pulitzer Prize for Drama.

Script Opportunities

- **Production**
- **Prizes**
- **Publication**
- **Development**

Production

What theatres are included in this section?

The overwhelming majority of the nonprofit professional theatres throughout the United States are represented here. In order to be included, a theatre must have been operating for at least two years and must meet professional standards of staffing, programming and budget. *Commercial and amateur producers are not included.*

How should I go about deciding where to submit my play?

Don't send it out indiscriminately. Take time to study the listings and select those theatres most likely to be receptive to your material. Find out all you can about each of the theatres you select. Look to TCG's *Theatre Profiles 12* for information on most of these theatres, including seasonal lists of plays each performed from 1993–95. Read *American Theatre* to see what plays the theatres are currently presenting and what their other activities are. (See Useful Publications for more information.) Whenever possible, go to see the theatre's work.

When I submit my play, what can I do to maximize its chances?

First, read carefully the Simple Working Guide for Playwrights in the Prologue of this *Sourcebook* for good advice on script submission. Then follow each theatre's guidelines meticulously. Pay particular attention to the Special Interests section: If a theatre specifies "gay and lesbian themes only," do not send them your heterosexual romantic comedy, however witty and well-written it is. Also, bear in mind the following points about the various submission procedures:

1) "Accepts unsolicited scripts": Don't waste the theatre's time and yours by writing to ask permission to submit your play—just send it. If you want an acknowledgment of receipt, say so and enclose a self-addressed stamped postcard (SASP) for this purpose. *Always* enclose a self-addressed stamped envelope (SASE) for the return of the script. Note that you may not receive any response to your work if you don't include this SASE. Many theatres enclose their response letter with the script when returning it.

2) "Synopsis and letter of inquiry": An increasing number of theatres require a synopsis rather than the script itself. Never send an unsolicited script to these theatres. Prepare a clear, cogent and *brief* synopsis of your play and send it along with any other materials requested in the listing. The letter of inquiry is a cover note asking for permission to submit the script; if there is something about your play or about yourself as a writer that you think may spark the theatre's interest, by all means mention it, but keep the letter brief. Unless the theatre specifies that it only responds if it wants to see the script, always enclose an SASP for the theatre's response.

3) "Professional recommendation": Send a script (not a letter of inquiry) accompanied by a letter of recommendation from a theatre professional. Wait until you can obtain such a letter before approaching these theatres.

4) "Agent submission": If you do not have an agent yet, do not submit to these theatres. Wait until you have had a production or two and have acquired a representative who can submit your script for you.

5) "Direct solicitation to playwright or agent": Do not submit to these theatres. If they are interested in your work you will hear from them!

Note that we've persuaded theatres requiring letters and synopses to give us two response times—one for letters and one for scripts they ask to see. All response times are average and approximate. Even if it takes the theatres longer to respond than they say it will, don't pester them; practice patience, and get on with your life and your art.

A CONTEMPORARY THEATRE

The Eagles Building, 700 Union St; Seattle, WA 98101-2330; (206) 292-7670,
    FAX 292-7670
Peggy Shannon, *Artistic Director*

Submission procedure: no unsolicited scripts; agent submission; will accept synopsis, 10 pages of dialogue and letter of inquiry from Northwest playwrights only. **Types of material:** full-length plays, one-acts, translations, adaptations, musicals, solo pieces. **Special interests:** current social, political and psychological issues; plays theatrical in imagination and execution; multicultural themes; not keen on "kitchen-sink" realism or "message" plays. **Facilities:** 390 seats, thrust stage; 390 seats, arena stage; 150 seats, cabaret. **Best submission time:** Sep–Apr. **Response time:** 1 month letter; 4–6 months script. **Special programs:** new play development workshops. FirstACT: play commissions and workshops for local playwrights. Young ACT Company: tours WA schools annually. Theatre As a Learning Tool: artist-led classroom workshops use drama to educate children in such issues as literacy and self-esteem.

A. D. PLAYERS

2710 West Alabama St; Houston, TX 77098; (713) 526-2721,
    FAX 439-0905
Literary Manager

Submission procedure: no unsolicited scripts; synopsis, resume and letter of inquiry. **Types of material:** full-length plays, one-acts, adaptations, plays for young audiences, musicals. **Special interests:** works that "state or affirm the centrality of God's love and power in the issue of life." **Facilities:** Grace Theater, 212 seats, proscenium stage. **Production considerations:** cast limit of 12, prefers less than 10; no more than 2 sets, maximum height 11′ 6″; no fly space, minimal lighting. **Best submission time:** year-round. **Response time:** 2 months letter; 12 months script. **Special programs:** staged reading series. Theater Arts Academy: includes playwriting classes; contact theatre for information.

ACADEMY THEATRE

501 Means St NW; Atlanta, GA 30318; (404) 525-4111, FAX 688-8009
Frank Wittow, *Artistic Director*

Submission procedure: accepts unsolicited scripts with bio and letter of inquiry with SASE for response; $20 fee or $10 fee for plays less than 20 minutes in length. **Types of material:** full-length plays, one-acts, solo pieces. **Special interests:** plays completed within last 2 years or plays-in-process; shorter works with current political themes; primarily by metro-Atlanta or Southeast-region playwrights. **Facilities:** Studio, 60 seats, black box. **Best submission time:** year-round. **Response time:** 3 months letter. **Special programs:** New Play Reading: most promising play-in-process receives rehearsed reading followed by audience discussion. New Play Workshop Production: most promising new play receives workshop production followed by audience discussion. New PlayShorts Revue: a touring series of short plays presented at various venues. Actors Ensemble. Theatre for Youth Touring

Company. Community Outreach Training Program. Academy Theatre New Play Development Program (see Development).

THE ACTING COMPANY

Box 898, Times Square Station; New York, NY 10108; (212) 564-3510,
     FAX 714-2643
Margot Harley, *Producing Director*
John Miller-Stephany, *Associate Producer*

Submission procedure: no unsolicited scripts; recommendation from professional familiar with company's work and goals. **Types of material:** full-length plays, one-acts, translations, adaptations, musicals. **Special interests:** mainly classical repertory but occasionally produces new works suited to acting ensemble of approximately 8 men, 3 women, age range 24–45; prefers works with poetic dimension and heightened language. **Facilities:** no permanent facility; touring company which plays in New York City for 1 or 2 weeks a year. **Production considerations:** productions tour in repertory; simple, transportable proscenium-stage set. **Best submission time:** Nov–Jan. **Response time:** 12 months.

ACTORS ALLEY

5269 Lankershim Blvd; North Hollywood, CA 91601; (818) 508-4200,
     FAX 508-5113
Jeremiah Morris, *Artistic Director*

Submission procedure: accepts unsolicited scripts. **Types of material:** full-length plays, one-acts, translations, adaptations, plays for young audiences. **Special interests:** works by southern CA-based writers. **Facilities:** Pavilion, 350 seats, proscenium/thrust stage; Circle Forum, 99 seats, flexible stage; Store Front Theatre, 42 seats, proscenium stage. **Production considerations:** small cast for Store Front. **Best submission time:** Nov. **Response time:** 12 months. **Special programs:** year-round reading series.

ACTORS ALLIANCE THEATRE COMPANY

Box 1579; Royal Oak, MI 48068-1579; (810) 559-4100, FAX 552-1225
Jeff Nahan, *Artistic Director*

Submission procedure: no unsolicited scripts; synopsis and letter of inquiry. **Types of material:** full-length plays, adaptations, plays for young audiences. **Facilities:** Millennium Theatre Center, 499 seats, thrust stage; Studio Space, 49 seats, flexible stage. **Production considerations:** simple set; no fly or wing space. **Best submission time:** Oct–Feb. **Response time:** 1–2 months letter; 3 months script.

ACTORS & PLAYWRIGHTS' INITIATIVE

Box 50051; Kalamazoo, MI 49005-0051; (616) 343-8310, FAX 343-8310
Robert C. Walker, *Artistic Director*

Submission procedure: no unsolicited scripts; synopsis, resume and letter of inquiry with SASE for response. **Types of material:** full-length plays, one-acts, translations, adaptations, plays for young audiences, musicals, solo pieces. **Special interests:** aggressive and provocative social-political plays; plays that explore heterosexual, gay and bisexual relationships. **Facilities:** API Theatre, 60 seats, thrust stage. **Production considerations:** cast limit of 10; minimal set, costumes, props; no fly space. **Best submission time:** Oct–Feb. **Response time:** 2 months letter; 6 months script. **Special programs:** Firstage Script Development Reader's Theatre: developmental year-round reading series.

THE ACTOR'S EXPRESS

King Plow Arts Center, J-107; 887 West Marietta St NW; Atlanta, GA 30318;
(404) 875-1606
Literary Manager

Submission procedure: no unsolicited scripts; synopsis and letter of inquiry, accompanied by professional recommendation if possible. **Types of material:** full-length plays, translations, adaptations, musicals. **Special interests:** socially relevant material; minority and gay themes; works with poetic dimension. **Facilities:** Actor's Express, 200 seats, black box. **Production considerations:** no fly space. **Best submission time:** Nov–Jan. **Response time:** 1 month letter; 4–6 months script.

ACTORS' GANG THEATER

6201 Santa Monica Blvd; Hollywood, CA 90038; (213) 465-0566,
FAX 467-1245; E-mail mksd@aol.com
Jason Reed, *Submissions Coordinator*

Submission procedure: no unsolicited scripts; direct solicitation to agent. **Types of material:** full-length plays, plays for young audiences. **Special interests:** highly theatrical political or avant-garde works. **Facilities:** Actors' Gang Theater, 99 seats, flexible stage; Actors' Gang Workshop Space, 30 seats, flexible stage. **Response time:** 1 month.

THE ACTORS THEATER

Box 5858; Providence, RI 02903; (401) 823-0203
David Tulli, *Associate Artistic Director*

Submission procedure: accepts unsolicited scripts. **Types of material:** full-length plays, one-acts, solo pieces, performance art (short pieces only). **Special interests:** works that "provide hopeful, innovative solutions to social and cultural problems." **Facilities:** Columbus Theater, 200 seats, thrust stage. **Production considerations:** minimal production demands. **Best submission time:** year-round. **Response time:** 1–2 months. **Special programs:** Men's Stories Short Play Festival: festival of plays 10–30 min in length that depict "nonstereotypical men" exploring feelings about relationships, sex, self-image and violence; selected plays are given full production in annual fall festival; *deadline:* 1 Oct 1996; *dates:* fall 1996.

ACTORS THEATRE OF LOUISVILLE

316 West Main St; Louisville, KY 40202-4218; (502) 584-1265, FAX 561-3300
Michael Bigelow Dixon, *Literary Manager*
Michele Volansky, *Assistant Literary Manager*

Submission procedure: accepts unsolicited 10-page one-acts for contest only (see below); professional recommendation for all other plays. **Types of material:** full-length plays, one-acts, translations, adaptations, solo pieces. **Special interests:** plays of ideas; language-oriented plays; passion, humor and experimentation. **Facilities:** Pamela Brown Auditorium, 637 seats, thrust stage; Bingham Theatre, 340 seats, arena stage; Victor Jory Theatre, 159 seats, 3/4-arena stage. **Best submission time:** year-round. **Response time:** 6–9 months (most scripts returned in fall). **Special programs:** National Ten-Minute Play Contest (see Prizes).

ALABAMA SHAKESPEARE FESTIVAL

1 Festival Dr; Montgomery, AL 36117-4605; (334) 271-5300
Kent Thompson, *Artistic Director*
Eric Schmiedl, *Literary Associate*

Submission procedure: accepts unsolicited scripts with letter of inquiry for Southern Writers' Project only (see below); agent submission for all other plays. **Types of material:** full-length plays, adaptations, plays for young audiences. **Special interests:** new plays with southern or African-American themes, especially plays dealing with the Civil Rights movement; plays for young audiences. **Facilities:** Festival Stage, 750 seats, modified thrust stage; Octagon, 225 seats, flexible space. **Best submission time:** year-round. **Response time:** 2 months letter; 8–10 months script. **Special programs:** Southern Writers' Project: project to commission and develop plays based on southern and/or African-American issues; address submissions to Southern Writers' Project.

ALLEY THEATRE

615 Texas Ave; Houston, TX 77002; (713) 228-9341
Gregory Boyd, *Artistic Director*

Submission procedure: no unsolicited scripts; professional recommendation. **Types of material:** full-length plays, translations, adaptations, musicals. **Facilities:** Main Stage, 800 seats, thrust stage; Arena Stage, 300 seats, arena stage. **Best submission time:** year-round. **Response time:** 2–6 months.

ALLIANCE THEATRE COMPANY

1280 Peachtree St NE; Atlanta, GA 30309; (404) 733-4650,
        FAX 733-4625
Literary Department

Submission procedure: no unsolicited scripts; synopsis, dialogue sample if possible, and letter of inquiry. **Types of material:** full-length plays, musicals. **Special interests:** new musicals; southern themes; works that deal with moral and/or spiritual questions of life in multicultural America. **Facilities:** Alliance Theatre,

864 seats, proscenium stage; Studio Theatre, 200 seats, flexible stage. **Best submission time:** Mar–Sep. **Response time:** 1–2 months letter; 6 months script.

AMAS MUSICAL THEATRE, INC.

450 West 42nd St, Suite 2J; New York, NY 10036; (212) 563-2565,
    FAX 268-5501
Rosetta LeNoire, *Founder/Artistic Director*

Submission procedure: accepts unsolicited scripts. **Types of material:** musicals, cabaret/revues. **Special interests:** multicultural casts and themes. **Facilities:** no permanent facility; company performs in various proscenium or black box venues with 74–99 seats. **Production considerations:** cast limit of 15. **Best submission time:** summer, winter. **Response time:** 3–6 months. **Special programs:** The AMAS Six O'Clock Musical Theatre Lab: a reading series for new musicals open to composers, lyricists and librettists; writer must supply cast and musical director; AMAS provides theatre and publicity.

AMERICAN CONSERVATORY THEATER

30 Grant Ave, 6th Floor; San Francisco, CA 94108-5800; (415) 834-3200,
    FAX 834-3360
Literary Manager

Submission procedure: no unsolicited scripts; agents and theatre professionals only may send synopsis, maximum 10 pages of dialogue and letter of inquiry. **Types of material:** full-length plays, translations, adaptations. **Special interests:** theatre plans to work with selected playwrights on company projects and adaptations. **Facilities:** Geary Theater, 1,000 seats, proscenium stage. **Best submission time:** year-round. **Response time:** 1–2 months letter; 3 months script.

AMERICAN JEWISH THEATRE

307 West 26th St; New York, NY 10001; (212) 633-9797
Martin Blank, *Artistic Associate*

Submission procedure: accepts unsolicited scripts. **Types of material:** full-length plays, musicals. **Special interests:** works with Jewish themes. **Facilities:** American Jewish Theatre, 150 seats, flexible stage. **Production considerations:** cast limit of 8. **Best submission time:** year-round. **Response time:** 3 months.

AMERICAN MUSIC THEATER FESTIVAL

123 South Broad St, 25th Floor; Philadelphia, PA 19109; (215) 893-1570,
    FAX 893-1233; E-mail amtf.libertynet.org
Ben Levit, *Artistic Director*

Submission procedure: no unsolicited scripts; direct solicitation to playwright or agent. **Types of material:** music-theatre works including musical comedy, music drama, opera, experimental works, solo pieces. **Special interests:** contemporary music works using popular forms and styles, e.g., country and western, jazz, Cuban rhythms; works by minority writers. **Facilities:** Walnut Street Theatre, 1050 seats, proscenium stage; Annenberg Center's Zellerbach Theatre, 900 seats, thrust stage; Plays and Players Theatre, 300 seats, proscenium stage.

THE AMERICAN PLACE THEATRE
111 West 46th St; New York, NY 10036; (212) 840-2960
Literary Department

Submission procedure: no unsolicited scripts; synopsis, first 20 pages of script and letter of inquiry with SASE for response. **Types of material:** full-length plays, adaptations, performance art. **Special interests:** works by American playwrights only; works innovative in form and perspective; multicultural themes. **Facilities:** Main Stage, 180–299 seats, flexible stage; Cabaret Space, 75 seats, flexible stage; First Floor Theatre, 75 seats, flexible stage. **Best submission time:** Sep–Jun. **Response time:** 2 months letter; 3–4 months script. **Special programs:** The Humor Hatchery: developmental program of humorous plays by American playwrights. American Humorist Series: development of works by or about American humorists. First Floor Theatre: program of new experimental works and performance pieces.

AMERICAN REPERTORY THEATRE
64 Brattle St; Cambridge, MA 02138; (617) 495-2668
Steven Maler, *Artistic Associate*

Submission procedure: no unsolicited scripts; agent submission. **Types of material:** full-length plays, translations, adaptations, musicals, cabaret/revues. **Special interests:** prefers plays "which lend themselves to poetic use of the stage." **Facilities:** Loeb Drama Center, 556 seats, flexible stage; 12 Holyoke Street, 350 seats, proscenium stage; 0 Church Street, 200 seats, black box. **Production considerations:** cast limit of 15.

AMERICAN STAGE
Box 1560; St. Petersburg, FL 33731; (813) 823-1600, FAX 823-7529
Lisa Powers, *Artistic Director*

Submission procedure: no unsolicited scripts; professional recommendation. **Types of material:** full-length plays, adaptations, plays for young audiences. **Facilities:** American Stage, 130 seats, thrust stage. **Production considerations:** cast limit of 6; 1 set. **Best submission time:** year-round. **Response time:** 3 months letter; 12 months script. **Special programs:** New Visions: new play festival.

AMERICAN STAGE COMPANY
Box 336; Teaneck, NJ 07666
James Vagias, *Executive Producer*

Submission procedure: no unsolicited scripts. **Types of material:** full-length plays, musicals. **Facilities:** American Stage in Residence at Fairleigh Dickinson University, 270 seats, proscenium stage. **Production considerations:** cast limit of 6–8.

AMERICAN STAGE FESTIVAL
Box 225; Milford, NH 03055-0225; FAX (603) 889-2336
Attn: New Scripts, EARLY STAGES

Submission procedure: no unsolicited scripts; synopsis, 10 pages of dialogue and letter of inquiry with SASE for response; include cassette of 2–3 songs for musicals. **Types of material:** full-length plays, musicals. **Special interests:** material with strong emotional content that tells a compelling story; material that encourages new theatrical techniques and a new sense of theatrical reality. **Facilities:** American Stage Festival, 497 seats, proscenium stage. **Production considerations:** cast limit of 10 for plays, 15 plus 5 musicians for musicals. **Best submission time:** Sep–Dec. **Response time:** 2–3 months letter; 4–6 months script.

AMERICAN THEATRE OF ACTORS, INC.
314 West 54th St; New York, NY 10019; (212) 581-3044
James Jennings, *Artistic Director*

Submission procedure: accepts unsolicited scripts. **Types of material:** full-length plays, one-acts. **Facilities:** Chernuchin Theatre, 140 seats, proscenium stage; Sargent Theatre, 65 seats, proscenium stage; Beckmann Theatre, 35 seats, arena stage. **Production considerations:** cast limit of 8; minimal sets. **Best submission time:** year-round. **Response time:** 2 weeks.

APPLE TREE THEATRE
595 Elm Pl, Suite 210; Highland Park, IL 60035; (847) 432-8223,
    FAX 432-5214
Beth Larson, *Literary Manager*

Submission procedure: no unsolicited scripts; will accept synopsis and letter of inquiry; include cassette for musicals. **Types of material:** full-length plays, adaptations, plays for young audiences, musicals. **Facilities:** Apple Tree Theatre, 171 seats, modified thrust stage. **Production considerations:** cast limit of 9, unit set. **Best submission time:** year-round. **Response time:** 1 month letter; 4 months script. **Special programs:** staged readings.

ARDEN THEATRE COMPANY
40 North 2nd St; Philadelphia, PA 19106; (215) 922-8900;
    Web http://www.libertynet.org/~arden
Terrence J. Nolen, *Producing Artistic Director*
Aaron Posner, *Artistic Director*

Submission procedure: no unsolicited scripts; synopsis and letter of inquiry. **Types of material:** full-length plays, translations, adaptations, musicals. **Special interests:** new adaptations of literary works. **Facilities:** Mainstage, 400 seats, flexible stage; Arcadia Stage/Studio Theatre, 175 seats, flexible stage. **Best submission time:** year-round. **Response time:** 3 months letter; 6 months script.

ARENA STAGE

6th and Maine Ave SW; Washington, DC 20024; (202) 554-9066, FAX 488-4056
Cathy Madison, *Literary Manager*

Submission procedure: no unsolicited scripts; synopsis, 10 pages of dialogue, bio and letter of inquiry. **Types of material:** full-length plays, translations, adaptations, musicals. **Special interests:** unproduced works only; plays for a multicultural company; plays by women and writers of color. **Facilities:** Fichandler Stage, 827 seats, arena stage; The Kreeger Theater, 514 seats, modified thrust stage; The Old Vat Room, 110 seats, cabaret stage. **Best submission time:** spring–early fall. **Response time:** 1 day letter; 6 months script. **Special programs:** PlayQuest (see Development).

ARIZONA THEATRE COMPANY

Box 1631; Tucson, AZ 85702-1631; (520) 884-8210
Rebecca Million, *Literary Manager*

Submission procedure: accepts unsolicited scripts from Southwest playwrights only. **Types of material:** full-length plays, translations, adaptations, musicals. **Facilities:** Herberger Theater Center (in Phoenix), 800 seats, proscenium stage; Temple of Music and Art (in Tucson), 600 seats, proscenium stage. **Best submission time:** spring–summer. **Response time:** 6–12 months. **Special programs:** New Play Reading Series: rehearsed readings followed by discussion with audience. National Hispanic Playwriting Contest (see Prizes).

ARKANSAS REPERTORY THEATRE

Box 110; Little Rock, AR 72203-0110; (501) 378-0445, FAX 378-0012
Brad Mooy, *Literary Manager*

Submission procedure: no unsolicited scripts; synopsis and letter of inquiry. **Types of material:** full-length plays, musicals, cabaret/revues, solo pieces. **Facilities:** Arkansas Repertory Theatre, 354 seats, proscenium stage; Second Stage, 99 seats, black box. **Production considerations:** prefers small cast. **Best submission time:** year-round. **Response time:** 3 months letter; 3 months script. **Special programs:** New Playreading Series.

ARROW ROCK LYCEUM THEATRE

High St; Arrow Rock, MO 65320; (816) 837-3311, FAX (573) 815-7564
Michael Bollinger, *Artistic Producing Director*

Submission procedure: no unsolicited scripts; direct solicitation to playwright or agent. **Types of material:** full-length plays, translations, adaptations, musicals. **Facilities:** Arrow Rock Lyceum Theatre, 410 seats, semithrust stage.

ART STATION

Box 1998; Stone Mountain, GA 30086; (770) 469-1105, FAX 469-0355
Pamella McClure, *Literary Manager*

Submission procedure: accepts unsolicited scripts. **Types of material:** full-length plays, adaptations, musicals, solo pieces. **Special interests:** new works by southern playwrights. **Facilities:** Art Station Theatre, 100 seats, proscenium/thrust stage. **Production considerations:** cast limit of 6; single set; no fly space. **Best submission time:** Jun–Dec. **Response time:** 2 months. **Special programs:** I.T.C. Playwrights Project: year-round playwrights group meets bimonthly to critique and develop new works; presents quarterly staged readings.

ARTISTS REPERTORY THEATRE

1111 Southwest 10th Ave; Portland, OR 97205; (503) 294-7373
Allen Nause, *Artistic Director*

Submission procedure: no unsolicited scripts; synopsis and letter of inquiry. **Types of material:** full-length plays, adaptations. **Facilities:** Winningstadt Theatre, 275 seats, flexible stage; Wilson Center for the Performing Arts, 110 seats, thrust stage. **Production considerations:** cast limit of 10, 1 set or unit set. **Best submission time:** year-round. **Response time:** 6 months. **Special programs:** Play Lab: staged reading series.

ARTREACH TOURING THEATRE

3074 Madison Rd; Cincinnati, OH 45209; (513) 871-2300, FAX 871-2501
Kathryn Schultz Miller, *Artistic Director*

Submission procedure: accepts unsolicited scripts. **Types of material:** plays for young audiences. **Special interests:** intelligent, well-plotted plays; subjects not usually explored in children's theatre, e.g., Vietnam, Hiroshima. **Facilities:** touring company. **Production considerations:** cast limit of 3; plays must be 50–60 minutes in length and easy to tour. **Best submission time:** Jan–Mar. **Response time:** 3 months.

ARTS AT ST. ANN'S

157 Montague St; Brooklyn, NY 11201; (718) 834-8794, FAX 522-2470
Susan Feldman, *Artistic Director*

Submission procedure: no unsolicited scripts; synopsis and letter of inquiry. **Types of material:** full-length plays, musicals. **Special interests:** musical theatre works. **Facilities:** Church of St. Ann and Holy Trinity, 652 seats, flexible stage; Parish Hall, 100 seats, flexible stage. **Best submission time:** year-round. **Response time:** 2 months letter; 3 months script.

ASIAN AMERICAN THEATER COMPANY

403 Arguello Blvd; San Francisco, CA 94118; FAX (415) 751-3842
Karen Amano, *Artistic Director*

Submission procedure: accepts unsolicited scripts with synopsis, character breakdown, resume and letter of inquiry. **Types of material:** full-length plays, adaptations, plays for young audiences. **Special interests:** plays that explore diversity of the Asian-Pacific–American experience. **Facilities:** Mainstage, 130 seats, proscenium stage; Second Stage, 40 seats, black box. **Production considerations:** cast limit of 8. **Best submission time:** year-round. **Response time:** 3–6 months.

ASOLO THEATRE COMPANY

Asolo Center for the Performing Arts; 5555 North Tamiami Trail;
    Sarasota, FL 34243; (941) 351-9010, FAX 351-5796;
    E-mail brodge@netline.net
Bruce E. Rodgers, *Associate Artistic Director*

Submission procedure: no unsolicited scripts; 1-page synopsis and letter of inquiry with SASE for response. **Types of material:** full-length plays, translations, adaptations, solo pieces. **Facilities:** The Mertz Theatre, 499 seats, proscenium stage; The Conservatory Theatre, 161 seats, proscenium stage. **Best submission time:** Jun–Aug. **Response time:** 2 months letter; 6 months script.

ATLANTIC THEATER COMPANY

336 West 20th St; New York, NY 10011; (212) 645-8015, FAX 645-8755
Neil Pepe, *Artistic Director*

Submission procedure: no unsolicited scripts; agent submission. **Types of material:** full-length plays, one-acts, adaptations. **Facilities:** Atlantic Theater, 150 seats, proscenium stage.

BAILIWICK REPERTORY

1229 West Belmont; Chicago, IL 60657-3205; (312) 883-1090
David Zak, *Executive Director*
Cecilie D. Keenan, *Artistic Director*

Submission procedure: send SASE for manuscript submission guidelines. **Types of material:** full-length plays, translations, adaptations, musicals, solo pieces. **Special interests:** translations and adaptations; theatrically inventive and/or politically intriguing works; plays by women for Women's Work series. **Facilities:** Bailiwick Arts Center: mainstage, 160 seats, flexible/thrust stage; cabaret/studio, 100 seats, flexible stage. **Best submission time:** year-round. **Response time:** 4 months. **Special programs:** note: all playwrights submitting to these programs must first send SASE for manuscript submission guidelines. Pride Performance Series: year-round exploration of works of interest to the lesbian and gay communities, culminating in summer festival. New Directions Series: fully staged performances of works that experiment boldly with form and content. Director's Festival: annual directors' showcase of 48 plays, 10–50 minutes long, staged in black-box setting. Studio series to include workshops and readings of plays, performance pieces and musicals to be instituted during 1996–97.

BARKSDALE THEATRE

Box 7; Hanover, VA 23069; (804) 537-5201
John Glenn, *Artistic Director*

Submission procedure: no unsolicited scripts; synopsis and letter of inquiry. **Types of material:** full-length plays, one-acts, translations, adaptations, plays for young audiences, musicals, cabaret/revues, solo pieces. **Facilities:** Hanover Tavern, 199 seats, thrust stage. **Production considerations:** small cast, minimal production demands; no fly or wing space. **Best submission time:** summer. **Response time:** 2 months letter; 6 months script.

THE BARROW GROUP

Box 5112; New York, NY 10185; (212) 522-1421, FAX 522-1402
Steve Vierk, *Company Manager*

Submission procedure: no unsolicited scripts; professional recommendation. **Types of material:** full-length plays, translations, adaptations. **Facilities:** no permanent facility. **Production considerations:** cast limit of 12; minimal sets. **Best submission time:** year-round. **Response time:** 1 month letter; 6 months script.

BARTER THEATRE

Box 867; Abingdon, VA 24210-0867; (540) 628-2281, FAX 628-4551
Richard Rose, *Producing Artistic Director*

Submission procedure: no unsolicited scripts; synopsis, dialogue sample and letter of inquiry. **Types of material:** full-length plays, translations, adaptations, plays for young audiences. **Special interests:** social issues and current events; works that expand theatrical form. **Facilities:** Barter Theatre, 508 seats, proscenium stage; Barter's Stage II, 150 seats, flexible stage. **Production considerations:** cast of 4–12. **Best submission time:** Mar, Sep. **Response time:** 6 months letter; 9 months script. **Special programs:** Barter's Early Stages: script development program.

BAY STREET THEATRE

Box 810; Sag Harbor, NY 11963; (516) 725-0818, FAX 725-0906;
    Web http://www.baystreet.org
Mia Emlen Grosjean, *Literary Manager*

Submission procedure: no unsolicited scripts; agent submission. **Types of material:** full-length plays, musicals, solo pieces. **Special interests:** plays that challenge as well as entertain; plays that "address the heart of our community and champion the human spirit." **Facilities:** Mainstage, 299 seats, thrust stage. **Production considerations:** cast limit of 8–9; prefers unit set; no fly or wing space; small-scale musicals only. **Best submission time:** year-round. **Response time:** 3–6 months. **Special programs:** Reading series: readings of 2 new plays each fall and spring; playwright receives $50 honorarium and travel from New York City; scripts for special programs selected through theatre's normal submission procedure.

BERKELEY REPERTORY THEATRE

2025 Addison St; Berkeley, CA 94704; (510) 204-8901, FAX 841-7711;
E-mail litman@berkeleyrep.com
Tony Kelly, *Literary Manager*

Submission procedure: no unsolicited scripts; agent submission. **Types of material:** full-length plays, translations, adaptations. **Facilities:** Mark Taper Mainstage, 400 seats, thrust stage. **Best submission time:** Sep–May. **Response time:** 4–6 months. **Special programs:** Parallel Season: productions of 2–3 new plays each season. Commissioning program. In-house readings.

BERKSHIRE THEATRE FESTIVAL

Box 797; Stockbridge, MA 01262; (413) 298-5536, FAX 298-3368
Arthur Storch, *Artistic Director*

Submission procedure: no unsolicited scripts; agent submission. **Types of material:** full-length plays, one-acts, musicals, solo pieces. **Special interests:** thought-provoking vacation entertainment; theatre on the "cutting edge." **Facilities:** Playhouse, 413 seats, proscenium stage; Unicorn Theatre, 99 seats, thrust stage. **Production considerations:** cast limit of 8 for plays; small orchestra for musicals; prefers simple set. **Best submission time:** Nov–Dec. **Response time:** 3 months. **Special programs:** staged reading series.

BILINGUAL FOUNDATION OF THE ARTS

421 North Ave 19; Los Angeles, CA 90031; (213) 225-4044, FAX 225-1250
Guillermo Reyes, *Dramaturg/Literary Manager*

Submission procedure: accepts unsolicited scripts. **Types of material:** full-length plays, translations, adaptations, plays for young audiences. **Special interests:** plays with Hispanic themes or by Hispanic playwrights only. **Facilities:** BFA's Little Theatre, 99 seats, thrust stage; uses theatres at Los Angeles Center for the Arts for some mainstage productions. **Production considerations:** cast limit of 10, simple set. **Best submission time:** year-round. **Response time:** 3–6 months.

BIRMINGHAM CHILDREN'S THEATRE

Box 1362; Birmingham, AL 35201; (205) 324-0470, FAX 324-0494
Charlotte Lane Dominick, *Executive Director*

Submission procedure: accepts scripts; prefers synopsis and letter of inquiry. **Types of material:** plays for young audiences. **Special interests:** interactive plays for preschool–grade 2; presentational plays for K–6. **Facilities:** Birmingham-Jefferson Civic Center Theatre, 1073 seats, thrust stage; Studio Theatre, up to 250 seats, lab space. **Production considerations:** prefers cast of 4–6. **Best submission time:** Sep–Dec. **Response time:** 2 weeks letter; several months script.

BLOOMSBURG THEATRE ENSEMBLE

Box 66; Bloomsburg, PA 17815; (717) 784-5530, FAX 784-4912
Tom Byrn, *Play Selection Chair*

Submission procedure: no unsolicited scripts; synopsis, dialogue sample, letter of recommendation from theatre professional and letter of inquiry. **Types of material:** full-length plays, translations, adaptations. **Special interests:** new translations of classics; plays suitable for 9-member acting ensemble. **Facilities:** Alvina Krause Theatre, 369 seats, proscenium stage. **Production considerations:** small to mid-sized cast, 1 set or unit set. **Best submission time:** year-round. **Response time:** 3 months letter; 6 months script.

BOARSHEAD: MICHIGAN PUBLIC THEATER

425 South Grand Ave; Lansing, MI 48933; (517) 484-7800
John Peakes, *Artistic Director*

Submission procedure: no unsolicited scripts; synopsis, character breakdown, 10 pages of dialogue and letter of inquiry with SASP for response. **Types of material:** full-length plays, plays for young audiences. **Special interests:** plays that make use of theatrical conventions or create new ones; social issues; comedies. **Facilities:** Center for the Arts, 249 seats, thrust stage. **Best submission time:** year-round. **Response time:** 1 month letter; 3–6 months script. **Special programs:** staged readings of 5 new plays a year.

BORDERLANDS THEATER

Box 2791; Tucson, AZ 85702; (520) 882-8607, FAX 882-7406 (call first)

Submission procedure: no unsolicited scripts; synopsis and letter of iquiry. **Types of material:** full-length plays, translations, adaptations. **Special interests:** cultural diversity; race relations; "border" issues, including concerns of the geographical border region as well as the metaphorical borders of gender, class and race. **Facilities:** Pima Community College Center for the Arts: 1st theatre, 400 seats, proscenium stage; 2nd theatre, 160 seats, black box. **Production considerations:** cast limit of 12, minimal set. **Best submission time:** year-round. **Response time:** 3–6 months. **Special programs:** Border Playwrights Project (see Development).

BRAVE NEW WORKSHOP & INSTANT THEATRE COMPANY

2605 Hennepin Ave S; Minneapolis, MN 55408-1150; (612) 377-8445,
    FAX 377-8472
Dudley Riggs, *Producing Director*
Linda Jacobs, *Associate Producer*

Submission procedure: accepts unsolicited scripts with synopsis and letter of inquiry; include cassette for musicals. **Types of material:** capsule musicals/songs, cabaret/revues, solo pieces, comedy sketches. **Special interests:** current-event-driven satirical revues. **Facilities:** Dudley Riggs Theatre, 230 seats, modified thrust stage. **Production considerations:** cast limit of 7; minimal production demands; small stage. **Best submission time:** year-round. **Response time:** 6 months.

BRISTOL RIVERSIDE THEATRE
Box 1250; Bristol, PA 19007; (215) 785-6664, FAX 785-2762
David J. Abers, *Assistant to Artistic Director*

Submission procedure: accepts unsolicited scripts. **Types of material:** full-length plays, one-acts, translations, adaptations, musicals, solo pieces, performance art. **Special interests:** cutting-edge works; plays that experiment with form; translations; musicals. **Facilities:** Bristol Riverside Theatre, 302 seats, flexible stage. **Production considerations:** cast limit of 10 for plays, 18 for musicals, 9 for orchestra; minimal production demands. **Best submission time:** spring. **Response time:** 4–6 months letter; 6–8 months script. **Special programs:** year-round reading series.

CALIFORNIA REPERTORY COMPANY
1250 Bellflower Blvd; Long Beach, CA 90840; (310) 985-5357, FAX 985-2263
Ron Lindblom, *Associate Artistic Producing Director*

Submission procedure: direct solicitation to playwright or agent. **Types of material:** full-length plays, translations, adaptations. **Special interests:** international works. **Facilities:** UT Theatre, 400 seats, proscenium stage; Studio Theatre, 225 seats, flexible stage; Cal Rep Theatre, 90 seats, proscenium stage. **Production considerations:** cast of 8–18. **Best submission time:** Sep, Mar. **Response time:** 3 weeks letter; 2 months script.

CALIFORNIA THEATRE CENTER
Box 2007; Sunnyvale, CA 94087; (408) 245-2979, FAX 245-0235
Will Huddleston, *Resident Director*

Submission procedure: accepts unsolicited scripts; prefers synopsis and letter of inquiry. **Types of material:** plays for young audiences. **Special interests:** classics adapted for young audiences; comedies; historical material. **Facilities:** company primarily tours to large proscenium-stage theatres; home base: Sunnyvale Performing Arts Center, 200 seats, proscenium stage. **Production considerations:** cast limit of 8 for professional touring productions; minimum cast of 15 for conservatory productions; modest production demands. **Best submission time:** year-round. **Response time:** 4–6 months.

CAPITAL REPERTORY COMPANY
Box 399; Albany, NY 12201-0399; (518) 462-4531, FAX 465-0213

Submission procedure: no unsolicited scripts; agent submission. **Types of material:** full-length plays, translations, adaptations, music-theatre works. **Facilities:** Market Theatre, 299 seats, thrust stage. **Production considerations:** cast limit of 10, simple set; modest musical requirements. **Best submission time:** late spring. **Response time:** 4–6 months.

CAPITOL CITY PLAYHOUSE

214 West 4th St; Austin, TX 78701; (512) 472-1855, FAX 472-4737
Emily Ball Cicchini, *Associate Artistic Director*

Submission procedure: accepts unsolicited scripts from Texas playwrights only; all others send synopsis and letter of inquiry. **Types of material:** full-length plays, adaptations, musicals, cabaret/revues. **Special interests:** innovative, well-structured plays with powerful images and language; social themes; historical subjects. **Facilities:** Capitol City Playhouse, 200 seats, thrust stage. **Production considerations:** prefers minimal production demands. **Best submission time:** Aug, Dec. **Response time:** 2 weeks letter; 2 months script. **Special programs:** Imagewrighters/New Play Development Program: monthly reading series in spring and fall; plays selected from program receive workshop production and possible full production with $500 royalty; scripts selected through theatre's regular submission process; *deadline:* 15 Dec 1996 for spring, 15 Aug 1997 for fall. Texas Young Playwrights Festival: developmental workshops of plays by Texan playwrights 19 or younger; selected plays receive full production; write or call for details: Texas Young Playwrights Festival, Dougherty Arts Center, 1110 Barton Springs Rd, Austin, TX 78704, (512) 397-1457; *deadline:* 2 Feb 1997.

THE CAST THEATRE

804 North El Centro Ave; Hollywood, CA 90038; (213) 462-0265
Literary Manager

Submission procedure: accepts unsolicited scripts. **Types of material:** full-length plays. **Special interests:** previously unproduced works. **Facilities:** Cast of the Circle, 99 seats, proscenium stage; Cast, 65 seats, proscenium stage. **Best submission time:** year-round. **Response time:** 6 months

CASTILLO THEATRE

500 Greenwich St, Suite 201; New York, NY 10013; (212) 941-5800,
        FAX 941-8340; E-mail street@pipeline.com; Web http://www.castillo.org
Fred Newman, *Artistic Director*

Submission procedure: no unsolicited scripts; synopsis, 5–10 page dialogue sample and letter of inquiry; prefers playwright see theatre production before submitting. **Types of material:** full-length plays, one-acts. **Special interests:** plays that address social, cultural and political concerns and challenge theatrical and social convention; multiracial/multicultural issues. **Facilities:** Castillo Theatre, 71 seats, 3/4-arena stage. **Best submission time:** year-round. **Response time:** 2 months letter; 6 months script. **Special programs:** weekly playwriting workshop in spring; contact Dan Friedman, dramaturg, for information.

CENTER STAGE

700 North Calvert St; Baltimore, MD 21202-3686; (410) 685-3200,
    FAX 539-3912
James Magruder, *Resident Dramaturg*

Submission procedure: no unsolicited scripts; synopsis, sample pages and letter of inquiry. **Types of material:** full-length plays, translations, adaptations, music-theatre works, solo pieces. **Facilities:** Pearlstone Theater, 541 seats, modified thrust stage; Head Theater, 100–400 seats, flexible space. **Best submission time:** year-round. **Response time:** 5–7 weeks letter; 4–6 months script.

CENTER THEATER ENSEMBLE

1346 West Devon Ave; Chicago, IL 60660; (312) 508-0200
Dale Calandra, *Literary Manager*

Submission procedure: no unsolicited scripts; synopsis, resume and letter of inquiry with SASE for response. **Types of material:** full-length plays, translations, adaptations, musicals, solo pieces. **Special interests:** comedies; plays creating a heightened reality; language-oriented plays; dramas of substance; original musicals only. **Facilities:** Mainstage, 75 seats, modified thrust stage; Studio, 35 seats, black box. **Production considerations:** cast limit of approximately 12; limited wing space, no fly loft. **Best submission time:** year-round. **Response time:** 3 months letter; 3 months script. **Special programs:** Playwrights Workshop Series: participation by invitation only. Actor/Director/Playwright Unit: participants meet monthly to work on scripts; some scripts given staged reading, possibly leading to 2-week developmental workshop and performances and/or full production; participants selected through personal interview; Chicago-area playwrights contact Dale Calandra, Workshop Coordinator, for appointment. Center Theater International Playwrighting Contest (see Prizes).

THE CHANGING SCENE

1527½ Champa St; Denver, CO 80202; (303) 893-5775
Maxine Munt, *Literary Manager*

Submission procedure: accepts unsolicited scripts. **Types of material:** full-length plays, performance art. **Special interests:** nonrealistic plays. **Facilities:** The Changing Scene, 76 seats, black box. **Production considerations:** cast limit of 10; prefers single adjustable set. **Best submission time:** year-round. **Response time:** 4–6 months.

CHARLOTTE REPERTORY THEATRE

2040 Charlotte Plaza; Charlotte, NC 28244; (704) 333-8587, FAX 333-0224
Claudia Carter Covington, *Literary Manager*

Submission procedure: accepts unsolicited scripts. **Types of material:** professionally unproduced full-length plays; no children's works. **Facilities:** Booth Theatre at North Carolina Blumenthal Performing Arts Center, 450 seats, flexible stage. **Best submission time:** year-round. **Response time:** 3–6 months. **Special programs:**

Festival of New American Plays: annual festival of staged readings; stipend, transportation and housing provided.

CHELTENHAM CENTER FOR THE ARTS

439 Ashbourne Rd; Cheltenham, PA 19012; (215) 379-4660

Submission procedure: no unsolicited scripts; synopsis/description of play and letter of inquiry. **Types of material:** full-length plays, translations, adaptations. **Facilities:** Bernard H. Berger Theater, 140 seats, proscenium stage. **Production considerations:** cast limit of 10. **Best submission time:** Jul–Feb. **Response time:** 1 month letter; 6 months script.

CHICAGO DRAMATISTS WORKSHOP

See Membership and Service Organizations.

THE CHILDREN'S THEATRE COMPANY

2400 Third Ave S; Minneapolis, MN 55404-3597; (612) 874-0500,
    FAX 874-8119
Jon Cranney, *Executive Producer*

Submission procedure: no unsolicited scripts; synopsis, resume and letter of inquiry. **Types of material:** full-length plays, one-acts, translations, adaptations, plays for young audiences, musicals. **Special interests:** adaptations or original plays for young audiences. **Facilities:** Children's Theatre Company, 745 seats, proscenium stage; Studio Theatre, 80–100 seats, black box. **Best submission time:** Oct–Apr. **Response time:** 2 weeks letter; 5 months script.

CHILDSPLAY

Box 517; Tempe, AZ 85280; (602) 350-8101, FAX 350-8584
David Saar, *Artistic Director*

Submission procedure: no unsolicited scripts; synopsis and letter of inquiry. **Types of material:** plays for young audiences, including full-length plays, adaptations, musicals, performance pieces. **Special interests:** nontraditional plays; material that entertains and challenges both performers and audiences; new work; 2nd and 3rd productions prior to publication. **Facilities:** Herberger Theater Center: Center Stage, 800 seats, proscenium stage; Scottsdale Center for the Arts, 800 seats, proscenium stage; Stage West, 350 seats, proscenium stage; Tempe Performing Arts Center, 175 seats, black box; also performs in Tucson (no permanent space). **Production considerations:** some van-sized touring productions. **Best submission time:** Jun–Oct. **Response time:** 1 month letter; 3 months script. **Special programs:** 1–3 works commissioned each season; each receives minimum 2 years of development.

CINCINNATI PLAYHOUSE IN THE PARK

Box 6537; Cincinnati, OH 45206-0537; (513) 345-2242
Edward Stern, *Producing Artistic Director*

Submission procedure: no unsolicited scripts; maximum 2-page abstract including synopsis, character breakdown and playwright's bio, 5 pages of dialogue and letter of inquiry, submitted by playwright or agent. **Types of material:** full-length plays, translations, adaptations, musicals. **Facilities:** Robert S. Marx Theatre, 629 seats, thrust stage; Thompson Shelterhouse, 220 seats, thrust stage. **Best submission time:** year-round. **Response time:** 2 months letter; 8 months script. **Special programs:** Lois and Richard Rosenthal New Play Prize (see Prizes).

CIRCLE IN THE SQUARE

1633 Broadway; New York, NY 10019-6795; (212) 307-2700, FAX 581-6371
Michael Breault, *Artistic Associate*

Submission procedure: no unsolicited scripts; agent submission. **Types of material:** full-length plays, translations, adaptations. **Special interests:** contemporary American or British plays. **Facilities:** Circle in the Square, 724 seats, arena stage. **Production considerations:** all productions performed in the round.

CIRCLE REPERTORY COMPANY

632 Broadway, 6th Floor; New York, NY 10012-2614; (212) 505-6010,
    FAX 505-8520
David Sisson, *Literary Coordinator*

Submission procedure: no unsolicited scripts; agents and theatre professionals only may send script with resume and reviews; no letters of inquiry. **Types of material:** full-length plays. **Facilities:** Circle Repertory, 199 seats, flexible stage. **Best submission time:** year-round. **Response time:** 4–8 months. **Special programs:** weekly reading series. Playwrights Project: participation by invitation only.

CITY THEATRE COMPANY

57 South 13th St; Pittsburgh, PA 15203; (412) 431-4400, FAX 431-5535
Marc Masterson, *Producing Director*

Submission procedure: no unsolicited scripts; synopsis, dialogue sample and letter of inquiry. **Types of material:** full-length plays, translations, adaptations, chamber musicals, solo pieces. **Special interests:** comedies of substance; plays with strong storyline; American themes. **Facilities:** mainstage, 250 seats, proscenium-thrust stage; laboratory theatre, 99 seats, black box. **Best submission time:** year-round. **Re-sponse time:** 2 months letter; 4 months script.

CLARENCE BROWN THEATRE COMPANY

206 McClung Tower; Knoxville, TN 37996; (423) 974-6011
Thomas P. Cooke, *Producing Artistic Director*

Submission procedure: no unsolicited scripts; synopsis, character breakdown, 1–2 pages of dialogue and letter of inquiry. **Types of material:** full-length plays. **Special interests:** contemporary American plays. **Facilities:** Clarence Brown Theatre, 600 seats, proscenium stage; Carousel Theatre, 250 seats, arena stage.

CLASSIC STAGE COMPANY (CSC)
136 East 13th St; New York, NY 10003; (212) 677-4210, FAX 477-7504
Lenora Champagne, *Artistic Associate*

Submission procedure: no unsolicited scripts; synopsis, dialogue sample and letter of inquiry. **Types of material:** translations and adaptations of "classic literature and themes only." **Special interests:** translations and adaptations of classic plays; adaptations of major nondramatic classics; prefers highly theatrical work. **Facilities:** CSC, 180 seats, flexible stage. **Production considerations:** cast limit of 8. **Best submission time:** year-round. **Response time:** 1 month letter; 3 months script. **Special programs:** developmental program of rehearsed readings.

THE CLEVELAND PLAY HOUSE
8500 Euclid Ave; Cleveland, OH 44106-0189; (216) 795-7010, FAX 795-7005; E-mail skryt@aol.com
Scott Kanoff, *Literary Manager/Dramaturg*

Submission procedure: no unsolicited scripts; resume and letter of inquiry. **Types of material:** full-length plays, adaptations, musicals. **Facilities:** Kenyon C. Bolton Theatre, 612 seats, proscenium stage; Francis E. Drury Theatre, 501 seats, proscenium stage. **Best submission time:** 1 Jul–30 Nov. **Response time:** 2–4 weeks letter; 1–3 months script. **Special programs:** The Next Stage (see Development).

CLEVELAND PUBLIC THEATRE
6415 Detroit Ave; Cleveland, OH 44102-3011; (216) 631-2727, FAX 631-2575; E-mail cpt@en.com
James A. Levin, *Artistic Director*

Submission procedure: no unsolicited scripts except for New Plays Festival (see below); synopsis and letter of inquiry; 5–10 sample pages optional. **Types of material:** full-length plays, one-acts, solo pieces. **Special interests:** experimental, alternative, poetic, political works; voices not heard in the mainstream (people of color, women, gays and lesbians); "no sitcoms or made-for-TV movies." **Facilities:** Cleveland Public Theatre, 150–175 seats, adaptable stage (arena/proscenium). **Production considerations:** simple set; cast limit of 10. **Best submission time:** 1 Feb–31 Oct; New Plays Festival, 1 Mar–1 Sep. **Response time:** 6 weeks letter; 9 months script. **Special programs:** Katherine and Lee Chilcote Award (see Prizes). New Plays Festival: staged readings of 10–13 full-length and one-act plays; submit script and $10 reading fee to Terence Cranendonk, Director, New Plays Festival; *deadline:* 1 Sep 1996; *notification:* Dec 1996; *dates:* Jan 1997.

Coconut Grove Playhouse
3500 Main Highway; Miami, FL 33133; (305) 442-2662, FAX 444-6437
Arnold Mittelman, *Producing Artistic Director*

Submission procedure: no unsolicited scripts; synopsis and letter of inquiry. **Types of material:** full-length plays, translations, musicals, cabaret/revues. **Special interests:** dramas, musicals. **Facilities:** Mainstage, 1100 seats, proscenium stage; Encore Room, 150 seats, cabaret. **Best submission time:** year-round. **Response time:** 1 week letter; 2 months script.

The Colony Studio Theatre
1944 Riverside Dr; Los Angeles, CA 90039
Judith Goldstein, *New Play Selection Committee*

Submission procedure: no unsolicited scripts; send SASE for submission guidelines. **Types of material:** full-length plays, adaptations. **Facilities:** Studio Theatre, 99 seats, thrust stage. **Production considerations:** cast of 4–12; plays cast from resident company. **Best submission time:** year-round. **Response time:** 12 months.

Coney Island, USA
1208 Surf Ave; Coney Island, NY 11224; (718) 372-5159
Dick D. Zigun, *Artistic Director*

Submission procedure: no unsolicited scripts; synopsis, resume, reviews of prior work and letter of inquiry. **Types of material:** company books in already existing productions of plays and performance art. **Special interests:** new and old vaudeville; pop music; pop culture; Americana bizarro. **Facilities:** Sideshows by the Seashore, 150 seats, arena stage; also open-air performances on streets, boardwalk, beach. **Best submission time:** year-round. **Response time:** 1 month letter; 6 months script.

Contemporary American Theater Festival
Box 429; Shepherdstown, WV 25443; (304) 876-3473, FAX 876-0955
Ed Herendeen, *Producing Director*

Submission procedure: no unsolicited scripts; synopsis and letter of inquiry. **Types of material:** full-length plays. **Special interests:** new American plays; contemporary issues. **Facilities:** Main Stage, 350 seats, proscenium stage; Studio Theater, 99 seats, black box. **Best submission time:** fall. **Response time:** 1 month letter; 2 months script. **Special programs:** staged readings each Tuesday night during summer season.

Cornerstone Theater Company
1653 18th St, #6; Santa Monica, CA 90404; (310) 449-1700, FAX 453-4347
Deb Piver, *Administrative Associate*

Submission procedure: no unsolicited scripts; letter of inquiry only. **Types of material:** full-length plays, adaptations, musicals. **Special interests:** company primarily interested in collaborating with playwrights to develop new works or contemporary adaptations of classics, focusing on specific communities. **Facilities:** no permanent facility. **Best submission time:** year-round. **Response time:** 2 months.

THE COTERIE THEATRE

2450 Grand Ave; Kansas City, MO 64108-2520; (816) 474-6785, FAX 474-7112
Jeff Church, *Producing Artistic Director*

Submission procedure: accepts unsolicited scripts from established playwrights in youth-theatre field; others send brief synopsis, dialogue sample, resume and letter of inquiry. **Types of material:** works for young and family audiences, including adaptations, musicals and solo pieces. **Special interests:** ground-breaking works only; plays with culturally diverse casts or themes; social issues; adaptations of classic or contemporary literature; musicals. **Facilities:** The Coterie Theatre, 240 seats, flexible stage. **Production considerations:** cast limit of 12, prefers 5–7; no fly or wing space. **Best submission time:** year-round. **Response time:** 4 months letter; 8 months script.

COURT THEATRE

5535 South Ellis; Chicago, IL 60637; (312) 702-7005, FAX 702-6417;
        E-mail ghwitt@midway.uchicago.edu
Gavin Witt, *Dramaturg*

Submission procedure: accepts unsolicited scripts; prefers synopsis and letter of inquiry. **Types of material:** full-length plays, translations, adaptations. **Special interests:** translations or adaptations of classic, literary or dramatic sources. **Facilities:** Abelson Auditorium, 253 seats, thrust stage. **Production considerations:** cast of 6–8; 1–2 sets; limited fly space. **Best submission time:** year-round; prefers fall. **Response time:** 3 weeks letter; 1–6 months script.

CROSSROADS THEATRE COMPANY

7 Livingston Ave; New Brunswick, NJ 08901; (908) 249-5581, FAX 249-1861
Fadra N. Chatard, *Literary Manager*
Sydné Mahone, *Director of Play Development*

Submission procedure: no unsolicited scripts; synopsis, 10-page dialogue sample, bio and/or resume and letter of inquiry. **Types of material:** full-length plays, one-acts, translations, adaptations, musicals, cabaret/revues, performance art. **Special interests:** African-American, African and West Indian issue-oriented, experimental plays that examine the complexity of the human experience. **Facilities:** Crossroads Theatre, 264 seats, thrust stage. **Best submission time:** year-round. **Response time:** 2 months letter; 12 months script. **Special programs:** The Genesis Festival: A Celebration of New Voices in African American Theatre: spring series of public readings and special events for the purpose of developing new plays; scripts selected through theatre's normal submission procedure.

CUMBERLAND COUNTY PLAYHOUSE

Box 830; Crossville, TN 38557; (615) 484-4324, FAX 484-6299
Jim Crabtree, *Producing Director*

Submission procedure: no unsolicited scripts; synopsis and letter of inquiry. **Types of material:** full-length plays, adaptations, plays for young audiences, musicals. **Special interests:** works for family audiences; works with southern or rural background; works about Tennessee history or culture. **Facilities:** Cumberland County Playhouse, 490 seats, proscenium stage; Theater-in-the-Woods, 200 seats, outdoor arena; Adventure Theater, 180–220 seats, flexible black box. **Best submission time:** Aug–Dec. **Response time:** 2 weeks letter (if interested); 6–12 months script.

DALLAS CHILDREN'S THEATER

2215 Cedar Springs; Dallas, TX 75201; (214) 978-0110, FAX 978-0118
Artie Olaisen, *Administrative Artist*

Submission procedure: accepts unsolicited scripts with synopsis, character breakdown and letter of inquiry; include production history and professional recommendation if available. **Types of material:** full-length plays, adaptations, plays for young audiences. **Special interests:** works for family audiences; adaptations of classics; historical plays; socially relevant works. **Facilities:** El Centro Theater, 500 seats, proscenium stage; Crescent Theater, 180 seats, flexible stage. **Best submission time:** year-round. **Response time:** 3–6 months.

DALLAS THEATER CENTER

3636 Turtle Creek Blvd; Dallas, TX 75219-5598; (214) 526-8210, FAX 521-7666
Stefan Novinski, *Artistic Administrator*

Submission procedure: no unsolicited scripts; professional recommendation. **Types of material:** full-length plays, adaptations, translations, solo pieces. **Special interests:** plays that explore language or form; African-American or Hispanic material. **Facilities:** Kalita Humphreys Theater, 466 seats, thrust stage; Arts District Theater, 530 seats, flexible stage. **Best submission time:** year-round. **Response time:** 6–9 months.

DELAWARE THEATRE COMPANY

200 Water St; Wilmington, DE 19801-5030; (302) 594-1104, FAX 594-1107
Cleveland Morris, *Artistic Director*

Submission procedure: accepts unsolicited scripts. **Types of material:** full-length plays, translations, adaptations. **Facilities:** Delaware Theatre Company, 300 seats, thrust stage. **Production considerations:** cast limit of 10. **Best submission time:** Feb–May. **Response time:** 6 months. **Special programs:** Connections (see Prizes).

DELL'ARTE PLAYERS COMPANY
Box 816; Blue Lake, CA 95525; (707) 668-5663, FAX 668-5663;
    E-mail dellarte@aol.com
Michael Fields, *Managing Artistic Director*

Submission procedure: no unsolicited scripts; synopsis and letter of inquiry (company customarily creates its own original works but may from time to time produce plays by or collaborate with other writers). **Types of material:** full-length plays, translations, adaptations, plays for young audiences, solo pieces. **Special interests:** comedies; issue-oriented works in commedia dell'arte style; Christmas plays for young audiences. **Facilities:** Dell'Arte Players, 100 seats, flexible stage. **Production considerations:** company of 3–4 actors; production demands adaptable to touring. **Best submission time:** Jan–Mar. **Response time:** 3 weeks letter; 6 weeks script.

DENVER CENTER THEATRE COMPANY
1050 13th St; Denver, CO 80204; (303) 893-4000
Tom Szentgyorgyi, *Associate Artistic Director/New Play Development*

Submission procedure: accepts unsolicited scripts from Rocky Mountain region playwrights only; others send synopsis, 10 pages of dialogue, resume of writing experience and letter of inquiry. **Types of material:** full-length plays. **Facilities:** The Stage, 642 seats, thrust stage; The Space, 450 seats, arena stage; The Ricketson, 196 seats, proscenium stage; The Source, 155 seats, thrust stage. **Best submission time:** year-round. **Response time:** 4–6 weeks letter; 4–6 months script. **Special programs:** Denver Center Theatre Company U S WEST Workshops (see Development).

DETROIT REPERTORY THEATRE
13103 Woodrow Wilson Ave; Detroit, MI 48238; (313) 868-1347, FAX 868-1705
Barbara Busby, *Literary Manager*

Submission procedure: accepts unsolicited scripts. **Types of material:** full-length plays. **Special interests:** issue-oriented plays. **Facilities:** Detroit Repertory Theatre, 194 seats, proscenium stage. **Production considerations:** prefers cast limit of 8. **Best submission time:** Sep–Feb. **Response time:** 3–6 months.

DIAMOND HEAD THEATRE
See Diamond Head Theatre Development Programs in Development.

DIXON PLACE
258 Bowery; New York, NY 10012; (212) 219-3088, FAX 274-9114
Bru Dye, *Curator of Play Reading Series*

Submission procedure: accepts unsolicited scripts; prefers 10-page writing sample and letter of inquiry. **Types of material:** full-length plays, one-acts. **Special interests:** works by New York City–based writers only; works by women; writers of color; "adventurous settings"; no "kitchen-sink soap operas." **Facilities:** Dixon Place, 50 seats, 3/4-stage. **Production considerations:** readings only; small stage; no sets; minimal lighting. **Best submission time:** year-round. **Response time:** 6 months.

DOBAMA THEATRE

1846 Coventry Rd; Cleveland Heights, OH 44118; (216) 932-6838,
    FAX 932-3259
Sue Ott Rowlands, *Literary Manager*

Submission procedure: accepts unsolicited scripts with synopsis. **Types of material:** full-length plays, solo pieces. **Special interests:** plays with opportunities for ethnically diverse casting; plays that make a statement about contemporary life. **Facilities:** Dobama Theatre, 200 seats, thrust stage. **Production considerations:** prefers cast limit of 9; limited production demands; no fly space. **Best submission time:** year-round. **Response time:** 9 months. **Special programs:** One World Premiere: production of 1 new play included in mainstage season each year; *deadline:* 1 Feb 1997; *notification:* 15 May 1997 for 1997–98 season. Owen Kelly Adopt-a-Playwright Program: 2 full-length plays by OH residents each given 2 weeks of developmental work with director, dramaturg and cast, culminating in workshop production; playwright must be available to participate; to apply, submit script to the attention of the program; *deadline:* 1 Feb 1997; *notification:* 15 May 1997; *dates:* Jul 1997. Marilyn Bianchi Kids' Playwriting Festival: annual short-play competition open to students attending Cuyahoga County schools, grades 1–12; several winners may receive savings bonds, publication and/or full production; write for application in Sep 1996; *deadline:* Feb 1997; exact date TBA.

DORSET THEATRE FESTIVAL

Box 510; Dorset, VT 05251; (802) 867-2223, FAX 867-0144;
    E-mail theatre@sover.net
Jill Charles, *Artistic Director*

Submission procedure: no unsolicited scripts; synopsis, character/set breakdown and letter of inquiry with SASP for response; include production history of readings in New York City–New England area if available. **Types of material:** full-length plays. **Special interests:** plays with broad commercial appeal. **Facilities:** Dorset Playhouse, 218 seats, proscenium stage. **Production considerations:** cast limit of 8; prefers 1 set or unit set. **Best submission time:** Sep–Dec. **Response time:** 1–2 months letter; 3 months script. **Special programs:** Dorset Colony for Writers (see Colonies).

EAST WEST PLAYERS

4424 Santa Monica Blvd; Los Angeles, CA 90029; (213) 660-0366,
    FAX 666-0896
Ken Narasaki, *Literary Manager*

Submission procedure: accepts unsolicited scripts with SASE for response. **Types of material:** full-length plays, translations, adaptations, plays for young audiences, musicals. **Special interests:** plays by or about Asian-Pacific–Americans. **Facilities:** East West Players, 99 seats, thrust stage. **Production considerations:** minimal production demands. **Best submission time:** year-round. **Response time:** 3–8 months.

ECLIPSE THEATRE COMPANY

2074 North Leavitt St; Chicago, IL 60647; (312) 862-7415
Literary Department

Submission procedure: no unsolicited scripts; synopsis and letter of inquiry. **Types of material:** full-length plays, one-acts, translations, adaptations, cabaret/revues, solo pieces. **Special interests:** adaptations; plays with environmental themes. **Facilities:** Mainstage, 40 seats, black box. **Production considerations:** cast limit of 12; small stage. **Best submission time:** year-round. **Response time:** 1 month letter; 4–6 months script.

EL TEATRO CAMPESINO

Box 1240; San Juan Bautista, CA 95045; (408) 623-2444, FAX 623-4127
Managing Director

Submission procedure: no unsolicited scripts; synopsis, character breakdown, resume and letter of inquiry. **Types of material:** full-length plays, one-acts, translations, adaptations, plays for young audiences, musicals, cabaret/revues, solo pieces. **Special interests:** socially relevant works; works that reflect a multiethnic world; contemporary adaptations of classics. **Facilities:** El Teatro Campesino Playhouse, 150 seats, flexible stage. **Best submission time:** Jan–Apr. **Response time:** 6 months letter; 12 months script.

THE EMELIN THEATRE FOR THE PERFORMING ARTS

Library Lane; Mamaroneck, NY 10543; (914) 698-3045
David G. Watson, *Executive Director*

Submission procedure: accepts unsolicited scripts with professional recommendation only; include video for solo pieces. **Types of material:** full-length plays, chamber musicals, cabaret/revues, solo pieces. **Facilities:** The Emelin Theatre, 280 seats, proscenium stage. **Production considerations:** small cast; no fly space. **Best submission time:** year-round. **Response time:** 2 months.

THE EMPTY SPACE THEATRE

3509 Fremont Ave N; Seattle, WA 98103-8813; (206) 547-7633, FAX 547-7635;
    Web http://emptyspace.com
Eddie Levi Lee, *Artistic Director*

Submission procedure: accepts unsolicited scripts from regional playwrights (AK, ID, MT, OR, WA, WY and BC); others send synopsis and letter of inquiry. **Types of material:** full-length plays, one-acts, translations, adaptations, musicals, solo pieces. **Facilities:** The Empty Space Theatre at the Fremont Palace, 150 seats, endstage. **Production considerations:** prefers small casts. **Best submission time:** year-round. **Response time:** 6–10 weeks letter; 4–6 months script.

EN GARDE ARTS

509 Greenwich; New York, NY 10013; (212) 941-9793, FAX 343-1137;
E-mail engardeart@aol.com
Carol Bixler, *Managing Director/Associate Producer*

Submission procedure: professional recommendation. **Types of material:** full-length plays, translations, adaptations, musicals, solo pieces, performance art. **Special interests:** site-specific works only. **Facilities:** no permanent facility; various sites in and outside of New York City, e.g., Central Park Lake, Chelsea Hotel, Victory Theatre, meatpacking district. **Best submission time:** Aug. **Response time:** 6–8 months.

ENSEMBLE STUDIO THEATRE

549 West 52nd St; New York, NY 10019; (212) 247-4982, FAX 664-0041
Jamie Richards, *Executive Producer*

Submission procedure: accepts unsolicited scripts. **Types of material:** full-length plays, one-acts. **Facilities:** Mainstage, 99 seats, black box; Studio, 60 seats, proscenium stage. **Best submission time:** year-round. **Response time:** 6 months. **Special programs:** summer reading series and playwriting workshops. First Look: reading series of full-length plays. Annual Marathon of One-Act Plays: one-act play festival; *deadline:* 1 Dec 1996.

THE ENSEMBLE THEATRE

3535 Main St; Houston, TX 77002-9529; (713) 520-0055, FAX 520-1269
Eileen J. Morris, *Artistic Director*

Submission procedure: accepts unsolicited scripts. **Types of material:** full-length plays, adaptations, plays for young audiences, musicals, solo pieces. **Special interests:** works reflecting the African-American experience. **Facilities:** Hawkins Stage, 199 seats, proscenium stage; Arena Stage, 80 seats, black box. **Production considerations:** cast limit of 10, maximum 2 sets. **Best submission time:** Oct–Apr. **Response time:** 2–3 months.

ENSEMBLE THEATRE OF CINCINNATI

1127 Vine St; Cincinnati, OH 45210; (513) 421-3555
D. Lynn Meyers, *Interim Artistic Director*

Submission procedure: no unsolicited scripts; synopsis, dialogue sample, resume and letter of inquiry. **Types of material:** full-length plays, adaptations, plays for young audiences. **Special interests:** contemporary and social issues. **Facilities:** Ensemble Theatre of Cincinnati, 202 seats, 3/4-arena stage. **Production considerations:** cast limit of 6, simple set. **Best submission time:** Sep. **Response time:** 1 month letter; 4 months script.

EUREKA THEATRE COMPANY
330 Townsend St, Suite 210; San Francisco, CA 94107; (415) 243-9899,
    FAX 243-0789
Nicole Galland, *Literary Manager*

Submission procedure: no unsolicited scripts; synopsis, 15 pages of dialogue, resume and letter of inquiry. **Types of material:** full-length plays, one-acts, translations, adaptations, solo pieces. **Special interests:** dynamic contemporary plays "strongly theatrical with an eye toward the millennium." **Facilities:** no permanent facility. **Best submission time:** year-round. **Response time:** 2 months letter; 6 months script. **Special programs:** Discovery Series: regularly scheduled rehearsed readings of new plays presented for public and followed by audience discussion.

FIRST STAGE MILWAUKEE
929 North Water St; Milwaukee, WI 53202; (414) 273-7121, FAX 273-5595
Rob Goodman, *Producer/Artistic Director*

Submission procedure: no unsolicited scripts; synopsis, resume and letter of inquiry. **Types of material:** works for young audiences, including translations, adaptations and musicals. **Facilities:** Marcus Center for the Performing Arts's Todd Wehr Theater, 500 seats, thrust stage. **Best submission time:** spring–summer. **Response time:** 1 month letter; 3 months script.

FLORIDA STUDIO THEATRE
1241 North Palm Ave; Sarasota, FL 34236; (941) 366-9017
Chris Angermann, *Associate Director*

Submission procedure: no unsolicited scripts; synopsis and letter of inquiry. **Types of material:** full-length plays, one-acts, translations, adaptations, musicals, cabaret/revues, solo pieces. **Facilities:** Florida Studio Theatre, 170 seats, semi-thrust stage; FST Cabaret Club, 100 seats, cabaret space. **Best submission time:** Apr–Nov. **Response time:** 1–2 weeks letter; 6 months script. **Special programs:** Sarasota Festival of New Plays: 4-tier festival includes Young Playwrights Festival (May): workshop productions of plays by playwrights grades 2–12; *deadline:* 15 Mar 1997. Florida Playwrights Festival (Jul–Aug): workshops, seminars, staged readings and cabaret performances in conjunction with workshop productions of 3 plays by FL playwrights; scripts selected through theatre's normal submission procedure. National Playwrights Festival (May): workshop productions of 3 new plays; playwright receives stipend, travel, housing; scripts selected through theatre's normal submission procedure. Vanguard Festival: workshop productions of 3 new plays; "cutting-edge" material; scripts selected through theatre's normal submission procedure. Fall reading series. American Shorts Contest (see Prizes).

THE FOOTHILL THEATRE COMPANY
Box 1812; Nevada City, CA 95959; (916) 265-9320
Philip Charles Sneed, *Artistic Director*

Submission procedure: accepts unsolicited scripts. **Types of material:** full-length plays, one-acts, translations, adaptations, plays for young audiences, solo pieces. **Special interests:** plays dealing with history of northern CA and/or the western U.S. **Facilities:** The Nevada Theatre, 246 seats, proscenium stage; also rents small spaces with 50–100 seats. **Production considerations:** very limited fly and wing space. **Best submission time:** year-round. **Response time:** 3–6 months.

FORD'S THEATRE
511 Tenth Ave NW; Washington, DC 20004; (202) 638-2941, FAX 347-6269
Ellen Hause, *Literary Associate*

Submission procedure: no unsolicited scripts; synopsis, sample pages and letter of inquiry. **Types of material:** full-length plays, musicals. **Special interests:** small-scale musicals and works celebrating the African-American experience. **Facilities:** Ford's Theatre, 699 seats, proscenium/thrust stage. **Production considerations:** cast limit of 15. **Best submission time:** spring–summer. **Response time:** 3 weeks letter; 6 months script.

THE FOUNTAIN THEATRE
5060 Fountain Ave; Los Angeles, CA 90029; (213) 663-2235, FAX 663-1629
Simon Levy, *Producing Director/Dramaturg*

Submission procedure: no unsolicited scripts; synopsis, and letter of inquiry. **Types of material:** full-length plays, translations, adaptations, musicals. **Special interests:** lyrical dramas; contemporary comedies; works with dance; adaptations of American literature. **Facilities:** Fountain Theatre Mainstage, 78 seats, thrust stage; The Lab, 22 seats, black box. **Production considerations:** cast limit of 12; 1 set; no fly space; low ceiling. **Best submission time:** year-round. **Response time:** 2 months letter; 6 months script.

FREE STREET PROGRAMS
1419 West Blackhawk St; Chicago, IL 60622; (312) 772-7248, FAX 772-7248
Ron Bieganski, *Artistic Director*
David Schein, *Executive Director*

Submission procedure: no unsolicited scripts; letter from writer with "a concept for a show or a brilliant idea for a new theatre program for inner-city kids/teens." **Types of material:** plays and performance pieces, including shows to be performed in public places or out of doors. **Special interests:** inner-city kids/teenagers; "cultural empowerment of new populations"; developing works with communities; enhancing literacy through the arts; new work by Chicago-area artists. **Facilities:** national/international touring company (teens). **Production considerations:** no expensive production demands. **Response time:** 2 months letter; two months script.

FREEDOM REPERTORY THEATRE

1346 North Broad St; Philadelphia, PA 19121; (215) 765-2791, FAX 765-4191
Walter Dallas, *Artistic Director*

Submission procedure: no unsolicited scripts; professional recommendation. **Types of material:** full-length plays, musicals, cabaret/revues. **Special interests:** contemporary plays with African-American themes. **Facilities:** John E. Allen Theatre, 298 seats, proscenium stage; Freedom Cabaret Theatre, 120 seats, flexible stage. **Special programs:** Freedom Fest: play reading series; resident playwright program; commissioning program; all programs are by invitation only.

FULTON THEATRE COMPANY

Box 1865; Lancaster, PA 17603-1865; (717) 394-7133, FAX 397-3780
Kathleen A. Collins, *Artistic Director*

Submission procedure: no unsolicited scripts; accepts synopsis and letter of inquiry; prefers professional recommendation. **Types of material:** full-length plays, musicals. **Special interests:** contemporary themes. **Facilities:** Fulton Opera House, 684 seats, proscenium stage. **Production considerations:** cast limit of 10, unit set. **Best submission time:** year-round. **Response time:** 3 weeks letter; 4 months script.

GALA HISPANIC THEATRE

Box 43209; Washington, DC 20010; (202) 234-7174, FAX 332-1247
Hugo J. Medrano, *Producing/Artistic Director*

Submission procedure: accepts unsolicited scripts; prefers synopsis/description of play and letter of inquiry. **Types of material:** full-length plays, solo pieces. **Special interests:** plays by Spanish, Latino or Hispanic-American writers in Spanish or English only; prefers Spanish-language works with accompanying English translation; works that reflect sociocultural realities of Hispanics in Latin America, the Caribbean or Spain, as well as the Hispanic-American experience. **Facilities:** GALA Hispanic Theatre, 200 seats, proscenium stage. **Production considerations:** cast of 6–8. **Best submission time:** Apr–May. **Response time:** 1 month letter; 1 month script. **Special programs:** poetry onstage.

GEORGE STREET PLAYHOUSE

9 Livingston Ave; New Brunswick, NJ 08901; (908) 846-2895, FAX 247-9151;
        E-mail trishroche@aol.com
Tricia Roche, *Literary Manager*

Submission procedure: no unsolicited scripts; professional recommendation. **Types of material:** full-length plays, one-acts for young audiences, musicals. **Special interests:** comedies and dramas that present a fresh perspective on our society and challenge our expectations of theatre; voices not traditionally heard on America's main stages; social-issue one-acts suitable for touring to schools (not seeking any other type of one-act for young audiences). **Facilities:** Mainstage, 367 seats, proscenium-thrust stage. **Production considerations:** prefers cast limit of 6 for plays, 10 for musicals. **Best submission time:** year-round. **Response time:** 6–8 months. **Special programs:** staged reading series.

GEORGIA REPERTORY THEATRE
Department of Drama, University of Georgia; Athens, GA 30602-3154;
　　　　(706) 542-2836, FAX 542-2080; E-mail longman@uga.cc.uga.edu
Stanley V. Longman, *Dramaturg*

Submission procedure: accepts unsolicited scripts. **Types of material:** full-length plays. **Special interests:** unproduced plays. **Facilities:** Fine Arts Theatre, 750 seats, proscenium stage; Cellar Theatre, 100 seats, proscenium stage. **Production considerations:** cast limit of 8; minimal set. **Best submission time:** late spring. **Response time:** 3–6 months.

GERMINAL STAGE DENVER
2450 West 44th Ave; Denver, CO 80211; (303) 455-7108
Edward Baierlein, *Director/Manager*

Submission procedure: no unsolicited scripts; synopsis, 5 pages of dialogue and letter of inquiry with SASP for response. **Types of material:** full-length plays, translations, adaptations. **Special interests:** adaptations that use both dialogue and narration. **Facilities:** Germinal Stage Denver, 100 seats, thrust stage. **Production considerations:** cast limit of 10, minimal production requirements. **Best submission time:** year-round. **Response time:** 2 weeks letter; 6 months script.

GeVa THEATRE
75 Woodbury Blvd; Rochester, NY 14607-1717; (716) 232-1366
Jean Ryon, *New Plays Coordinator*

Submission procedure: no unsolicited scripts; synopsis and letter of inquiry. **Types of material:** full-length plays, translations, adaptations. **Facilities:** GeVa Theatre, 552 seats, modified thrust stage. **Best submission time:** year-round. **Response time:** 1 week letter; 6 months script.

THE GLINES
240 West 44th St; New York, NY 10036; (212) 354-8899

Submission procedure: accepts unsolicited scripts. **Types of material:** full-length plays. **Special interests:** plays dealing with gay experience only. **Facilities:** no permanent facility. **Best submission time:** year-round. **Response time:** 2 months.

GOODMAN THEATRE
200 South Columbus Dr; Chicago, IL 60603-6491; (312) 443-3811,
　　　FAX 263-6004; E-mail staff@goodman-theatre.org
Susan V. Booth, *Literary Manager*

Submission procedure: no unsolicited scripts; synopsis, professional recommendation and letter of inquiry. **Types of material:** full-length plays, translations, musicals, solo pieces. **Special interests:** social or political themes. **Facilities:** Goodman Mainstage, 683 seats, proscenium stage; Goodman Studio, 135 seats, proscenium stage. **Best submission time:** year-round. **Response time:** 2–3 months letter; 6–8 months script.

GOODSPEED OPERA HOUSE

Box A; East Haddam, CT 06423; (860) 873-8664, FAX 873-2329
Sue Frost, *Associate Producer*

Submission procedure: no unsolicited scripts; synopsis and letter of inquiry. **Types of material:** original musicals only. **Facilities:** Goodspeed Opera House, 400 seats, proscenium stage; Goodspeed-at-Chester, 200 seats, adaptable proscenium stage. **Best submission time:** Jan–Mar. **Response time:** 3 months letter; 12 months script.

GREAT AMERICAN HISTORY THEATRE

30 East Tenth St; St. Paul, MN 55101; (612) 292-4323, FAX 292-4322
Ron Peluso, *Artistic Director*

Submission procedure: no unsolicited scripts; synopsis and letter of inquiry. **Types of material:** full-length plays, adaptations, musicals, solo pieces. **Special interests:** works involving people, events, issues, ideas and places in history; nonrealistic works preferred; no pageants. **Facilities:** Crawford Livingston Theatre, 597 seats, thrust stage. **Production considerations:** cast limit of 10; moderate production demands; small musicals only. **Best submission time:** winter–spring. **Response time:** 1 month letter; 2–6 months script.

GRETNA THEATRE

Box 578; Mt. Gretna, PA 17064; (717) 964-3322, FAX 964-2189

Submission procedure: no unsolicited scripts; synopsis, 5 pages of dialogue, character list with descriptions, production history and letter of inquiry; include cassette for musicals. **Types of material:** full-length plays, plays for young audiences, musicals. **Special interests:** plays suitable for conservative community; prefers comedies; small-cast musicals only. **Facilities:** Mt. Gretna Playhouse, 700 seats, proscenium stage. **Production considerations:** open-air facility; 14′ ceiling over stage. **Best submission time:** Aug–Apr. **Response time:** 1 month letter; 3 months script.

THE GROUP: SEATTLE'S MULTICULTURAL THEATRE

305 Harrison St; Seattle, WA 98109; (206) 441-9480, FAX 441-9839
Literary Department

Submission procedure: no unsolicited scripts; synopsis, 10–15 pages of dialogue, resume and letter of inquiry with SASE for response. **Types of material:** full-length plays, translations, adaptations, plays for young audiences, musicals, solo pieces. **Special interests:** plays suitable for multiethnic casts; serious plays on social/cultural issues; satires, musicals or comedies with bite. **Facilities:** Seattle Center's Carlton Playhouse, 200 seats, modified thrust stage. **Production consider-**

ations: cast limit of 10; prefers unit set or simple sets. **Best submission time:** year-round. **Response time:** 4–6 months.

THE GUTHRIE THEATER
725 Vineland Pl; Minneapolis, MN 55403; (612) 347-1100, FAX 347-1188
Literary Department

Submission procedure: no unsolicited scripts; professional recommendation and letter of inquiry with SASE for response. **Types of material:** full-length plays, translations, adaptations. **Special interests:** folktales of diverse cultures; well-crafted and highly theatrical plays of "depth and significance" dealing with universal themes; contemporary international plays, translations and adaptations of classic literature only; no sitcoms. **Facilities:** Guthrie Theater, 1309 seats, thrust stage; Guthrie Laboratory, 350 seats, flexible stage. **Best submission time:** year-round. **Response time:** 3–4 months letter; scripts vary.

HAHN COSMOPOLITAN THEATRE
444 Fourth Ave; San Diego, CA 92101; (619) 232-9608,
      FAX 239-3823 (must address to attention of Ginger)
Ginger Sparkman, *Manager*

Submission procedure: accepts unsolicited scripts. **Types of material:** full-length plays, one-acts, translations, adaptations, musicals, solo pieces, performance art. **Facilities:** Hahn Cosmopolitan Theatre, 250 seats, proscenium stage. **Production considerations:** minimal wing space. **Best submission time:** year-round. **Response time:** 6 months.

HARTFORD STAGE COMPANY
50 Church St; Hartford, CT 06103; (860) 525-5601, FAX 525-4420
Kim Euell, *Director of New Play Development*

Submission procedure: no unsolicited scripts; synopsis, 10 pages of dialogue and letter of inquiry. **Types of material:** full-length plays, translations, adaptations. **Facilities:** John W. Huntington Theatre, 489 seats, thrust stage. **Best submission time:** year-round. **Response time:** 10–14 days letter; 6–9 months script.

HEDGEROW THEATRE
146 West Rose Valley Rd; Rose Valley, PA 19065; (610) 565-4211
Margaret Royal, *Literary Director*

Submission procedure: accepts unsolicited scripts. **Types of material:** full-length plays, translations, adaptations, plays for young audiences. **Special interests:** comedies; language-oriented plays. **Facilities:** Hedgerow Theatre, 144 seats, proscenium stage. **Production considerations:** small stage; minimal production demands. **Best submission time:** year-round. **Response time:** 3 months.

HIP POCKET THEATRE
1627 Fairmount Ave; Fort Worth, TX 76104-4237; (817) 927-2833,
    FAX 927-8051
Johnny Simons, *Artistic Director*

Submission procedure: accepts unsolicited scripts; include cassette for musicals. **Types of material:** full-length plays, translations, adaptations, plays for young audiences, musicals, solo pieces, multi-media works. **Special interests:** well-crafted stories with poetic, mythic slant that incorporate ritual and ensemble; works utilizing masks, puppetry, music, dance, mime and strong visual elements. **Facilities:** Oak Acres Amphitheatre, 175 seats, outdoor amphitheatre; Magnolia Theatre, 85 seats, black box. **Production considerations:** prefers cast limit of 10–15; simple sets; no fly space in Magnolia. **Best submission time:** Oct–Feb. **Response time:** 6 weeks.

THE HIPPODROME STATE THEATRE
25 Southeast Second Pl; Gainesville, FL 32601-6596; (352) 373-5968
David Boyce, *Dramaturg*

Submission procedure: no unsolicited scripts; professional recommendation or agent submission. **Types of material:** full-length plays, translations, adaptations. **Facilities:** Mainstage Theatre, 266 seats, thrust stage; Second Stage, 87 seats, flexible stage. **Production considerations:** prefers small cast, unit set. **Best submission time:** summer–fall. **Response time:** 8 months.

HONOLULU THEATRE FOR YOUTH
2846 Ualena St; Honolulu, HI 96819-1910; (808) 839-9885, FAX 839-9885
Peter C. Brosius, *Artistic Director*

Submission procedure: no unsolicited scripts; synopsis, resume and letter of inquiry. **Types of material:** one-acts, plays for young audiences. **Special interests:** plays for audiences up to high school age, with contemporary themes; adaptations of literary classics; new works based on Pacific Rim cultures; plays with compelling language that are imaginative and socially relevant. **Facilities:** Leeward Community College Theatre, 650 seats, proscenium stage; McCoy Pavilion, 300 seats, flexible stage. **Production considerations:** cast limit of 10. **Best submission time:** year-round. **Response time:** 1 month letter; 4–5 months script.

HORIZON THEATRE COMPANY

Box 5376, Station E; Atlanta, GA 30307; (404) 523-1477,
    FAX 523-1477 (call first)
Lisa Adler, *Co-Artistic Director*

Submission procedure: accepts unsolicited scripts from GA playwrights only; others send synopsis, resume and letter of inquiry. **Types of material:** full-length plays, translations, adaptations, musicals. **Special interests:** contemporary issues; plays by women; southern urban themes; comedies. **Facilities:** Horizon Theatre, 170–200 seats, flexible stage. **Production considerations:** plays cast from ensemble of up to 12 actors aged 20–40. **Best submission time:** May–Jun. **Response time:** 6 months letter; 12 months script. **Special programs:** Teen Ensemble: one-acts about teen issues to be performed by teens. Senior Citizens Ensemble: one-acts about senior-citizen issues to be performed by senior citizens.

HORSE CAVE THEATRE

Box 215; Horse Cave, KY 42749; (502) 786-1200, FAX 786-5298
Warren Hammack, *Artistic Director*

Submission procedure: no unsolicited scripts; professional recommendation. **Types of material:** full-length plays. **Special interests:** KY-based plays by KY playwrights. **Facilities:** Horse Cave Theatre, 345 seats, thrust stage. **Production considerations:** cast limit of 10, 1 set. **Best submission time:** Oct–Apr. **Response time:** varies.

THE HUMAN RACE THEATRE COMPANY

126 North Main St, Suite 300; Dayton, OH 45402-1710; (513) 461-3823,
    FAX 461-7223
Tony Dallas, *Playwright in Residence*

Submission procedure: no unsolicited scripts; professional recommendation. **Types of material:** full-length plays, one-acts, plays for young audiences. **Special interests:** OH playwrights; works for junior and senior high school audiences; contemporary issues. **Facilities:** The Loft, 219 seats, thrust stage. **Production considerations:** small casts; no fly space; plays for young audiences tour to schools. **Best submission time:** year-round. **Response time:** 6 months.

HUNTINGTON THEATRE COMPANY

264 Huntington Ave; Boston MA 02115-4606; (617) 266-7900, FAX 353-8300
Jayme Koszyn, *Literary Associate*

Submission procedure: no unsolicited scripts; synopsis and letter of inquiry. **Types of material:** full-length plays, translations, adaptations, solo pieces. **Special interests:** New England playwrights; plays of regional relevance; plays based on literary sources. **Facilities:** Huntington Theatre, 850 seats, proscenium stage. **Best submission time:** May–Sep. **Response time:** 3 months letter; 6 months script.

ILLINOIS THEATRE CENTER
400A Lakewood Blvd; Park Forest, IL 60466; (708) 481-3510
Steve S. Billig, *Artistic Director*

Submission procedure: no unsolicited scripts; synopsis and letter of inquiry with SASE for response. **Types of material:** full-length plays, musicals. **Facilities:** Illinois Theatre Center, 200 seats, proscenium-thrust stage. **Production considerations:** cast limit of 9 for plays, 14 for musicals. **Best submission time:** year-round. **Response time:** 1 month letter; 2 months script.

ILLUSION THEATER
528 Hennepin Ave, Suite 704; Minneapolis, MN 55403; (612) 339-4944,
    FAX 337-8042
Michael Robins, *Executive Producing Director*

Submission procedure: no unsolicited scripts; professional recommendation. **Types of material:** full-length plays, one-acts, translations, adaptations, musicals, solo pieces. **Special interests:** writers to collaborate on new works with company. **Facilities:** Illusion Theater, 250 seats, semi-thrust stage. **Best submission time:** Jul–Nov. **Response time:** 6–12 months. **Special programs:** Fresh Ink Series: 5–6 plays each presented with minimal set and costumes for 1 weekend; post-performance discussion with audience, who are seated onstage; scripts selected through theatre's normal submission procedure.

INDIANA REPERTORY THEATRE
140 West Washington St; Indianapolis, IN 46204-3465; (317) 635-5277,
    FAX 236-0767
Richard J. Roberts, *Literary Manager*

Submission procedure: no unsolicited scripts; synopsis and letter of inquiry from playwright with SASE for response; inquiries only from agents (no scripts). **Types of material:** full-length plays, translations, adaptations, solo pieces. **Special interests:** adaptations of classic literature; plays that explore cultural/ethnic issues. **Facilities:** Mainstage, 600 seats, modified thrust stage; Upperstage, 250 seats, modified proscenium stage. **Production considerations:** cast limit of 6–8. **Best submission time:** year-round (season chosen by Jan each year). **Response time:** 3–4 months letter; 6 months script. **Special programs:** Family Plays: presentation of plays for family audiences with a focus on youth and culturally/ethnically diverse plays with an emphasis on history and literature; follow theatre's normal submission procedure above.

INTAR HISPANIC AMERICAN ARTS CENTER
Box 788; New York, NY 10108; (212) 695-6134, -6135, FAX 268-0102
Lorenzo Mans, *Literary Manager*

Submission procedure: accepts unsolicited scripts. **Types of material:** full-length plays, one-acts, translations, adaptations, musicals, solo pieces. **Special interests:** new plays by Hispanic-American writers and translations and adaptations of

Hispanic works only. **Facilities:** INTAR on Theatre Row, 99 seats, proscenium stage; INTAR Stage Two, 75 seats, proscenium stage. **Production considerations:** prefers cast limit of 8; no wing space. **Best submission time:** year-round (season chosen late summer–early fall). **Response time:** 3–6 months. **Special programs:** New Works Lab: workshop productions. Reading series.

INTERACT THEATRE COMPANY
Box 42138; Philadelphia, PA 19101; (215) 568-8077, FAX 568-8095
Seth Rozin, *Artistic Director*
Tom Gibbons, *Literary Manager*

Submission procedure: no unsolicited scripts; synopsis, resume and letter of inquiry. **Types of material:** full-length plays. **Special interests:** plays that theatrically explore issues of cultural conflict only (political, social, historical, etc.). **Facilities:** Arts Bank, 200 seats, proscenium stage. **Production considerations:** cast limit of 10. **Best submission time:** year-round. **Response time:** 2 months letter; 4 months script. **Special programs:** script-in-hand reading series.

INTIMAN THEATRE
Box 19760; Seattle, WA 98109; (206) 269-1901, FAX 269-1928
Robert Menna, *Dramaturg/Literary Manager*

Submission procedure: no unsolicited scripts; synopsis, sample pages and letter of inquiry with SASE for response (indicate if play is unproduced). **Types of material:** full-length plays, translations, adaptations. **Special interests:** well-crafted plays that fully utilize the power of language and character relationships to explore enduring themes. **Facilities:** Intiman Playhouse, 424 seats, thrust stage. **Production considerations:** prefers cast limit of 12. **Best submission time:** year-round. **Response time:** 1 month letter; 4 months script. **Special programs:** New Voices at Intiman: developmental readings of unproduced new plays; scripts selected through theatre's normal submission procedure.

INVISIBLE THEATRE
1400 North 1st Ave; Tucson, AZ 85719; (520) 882-9721, FAX 884-0672
Deborah Dickey, *Literary Manager*

Submission procedure: no unsolicited scripts; professional recommendation. **Types of material:** full-length plays, one-acts, musicals, solo pieces. **Special interests:** mainly but not exclusively works with contemporary settings; works with strong female roles; social and political issues. **Facilities:** Invisible Theatre, 78 seats, black box. **Production considerations:** cast limit of 10; simple set; minimal props; small-cast musicals only. **Best submission time:** after 1 Sep 1996 only. **Response time:** 6–12 months.

IRONDALE ENSEMBLE PROJECT
Box 1314, Old Chelsea Station; New York, NY 10011-1314; (212) 633-1292,
    FAX 633-2078; E-mail irondalert@aol.com
Jim Niesen, *Artistic Director*

Submission procedure: no unsolicited scripts; letter of inquiry from playwright interested in developing work with ensemble through ongoing workshop process. **Types of material:** full-length plays, adaptations, plays with music. **Special interests:** works with political or social relevance. **Facilities:** no permanent facility. **Production considerations:** cast limit of 8–9. **Best submission time:** Sep–Jun. **Response time:** 10 weeks.

JEWISH ENSEMBLE THEATRE
6600 West Maple Rd; West Bloomfield, MI 48322-3002; (810) 788-2900,
    FAX 661-3680
Evelyn Orbach, *Artistic Director*

Submission procedure: accepts unsolicited scripts. **Types of material:** full-length plays, one-acts, plays for young audiences. **Special interests:** works on Jewish themes and/or by Jewish writers. **Facilities:** Aaron DeRoy Theatre, 194 seats, thrust stage. **Production considerations:** no fly space. **Best submission time:** late spring–early fall. **Response time:** 6 months. **Special programs:** Festival of New Plays in Staged Readings: 4 plays given readings during Feb series, possibly leading to main stage production; scripts selected through theatre's normal submission procedure.

JEWISH REPERTORY THEATRE
92nd Street Y; 1395 Lexington Ave; New York, NY 10128; (212) 415-5550
Ran Avni, *Artistic Director*

Submission procedure: accepts unsolicited scripts. **Types of material:** full-length plays, one-acts, musicals. **Special interests:** works that address some aspect of Jewish life. **Facilities:** Playhouse 91, 299 seats, thrust stage. **Production considerations:** small cast. **Best submission time:** Sep–May. **Response time:** 1 month. **Special programs:** Lee Guber Playwrights' Lab: readings of new plays.

JOMANDI PRODUCTIONS
1444 Mayson St NE; Atlanta, GA 30324; (404) 876-6346, FAX 872-5764
Julie Pradia, *Literary Manager*

Submission procedure: no unsolicited scripts; synopsis, dialogue sample, resume and letter of inquiry. **Types of material:** full-length plays, adaptations, plays for young audiences, musicals, solo pieces. **Special interests:** historical or contemporary portrayals of the African-American experience; adaptations of African-American literature. **Facilities:** 14th Street Playhouse main stage, 385 seats, proscenium/thrust stage. **Production considerations:** produces some large-cast plays but prefers average cast of 7; prefers unit set. **Best submission time:** spring–summer. **Response time:** 1 month letter; 4–6 months script.

JUNGLE THEATER
709 West Lake St; Minneapolis, MN 55408; (612) 822-7063, FAX 822-9408
Bain Boehlke, *Artistic Director*

Submission procedure: no unsolicited scripts; synopsis, sample pages, resume and letter of inquiry. **Types of material:** full-length plays. **Facilities:** Jungle Theater, 95 seats, proscenium stage. **Best submission time:** year-round. **Response time:** 1 month letter; 3 months script.

L. A. THEATRE WORKS
681 Venice Blvd; Venice, CA 90291; (310) 827-0808, FAX 827-4949;
    E-mail latworks@aol.com
Kirsten Dahl, *Literary Manager*

Submission procedure: no unsolicited scripts; agent submission. **Types of material:** full-length plays, one-acts, adaptations. **Special interests:** highly theatrical, nonrealistic new plays; contemporary adaptations of classic themes. **Facilities:** no permanent facility. **Best submission time:** year-round. **Response time:** 4–6 months. **Special programs:** Radio Theatre Series for New Plays: bimonthly performances; scripts selected from among those received through theatre's normal submission procedure. Writers Dialogue: series of advanced playwriting workshops; $300 fee for 10-week session; contact theatre for information.

LA JOLLA PLAYHOUSE
Box 12039; La Jolla, CA 92039; (619) 550-1070, FAX 550-1075
Robert Blacker, *Associate Artistic Director*
Gregory Gunter, *Literary Manager/Dramaturg*

Submission procedure: no unsolicited scripts; professional recommendation. **Types of material:** full-length plays, translations, musicals. **Special interests:** material pertinent to the lives we are leading at the end of this century; innovative form and language. **Facilities:** Mandell Weiss Center for the Performing Arts, 500 seats, proscenium stage; Weiss Forum, 400 seats, thrust stage. **Best submission time:** Feb–Nov. **Response time:** 4 months.

LA MAMA EXPERIMENTAL THEATER CLUB
74A East 4th St; New York, NY 10003; (212) 254-6468, FAX 254-7908
Ellen Stewart, *Artistic Director*
Meryl Vladimer, *Associate Director*

Submission procedure: no unsolicited scripts; accepts unsolicited videotapes of projects with synopsis; prefers professional recommendation. **Types of material:** full-length plays, one-acts, musicals, solo pieces, performance art. **Special interests:** culturally diverse works with music, movement and media. **Facilities:** Annex Theater, 299 seats, flexible stage; Club, 125 seats, black box; 1st Floor Theater, 99 seats, black box. **Best submission time:** year-round. **Response time:** 2–6 months. **Special programs:** New Voices/New Plays: weekly series of readings followed by informal audience-response sessions. One Night Stand Series: weekly performance series for emerging multidisciplinary performance artists, including writers, who perform own work; theatre provides lighting, sound and stage management. Cross Cultural Institute of Theater Art Studies: promotes intercultural understanding and artistic exchange developed or created through theatrical workshops, artistic explorations and premiere productions involving collaboration among artists of varying geographic and ethnic origins.

LAGUNA PLAYHOUSE
606 Laguna Canyon Rd; Laguna Beach, CA 92651; (714) 494-8022,
    FAX 497-6948
Andrew Barnicle, *Artistic Director*

Submission procedure: accepts unsolicited scripts; no synopses. **Types of material:** full-length plays, plays for young audiences, musicals. **Facilities:** Moulton Theater, 418 seats, proscenium stage. **Best submission time:** year-round. **Response time:** 6–12 months.

LINCOLN CENTER THEATER
150 West 65th St; New York, NY 10023; (212) 362-7600
Anne Cattaneo, *Dramaturg*

Submission procedure: no unsolicited scripts; agent submission. **Types of material:** full-length plays, one-acts, translations, adaptations, musicals. **Facilities:** Vivian Beaumont, 1000 seats, thrust stage; Mitzi E. Newhouse, 300 seats, thrust stage. **Best submission time:** year-round. **Response time:** 2–4 months.

LIVE BAIT THEATRICAL COMPANY
3914 North Clark; Chicago, IL 60613; (312) 871-1212, FAX 871-3191
Edward Thomas-Herrera, *Managing Director*

Submission procedure: no unsolicited scripts; synopsis and letter of inquiry from Chicago-area playwrights only; no other submissions accepted. **Types of material:** full-length plays, translations, adaptations, solo pieces, performance art. **Special interests:** nonrealistic plays; performance poetry; performance art; multimedia works; works that emphasize visual aspects of staging. **Facilities:** Live Bait Theater, 70 seats, black box. **Production considerations:** prefers cast limit of 9; 1 set; no fly or wing space. **Best submission time:** year-round. **Response time:** 6 weeks letter; 6 months script.

LIVE OAK THEATRE
200 Colorado St; Austin, TX 78701; (512) 472-5143, FAX 472-7199
Michael Hankin, *Associate Director*

Submission procedure: accepts unsolicited scripts or synopsis, dialogue sample and letter of inquiry; include cassette for musicals. **Types of material:** full-length plays, adaptations, solo pieces. **Special interests:** Texas plays. **Facilities:** Live Oak Theatre, 400 seats, proscenium stage. **Production considerations:** limited wing space; small stage. **Best submission time:** year-round. **Response time:** scripts chosen in summer of year after submission. **Special programs:** Live Oak Theatre's Harvest Festival of New American Plays (see Prizes).

THE LIVING THEATRE

800 West End Ave, #5A; New York, NY 10025; (212) 865-3957, FAX 865-3234
Craig Peritz, *Administrative Assistant*

Submission procedure: no unsolicited scripts; synopsis and letter of inquiry. **Types of material:** full-length plays, translations, adaptations. **Special interests:** plays that creatively incorporate audience participation; experimental works; new theatre forms; nonfictional plays dealing with current issues performed by actors who play themselves. **Facilities:** no permanent facility; touring company; street and various outdoor venues. **Production considerations:** plays must accommodate ensemble of 12. **Best submission time:** year-round. **Response time:** 2 months letter; 6 months script.

THE LOFT PRODUCTION COMPANY

1441 East Fletcher Ave, Suite 413; Tampa, FL 33612; (813) 972-1200,
    FAX 977-8485
(Mr.) Kelly Smith, *Artistic Director*

Submission procedure: accepts unsolicited scripts with maximum 1-page synopsis, scene/set breakdown and $5 fee; playwright's name, address and phone number must appear on title page; submissions not returned. **Types of material:** unproduced and unpublished full-length plays, adaptations, musicals, performance art. **Special interests:** gay and lesbian works; women's works. **Facilities:** Resident Theatre Company of the Off-Center Theater at Tampa Bay Performing Arts Center, 130 seats, black box. **Production considerations:** cast limit 8; cast age of 20–40; simple set; minimal production demands. **Best submission time:** year-round. **Response time:** 3 months. **Special programs:** The Loft Fest '97—Festival of Shorts (see Development).

LONG WHARF THEATRE

222 Sargent Dr; New Haven, CT 06511; (203) 787-4284, FAX 776-2287
John Tillinger, *Literary Consultant*

Submission procedure: no unsolicited scripts; professional recommendation. **Types of material:** full-length plays, translations, adaptations. **Special interests:** plays about human relationships, social concerns, ethical and moral dilemmas; will also consider farces and comedies of manners. **Facilities:** Long Wharf Theatre, 484 seats, thrust stage; Stage II, 199 seats, flexible stage. **Best submission time:** year-round. **Response time:** 6 months. **Special programs:** in-house readings of new plays. Long Wharf Theatre Stage II Workshops (see Development).

Mabou Mines

150 First Ave; New York, NY 10009; (212) 473-0559, FAX 473-2410
Sharon Fogarty, *Company Manager*

Submission procedure: no unsolicited scripts; professional recommendation.
Types of material: full-length plays, one-acts, translations, adaptations. **Special
interests:** contemporary works on contemporary issues. **Facilities:** no permanent
facility. **Best submission time:** year-round. **Response time:** 6 months.

Mad River Theater Works

Box 248; West Liberty, OH 43357; (513) 465-6751
Jeff Hooper, *Producing Director*

Submission procedure: no unsolicited scripts; professional recommendation.
Types of material: full-length plays, one-acts, adaptations. **Special interests:**
midwestern or rural subject matter. **Facilities:** Center Stage, 150 seats, flexible
stage. **Production considerations:** cast limit of 6, simple set and costumes. **Best
submission time:** year-round. **Response time:** 3–4 months.

Madison Repertory Theatre

122 State St, Suite 201; Madison, WI 53703-2500; (608) 256-0029,
   FAX 256-7433; E-mail madisonrep@aol.com
D. Scott Glasser, *Artistic Director*

Submission procedure: no unsolicited scripts; synopsis and letter of inquiry. **Types
of material:** full-length plays, one-acts, translations, adaptations, musicals. **Special
interests:** works with midwestern themes. **Facilities:** Isthmus Playhouse, 335 seats,
thrust stage. **Production considerations:** cast limit of 15; no fly space. **Best
submission time:** year-round. **Response time:** 3–4 months letter; 3–4 months
script. **Special programs:** reading series for plays in development.

Magic Theatre

Fort Mason Center, Bldg D; San Francisco, CA 94123; (415) 441-8001,
   FAX 771-5505
Literary Manager

Submission procedure: no unsolicited scripts; synopsis, first 10 pages of play,
resume and letter of inquiry. **Types of material:** full-length plays, solo pieces.
Special interests: new plays that are innovative and/or nonlinear in form and
content; political themes. **Facilities:** Magic Theatre Southside, 170 seats,
proscenium stage; Magic Theatre Northside, 155 seats, thrust stage. **Production
considerations:** prefers cast limit of 6. **Best submission time:** Sep–May. **Response
time:** 6 weeks letter; 6–8 months script.

MANHATTAN THEATRE CLUB

453 West 16th St; New York, NY 10011; (212) 645-5590, FAX 691-9106;
E-mail 76735.3316@compuserve.com
Kate Loewald, *Director of Play Development*
Clifford Lee Johnson III, *Director of Musical Theatre Program*

Submission procedure: no unsolicited scripts; agent submission. **Types of material:** full-length plays, musicals. **Facilities:** Stage I at City Center, 299 seats, proscenium stage; Stage II, 150 seats, thrust stage. **Production considerations:** cast of 6–8; 1 set or unit set. **Best submission time:** year-round. **Response time:** 6 months. **Special programs:** readings and workshop productions of new musicals. "First-hearing" readings: in-house readings of new plays or first drafts. Manhattan Theatre Club Playwriting Fellowships (see Fellowships and Grants).

MARIN THEATRE COMPANY

397 Miller Ave; Mill Valley, CA 94941; (415) 388-5200, FAX 388-0768
Lee Sankowich, *Artistic Director*

Submission procedure: no unsolicited scripts; agent submission. **Types of material:** full-length plays, translations, adaptations, plays for young audiences. **Facilities:** Marin Theatre, 250 seats, proscenium stage; 2nd theatre, 109 seats, black box. **Best submission time:** Jun–Aug. **Response time:** 6 months.

MARK TAPER FORUM

135 North Grand Ave; Los Angeles, CA 90012; (213) 972-7574
Oliver Mayer, *Associate Literary Manager*

Submission procedure: no unsolicited scripts; description of work, 5–10 sample pages and letter of inquiry. **Types of material:** full-length plays, one-acts, translations, adaptations, plays for young audiences, musicals, literary cabaret, solo pieces, performance art. **Facilities:** Mark Taper Forum, 742 seats, thrust stage; Taper, Too, 80–90 seats, flexible stage. **Best submission time:** call for information. **Response time:** 4–6 weeks letter; 8–10 weeks script. **Special programs:** Mark Taper Forum Developmental Programs (see Development).

McCARTER THEATRE CENTER FOR THE PERFORMING ARTS

91 University Pl; Princeton, NJ 08540; (609) 683-9100, FAX 497-0369
Janice Paran, *Literary Manager/Dramaturg*

Submission procedure: no unsolicited scripts; synopsis and letter of inquiry. **Types of material:** full-length plays, musicals. **Facilities:** McCarter Theatre, 1077 seats, proscenium stage. **Best submission time:** Sep–May. **Response time:** 1 month letter; 3 months script.

MEADOW BROOK THEATRE
Oakland University; Rochester, MI 48309-4401; (810) 370-3310, FAX 370-3108
Literary Manager

Submission procedure: no unsolicited scripts; synopsis, sample pages and letter of inquiry. **Types of material:** full-length plays, translations, adaptations, musicals. **Facilities:** Meadow Brook Theatre, 608 seats, proscenium stage. **Best submission time:** year-round. **Response time:** 1–2 months letter; 3–5 months script.

MERRIMACK REPERTORY THEATRE
50 East Merrimack St; Lowell, MA 01852; (508) 454-6324, FAX 934-0166
David G. Kent, *Artistic Director*

Submission procedure: no unsolicited scripts; synopsis and letter of inquiry. **Types of material:** full-length plays, translations, adaptations, plays for young audiences, musicals. **Special interests:** well-crafted stories with a poetic and human focus; varied ethnic tapestries of American life and love. **Facilities:** Liberty Hall, 386 seats, thrust stage. **Production considerations:** moderate cast size, simple set. **Best submission time:** spring–summer. **Response time:** 1 month letter (if interested); 6 months script.

MERRY-GO-ROUND PLAYHOUSE
Box 506; Auburn, NY 13021; (315) 255-1305, FAX 252-3815
Emily Mattina, *Literary Manager*

Submission procedure: accepts unsolicited scripts. **Types of material:** full-length plays, translations, adaptations, plays for young audiences, musicals. **Special interests:** participatory plays for young audiences with cast limit of 3–4; plays for grades K–12. **Facilities:** Merry-Go-Round Playhouse (adaptable), 325 seats, proscenium stage or 100 seats, thrust stage. **Production considerations:** cast limit of 5. **Best submission time:** Jan–Feb. **Response time:** 2 months.

METRO THEATER COMPANY
524 Trinity Ave; St. Louis, MO 63130; (314) 727-3552, FAX 727-7811
Carol North, *Producing Director*

Submission procedure: no unsolicited scripts; professional recommendation. **Types of material:** plays and musicals for young audiences. **Special interests:** no works longer than 60 minutes; plays with music and musicals that are not dramatically limited by traditional concepts of "children's theatre." **Facilities:** touring company. **Production considerations:** works cast from ensemble of 5; sets suitable for touring. **Best submission time:** year-round. **Response time:** 2–3 months. **Special programs:** new plays readings; commissioning program; interested writers send letter of inquiry with recommendations from theatres who have produced writer's work.

METROSTAGE

1816 Duke St; Alexandria, VA 22314; (703) 548-9044, FAX 548-9089
Carolyn Griffin, *Producing Director*

Submission procedure: no unsolicited scripts; synopsis, first 10 pages of dialogue, list of productions and readings, and letter of inquiry. **Types of material:** full-length plays, one-acts, musicals. **Facilities:** MetroStage, 100 seats, thrust stage. **Production considerations:** cast limit of 8, prefers 4; prefers 1 set. **Best submission time:** year-round. **Response time:** 1 month letter; 1 month script. **Special programs:** First Stage: staged reading series Jan–May.

MILL MOUNTAIN THEATRE

1 Market Square SE; Roanoke, VA 24011-1437; (703) 342-5730,
      FAX (540) 342-5749
Jo Weinstein, *Literary Manager*

Submission procedure: accepts unsolicited one-acts only; synopsis, 10 pages of dialogue and letter of inquiry for all other submissions. **Types of material:** full-length plays, one-acts, musicals, solo pieces. **Special interests:** plays with racially mixed casts. **Facilities:** Mill Mountain Theatre, 400 seats, flexible proscenium stage; Theatre B, 125 seats, flexible space. **Production considerations:** cast limit of 15 for plays, 24 for musicals; prefers unit set. **Best submission time:** year-round. **Response time:** 6 weeks letter; 6–8 months script. **Special programs:** Centerpieces: monthly lunchtime staged readings of one-acts by emerging playwrights; unpublished one-acts 25–35 minutes long (no 10-minute plays). The Mill Mountain Theatre New Play Competition: The Norfolk Southern Festival of New Works (see Prizes).

MILWAUKEE CHAMBER THEATRE

158 North Broadway; Milwaukee, WI 53202; (414) 276-8842, FAX 277-4477;
      E-mail mct@execpc.com
Montgomery Davis, *Artistic Director*

Submission procedure: no unsolicited scripts; professional recommendation. **Types of material:** full-length plays, one-acts, translations, adaptations. **Special interests:** strong, well-crafted plays; plays about Shaw for annual Shaw Festival. **Facilities:** Broadway Theatre Center: Cabot Theatre, 372 seats, proscenium stage; studio, 99 seats, black box. **Production considerations:** 1 set or unit set. **Best submission time:** summer. **Response time:** 2 months.

MILWAUKEE PUBLIC THEATRE

626 East Kilbourn Ave, #802; Milwaukee, WI 53202-3237; (414) 347-1685,
      FAX 347-1685 (call first); E-mail bleigh@omnifest.uwm.edu
Barbara Leigh, *Co-Artistic/Producing Director*

Submission procedure: no unsolicited scripts; synopsis and letter of inquiry with SASE for response. **Types of material:** full-length plays, one-acts, translations, adaptations, plays for young audiences, cabaret/revues, clown/vaudeville shows.

Special interests: works with cast of 1–3 playing multiple roles; political satire; social-political and regional or local themes; plays dealing with disabilities; interart works; new clown/vaudeville shows; works for young and family audiences. **Facilities:** no permanent facility. **Production considerations:** simple production demands; productions tour. **Best submission time:** year-round for plays dealing with disabilities; Sep only for all other submissions. **Response time:** 6 months letter; 12 months script. **Special programs:** outdoor park performances.

MILWAUKEE REPERTORY THEATER

108 East Wells St; Milwaukee, WI 53202; (414) 224-1761
Joseph Hanreddy, *Artistic Director*

Submission procedure: no unsolicited scripts; agent submission. **Types of material:** full-length plays, translations, adaptations, cabaret/revues. **Facilities:** Powerhouse Theatre, 720 seats, thrust stage; Stiemke Theatre, 200 seats, flexible stage; Stackner Cabaret, 100 seats, cabaret stage. **Production considerations:** works for cabaret must not exceed 80 minutes in length. **Best submission time:** year-round. **Response time:** 2–3 months.

MISSOURI REPERTORY THEATRE

4949 Cherry St; Kansas City, MO 64110-2499; (816) 235-2727, FAX 235-5367;
    E-mail kreece@cctr.umkc.edu
George Keathley, *Artistic Director*

Submission procedure: no unsolicited scripts; synopsis and letter of inquiry. **Types of material:** full-length plays, translations, adaptations. **Facilities:** Helen F. Spencer Theatre, 740 seats, modified thrust stage. **Best submission time:** year-round. **Response time:** 1 month letter; script varies. **Special programs:** Playwrights' Stage: scripts developed through series of readings leading to production.

MIXED BLOOD THEATRE COMPANY

1501 South Fourth St; Minneapolis, MN 55454; (612) 338-0937
David Kunz, *Script Czar*

Submission procedure: no unsolicited scripts; synopsis and letter of inquiry. **Types of material:** full-length plays, translations, musicals, cabaret/revues. **Facilities:** Main Stage, 200 seats, flexible stage. **Best submission time:** year-round. **Response time:** 1 month letter; 2–6 months script. **Special programs:** Mixed Blood Versus America (see Prizes).

THE MONTANA REPERTORY THEATRE

Department of Drama and Dance; The University of Montana;
    Missoula, MT 59812-1582; (406) 243-6809, FAX 243-5726
Greg Johnson, *Artistic Director*

Submission procedure: no unsolicited scripts; synopsis, resume and letter of inquiry. **Types of material:** full-length plays, one-acts, musicals. **Special interests:** plays by and about Native Americans. **Facilities:** touring company. **Best submission**

time: summer. **Response time:** 3 months letter; 6 months script.

MUSIC-THEATRE GROUP
29 Bethune St; New York, NY 10014; (212) 924-3108, FAX 255-1981
Jun–Aug: Box 641; Stockbridge, MA 01262
Lyn Austin, *Producing Director*
Diane Wondisford, *General Director*

Submission procedure: no unsolicited scripts; direct solicitation to playwright or agent. **Types of material:** music-theatre works, operas, cabaret. **Special interests:** experimental musical works; collaborations between music-theatre, dance and the visual arts. **Facilities:** no permanent facility.

NATIONAL JEWISH THEATER
5050 West Church St; Skokie, IL 60077; (847) 329-9443, FAX 329-9421
Jeff Ginsberg and Susan Padveen, *Co-Artistic Directors*

Submission procedure: no unsolicited scripts; synopsis and letter of inquiry with SASE for response. **Types of material:** full-length plays, translations, adaptations, musicals. **Special interests:** American Jewish experience from early immigration to contemporary problems. **Facilities:** Mainstage, 250 seats, open stage. **Production considerations:** prefers cast limit of 8–10; no more than 2 sets; no fly space. **Best submission time:** year-round. **Response time:** 2 months letter; 4 months script.

NATIONAL THEATRE OF THE DEAF
Box 659; Chester, CT 06412; (203) 526-4971 (voice), -4974 (TTY)
Will Rhys, *Artistic Director*

Submission procedure: no unsolicited scripts; synopsis, character breakdown, sample pages and letter of inquiry with SASE for response. **Types of material:** full-length plays, adaptations, plays for young audiences. **Special interests:** deaf issues; culturally diverse plays. **Facilities:** touring company. **Production considerations:** cast limit of 10; production must tour. **Best submission time:** year-round. **Response time:** 1 month letter; 3–6 months script.

NEBRASKA REPERTORY THEATRE
215 Temple Bldg; 12th and R Sts; Lincoln, NE 68588-0201; (402) 472-2072, FAX 472-9055; E-mail jeh@unlgrad1.unl.edu
Randall Wheatley, *Literary Manager*

Submission procedure: no unsolicited scripts; synopsis and letter of inquiry with SASE for response. **Types of material:** full-length plays, one-acts, musicals. **Special interests:** unpublished scripts for NEW THEATRE series (see below); plays that contribute to multicultural awareness. **Facilities:** Howell Theatre, 380 seats, proscenium stage; Studio Theatre, 180 seats, black box. **Production considerations:** simple set for Studio Theatre. **Best submission time:** Aug–Feb. **Response time:** 1 month letter; 2–6 months script. **Special programs:** NEW THEATRE:

reading and performance series.

NEBRASKA THEATRE CARAVAN

6915 Cass St; Omaha, NE 68132; (402) 553-4890, FAX 553-6288;
      E-mail necaravan@aol.com
Richard L. Scott, *Managing Director*

Submission procedure: no unsolicited scripts; synopsis and letter of inquiry. **Types of material:** full-length plays, adaptations, plays for young audiences, musicals. **Facilities:** touring company. **Production considerations:** cast limit of 12, 1 set. **Best submission time:** year-round. **Response time:** 1 month letter; 3 months script.

NEW DRAMATISTS

See Membership and Service Organizations.

NEW FEDERAL THEATRE

292 Henry St; New York, NY 10002; (212) 353-1176, FAX 353-1088
Woodie King, Jr., *Producing Director*
Pat White, *Company Manager*

Submission procedure: no unsolicited scripts; professional recommendation. **Types of material:** full-length plays. **Special interests:** social and political issues; family and community themes related to minorities. **Facilities:** Henry Street Settlement Abron Arts Center: Theatre 1, 350 seats, proscenium stage; Theatre 2, 100 seats, 3/4-arena stage; Theatre 3, 100 seats, endstage. **Production considerations:** small cast, no more than 2 sets. **Best submission time:** year-round. **Response time:** 5 months.

NEW JERSEY SHAKESPEARE FESTIVAL

c/o Drew University; 36 Madison Ave; Madison, NJ 07940; (201) 408-3278,
      FAX 408-3361
Bonnie J. Monte, *Artistic Director*

Submission procedure: no unsolicited scripts; synopsis and letter of inquiry. **Types of material:** full-length plays, translations, adaptations, solo pieces. **Special interests:** translations and/or adaptations of classic works only. **Facilities:** Festival Theatre, 238 seats, thrust stage. **Production considerations:** modest technical demands; limited wing space. **Best submission time:** early fall. **Response time:** 2 months letter; 1 month script.

NEW MUSIC-THEATER ENSEMBLE

308 Prince St, #250; St. Paul, MN 55101; (612) 298-9913
Marge Betley, *Managing Director*

Submission procedure: no unsolicited scripts; direct solicitation to playwright or agent. **Types of material:** musicals, music-theatre works, opera. **Facilities:** Southern Theater, 150 seats, proscenium stage; New Music-Theater Ensemble

Studio, 40 seats, black box. **Special programs:** Composer/Librettist Studio: annual 2-week music-theatre lab for Minnesota composers and writers only; send postcard with name and address for information.

NEW REPERTORY THEATRE

Box 418; Newton Highlands, MA 02161; (617) 332-7058, FAX 527-5217
Rick Lombardo, *Artistic Director*

Submission procedure: no unsolicited scripts; direct solicitation to playwright or agent. **Types of material:** full-length plays, translations, adaptations. **Special interests:** multicultural themes; intimate, interpersonal themes. **Facilities:** New Repertory Theatre, 170 seats, thrust stage.

NEW STAGE THEATRE

Box 4792; Jackson, MS 39296-4792; (601) 948-0143, FAX 948-3538
John Maxwell, *Artistic Director*

Submission procedure: no unsolicited scripts; synopsis and letter of inquiry. **Types of material:** full-length plays, solo pieces. **Facilities:** Meyer Crystal Auditorium, 364 seats, proscenium stage. **Production considerations:** cast of 3–8. **Best submission time:** summer–fall. **Response time:** 4 weeks letter; 3 months script. **Special programs:** New Play Series: public readings of 8 new plays every year; full production of a new play every season.

NEW YORK STAGE AND FILM

515 Madison Ave, 28th Floor; New York, NY 10022; (212) 750-6703,
    FAX 750-6784
Peter Manning, *Producer*

Submission procedure: accepts unsolicited scripts with letter of inquiry. **Types of material:** full-length plays. **Facilities:** Powerhouse Theatre, 135 seats, proscenium stage; Coalbin, 110 seats, black box. **Best submission time:** 1 Sep–31 Oct only. **Response time:** 3 months.

NEW YORK STATE THEATRE INSTITUTE

155 River St; Troy, NY 12180; (518) 274-3200, FAX 274-3815
Patricia Di Benedetto Snyder, *Producing Artistic Director*

Submission procedure: no unsolicited scripts; synopsis, cast/scene breakdown and letter of inquiry. **Types of material:** full-length plays, adaptations, musicals. **Special interests:** mainly presents works for family audiences. **Facilities:** Schacht Fine Arts Center, 900 seats, proscenium stage. **Best submission time:** Mar–Sep. **Response time:** 2–4 weeks. **Special programs:** new works developmental workshops; playwrights receive staged reading or workshop production, negotiable remuneration, travel and housing.

NEW YORK THEATRE WORKSHOP
79 East 4th St; New York, NY 10003; (212) 780-9037
Mandy Mishell, *Artistic Associate, Literary*

Submission procedure: no unsolicited scripts; synopsis, 10-page sample scene, resume and letter of inquiry. **Types of material:** full-length plays, one-acts, translations, music-theatre works, solo pieces, proposals for performance projects. **Special interests:** large issues; socially relevant and/or minority issues; innovative form and language. **Facilities:** 79 East 4th Street Theatre, 150 seats, proscenium stage. **Best submission time:** fall–spring. **Response time:** 4 weeks letter; 3–5 months script. **Special programs:** Mondays at Three: reading series, developmental workshops and symposiums. Playwrights Circle. Summer writing residency.

NEXT THEATRE COMPANY
927 Noyes St; Evanston, IL 60201; (847) 475-6763, FAX 475-6767
Sarah Tucker, *Associate Artistic Director*

Submission procedure: no unsolicited scripts; synopsis, 10–15 pages of dialogue and letter of inquiry. **Types of material:** full-length plays, translations, adaptations. **Facilities:** Mainstage, 175 seats, proscenium stage. **Production considerations:** no fly space; limited wing space. **Best submission time:** year-round. **Response time:** 1 month letter; 1–3 months script.

NORTHLIGHT THEATRE
600 Davis St; Evanston, IL 60201; (847) 869-7732, FAX 869-9445
Brian Russell, *Associate Artistic Director*

Submission procedure: no unsolicited scripts; synopsis and letter of inquiry. **Types of material:** full-length plays, translations, adaptations, musicals, solo pieces. **Special interests:** translations and adaptations of "lost" plays; the public world and public issues; plays of ideas; works that are passionate and/or hilarious; stylistic exploration and complexity; no domestic realism. **Facilities:** no permanent facility; company performs in various proscenium- or thrust-stage venues with 250–500 seats. **Best submission time:** Sep–Feb. **Response time:** 1 month letter; 2–4 months script.

NOVEL STAGES
Box 58879; Philadelphia, PA 19102-8879; (215) 844-8868, FAX 844-2060
Clista Townsend, *Artistic Associate*

Submission procedure: no unsolicited scripts; synopsis and letter of inquiry with SASP for response. **Types of material:** full-length plays, one-acts, translations, adaptations, plays for young audiences, solo pieces. **Facilities:** Stage III at 1619 Walnut St, 130 seats, endstage. **Production considerations:** simple set; no fly space, very little wing space. **Best submission time:** year-round. **Response time:** 6 months letter; 9–12 months script.

ODYSSEY THEATRE ENSEMBLE

2055 South Sepulveda Blvd; Los Angeles, CA 90025; (310) 477-2055
Jan Lewis, *Director of Literary Programs*

Submission procedure: no unsolicited scripts; synopsis, 8–10 pages of dialogue, play's production history (if any), resume and letter of inquiry; include cassette for musicals. **Types of material:** full-length plays, translations, adaptations, musicals. **Special interests:** culturally diverse works; works with innovative form or provocative subject matter; works exploring the enduring questions of human existence and the possibilities of the live-theatre experience; works with political or sociological impact. **Facilities:** Odyssey 1, 99 seats, flexible stage; Odyssey 2, 99 seats, thrust stage; Odyssey 3, 99 seats, endstage. **Production considerations:** plays must be 90 minutes or longer. **Best submission time:** year-round. **Response time:** 2–4 weeks letter; 6 months script.

OLD GLOBE THEATRE

Box 2171; San Diego, CA 92112-2171; (619) 231-1941
Raúl Moncada, *Literary Manager*

Submission procedure: no unsolicited scripts; synopsis and letter of inquiry with SASE for response. **Types of material:** full-length plays, translations, adaptations, musicals. **Special interests:** well-crafted plays; strongly theatrical material. **Facilities:** Lowell Davies Festival Stage, 620 seats, outdoor stage; Old Globe Theatre, 581 seats, modified thrust stage; Cassius Carter Centre Stage, 225 seats, arena stage. **Production considerations:** prefers cast limit of 8. **Best submission time:** year-round. **Response time:** 2–3 months letter; 6–10 months script.

OLDCASTLE THEATRE COMPANY

Box 1555; Bennington, VT 05201; (802) 447-1267, FAX 442-3704
Eric Peterson, *Producing Artistic Director*

Submission procedure: accepts unsolicited scripts. **Types of material:** full-length plays, musicals. **Facilities:** Bennington Center for the Arts, 300 seats, modified proscenium stage. **Best submission time:** winter. **Response time:** 4–6 months.

OLNEY THEATRE CENTER FOR THE ARTS

2001 Olney-Sandy Spring Rd; Olney, MD 20832; (301) 924-4485, FAX 924-2654
Jim Petosa, *Artistic Director*

Submission procedure: no unsolicited scripts; professional recommendation. **Types of material:** full-length plays, translations, adaptations, solo pieces. **Facilities:** Mainstage, 500 seats, proscenium stage. **Production considerations:** cast limit of 8. **Best submission time:** year-round. **Response time:** 6 months.

OMAHA THEATER COMPANY FOR YOUNG PEOPLE

2001 Farnam St; Omaha, NE 68102; (402) 345-9718, FAX 345-7255
James Larson, *Artistic Director*

Submission procedure: no unsolicited scripts; professional recommendation.
Types of material: full-length plays. **Special interests:** plays for family audiences
only; plays based on children's literature and contemporary issues; multicultural
themes. **Facilities:** Omaha Theater Company, 932 seats, proscenium stage; second
stage, 150 seats, black box. **Production considerations:** cast limit of 15; prefers
unit set. **Best submission time:** year-round. **Response time:** 6 months.

ONTOLOGICAL-HYSTERIC THEATER

260 West Broadway; New York, NY 10013; (212) 941-8911, FAX 334-5149

Submission procedure: no unsolicited scripts; direct solicitation to playwright or
agent. **Types of material:** full-length plays. **Facilities:** Ontological at St. Mark's
Theater, 80 seats, black box.

THE OPEN EYE THEATER

Box 204; Denver, NY 12421; (607) 326-4986, FAX 326-4986
Amie Brockway, *Producing Artistic Director*

Submission procedure: no unsolicited scripts; synopsis and letter of inquiry with
self-addressed, unstamped envelope for possible response. **Types of material:** full-
length plays, one-acts, translations, adaptations. **Special interests:** plays for
multigenerational audiences only; culturally diverse themes; plays with music;
ensemble plays; plays of any length (10 minutes or more) by upstate NY residents,
especially Catskill Mountain-area writers, about life in rural upstate NY. **Facilities:**
no permanent facility. **Production considerations:** minimal set. **Best submission
time:** Oct–Apr. **Response time:** 1 week letter (if interested); 3–6 months script.
Special programs: New Play Works: new-play developmental program of readings
and workshop productions.

OREGON SHAKESPEARE FESTIVAL

Box 158; Ashland, OR 97520; (541) 482-2111, FAX 482-0446
Cynthia White, *Associate Director/Play Development*

Submission procedure: no unsolicited scripts; professional recommendation.
Types of material: full-length plays, translations. **Special interests:** plays of ideas;
language-oriented plays; submissions by women and minorities encouraged.
Facilities: Elizabethan Theatre, 1194 seats, outdoor Elizabethan stage; Angus
Bowmer Theatre, 600 seats, thrust stage; Black Swan, 140 seats, black box. **Best
submission time:** year-round. **Response time:** varies. **Special programs:** reading
series; commissioning programs; developmental workshops.

ORGANIC THEATER COMPANY

3319 North Clark St; Chicago, IL 60657; (312) 327-2427, FAX 327-8947
Paul Frellick, *Artistic Director*

Submission procedure: no unsolicited scripts; synopsis, 10 pages of dialogue and letter of inquiry. **Types of material:** full-length plays, long one-acts. **Special interests:** unproduced works only; imaginative plays that explore the theatrical medium; scripts by women and minorities; writers willing to work a year or more to bring script from initial idea through workshop to limited or full production. **Facilities:** Mainstage, 400 seats, modified thrust stage; Organic Greenhouse, 90 seats, proscenium stage; South Hall, up to 60 seats, flexible space. **Best submission time:** year-round. **Response time:** 4–6 weeks letter; 2–4 months script.

PA STAGE

837 Linden St; Allentown, PA 18101; (610) 434-6110, FAX 433-6086
Charles Richter, *Producing Artistic Director*

Submission procedure: no unsolicited scripts; synopsis, cast list, 10 pages of dialogue and letter of inquiry. **Types of material:** full-length plays, musicals, solo pieces. **Facilities:** J. I. Rodale Theatre, 274 seats, proscenium stage. **Production considerations:** cast limit of 10 for musicals, 11 for plays; prefers 1 set. **Best submission time:** year-round. **Response time:** 1 month letter; 3 months script. **Special programs:** New Evolving Works Program: staged reading series.

PAN ASIAN REPERTORY THEATRE

47 Great Jones St; New York, NY 10012; (212) 505-5655, FAX 505-6014
Tisa Chang, *Artistic/Producing Director*

Submission procedure: accepts unsolicited scripts with resume. **Types of material:** full-length plays, translations, adaptations, musicals. **Special interests:** Asian or Asian-American themes only. **Facilities:** St. Clement's Theatre, 150 seats, 38' x 40' open stage. **Production considerations:** prefers cast limit of 8. **Best submission time:** summer. **Response time:** 9 months. **Special programs:** staged readings and workshops.

THE PASADENA PLAYHOUSE

39 South El Molino Ave; Pasadena, CA 91101; (818) 792-8672

Submission procedure: no unsolicited scripts; synopsis, character breakdown, first 15 pages of text and letter of inquiry. **Types of material:** full-length plays, musicals. **Special interests:** works with broad commercial appeal. **Facilities:** The Pasadena Playhouse, 670 seats, proscenium stage. **Production considerations:** cast limit of 7; 1 set or unit set; modest musical requirements. **Best submission time:** year-round. **Response time:** 2–3 months letter; 12 months script.

PEGASUS PLAYERS

1145 West Wilson; Chicago, IL 60640; (312) 878-9761, FAX 271-8057;
E-mail uwcrocker@uxa.ecn.bgu.edu
Warner Crocker, *Artistic Director*

Submission procedure: no unsolicited scripts; synopsis and letter of inquiry. **Types of material:** full-length plays, translations, adaptations, musicals, solo pieces. **Facilities:** The O'Rourke Center for the Performing Arts, 250 seats, proscenium stage. **Best submission time:** year-round. **Response time:** 1 month letter; 4–6 months script. **Special programs:** Chicago Young Playwrights Festival: annual Jan festival of plays by Chicago-area high school students; write for information.

PENGUIN REPERTORY COMPANY

Box 91; Stony Point, NY 10980; (914) 786-2873, FAX 786-5919
Joe Brancato, *Artistic Director*

Submission procedure: accepts unsolicited scripts. **Types of material:** full-length plays, adaptations. **Facilities:** Barn Playhouse, 108 seats, proscenium stage. **Production considerations:** cast limit of 5; simple set. **Best submission time:** Jun–Sep. **Response time:** 3 months.

PENNSYLVANIA SHAKESPEARE FESTIVAL

2755 Station Ave; Center Valley, PA 18034; (610) 282-9455, FAX 282-2240
Jay Kline, *Assistant Professor*

Submission procedure: no unsolicited scripts; synopsis and letter of inquiry. **Types of material:** full-length plays. **Facilities:** Mainstage, 473 seats, modified thrust stage; Arena Stage, 215 seats, arena stage. **Best submission time:** year-round. **Response time:** 2 months letter; 6 months script.

PENOBSCOT THEATRE COMPANY

183 Main St; Bangor, ME 04401; (207) 942-3333, FAX 947-6678
Mark Torres, *Producing Artistic Director*

Submission procedure: no unsolicited scripts; synopsis and letter of inquiry. **Types of material:** full-length plays, plays for young audiences. **Special interests:** new American plays. **Facilities:** Penobscot Theatre, 132 seats, proscenium/thrust stage. **Production considerations:** small cast, limited production requirements; small performance space. **Best submission time:** late fall. **Response time:** 1 month letter; 2 months script. **Special programs:** play reading series in late spring; scripts selected through theatre's normal submission procedure.

THE PENUMBRA THEATRE COMPANY

The Martin Luther King Bldg; 270 North Kent St; St. Paul, MN 55102-1794;
(612) 224-4601, FAX 224-7074
Lou Bellamy, *Artistic Director*

Submission procedure: accepts unsolicited scripts with resume. **Types of material:**

full-length plays, one-acts, translations, adaptations, plays for young audiences, musicals. **Special interests:** works that address the African-American experience. **Facilities:** Hallie Q. Brown Theatre, 260 seats, proscenium/thrust stage. **Best submission time:** year-round. **Response time:** 6–9 months. **Special programs:** Cornerstone Dramaturgy and Development Project (see Development).

THE PEOPLE'S LIGHT AND THEATRE COMPANY
39 Conestoga Rd; Malvern, PA 19355-1798; (215) 647-1900
Alda Cortese, *Literary Manager*

Submission procedure: no unsolicited scripts; synopsis, cast list, 10 pages of dialogue and letter of inquiry. **Types of material:** full-length plays, translations, adaptations. **Facilities:** People's Light and Theatre, 350 seats, flexible stage; Steinbright Stage, 99–150 seats, flexible stage. **Production considerations:** prefers cast limit of 12, 1 set or unit set. **Best submission time:** year-round. **Response time:** 2 weeks letter; 8–10 months script.

PERSEVERANCE THEATRE
914 3rd St; Douglas, AK 99824; (907) 364-2421, -2151, FAX 364-2603;
      E-mail persthr@ptialaska.net
Molly Smith, *Artistic Director*

Submission procedure: no unsolicited scripts; synopsis, resume, list of previous productions and letter of inquiry. **Types of material:** full-length plays, one-acts, solo pieces. **Special interests:** new plays by AK playwrights; plays about ethnic experiences, gender, sexual orientation and disabilities. **Facilities:** Mainstage, 150 seats, thrust stage; Phoenix Stage, 50–75 seats, flexible space. **Best submission time:** year-round. **Response time:** 2 months letter; 6 months script.

PETERBOROUGH PLAYERS
Box 118; Peterborough, NH 03458; (603) 924-7585
Gus Kaikkonem, *Artistic Director*

Submission procedure: no unsolicited scripts; synopsis and letter of inquiry. **Types of material:** full-length plays, one-acts, adaptations. **Facilities:** Hadley Barn, 207 seats, flexible stage. **Best submission time:** Sep–Dec. **Response time:** 2 months letter; 6 months script. **Special programs:** staged readings.

PHILADELPHIA FESTIVAL THEATRE FOR NEW PLAYS
AT ANNENBERG CENTER
3680 Walnut St; Philadelphia, PA 19104; (215) 898-3900, FAX 898-7240;
      E-mail pfr@libertynet.org
Sally de Sousa, *Producing Director*

Submission procedure: no unsolicited scripts; synopsis, 10 pages of dialogue, resume and letter of inquiry. **Types of material:** full-length plays. **Special interests:** only plays not previously given full production; plays that reflect larger social issues through strong character relationships. **Facilities:** Zellerbach Theatre, 900 seats, proscenium/thrust stage; Harold Prince Theatre, 200 seats, proscenium or 3/4-arena stage. **Best submission time:** year-round. **Response time:** 3–4 weeks letter; 6–9 months script. **Special programs:** Previewers: series of script-in-hand readings; scripts selected through theatre's normal submission procedure.

PHILADELPHIA THEATRE COMPANY
The Belgravia, Suite 300; 1811 Chestnut St; Philadelphia, PA 19103;
(215) 568-1920, FAX 568-1944
Sara Garonzik, *Producing Artistic Director*

Submission procedure: no unsolicited scripts; agent submission. **Types of material:** full-length plays, solo pieces. **Special interests:** new American plays; social/humanistic themes; sense of theatricality. **Facilities:** Plays and Players Theater, 324 seats, proscenium stage. **Best submission time:** Jan–Jun. **Response time:** 6–8 months. **Special programs:** STAGES: program of staged readings.

PHOENIX THEATRE
1625 North Central Ave, #2; Phoenix, AZ 85004; (602) 258-1974, FAX 253-3626
Michael Mitchell, *Artistic Director*

Submission procedure: no unsolicited scripts; synopsis and letter of inquiry with SASE for response; send production history if available. **Types of material:** plays for young audiences, musicals, cabaret/revues. **Facilities:** Mainstage, 346 seats, proscenium stage; Cookie Company, 175 seats, arena stage. **Best submission time:** Jan, Aug. **Response time:** 1 month letter; 3 months script.

THE PHOENIX THEATRE
749 North Park Ave; Indianapolis, IN 46202; (317) 635-7529, FAX 635-7529
Bryan Fonseca, *Producing Director*

Submission procedure: no unsolicited scripts. **Types of material:** full-length plays, one-acts. **Facilities:** Mainstage, 150 seats, proscenium stage; Underground, 75 seats, black box. **Special programs:** The Festival of Emerging American Theatre (FEAT) Competition (see Prizes).

THE PHOENIX THEATRE COMPANY
Box 544; Purchase, NY 10577; (914) 251-6288, FAX 251-6289
Bram Lewis, *Artistic Director*

Submission procedure: accepts unsolicited scripts. **Types of material:** full-length plays, one-acts, translations, adaptations, plays for young audiences, musicals, cabaret/revues, performance art. **Special interests:** mainstream works for main stage; more provocative works for second stage. **Facilities:** main stage, 516 seats, proscenium stage; second stage, 300 seats, black box. **Best submission time:** Jan. **Response time:** 10 weeks.

PILLSBURY HOUSE THEATRE
3501 Chicago Ave S; Minneapolis, MN 55407; (612) 824-0708, FAX 827-5818
Ralph Remington, *Producing Artistic Director*

Submission procedure: no unsolicited scripts; synopsis and letter of inquiry; resume and dialogue samples optional. **Types of material:** full-length plays, one-acts, translations, adaptations, plays for young audiences, musicals, performance art, solo pieces. **Special interests:** only works that speak to issues of sociopolitical change; works that address marginalized groups, e.g., people of color, women, lesbians, gays, the disabled and the economically disenfranchised; nonlinear works. **Facilities:** Pillsbury House Theatre, 120 seats, black box/proscenium stage. **Production considerations:** cast limit of 12; no fly space. **Best submission time:** year-round. **Response time:** 3 months letter; 3–6 months script.

PING CHONG & COMPANY
47 Great Jones St; New York, NY 10012; (212) 529-1557, FAX 529-1703

Submission procedure: no unsolicited scripts; direct solicitation to playwright. **Types of material:** full-length works by company only. **Facilities:** no permanent facility.

PIONEER THEATRE COMPANY
University of Utah; Salt Lake City, UT 84112; (801) 581-6356, FAX 581-5472
Charles Morey, *Artistic Director*

Submission procedure: no unsolicited scripts; synopsis and letter of inquiry. **Types of material:** full-length plays, translations, adaptations, musicals. **Facilities:** Pioneer Memorial Theatre, 1000 seats, proscenium stage. **Best submission time:** fall. **Response time:** 1 month letter; 6 months script.

PIRATE PLAYHOUSE—ISLAND THEATRE
2200 Periwinkle Way; Sanibel Island, FL 33957; (941) 472-4109, FAX 472-0055;
E-mail pirateplay@aol.com
Robert Cacioppo, *Artistic Director*

Submission procedure: no unsolicited scripts; synopsis, 10-page dialogue sample, character breakdown and letter of inquiry with SASP for response. **Types of material:** full-length plays, plays for young audiences, musicals, cabaret/revues, solo pieces. **Facilities:** Pirate Playhouse, 180 seats, thrust/proscenium/arena stage. **Best submission time:** year-round. **Response time:** 1–3 months letter; 3–5 months script.

PITTSBURGH PUBLIC THEATER
Allegheny Square; Pittsburgh, PA 15212-5349; (412) 323-8200, FAX 323-8550
Rob Zellers, *Literary Manager*

Submission procedure: no unsolicited scripts; synopsis, dialogue sample and letter of inquiry with SASE for response. **Types of material:** full-length plays, translations, adaptations, musicals. **Facilities:** Theodore L. Hazlett, Jr. Theater, 457 seats, thrust or arena stage. **Best submission time:** year-round. **Response time:** 1 month letter; 3 months script.

PLAYHOUSE ON THE SQUARE

51 South Cooper St; Memphis, TN 38104; (901) 725-0776, FAX 272-7530
Jackie Nichols, *Executive Producer*

Submission procedure: accepts unsolicited scripts. **Types of material:** full-length plays, musicals. **Facilities:** Playhouse on the Square, 250 seats, proscenium stage; Circuit Playhouse, 136 seats, proscenium stage. **Best submission time:** year-round. **Response time:** 3–5 months. **Special programs:** Playhouse on the Square New Play Competition (see Prizes).

PLAYMAKERS REPERTORY COMPANY

CB# 3235 Graham Memorial Bldg, 052A; Chapel Hill, NC 27599-3235;
    (919) 962-1132, FAX 962-4069
David Hammond, *Associate Producing Director*

Submission procedure: no unsolicited scripts; professional recommendation. **Types of material:** full-length plays, translations, adaptations, solo pieces. **Facilities:** Paul Green Theatre, 498 seats, thrust stage. **Best submission time:** Apr–Sep. **Response time:** 6 months.

THE PLAYWRIGHTS' CENTER

See Membership and Service Organizations.

PLAYWRIGHTS HORIZONS

416 West 42nd St; New York, NY 10036-6896; (212) 564-1235, FAX 594-0296
Sonya Sobieski, *Literary Manager*

Submission procedure: accepts unsolicited scripts with resume and cover letter; if necessary, will accept synopsis, dialogue sample and letter of inquiry; for musicals, send script and cassette (no synopses). **Types of material:** full-length plays, musicals; no one-person shows or children's theatre. **Special interests:** works by American writers only; works with strong sense of language that take theatrical risks. **Facilities:** Mainstage, 145 seats, proscenium stage; Studio Theater, 72 seats, black box. **Best submission time:** year-round. **Response time:** 6 weeks letter; 3–6 months script.

POPE THEATRE COMPANY

262 South Ocean Blvd; Manalapan, FL 33462; (407) 585-3404, FAX 588-4708
Louis Tyrrell, *Producing Director*

Submission procedure: no unsolicited scripts; agent submission. **Types of material:** full-length plays, plays for young audiences. **Special interests:** contemporary issues and ideas. **Facilities:** Lois Pope Theatre, 250 seats, thrust stage. **Production**

considerations: cast of 2–6; 1 set. **Best submission time:** year-round. **Response time:** 3–4 months. **Special programs:** reading series.

PORTLAND CENTER STAGE

1111 Southwest Broadway; Portland, OR 97205; (503) 248-6309
Elizabeth Huddle, *Producing Artistic Director*

Submission procedure: no unsolicited scripts; synopsis and letter of inquiry. **Types of material:** full-length plays, translations, adaptations. **Facilities:** Intermediate Theatre, Portland Center for the Performing Arts, 860 seats, proscenium stage. **Production considerations:** prefers cast of 8–12. **Best submission time:** year-round. **Response time:** 1–2 months letter; 2–3 months script.

PORTLAND REPERTORY THEATRE

2 World Trade Center; 25 Southwest Salmon St; Portland, OR 97204-3233;
   (503) 224-4491, FAX 224-1316
Kit Koenig, *Literary Manager/Dramaturg*

Submission procedure: no unsolicited scripts; synopsis, first 10–15 pages of script, character breakdown, set description and letter of inquiry with SASE for response. **Types of material:** full-length plays, translations, adaptations. **Facilities:** Portland Repertory Theatre, 230 seats, proscenium stage. **Production considerations:** cast limit of 10; maximum 2 sets. **Best submission time:** May–Aug. **Response time:** 4 months letter; 6–12 months script. **Special programs:** staged reading series; play development for Portland-area playwrights.

PORTLAND STAGE COMPANY

Box 1458; Portland, ME 04104; (207) 774-1043
Matthew Arbour, *Literary Manager*

Submission procedure: no unsolicited scripts; synopsis, dialogue sample and letter of inquiry. **Types of material:** full-length plays, translations, adaptations. **Facilities:** Performing Arts Center Theatre, 290 seats, proscenium stage; PSC Rehearsal Hall, 90 seats, flexible space (readings only). **Best submission time:** year-round. **Response time:** 2 months letter; 3–6 months script. **Special programs:** in-house play readings.

PRIMARY STAGES COMPANY

584 9th Ave; New York, NY 10027; (212) 333-7471, FAX 333-2025
Andrew Leynse, *Literary Manager*

Submission procedure: accepts unsolicited scripts; also accepts synopsis, 10 pages of dialogue and letter of inquiry with SASE for response. **Types of material:** full-length plays, musicals, solo pieces. **Special interests:** new American plays and musicals previously unproduced in New York City. **Facilities:** Primary Stages Theatre, 99 seats, proscenium stage; Phil Bosakowski Theatre, 65 seats, proscenium stage. **Production considerations:** prefers small cast; single set or unit set; no fly or wing space. **Best submission time:** Sep–Jun. **Response time:** 1 month letter; 3–5 months script. **Special programs:** Ten-Minute Play Festival: festival of single-theme 10-minute plays; by invitation only; *dates:* Oct 1996.

THE PUBLIC THEATER/NEW YORK SHAKESPEARE FESTIVAL

Joseph Papp Public Theater; 425 Lafayette St; New York, NY 10003;
(212) 539-8530, FAX 539-8505
Shelby Jiggetts, *Play Development Department*
Wiley Hausam, *Associate Producer, Musicals*

Submission procedure: no unsolicited scripts; synopsis, 10-page sample scene and letter of inquiry; include cassette of 3–5 songs for musicals and operas. **Types of material:** full-length plays, translations, adaptations, musicals, operas, solo pieces. **Facilities:** Newman Theater, 299 seats, proscenium stage; Anspacher Theater, 275 seats, thrust stage; Martinson Hall, 200 seats, proscenium stage; LuEsther Hall, 150 seats, flexible stage; Shiva Theater, 100 seats, flexible stage. **Best submission time:** year-round. **Response time:** 1 month letter; 6 months script.

THE PURPLE ROSE THEATRE COMPANY

137 Park St; Chelsea, MI 48118; (313) 475-5817, FAX 475-0802
Anthony Caselli, *Literary Manager*

Submission procedure: accepts unsolicited scripts. **Types of material:** full-length plays. **Special interests:** plays that speak to a middle-American audience. **Facilities:** Garage Theatre, 119 seats, thrust stage. **Production considerations:** cast limit of 10; no fly or wing space. **Best submission time:** year-round. **Response time:** 6–9 months. **Special programs:** Playwrights Unit: area playwrights meet monthly to discuss works; interested playwrights send letter of introduction addressed to unit. Developmental workshops: members of Playwrights Unit or playwrights found through theatre's normal submission procedure work with company to develop scripts through readings and conferences.

REPERTORIO ESPAÑOL

138 East 27th St; New York, NY 10016; (212) 889-2850, FAX 686-3732
Robert Weber Federico, *Artistic Associate Producer*

Submission procedure: no unsolicited scripts; synopsis and letter of inquiry. **Types of material:** full-length plays, adaptations, plays for young audiences, musicals, operas. **Special interests:** plays dealing with Hispanic themes. **Facilities:** Gramercy Arts Theatre, 135 seats, proscenium stage. **Production considerations:** small cast. **Best submission time:** summer. **Response time:** 1 month letter; 6 months script.

THE REPERTORY THEATRE OF ST. LOUIS

Box 191730; St. Louis, MO 63119; (314) 968-7340
Susan Gregg, *Associate Artistic Director*

Submission procedure: no unsolicited scripts; synopsis, character breakdown, technical requirements and letter of inquiry. **Types of material:** full-length plays. **Special interests:** nonnaturalistic plays; contemporary social and political issues.

Facilities: Main Stage, 750 seats, thrust stage; Studio Theatre, 130 seats, black box. **Production considerations:** small cast, modest production demands. **Best submission time:** year-round. **Response time:** 1 month letter; 2 years script. **Special programs:** developmental workshop for new plays; scripts selected through theatre's normal submission procedure.

RIVERSIDE THEATRE
Box 3788; Vero Beach, FL 32964; (407) 231-5860
Jennie L. Davis, *Production Stage Manager*

Submission procedure: no unsolicited scripts; synopsis and letter of inquiry. **Types of material:** full-length plays, translations, adaptations, plays for young audiences, musicals. **Facilities:** Riverside Theatre, 633 seats, proscenium stage; Agnes Wahlstrom Youth Playhouse, 200 seats, flexible stage. **Production considerations:** cast limit of 10. **Best submission time:** fall. **Response time:** 1 month letter (if interested); 3–5 months script.

RIVERSIDE THEATRE
Box 1651; Iowa City, IA 52244; (319) 338-7672, FAX 338-7672
Ron Clark, *Artistic Director*

Submission procedure: no unsolicited scripts; synopsis and letter of inquiry. **Types of material:** full-length plays, translations, adaptations, cabaret/revues, solo pieces. **Facilities:** Riverside Theatre, 110 seats, flexible stage. **Production considerations:** small cast; simple set. **Best submission time:** year-round. **Response time:** 1 month letter (if interested); 3–5 months script.

THE ROAD COMPANY
Box 5278 EKS; Johnson City, TN 37603-5278; (423) 926-7726
Christine Murdock, *General Manager*

Submission procedure: no unsolicited scripts. **Types of material:** full-length plays, one-acts, adaptations, cabaret/revues. **Special interests:** southern playwrights; experimental work. **Facilities:** Beeson Hall, 100–150 seats, flexible space. **Production considerations:** small cast; simple sets. **Special programs:** salaried writer-in-residence each season.

ROADSIDE THEATER
306 Madison St; Whitesburg, KY 41858; (606) 633-0108, FAX 633-1009;
    E-mail roadsideth@aol.com
Dudley Cocke, *Director*

Submission procedure: no unsolicited scripts; synopsis, dialogue sample and letter of inquiry. **Types of material:** full-length plays. **Special interests:** plays about the Appalachian region only. **Facilities:** Appalshop Theater, 150 seats, thrust stage. **Production considerations:** small cast; simple sets suitable for touring. **Best submission time:** year-round. **Response time:** 2 weeks letter; 1 month script. **Special programs:** reading and workshop series. Playwright residencies initiated by theatre; playwright may not apply.

ROUND HOUSE THEATRE

12210 Bushey Dr; Silver Spring, MD 20902; (301) 933-9530
Jerry Whiddon, *Producing Artistic Director*

Submission procedure: no unsolicited scripts; synopsis, dialogue sample, cast breakdown, technical requirements and letter of inquiry. **Types of material:** full-length plays, translations, adaptations, plays for young audiences, musicals. **Special interests:** contemporary issues; new translations of lesser-known classics; experimental works; humorous plays. **Facilities:** Round House Theatre, 216 seats, modified thrust stage. **Production considerations:** cast limit of 8; prefers 1 set. **Best submission time:** year-round. **Response time:** 2 months letter (if interested); at least 12 months script.

SACRAMENTO THEATRE COMPANY

1419 H St; Sacramento, CA 95814; (916) 446-7501, FAX 446-4066
Patrick Elkins-Zeglarski, *Artistic Coordinator*

Submission procedure: no unsolicited scripts; synopsis, resume and letter of inquiry with SASE for response. **Types of material:** full-length plays, adaptations, cabaret/revues. **Special interests:** contemporary social and political issues; craftsmanship; theatricality; vital language; "characters an audience will care about." **Facilities:** McClatchy Mainstage, 300 seats, proscenium stage; Stage II, 90 seats, black box. **Production considerations:** cast of 3–5. **Best submission time:** Jun–Dec. **Response time:** 1 month letter; 3 months script.

THE SALT LAKE ACTING COMPANY

168 West 500 N; Salt Lake City, UT 84103; (801) 363-0526
David Mong, *Literary Manager*

Submission procedure: no unsolicited scripts; synopsis, 5–10 pages of dialogue, resume and letter of inquiry with SASE for response. **Types of material:** full-length plays, translations, adaptations, musicals. **Special interests:** western American writers "who understand the unique synergistic effect that playwright, actor and audience enjoy when a work is produced for the stage." **Facilities:** Upstairs, 99–130 seats, thrust stage; Chapel Theatre, 90 seats, thrust stage. **Best submission time:** year-round. **Response time:** 4 months letter; 8 months script. **Special programs:** reading series in winter, spring and fall.

SAN DIEGO REPERTORY THEATRE

79 Horton Plaza; San Diego, CA 92101; (619) 231-3586, FAX 235-0939
Todd Salovey, *Literary Manager*

Submission procedure: no unsolicited scripts; synopsis and letter of inquiry. **Types of material:** full-length plays, translations, adaptations, musicals, literary cabaret, mixed-media events. **Special interests:** multiethnic work; hard-hitting social and political work; offbeat hip musicals; dramatic work with unusual incorporation of music; women's issues; sharp-edged comedy; poetic visions; Hispanic plays suitable for presentation in both Spanish and English. **Facilities:** Lyceum Stage, 570 seats, modified thrust stage; Lyceum Space, 270 seats, flexible stage. **Production considerations:** no fly loft in Lyceum Space. **Best submission time:** year-round. **Response time:** 3 months letter; 12 months script. **Special programs:** readings and workshop productions.

SAN JOSE REPERTORY THEATRE
Box 2399; San Jose, CA 95109-2399; (408) 291-2266, FAX 995-0737
J. R. Orlando, *Assistant to the Artistic Director*

Submission procedure: no unsolicited scripts; synopsis, dialogue sample and letter of inquiry with SASP for response. **Types of material:** full-length plays, translations, adaptations, musicals, solo pieces. **Special interests:** small-cast musicals. **Facilities:** Montgomery Theatre, 537 seats, proscenium stage; Louis B. Mayer Theatre, 505 seats, proscenium stage. **Best submission time:** Sep–Nov. **Response time:** 1 month letter; 6 months script.

SANTA FE STAGES
105 East Marcy St, Suite 107; Santa Fe, NM 87505; (505) 982-6680,
     FAX 982-6682; E-mail rr19@ix.netcom.com
Martin Platt, *Artistic Director*

Submission procedure: no unsolicited scripts; agent submission. **Types of material:** full-length plays, translations, adaptations. **Special interests:** cutting-edge works. **Facilities:** Greer Garson Theatre, 525 seats, proscenium stage; Weckesser Studio Theatre, 100 seats, flexible stage. **Best submission time:** Sep–Apr. **Response time:** 1 week letter; 3 months script.

SANTA MONICA PLAYHOUSE
1211 4th St; Santa Monica, CA 90401-1391; (310) 394-9779, FAX 393-5573
Chris DeCarlo, *Co-Artistic Director*
Evelyn Rudie, *Co-Artistic Director*

Submission procedure: no unsolicited scripts; synopsis and letter of inquiry. **Types of material:** full-length plays, one-acts, translations, adaptations, plays for young audiences, musicals. **Facilities:** Santa Monica Playhouse, 88 seats, arena/thrust stage. **Production considerations:** cast limit of 8, simple production demands. **Best submission time:** year-round. **Response time:** 3 months letter; 6 months script.

SEACOAST REPERTORY THEATRE
125 Bow St; Portsmouth, NH 03801; (603) 433-4793, FAX 431-7818
Roy M. Rogosin, *Producing Artistic Director*

Submission procedure: no unsolicited scripts; agent submission (1-page synopsis only; include cassette for musicals). **Types of material:** full-length plays, plays for young audiences, musicals. **Special interests:** new American plays; small-scale musicals; plays for young audiences. **Facilities:** Seacoast Repertory Theatre of the

Portsmouth Academy of Performing Arts, 175 seats, thrust stage. **Best submission time:** year-round. **Response time:** 3–6 months.

SEASIDE MUSIC THEATER
Box 2835; Daytona Beach, FL 32120; (904) 252-3394, FAX 252-8991;
    E-mail smthead@aol.com
Lester Malizia, *General Manager*

Submission procedure: no unsolicited scripts; synopsis, cassette of music and letter of inquiry. **Types of material:** musicals for young and adult audiences, cabaret/revues. **Facilities:** Winter Theater, 600 seats, proscenium stage; Summer Repertory Theater, 500 seats, proscenium stage; Theater for Children, 150 seats, modified thrust stage. **Production considerations:** cast limit of 8 for Winter Theater, 30 for Summer Repertory Theater, 10 for Theater for Children; small musical combo for Theater for Children and Winter Theater, 25-member orchestra for Summer Repertory Theater; no wing or orchestra space in Winter Theater; no fly space except in Summer Repertory Theater. **Best submission time:** Sep–Nov. **Response time:** 1 month letter; 3 months script.

SEATTLE CHILDREN'S THEATRE
Box 9640; Seattle, WA 98109-0640; (206) 443-0807
Deborah Frockt, *Dramaturg/Literary Manager*

Submission procedure: no unsolicited scripts; synopsis, 10-page dialogue sample, resume and letter of inquiry with SASP for response. **Types of material:** full-length plays for young audiences, including translations, adaptations, musicals, solo pieces. **Special interests:** sophisticated works for young audiences that also appeal to adults. **Facilities:** Charlotte Martin Theatre, 485 seats, proscenium stage; Eve Alvord Theatre, 280 seats, black box. **Best submission time:** year-round. **Response time:** 2 months letter; 6 months script.

SEATTLE REPERTORY THEATRE
155 Mercer St; Seattle, WA 98109; (206) 443-2210
Kurt Beattie, *Artistic Associate/Literary Manager*

Submission procedure: no unsolicited scripts; professional recommendation. **Types of material:** full-length plays, translations, adaptations, musicals, solo pieces. **Facilities:** Seattle Repertory Theatre, 856 seats, proscenium stage; second theatre, 284 seats, proscenium stage. **Best submission time:** year-round. **Response time:** 2–3 months. **Special programs:** New Plays in Process Project: program of workshop productions; playwright receives travel and per diem.

SECOND STAGE THEATRE
Box 1807, Ansonia Station; New York, NY 10023; (212) 787-8302,
    FAX 877-9886
(Mr.) Erin Sanders, *Literary Manager/Dramaturg*

Submission procedure: no unsolicited scripts; synopsis, 5–10-page dialogue sample, resume and letter of inquiry. **Types of material:** full-length plays, adaptations, musicals. **Special interests:** new and previously produced American plays (include production history with script); "heightened" realism; sociopolitical issues; plays by women and minority writers. **Facilities:** McGinn/Cazale Theatre, 108 seats, endstage. **Best submission time:** year-round. **Response time:** 1 month letter; 4–6 months script. **Special programs:** annual series of 4–6 readings of new and previously produced plays.

7 STAGES
1105 Euclid Ave NE; Atlanta, GA 30307; (404) 522-0911
Del Hamilton, *Artistic Director*

Submission procedure: no unsolicited scripts; synopsis, dialogue sample, resume and letter of inquiry. **Types of material:** full-length plays, translations, adaptations, performance pieces. **Special interests:** nontraditional plays and performance texts focusing on social, political or spiritual themes. **Facilities:** 7 Stages, 250 seats, thrust stage; Back Door, 100 seats, flexible stage. **Best submission time:** year-round. **Response time:** 4 months letter; 12 months script. **Special programs:** Workshop Program: year-round development of nontraditional, process-oriented pieces that involve collaboration with other theatre artists (dancers, musicians, designers, etc.); send letter of inquiry.

SHAKESPEARE & COMPANY
The Mount; Box 865; Lenox, MA 01240; (413) 637-1199, ext 112
Dennis Krausnick, *Director of Training*

Submission procedure: no unsolicited scripts; synopsis, 4-page dialogue sample and letter of inquiry. **Types of material:** full-length and one-act adaptations. **Special interests:** plays based on or adapted from works by Edith Wharton or Henry James only. **Facilities:** Mainstage Theatre, 500 seats, outdoor amphitheatre; Oxford Court, 250 seats, outdoor amphitheatre; Stables Theatre, 108 seats, thrust stage; Salon Theatre, 75–90 seats, endstage. **Production considerations:** minimal set pieces only; all theatre spaces part of historic estate (former home of Edith Wharton). **Best submission time:** fall–winter. **Response time:** 6 months letter (if interested); 6 months script.

SHAKESPEARE SANTA CRUZ
Performing Arts Complex; University of California–Santa Cruz;
     Santa Cruz, CA 95064; (408) 459-2121, FAX 459-3552;
      E-mail karin_magaldi-unger@macmail.ucsc.edu
Karin Magaldi-Unger, *Literary Manager*

Submission procedure: no unsolicited scripts; will accept synopsis, resume and letter of inquiry; prefers professional recommendation. **Types of material:** full-length plays, one-acts, plays for young audiences. **Special interests:** Shakespearean spinoffs, i.e., plays that use Shakespeare's characters or plots. **Facilities:** Sinsheimer-Stanley Glen, 500–800 seats, outdoor amphitheatre; Performing Arts Theater, 500 seats, thrust stage. **Production considerations:** small cast; minimal set. **Best submission time:** fall–winter. **Response time:** 1 month letter; 1 month script.

THE SHAKESPEARE THEATRE
301 East Capitol St SE; Washington, DC 20003; (202) 547-3230, FAX 546-9447;
    E-mail shakespearedc.org
Michael Kahn, *Artistic Director*

Submission procedure: no unsolicited scripts; professional recommendation. **Types of material:** translations, adaptations. **Special interests:** translations and adaptations of classics only. **Facilities:** Lansburgh Theatre, 449 seats, thrust stage. **Best submission time:** summer. **Response time:** 2 months.

SIGNATURE THEATRE
3806 South Four Mile Run Dr; Arlington, VA 22206; (703) 820-9771
Marcia Gardner, *Literary Manager*

Submission procedure: accepts unsolicited scripts that have not been professionally produced; no dialogue samples or synopses. **Types of material:** full-length plays, adaptations, musicals. **Special interests:** social issues; comedies. **Facilities:** Signature Theatre, 126 seats, black box. **Production considerations:** prefers cast limit of 10; no fly space. **Best submission time:** Sep–May. **Response time:** 4 months. **Special programs:** Stages: staged readings of new plays-in-process; scripts selected through theatre's normal submission procedure. Emerging Playwrights Series: full production of 1 new play a year.

SIGNATURE THEATRE COMPANY, INC.
422 West 42nd St, 2nd Floor; New York, NY 10036-6809; (212) 967-1913,
    FAX 268-1446
James Houghton, *Founding Artistic Director*

Submission procedure: no unsolicited scripts; direct solicitation to playwright or agent. **Types of material:** full-length plays. **Special interests:** playwrights with substantial body of work to be produced over course of season. **Facilities:** no permanent facility; company performs in various end- or proscenium-stage venues with 99–125 seats. **Production considerations:** cast limit of 8; 1 set; modest production demands.

SINGULAR PRODUCTIONS
10824 Lindblade St; Culver City, CA 90230; (310) 558-1555, FAX 558-0513
Patrick McGowan, *Literary Manager*

Submission procedure: no unsolicited scripts; synopsis, 10-page dialogue sample and letter of inquiry with SASE for response. **Types of material:** full-length plays, translations, adaptations. **Facilities:** The Ivy Substation, 99 seats, flexible stage. **Production considerations:** cast minimum of 6 to accommodate ensemble. **Best submission time:** year-round. **Response time:** 2 months letter; 6–8 months script.

SOCIETY HILL PLAYHOUSE
507 South 8th St; Philadelphia, PA 19147; (215) 923-0210, FAX 923-1789
Walter Vail, *Literary Manager*

Submission procedure: no unsolicited scripts; synopsis and letter of inquiry with SASE for response. **Types of material:** full-length plays, translations, adaptations, musicals. **Special interests:** musicals and comedies with casts of 5–7. **Facilities:** Society Hill Playhouse, 223 seats, proscenium stage; Second Space, 90 seats, flexible stage. **Production considerations:** prefers small cast. **Best submission time:** year-round. **Response time:** 1 month letter; 6 months script.

SOURCE THEATRE COMPANY
1835 14th St NW; Washington, DC 20009; (202) 462-1073
Elizabeth Robelen, *Director of Script Development*

Submission procedure: accepts unsolicited scripts that have not been professionally produced with synopsis, resume and letter-size SASE for response (scripts not returned); new works normally produced as part of Washington Theatre Festival (see below) before being considered for main stage production. **Types of material:** full-length plays, one-acts, musicals, solo pieces. **Facilities:** Source Theatre Company, 101 seats, thrust stage. **Best submission time:** 16 Sep–14 Jan only. **Response time:** 4–8 months. **Special programs:** 17th Annual Washington Theatre Festival: new-play workshop productions; scripts selected through competition (see below); *deadline:* 15 Jan 1997; *dates:* 9 Jul–9 Aug 1997. Source Theatre Company 1997 Literary Prize (see Prizes).

SOUTH COAST REPERTORY
Box 2197; Costa Mesa, CA 92628-2197; (714) 957-2602
Jerry Patch, *Dramaturg*
John Glore, *Literary Manager*

Submission procedure: no unsolicited scripts; synopsis and letter of inquiry; dialogue sample is optional. **Types of material:** full-length plays, one-acts, translations, adaptations, musicals. **Facilities:** Mainstage, 507 seats, modified thrust stage; Second Stage, 161 seats, thrust stage. **Best submission time:** year-round. **Response time:** 1–3 weeks letter; 2–4 months script. **Special programs:** COLAB (Collaboration Laboratory) New Play Program: developmental program involving readings, staged readings, workshop and full productions; participation and all commissions offered by David Emmes and Martin Benson, artistic directors; playwright receives grant, commission and/or royalties depending on nature of project. Hispanic Playwrights Project (see Development).

SPOKANE INTERPLAYERS ENSEMBLE
Box 1961; Spokane, WA 99210; (509) 455-7529, FAX 624-5902
Robert A. Welch, *Managing Director*

Submission procedure: no unsolicited scripts; synopsis with cast list, set requirements, play's production history and reviews (if any), dialogue sample and letter of inquiry. **Types of material:** full-length plays. **Facilities:** Spokane Interplayers Ensemble, 255 seats, thrust stage. **Production considerations:** prefers cast limit of 8, 1 set. **Best submission time:** year-round. **Response time:** 3 months letter (if interested); 3–6 months script.

ST. LOUIS BLACK REPERTORY COMPANY

634 North Grand Blvd, Suite 10-F; St. Louis, MO 63103; (314) 534-3807,
FAX 533-3345
Ronald J. Himes, *Producing Director*

Submission procedure: no unsolicited scripts; synopsis, 3–5-page dialogue sample, resume and letter of inquiry. **Types of material:** full-length plays, plays for young audiences, musicals. **Special interests:** works by African-American and Third World playwrights. **Facilities:** Grandel Square Theatre, 470 seats, thrust stage. **Best submission time:** Jun–Aug. **Response time:** 2 months letter; 2 months script. **Special programs:** touring company presenting works for young audiences.

STAGE ONE: THE LOUISVILLE CHILDREN'S THEATRE

425 West Market St; Louisville, KY 40202-3300; (502) 589-5946, FAX 585-5910;
E-mail kystageone@aol.com
Moses Goldberg, *Producing Director*

Submission procedure: accepts unsolicited scripts. **Types of material:** plays for young audiences. **Special interests:** plays about young people in the real world; good, honest treatments of familiar titles. **Facilities:** Moritz von Bomard Theater, 610 seats, thrust stage; Louisville Gardens, 300 seats, arena stage. **Production considerations:** prefers cast limit of 12; some productions tour. **Best submission time:** Oct–Dec. **Response time:** 3 months. **Special programs:** Tomorrow's Playwrights: annual one-act competition open to high school students throughout KY region; 3 finalists receive staged readings and prepare rewrite to determine placement; scholarship check for winner, cash awards for 2 runners-up and 3 sponsoring schools; submit play through school; *deadline:* 15 Jan 1997.

STAGE WEST

Box 2587; Fort Worth, TX 76113; (817) 924-9454, FAX 926-8650
Jerry Russell, *Artistic Director*

Submission procedure: no unsolicited scripts; synopsis and letter of inquiry. **Types of material:** full-length plays, translations, adaptations, solo pieces. **Special interests:** plays with universal themes; contemporary issues. **Facilities:** Stage West, 190 seats, thrust stage. **Production considerations:** prefers cast limit of 9. **Best submission time:** Jan–Mar. **Response time:** 1 month letter; 3 months script.

STAGES

1540 North McCadden Place; Hollywood, CA 90028; (213) 463-5356;
FAX (310) 440-3989
Marcella Meharg, *Dramaturg*

Submission procedure: no unsolicited scripts; synopsis and letter of inquiry. **Types of material:** full-length plays, one-acts, translations, adaptations. **Special interests:** plays by foreign writers both in original language and in translation; theatre regularly produces plays in Spanish, French and English but can also find actors fluent in other languages; challenging, experimental work. **Facilities:** Amphitheatre, 99 seats, outdoor flexible stage; Mainstage, 49 seats, proscenium stage; Lab, 25 seats, classroom. **Production considerations:** prefers cast limit of 5. **Best submission time:** year-round. **Response time:** 1 month letter; 3 months script.

STAGEWEST

One Columbus Center; Springfield, MA 01103; (413) 781-4470, FAX 781-3741
Albert Ihde, *Producing Director*

Submission procedure: no unsolicited scripts; synopsis and letter of inquiry. **Types of material:** full-length plays, translations, adaptations, solo pieces. **Special interests:** new translations or adaptations of neglected classic and 20th-century European plays; adaptations of nondramatic material. **Facilities:** Mainstage, 479 seats, thrust stage; Studio, 99 seats, flexible stage. **Best submission time:** year-round. **Response time:** 6 months letter; 3 months script.

STAMFORD THEATRE WORKS

95 Atlantic St; Stamford, CT 06901; (203) 359-4414, FAX 356-1846
Steve Karp, *Producing Director*

Submission procedure: no unsolicited scripts; synopsis, dialogue sample and letter of inquiry; include cassette for musicals. **Types of material:** full-length plays, translations, adaptations, musicals. **Special interests:** plays that are innovative and thought-provoking, socially and culturally relevant, challenging and entertaining. **Facilities:** Center Stage, 150 seats, modified thrust stage. **Production considerations:** prefers small cast, unit set. **Best submission time:** year-round. **Response time:** 2 months letter; 6 months script. **Special programs:** Plays-in-Process Series: 3 staged readings a year of unproduced plays or musicals for purpose of developing future STW productions.

STEPPENWOLF THEATRE COMPANY

1650 North Halsted; Chicago, IL 60614; (312) 335-1888, FAX 335-0808
Michele Volansky, *Dramaturg/Literary Manager*

Submission procedure: no unsolicited scripts; professional recommendation. **Types of material:** full-length plays, one-acts, translations, adaptations. **Special interests:** ensemble pieces with dynamic acting roles. **Facilities:** Mainstage, 510 seats, proscenium stage; Studio, 50–300 seats, flexible stage. **Best submission time:** year-round. **Response time:** 3–6 months letter; 3–6 months script.

STUDIO ARENA THEATRE

710 Main St; Buffalo, NY 14202-1990; (716) 856-8025, FAX 856-3415
Gavin Cameron-Webb, *Artistic Director*

Submission procedure: no unsolicited scripts; agent submission. **Types of material:** full-length plays, translations, adaptations. **Special interests:** plays of local interest; plays of a theatrical nature; American history and culture; ethnic cultures, including plays about minorities. **Facilities:** Studio Arena Theatre, 637 seats, thrust stage. **Production considerations:** cast limit of 12 (prefers smaller-cast plays); no fly system, limited wing space. **Best submission time:** year-round. **Response time:** 6 months.

THE STUDIO THEATRE

1333 P St NW; Washington, DC 20005; (202) 232-7267, FAX 588-5262;
      E-mail sseiden580@aol.com
Serge Seiden, *Literary Manager*

Submission procedure: no unsolicited scripts; direct solicitation to playwright or agent. **Types of material:** full-length plays, translations, adaptations, musicals, solo pieces. **Special interests:** American lyric realism; ethnic American themes; translations of new European and Asian plays. **Facilities:** The Studio Theatre, 200 seats, modified thrust stage; Secondstage, 50 seats, flexible stage.

SWINE PALACE PRODUCTIONS

217 M&DA Building; Baton Rouge, LA 70803; (504) 388-3533, FAX 388-4135
Lisa McEwen, *Artist/Administrator*

Submission procedure: accepts unsolicited scripts. **Types of material:** full-length plays, musicals. **Special interests:** works that explore issues pertinent to Louisiana. **Facilities:** LSU Theatre, 400 seats, proscenium stage. **Best submission time:** summer. **Response time:** 1 month.

SYRACUSE STAGE

820 East Genesee St; Syracuse, NY 13210-1508; (315) 443-4008, FAX 443-9846
Robert Moss, *Artistic Director*

Submission procedure: no unsolicited scripts; synopsis, 10-page dialogue sample, resume, character breakdown and letter of inquiry; include cassette for musicals. **Types of material:** full-length plays, translations, adaptations, musicals, solo pieces. **Facilities:** John D. Archbold Theatre, 499 seats, flexible stage. **Production considerations:** prefers cast limit of 8. **Best submission time:** early summer. **Response time:** 2 months letter; 6–9 months script.

TACOMA ACTORS GUILD
901 Broadway, 6th Floor; Tacoma, WA 98402-4404; (206) 272-3107,
    FAX 272-3358
Bruce K. Sevy, *Artistic Director*

Submission procedure: no unsolicited scripts; synopsis and letter of inquiry. **Types of material:** full-length plays, translations, adaptations, musicals. **Facilities:** Theatre on the Square, 302 seats, proscenium stage. **Production considerations:** prefers small cast; 1 set or unit set. **Best submission time:** spring–summer. **Response time:** 1–2 months letter; 8–12 months script.

TENNESSEE REPERTORY THEATRE
427 Chestnut St; Nashville, TN 37203-4826; (615) 244-4878, FAX 244-1232;
    E-mail tnrep@isdn.net
Don Jones, *Associate Artistic Director*

Submission procedure: no unsolicited scripts; synopsis, dialogue sample, cassette of music and lyrics, and letter of inquiry. **Types of material:** musicals, solo pieces. **Special interests:** new American musicals. **Facilities:** Polk Theatre, 1050 seats, proscenium stage. **Best submission time:** Jun–Sep. **Response time:** 4–6 weeks letter; 9–12 months script.

THALIA SPANISH THEATRE
Box 4368; Sunnyside, NY 11104; (718) 729-3880, FAX 729-3388
Silvia Brito, *Artistic/Executive Director*

Submission procedure: accepts unsolicited scripts. **Types of material:** full-length plays, translations, adaptations. **Special interests:** plays in Spanish only. **Facilities:** Thalia Spanish Theatre, 74 seats, proscenium stage. **Production considerations:** cast limit of 6; 1 set. **Best submission time:** Dec–Jan. **Response time:** 3 months.

THEATER AT LIME KILN
Lime Kiln Arts; Box 663; Lexington, VA 24450; (540) 463-7088, FAX 463-1082;
    E-mail limekiln@cfw.com
Barry Mines, *Artistic Director*

Submission procedure: accepts unsolicited scripts. **Types of material:** full-length plays, adaptations, musicals. **Special interests:** issues, language and music indigenous to VA and region; nontraditional staging. **Facilities:** The Kiln, 299 seats, outdoor amphitheatre. **Production considerations:** prefers cast limit of 9. **Best submission time:** fall. **Response time:** 3 months. **Special Programs:** Theater at Lime Kiln Regional Playwriting Contest (see Prizes).

THE THEATER AT MONMOUTH
Box 385; Monmouth, ME 04259-0385; (207) 933-2952, FAX 933-2952
Richard Sewell, *Artistic Director*

Submission procedure: no unsolicited scripts; synopsis and letter of inquiry. **Types**

of material: plays for young audiences. **Special interests:** small-cast traditional plays for young audiences (no musicals). **Facilities:** Cumston Hall, 275 seats, raked thrust stage. **Production considerations:** simple set. **Best submission time:** Nov. **Response time:** 4–6 weeks letter; 4–6 months script.

THEATRE DE LA JEUNE LUNE

105 First St N; Minneapolis, MN 55401; (612) 332-3968, FAX 332-0048
Barbara Berlovitz Desbois, *Co-Artistic Director*

Submission procedure: no unsolicited scripts; synopsis and letter of inquiry. **Types of material:** full-length plays, translations, adaptations, musicals, cabaret/revues. **Special interests:** large-cast plays dealing with universal themes. **Facilities:** Theatre de la Jeune Lune, 500 seats, flexible stage. **Best submission time:** year-round. **Response time:** 8–10 weeks letter; 4 months script.

THEATER EMORY

Annex C, Emory University; Atlanta, GA 30322; (404) 727-3465, FAX 727-6253;
    E-mail vmurphy@emory.edu
Vincent Murphy, *Artistic Producing Director*

Submission procedure: accepts unsolicited scripts through members of Southeast Playwrights Project, Atlanta, GA, only; professional recommendation from artistic director for all others. **Types of material:** full-length plays, one-acts, translations, adaptations. **Special interests:** adaptations and translations of literary and classic works. **Facilities:** MGM-I, 120 seats, flexible stage; MGM-II, 70 seats, flexible stage; Annex Studio, 60 seats, flexible stage. **Production considerations:** cast limit of 20; no fly or wing space. **Best submission time:** year-round. **Response time:** 2 months letter; 4 months script. **Special programs:** Brave New Works: annual staged reading marathon of new plays in conjunction with the Southeast Playwrights Project; scripts chosen through regular submission procedure; *deadline:* fall 1996; *dates:* spring 1997. The Playwriting Center of Theater Emory: biennial 5–13 week residency of major playwright to develop new work and teach playwriting workshop; remuneration: $25,000; first residency during 1996–97 academic year.

THEATRE FOR A NEW AUDIENCE

154 Christopher St, Suite 3D; New York, NY 10014-2839; (212) 229-2819

Submission procedure: no unsolicited scripts; direct solicitation to playwright or agent. **Types of material:** full-length plays, one-acts. **Special interests:** plays with compelling use of language. **Facilities:** Theatre at St. Clement's, 175 seats, proscenium stage. **Special programs:** commissioning program; participation by invitation only.

THEATER FOR THE NEW CITY

155 First Ave; New York, NY 10003-2906; (212) 254-1109
Crystal Field, *Artistic Director*

Submission procedure: accepts unsolicited scripts. **Types of material:** full-length plays. **Special interests:** experimental American works; plays with poetry, music and dance; social issues. **Facilities:** Joyce and Seward Johnson Theater, 200 seats, flexible space; 2nd theatre, 75 seats, flexible space; 3rd theatre, 100 seats, flexible space; also cabaret space. **Best submission time:** summer. **Response time:** 9–12 months.

THEATRE IV

114 West Broad St; Richmond, VA 23220; (804) 783-1688, FAX 775-2325
Bruce Miller, *Artistic Director*

Submission procedure: no unsolicited scripts; synopsis and letter of inquiry. **Types of material:** plays for young audiences only, including full-length plays, translations and adaptations. **Facilities:** Empire Theatre, 604 seats, proscenium stage. **Production considerations:** moderate budget for all productions. **Best submission time:** spring and summer. **Response time:** 6 months letter; 6 months script.

THEATRE GAEL

Box 77156; Atlanta, GA 30357; (404) 876-1138, FAX 733-4756
John Stephens, *Artistic Director*

Submission procedure: no unsolicited scripts; synopsis and letter of inquiry. **Types of material:** full-length plays, translations, adaptations, plays for young audiences, solo pieces. **Special interests:** plays depicting life in Ireland, Scotland, Wales; plays about Americans of Celtic heritage; plays that compare different cultural backgrounds, e.g., the African-American versus Irish-American experiences. **Facilities:** 14th Street Playhouse, 90–180 seats, flexible stage; company tours to 80–330-seat flexible-stage theatres. **Production considerations:** productions tour to local schools, festivals and churches. **Best submission time:** year-round. **Response time:** 1 month letter; 3 months script. **Special programs:** Worldsong Children's Theatre: company tours to local schools, recreational areas and libraries.

THEATRE IN THE SQUARE

11 Whitlock Ave; Marietta, GA 30064; (770) 422-8369, FAX 424-2637
Literary Manager

Submission procedure: no unsolicited scripts; synopsis and letter of inquiry. **Types of material:** full-length plays, one-acts, translations, musicals. **Special interests:** world and southeastern premieres. **Facilities:** Mainstage, 225 seats, proscenium stage; Alley Stage, up to 80 seats, flexible stage. **Production considerations:** cast limit of 9; unit set; no fly space. **Best submission time:** Dec–Feb. **Response time:** 1 month letter (if interested); 6 months script.

THEATER OF THE FIRST AMENDMENT

MS 3E6; George Mason University; Fairfax, VA 22030-4444; (703) 993-2195, FAX 993-2191; E-mail rdavi4@gmu.edu
Rick Davis, *Artistic Director*

Submission procedure: no unsolicited scripts; synopsis, sample pages, resume and letter of inquiry. **Types of material:** full-length plays, one-acts, translations, adaptations, solo pieces. **Special interests:** "cultural history made dramatic as opposed to history dramatized; large battles joined; hard questions asked; word and image stretched." **Facilities:** TheaterSpace, 150–200 seats, flexible space. **Production considerations:** roles for younger actors welcome as TFA works with training program. **Best submission time:** Aug–Jan. **Response time:** 2 weeks letter; 6 months script. **Special programs:** readings, workshops and other development activities tailored to work under serious consideration for production.

THEATRE ON THE SQUARE

450 Post St; San Francisco, CA 94102; (415) 433-6461, FAX 433-2910; E-mail tot@hooked.net
Jonathan Reinis, *Owner*

Submission procedure: no unsolicited scripts; synopsis and letter of inquiry. **Types of material:** full-length plays, musicals. **Facilities:** Theatre on the Square, 750 seats, proscenium/thrust stage. **Production considerations:** no fly space. **Best submission time:** year-round. **Response time:** 6 months letter; 12 months script.

THEATRE RHINOCEROS

2926 16th St; San Francisco, CA 94103; (415) 552-4100, FAX 558-9044
Doug Holsclaw, *Literary Manager*

Submission procedure: accepts unsolicited scripts. **Types of material:** full-length plays, one-acts, solo pieces. **Special interests:** gay and lesbian works only. **Facilities:** Theatre Rhinoceros, 112 seats, proscenium stage; The Studio at Theatre Rhinoceros, 60 seats, studio. **Best submission time:** year-round. **Response time:** 3–4 months.

THEATRE THREE

Box 512; Port Jefferson, NY 11777-0512; (516) 928-9202, FAX 928-9120
Jeffrey Sanzel, *Artistic Director*

Submission procedure: no unsolicited scripts; synopsis, resume, press clippings (if any) and letter of inquiry. **Types of material:** full-length plays, one-acts. **Facilities:** Main Stage, 400 seats, proscenium; Second Stage, 80–100 seats, black box. **Production considerations:** prefers cast of 2–6; 1 set; minimal production demands; no fly or wing space in Main Stage. **Best submission time:** Jan-Apr. **Response time:** 1 month letter; 2 months script.

THEATRE THREE, INC.
2800 Routh St; Dallas, TX 75201; (214) 871-2933, FAX 871-3139
Jac Alder, *Executive Producer/Director*

Submission procedure: accepts unsolicited scripts; prefers synopsis and letter of inquiry. **Types of material:** full-length plays, musicals. **Special interests:** musicals; sophisticated comedies with socially relevant themes. **Facilities:** Theatre Three, 242 seats, arena stage. **Production considerations:** cast of 6–15; modest production demands. **Best submission time:** year-round; prefers Sep–Dec. **Response time:** 1 week letter; 2 months script.

THEATRE WEST
3333 Cahuenga Blvd W; Los Angeles, CA 90068; (213) 851-4839, FAX 851-5286
Arden Lewis and Doug Haverty, *Workshop Moderators*

Submission procedure: no unsolicited scripts; scripts developed in weekly workshops open to member playwrights only; submit script, resume and letter of inquiry; dues of $40 per month upon acceptance. **Types of material:** full-length plays, one-acts, translations, adaptations, plays for young audiences, musicals. **Facilities:** Theatre West, 180 seats, proscenium stage. **Best submission time:** year-round. **Response time:** 4 months.

THEATRE X
Box 92206; Milwaukee, WI 53202; (414) 278-0555
John D. Schneider, *Artistic Director*

Submission procedure: no unsolicited scripts; recommendation from professional familiar with company's work. **Types of material:** full-length plays, solo pieces, performance art. **Special interests:** plays written for or with the company; performance art and avant-garde works. **Facilities:** Black Box, 99 seats, flexible stage. **Production considerations:** small cast. **Best submission time:** year-round. **Response time:** 6 months.

THE THEATRE-STUDIO INC.
750 Eighth Ave, #200; New York, NY 10036; (212) 719-0500
A. M. Raychel, *Artistic Director/Producer*

Submission procedure: accepts unsolicited scripts. **Types of material:** one-acts, plays for young audiences, solo pieces, performance art. **Special interests:** one-acts. **Facilities:** The Theatre-Studio, 60 seats, studio. **Best submission time:** year-round. **Response time:** 3 months. **Special programs:** Playtime Series: year-round developmental program.

THEATREVIRGINIA
2800 Grove Ave; Richmond, VA 23221-2466; (804) 353-6100
George Black, *Producing Artistic Director*

Submission procedure: no unsolicited scripts; agent submission. **Types of material:** full-length plays, musicals. **Facilities:** Main Stage, 500 seats, proscenium stage. **Best submission time:** year-round. **Response time:** 3–8 months. **Special programs:** New Voices for the Theatre: playwriting competition open to VA students grades 5–12; winners grades 9–12 attend 3-week summer residency program and receive dramaturgical assistance and professional staged reading; contact Education and Outreach Department for more information; *deadline:* 1 Feb 1997.

THEATREWORKS
470 San Antonio Rd; Palo Alto, CA 94306; (415) 842-0500, FAX 812-7562
Jeannie Barroga, *Literary Manager*

Submission procedure: accepts unsolicited full-length plays and musicals; also accepts synopsis, dialogue sample and letter of inquiry with SASP for response; for translations and adaptations, send only letter of inquiry with SASP for response. **Types of material:** full-length plays, translations, adaptations, musicals; no one-acts. **Special interests:** works offering opportunities for multicultural casting. **Facilities:** Mountain View Center, 625 seats, proscenium stage; Stage II, 117 seats, thrust stage. **Best submission time:** Aug–Nov. **Response time:** 1 month letter; 4 months script.

THEATREWORKS/USA
890 Broadway, 7th Floor; New York, NY 10003; (212) 677-5959, FAX 353-1632
Barbara Pasternack, *Associate Artistic Director*

Submission procedure: accepts unsolicited scripts; prefers synopsis, sample scene(s) and songs (include cassette and lyric sheet) and letter of inquiry. **Types of material:** plays and musicals for young audiences. **Special interests:** literary adaptations; historical/biographical themes; fairy tales; contemporary issues. **Facilities:** Promenade Theatre, 398 seats, proscenium stage; also tours. **Production considerations:** cast limit of 5 (can play multiple roles); sets suitable for touring. **Best submission time:** summer. **Response time:** 1 month letter; 6 months script. **Special programs:** developmental workshops. Theatreworks/USA Commissioning Program (see Prizes).

THEATRICAL OUTFIT
Box 7098; Atlanta, GA 30357; (404) 872-0665, -8077, FAX 872-1164
Kate Warner, *Managing Director*

Submission procedure: no unsolicited scripts; 1-page synopsis and letter of inquiry with SASP for reply. **Types of material:** full-length plays, adaptations, solo pieces. **Facilities:** Theatrical Outfit, 400 seats, proscenium stage. **Best submission time:** summer. **Response time:** 2 months letter; 2 months script.

Touchstone Theatre

321 East 4th St; Bethlehem, PA 18015; (610) 867-1689, FAX 867-0561;
E-mail ttheatre@aol.com
Mark McKenna, *Artistic Director*

Submission procedure: no unsolicited scripts; letter of inquiry. **Types of material:** proposals for works to be created in collaboration with company's ensemble only. **Facilities:** Touchstone Theatre, 74 seats, black box. **Production considerations:** 18′ x 21′ playing area. **Best submission time:** year-round. **Response time:** 1 month.

Trinity Repertory Company

201 Washington St; Providence, RI 02903; (401) 521-1100
Oskar Eustis, *Artistic Director*

Submission procedure: no unsolicited scripts; dialogue sample, resume and letter of inquiry. **Types of material:** full-length plays, translations, adaptations, solo pieces. **Facilities:** Upstairs Theatre, 500 seats, thrust stage; Downstairs Theatre, 297 seats, thrust stage. **Best submission time:** year-round. **Response time:** 4 months letter; 4 months script.

Trustus Theatre

See South Carolina Playwrights' Festival in Prizes.

Ubu Repertory Theater

15 West 28th St; New York, NY 10001; (212) 679-7540
Françoise Kourilsky, *Artistic Director*

Submission procedure: no unsolicited scripts; synopsis and letter of inquiry. **Types of material:** full-length plays, one-acts, translations. **Special interests:** French-language plays or their translations only; contemporary plays from French-speaking countries and regions. **Facilities:** Ubu Repertory Theater, 99 seats, proscenium stage. **Production considerations:** cast limit of 10; 1 set or simple sets. **Best submission time:** year-round. **Response time:** 2 months letter; 6 months script.

Unicorn Theatre

See Unicorn Theatre National Playwrights' Award in Prizes.

Utah Shakespearean Festival

351 West Center St; Cedar City, UT 84720-2498; (801) 586-7880, FAX 865-8003
Douglas N. Cook, *Producing Artistic Director*

Submission procedure: no unsolicited scripts; professional recommendation. **Types of material:** full-length plays for Aug staged reading series. **Special interest:** plays by writers from western intermountain region; plays about minorities or the underserved. **Facilities:** Thorley Recital Hall, 235 seats, modified thrust stage.

Production considerations: cast limit of 10–12; no sets, minimal props and costumes; 5-rehearsal limit per production. **Best submission time:** Sep–Dec. **Response time:** 3 months.

VICTORY GARDENS THEATER

2257 North Lincoln Ave; Chicago, IL 60614; (312) 549-5788, FAX 549-2779
Sandy Shinner, *Associate Artistic Director*

Submission procedure: accepts unsolicited scripts from Chicago-area writers only; others send synopsis, 10-page dialogue sample and letter of inquiry. **Types of material:** full-length plays, adaptations, musicals. **Special interests:** Chicago and Midwest playwrights; plays by women and writers of color. **Facilities:** Mainstage one, 195 seats, modified thrust stage; Mainstage two, 200 seats, thrust stage; Studio, 70 seats, proscenium stage. **Production considerations:** prefers cast limit of 10; simple set; small-cast musicals only. **Best submission time:** Mar–Jun. **Response time:** 1 month letter; 6 months script. **Special programs:** Readers Theater: staged readings of works-in-progress by area writers twice a month.

THE VINEYARD PLAYHOUSE

Box 2452, 10 Church St; Vineyard Haven, MA 02568; (508) 693-6450
(Ms.) M. J. Munafo, *Artistic Director*

Submission procedure: no unsolicited scripts; direct solicitation to playwright or agent. **Types of material:** full-length plays, translations, adaptations, plays for young audiences, solo pieces. **Special interests:** contemporary American works; culturally diverse plays; plays that address social issues. **Facilities:** The Vineyard Playhouse, 120 seats, black box. **Production considerations:** prefers cast limit of 10; simple sets. **Special programs:** New England New Play Competition and Showcase (see Prizes).

VINEYARD THEATRE

108 East 15th St; New York, NY 10003-9689; (212) 353-3366, FAX 353-3803
Douglas Aibel, *Artistic Director*

Submission procedure: accepts unsolicited scripts; prefers synopsis, 10-page dialogue sample and letter of inquiry; include cassette for musicals. **Types of material:** full-length plays, musicals. **Special interests:** plays that incorporate music in a unique way; musicals with strong narrative. **Facilities:** Vineyard at Union Square, 130 seats, flexible stage; Vineyard Theatre, 70 seats, thrust stage. **Best submission time:** year-round. **Response time:** 6 months letter; 6 months script. **Special programs:** New Works at the Vineyard: play reading series. The Lab Program: developmental workshops for new plays and musicals.

VIRGINIA STAGE COMPANY

Box 3770; Norfolk, VA 23514; (804) 627-6988, FAX 628-5958

Submission procedure: no unsolicited scripts; synopsis and letter of inquiry. **Types of material:** full-length plays, musicals. **Special interests:** world premieres; plays by VA writers; poetic drama and comedy; hard-hitting, issue-oriented plays; no "kitchen-sink" drama. **Facilities:** main stage, 700 seats, proscenium stage; laboratory theatre, 99 seats, flexible space. **Best submission time:** year-round. **Response time:** 1 month letter; 6 months script.

THE WALNUT STREET THEATRE COMPANY
825 Walnut St; Philadelphia, PA 19107-5107; (215) 574-3550, FAX 574-3598
Beverly Elliott, *Literary Manager*

Submission procedure: no unsolicited scripts; synopsis, cast list, 14-page dialogue sample and letter of inquiry with SASE for response from Dramatist Guild members only; include professional-quality cassette for musicals. **Types of material:** full-length plays, musicals. **Special interests:** original, socially relevant musicals with uplifting themes; commercially viable works for Main Stage; meaningful comedies and dramas with some broad social relevance for Studio 3. **Facilities:** Main Stage, 1050 seats, proscenium stage; Studio 3, 80 seats, flexible stage. **Production considerations:** cast limit of 4 for Studio 3. **Response time:** 3 months letter; 6 months script.

WATERTOWER THEATRE, INC.
15650 Addison Rd; Addison, TX 75248; (214) 404-0228, FAX 458-7529
Gayle Pearson, *Producing Director*

Submission procedure: accepts unsolicited scripts. **Types of material:** full-length plays, one-acts, plays for young audiences, musicals, solo pieces. **Special interests:** plays that make creative use of flexible space. **Facilities:** Addison Conference & Theatre Centre, 100–300 seats, flexible stage. **Response time:** 2 months.

WEISSBERGER THEATER GROUP
909 Third Ave, 27th Floor; New York, NY 10022-9998; (212) 339-5529,
    FAX 486-8996
Jay Harris, *Producer*

Submission procedure: no unsolicited scripts; synopsis and letter of inquiry. **Types of material:** full-length plays. **Special interests:** topical issue-oriented plays. **Facilities:** no permanent facility. **Production considerations:** cast limit of 7. **Best submission time:** year-round. **Response time:** 1 month letter; 2 months script.

WEST COAST ENSEMBLE
Box 38728; Los Angeles, CA 90038; (213) 871-8673
Les Hanson, *Artistic Director*

Submission procedure: accepts unsolicited scripts. **Types of material:** full-length plays, one-acts, translations, adaptations, musicals. **Special interests:** world premieres; musicals; short plays. **Facilities:** main stage, 85 seats, proscenium stage. **Production considerations:** simple set; no fly space. **Best submission time:** Jun–Dec. **Response time:** 6 months. **Special programs:** staged readings of new plays. West Coast Ensemble Contests (see Prizes).

WILLIAMSTOWN THEATRE FESTIVAL

Box 517; Williamstown, MA 01267-0517; (413) 458-3200, FAX 458-3147
Michael Ritchie, *Producer*

Submission procedure: no unsolicited scripts; agent submission only. **Types of material:** full-length plays, adaptations, musicals, solo pieces. **Facilities:** Main Stage, 521 seats, proscenium stage; 2nd stage, 96 seats, thrust stage. **Best submission time:** 1 Oct–15 Feb. **Response time:** several months script. **Special programs:** New Play Staged Readings Series.

WILLOWS THEATRE COMPANY

(formerly CitiArts Theatre)
1975 Diamond Blvd, Suite A-20; Concord, CA 94520; (510) 798-1300,
     FAX 676-5726; E-mail CitiArts@aol.com
Richard H. Elliott, *Artistic Director*

Submission procedure: accepts unsolicited scripts. **Types of material:** full-length plays, translations, adaptations, musicals. **Special interests:** small-scale plays, musicals and revues with an edge that will appeal to both urban and suburban audiences. **Facilities:** Willows Theatre, 203 seats, proscenium stage. **Production considerations:** cast of 2–15; limit of 8 musicians for musical works; prefers simple set, unit set or environmental staging which uses theatre space as setting. **Best submission time:** 1 Jul–1 Oct. **Response time:** 3 months. **Special programs:** staged readings and workshop productions.

THE WILMA THEATER

2030 Sansom St; Philadelphia, PA 19103-4417; (215) 963-0249, FAX 963-0377
Michael Hollinger, *Literary Manager/Dramaturg*

Submission procedure: no unsolicited scripts; synopsis, dialogue sample and letter of inquiry. **Types of material:** full-length plays, translations, adaptations, musicals, full-length solo pieces. **Special interests:** new translations and adaptations from the international repertoire with emphasis on innovative, bold staging; world premieres; ensemble works; works with poetic dimension; plays with music; multimedia works; social issues. **Facilities:** Wilma Theater, 300 seats, flexible/proscenium stage. **Production considerations:** prefers cast limit of 12; stage 44' x 46'. **Best submission time:** year-round. **Response time:** 2–3 months letter; 6–9 months script.

WOMEN'S PROJECT & PRODUCTIONS

55 West End Ave; New York, NY 10023; (212) 765-1706, FAX 765-2024
Sharon Houck Ross, *Literary Manager*

Submission procedure: no unsolicited scripts; synopsis, 10-page dialogue sample and letter of inquiry with SASE for response. **Types of material:** full-length plays, solo pieces. **Special interests:** plays by women only. **Facilities:** no permanent space. **Best submission time:** year-round. **Response time:** 2–4 weeks letter; 3–6 months script. **Special programs:** developmental program including play readings, work-in-progress presentations, playwright's lab and directors' forum; participation by invitation only. Commissioning program.

WOOLLY MAMMOTH THEATRE COMPANY

1401 Church St NW; Washington, DC 20005; (202) 393-3939, FAX 667-0904
Jim Byrnes, *Literary Manager*

Submission procedure: accepts unsolicited scripts. **Types of material:** full-length plays, translations, adaptations, solo pieces. **Special interests:** offbeat topics and styles; nonrealism. **Facilities:** Woolly Mammoth, 132 seats, thrust stage. **Production considerations:** small cast; minimal staging requirements. **Best submission time:** year-round. **Response time:** 4 months.

THE WOOSTER GROUP

Box 654, Canal Street Station; New York, NY 10013; (212) 966-9796,
   FAX 226-6576; E-mail woostergrp@aol.com
Adam Sobsey, *Administrative Director*

Submission procedure: no unsolicited scripts; writers interested in collaborating with The Wooster Group should send resume and letter of inquiry only. **Types of material:** full-length plays. **Special interests:** experimental works. **Facilities:** The Performing Garage, 99 seats, black box.

WORCESTER FOOTHILLS THEATRE COMPANY

100 Front St, Suite 137; Worcester, MA 01608; (508) 754-3314, FAX 767-0676
Marc P. Smith, *Executive Producer/Artistic Director*

Submission procedure: no unsolicited scripts; synopsis and letter of inquiry. **Types of material:** full-length plays, translations, adaptations, musicals. **Special interests:** plays suited to multigenerational audiences. **Facilities:** Worcester Foothills Theatre, 349 seats, proscenium stage. **Production considerations:** prefers cast limit of 10, simple set; small-scale musicals only. **Best submission time:** year-round. **Response time:** 3 months letter; 4 months script.

WORKHOUSE THEATER

41 White St; New York, NY 10013; (212) 431-9220, FAX 941-7124
Julie Bleha, *Literary Manager*

Submission procedure: no unsolicited scripts; professional recommendation. **Types of material:** translations. **Special interests:** nonrealistic works and settings; classic texts; modern plays with classic themes; poetic plays; 10-minute plays for ongoing series; imaginative use of space and light. **Facilities:** Workhouse Theater, 70 seats, proscenium stage. **Best submission time:** year-round. **Response time:** 1 month letter; 2 months script. **Special programs:** year-round reading series.

YALE REPERTORY THEATRE
Box 208244, Yale Station; New Haven, CT 06520-8244; (203) 432-1560,
FAX 432-1550
Resident Dramaturg

Submission procedure: no unsolicited scripts; synopsis and letter of inquiry. **Types of material:** full-length plays, translations, adaptations, solo pieces. **Special interests:** new work; new translations of classics; contemporary foreign plays. **Facilities:** Yale Repertory Theatre, 487 seats, modified thrust stage; University Theatre, 654 seats, proscenium stage. **Best submission time:** year-round. **Response time:** 6 weeks letter; 3 months script.

YOUNG PLAYWRIGHTS INC.
See Young Playwrights Festival in Prizes and Young Playwrights Inc. in Organizations.

ZACHARY SCOTT THEATRE CENTER (ZACH)
1510 Toomey Rd; Austin, TX 78704-1078; (512) 476-0594, FAX 476-0314
Alice Wilson, *Producing Artistic Director*

Submission procedure: no unsolicited scripts; synopsis, dialogue sample, resume and letter of inquiry. **Types of material:** full-length plays, plays for young audiences. **Facilities:** Mainstage 1, 200 seats, thrust stage; Mainstage 2, 130 seats, arena stage. **Production considerations:** plays for young audiences tour. **Best submission time:** Jul–Aug. **Response time:** 6 weeks letter; 4–6 months script.

Prizes

What competitions are included here?

All the playwriting contests we've heard of that offer prizes of at least $200 or, in the case of awards to playwrights under the age of 19, the equivalent in production or publication. Most awards for which the playwright cannot apply—the Joseph Kesselring Award, the Pulitzer Prize—are not listed. Exceptions are made when, as with the Susan Smith Blackburn Prize, the nominating process allows playwrights to encourage nomination of their work by theatre professionals who are familiar with it.

How can I give myself the best chance of winning?

When a prize entry lists a notification date, make sure you don't mistake it for the deadline for submission. (One prize sponsor asked us to delete their notification date because so many playwrights were confusing the two!) If a listing specifies "write for guidelines," be sure to follow this instruction. It usually means that we don't have space in our brief listing to give you all the information you'll need to enter the contest. Write for the guidelines (and entry form, where applicable) several months ahead. Don't wait till the last minute since contests may occasionally change their rules or their deadlines after this book has been published. Follow the guidelines precisely. Send your script in well before the deadline, when the readers are fresh and enthusiastic rather than buried by an avalanche of submissions. If you can't submit well in advance, assume the deadline is the date your script must be received (not the postmark date). Except in the few cases where sponsors note that scripts won't be returned, always send an SASE with your submission. Many competitions enclose their response letter with the script when returning it.

Should I enter contests that charge entry fees?

It's true that a number of listings in this section (and in other sections as well) require a payment of a fee. You need not conclude from this that the whole world is out to rip off playwrights. It is unfortunately the case that many contest sponsors do not secure sufficient funding to cover their costs, which are considerable. Some playwrights as a matter of principle will not pay fees, and are prepared to protest their imposition. Other writers are willing to add an entry fee to the costs of copying and postage as a part of doing business. It's up to you.

Aren't new playwriting contests being created all the time?

Yes. As soon as we hear about them, we publish details of major new contests in the "Opportunities" column of our monthly magazine *American Theatre*. See Membership and Service Organizations and Useful Publications for other sources of current contest news.

A couple of *Sourcebook* reminders:

Throughout the *Sourcebook*, "full-length play" means just that—a full-length, original work without a score or libretto. One-acts, musicals, adaptations, translations and plays for young audiences are not called full-length plays for our purposes. If an organization is interested in those dramatic works, we'll list them separately.

    Sourcebook entries are alphabetized by first word (excluding "the") even if the title starts with a proper name. So, for instance, you'll find the David James Ellis Memorial Award under D. In the index, you will also find this prize cross-listed under E. This section also includes full listings of biennial prizes whose next deadline falls after the dates of this *Sourcebook* (after August 1997). By providing this added information, we hope to give you as much lead time as possible, but please read the deadlines carefully—don't mistake a March 1998 deadline for 1997!

ACME ORIGINALS

ACME Acting Company; 3841 Northeast 2nd Ave, Suite 302A;
    Miami, FL 33137-3639; (305) 576-7500, FAX 576-7500;
    E-mail aaackme@aol.com
Betsy Cardwell, *Producing Director*

Types of material: full-length plays, one-acts, solo pieces. **Frequency:** annual. **Remuneration:** $500–1000, production, travel and housing to attend rehearsals, and publication in arts and entertainment magazine for 3 winners; staged reading for 10 runners-up. **Guidelines:** play not produced professionally; prefers contemporary issues. **Submission procedure:** script only; script will not be returned. **Deadline:** ongoing (plays to be produced in 1997 chosen by 15 Apr 1997). **Dates:** year-round.

ALASKA NATIVE PLAYS CONTEST

Department of Theatre; University of Alaska, Anchorage; 3211 Providence Dr;
    Anchorage, AK 99508-8120; (907) 786-1794, FAX 786-1799;
    E-mail afdpe@orion.alaska.edu
David Edgecombe, *Associate Professor*

Types of material: full-length plays, one-acts, adaptations, plays for young audiences. **Frequency:** annual. **Remuneration:** $500 1st prize; $300 2nd prize; $200 3rd prize; possible production, travel to performance for Alaska playwrights only. **Guidelines:** Native North American characters and/or themes. **Submission procedure:** script only. **Deadline:** 20 Mar 1997. **Notification:** 10 May 1997.

AMERICAN SHORTS CONTEST

Florida Studio Theatre; 1241 North Palm Ave; Sarasota, FL 34236

Types of material: very short plays and solo pieces. **Frequency:** annual. **Remuneration:** $500; production for winning script and up to 12 others as part of evening of short works. **Guidelines:** play of 5 pages or less on specified theme TBA; write for guidelines. **Submission procedure:** script only. **Deadline:** TBA (15 Mar in 1996).

AMERICAN TRANSLATORS ASSOCIATION AWARDS

1800 Diagonal Rd, Suite 220; Alexandria, VA 22134-2840; FAX (703) 683-6122;
    E-mail 73564.2032@compuserve.com
Eric McMillan, *Chair, ATA Honors and Awards*

German Literary Translation Prize

Types of material: translations of full-length and one-act plays. **Frequency:** biennial. **Remuneration:** $1000; up to $500 expenses to attend ATA annual conference. **Guidelines:** translation from German published in U.S. by American publisher during 2 years before deadline as single volume or in collection. **Submission procedure:** no submission by translator; publisher nominates translation and submits 2 copies of book plus 10 consecutive pages of German original, extra jacket and any advertising copy; brief vita of translator. **Deadline:** 15 May 1997. **Notification:** fall 1997.

Lewis Galantiere Literary Translation Prize

Types of material: translations of full-length plays and one-acts. **Frequency:** biennial. **Remuneration:** $1000; up to $500 expenses to attend ATA annual conference. **Guidelines:** translation from any language except German published in U.S. by American publisher during 2 years before deadline as single volume or in collection. **Submission procedure:** no submission by translator; publisher nominates translation and submits 2 copies of book plus 10 consecutive pages of original, extra jacket and any advertising copy; brief vita of translator. **Deadline:** 15 May 1998. **Notification:** fall 1998.

ANNA ZORNIO MEMORIAL CHILDREN'S THEATRE PLAYWRITING AWARD

Department of Theater and Dance; University of New Hampshire;
Paul Creative Arts Center; 30 College Rd; Durham, NH 03824-3538;
(603) 862-3046, FAX 862-0298
Carol J. Fisher

Types of material: plays and musicals for young audiences. **Frequency:** every 4 years. **Remuneration:** $1000; production by UNH Theatre in Education Program. **Guidelines:** U.S. or Canadian resident; unpublished work not produced professionally and not more than 1 hour long; prefers single or unit set; 2-submission limit; write for rules. **Submission procedure:** script with brief synopsis, character breakdown and statement of design/technical considerations; SASP for acknowledgment of receipt; include cassette for musical. **Deadline:** Dec 1997. **Notification:** Jun 1998.

THE ANNUAL BLANK THEATRE COMPANY YOUNG PLAYWRIGHTS FESTIVAL

1301 Lucile Ave; Los Angeles, CA 90026-1519; (213) 662-7734;
E-mail btc@primenet.com
April Dawn, *Producer*

Types of material: full-length plays, one-acts, plays for young audiences, musicals, solo pieces, operas. **Frequency:** annual. **Remuneration:** workshop production for approximately 9 playwrights; some winning scripts subsequently receive full production. **Guidelines:** playwright 19 years of age or younger as of deadline date; original play of any length on any subject. **Submission procedure:** script with cover sheet containing name, date of birth, home address, phone number, and name of school (if any). **Deadline:** Apr 1997 (exact date TBA). **Notification:** May 1997.

ASF Translation Prize

The American-Scandinavian Foundation; 725 Park Ave; New York, NY 10021;
(212) 879-9779, FAX 249-3444; E-mail agyongy@amscan.org
Publishing Office

Types of material: translations. **Frequency:** annual. **Remuneration:** $2000;
publication of excerpt in *Scandinavian Review*, $500 for runner-up. **Guidelines:**
unpublished translation from a Scandinavian language into English of work
written by a Scandinavian author after 1800; manuscript must be at least 50 pages
long if prose, 25 pages if poetry, and must be conceived as part of a book; write
for guidelines. **Submission procedure:** 4 copies of translation, 1 of original;
permission letter from copyright holder. **Deadline:** 2 Jun 1997. **Notification:** fall
1997.

Baker's Plays High School Playwriting Contest

Baker's Plays; 100 Chauncy St; Boston, MA 02111; (617) 482-1280,
FAX 482-7613
Raymond Pape, *Associate Editor*

Types of material: full-length plays, one-acts, plays for young audiences, musicals.
Frequency: annual. **Remuneration:** 1st prize $500 and publication; 2nd prize
$250; 3rd prize $100. **Guidelines:** high school student, sponsored by high school
drama or English teacher; prefers play which has been produced or given public
reading; write for guidelines. **Submission procedure:** script with signature of
sponsoring teacher. **Deadline:** 31 Jan 1997. **Notification:** May 1997.

Beverly Hills Theatre Guild–
Julie Harris Playwright Award

2815 North Beachwood Dr; Los Angeles, CA 90068-1923; (213) 465-2703
Marcella Meharg, *Coordinator*

Types of material: full-length plays, solo pieces. **Frequency:** annual. **Remuneration:** $5000 1st prize plus $2000 to help finance production in Los Angeles area
within 1 year; $2000 2nd prize; $1000 3rd prize. **Guidelines:** U.S. citizen; 1
submission, not previously submitted, published, produced or optioned, or winner
of major competition; send SASE for guidelines. **Submission procedure:**
completed entry form and script. **Deadline:** 1 Nov 1996. **Notification:** Jun 1997.

Biennial Promising Playwright Award

Colonial Players, Inc; 108 East St; Annapolis, MD 21401
Contest Coordinator

Types of material: full-length plays, bills of 2 related one-acts, adaptations.
Frequency: biennial. **Remuneration:** $750; production (playwright must be
available to attend rehearsals). **Guidelines:** resident of DC, DE, MD, PA, VA or
WV; play, not produced professionally, suitable for arena stage; between 90–120
minutes; 2-set limit; cast limit of 10; only adaptations of material in public
domain; send SASE for guidelines. **Submission procedure:** script and SASP for

acknowledgment of receipt. **Deadline:** 31 Dec 1996; no submission before 1 Sep 1996. **Notification:** Jun 1997.

CALIFORNIA PLAYWRIGHTS COMPETITION
South Coast Repertory; Box 2197; Costa Mesa, CA 92628; (714) 957-2602,
      FAX 545-0391
John Glore, *Literary Manager*

Types of material: full-length plays. **Frequency:** biennial. **Remuneration:** 1st prize: $3000; staged reading; possible production with royalty; travel and housing to attend rehearsals and opening; 2nd prize: cash award of approximately $2000. **Guidelines:** playwright whose principal residence is in CA; play not professionally produced or optioned; previous entries ineligible; 2-submission limit. **Submission procedure:** completed entry form, script, synopsis of no more than 300 words and brief bio including information on CA residency. **Deadline:** 1 Dec 1997. **Notification:** Mar 1998.

CALIFORNIA YOUNG PLAYWRIGHTS CONTEST
Playwrights Project; 1450 Frazee Rd, Suite 215; San Diego, CA 92108;
      (619) 298-9242, FAX 298-9244
Deborah Salzer, *Director*

Types of material: full-length plays, one-acts, musicals, solo pieces. **Frequency:** annual. **Remuneration:** $100, production or staged reading, travel and housing to attend rehearsals to each of several winners (4 in 1995); all entrants receive written evaluation of work. **Guidelines:** CA writer or collaborating writers under 19 years of age as of deadline date; work at least 10 pages long; previous submissions ineligible; write for guidelines. **Submission procedure:** script, cover letter and brief bio; script will not be returned. **Deadline:** 1 Apr 1997. **Notification:** late fall 1997.

CENTER THEATER INTERNATIONAL
PLAYWRIGHTING CONTEST
1346 West Devon Ave; Chicago, IL 60660; (312) 508-0200
Dale Calandra, *Literary Manager*

Types of material: full-length plays, solo pieces. **Frequency:** annual. **Remuneration:** $300; production; winner and runners-up receive listings in mailing sent to all TCG theatres. **Guidelines:** unpublished play, not produced or optioned; cast limit of 6, minimal technical requirements; send SASE for rules. **Submission procedure:** completed entry form, script, 1-page synopsis, character breakdown, resume, $15 fee per submission and SASE for response; script will not be returned. **Deadline:** TBA (30 Jun in 1996). **Notification:** Sep 1997.

CHICANO/LATINO LITERARY CONTEST

Department of Spanish and Portuguese; University of California at Irvine;
Irvine, CA 92717; (714) 824-5702
Alejandro Morales, *Director*

Prize awarded for different genres (novel, short story, poetry, drama) in successive
years; next deadline for drama 30 Apr 1998.

CHRISTOPHER COLUMBUS
SCREENPLAY DISCOVERY AWARDS

Christopher Columbus Society; 433 North Camden Dr, Suite 600;
Beverly Hills, CA 90210; (310) 288-1881, FAX 288-0257;
E-mail writing@screenwriters.com
Carlos de Abreu and Janice Pennington, *Co-Founders*

Types of material: screenplays. **Frequency:** annual. **Remuneration:** Discovery of
the Month Award: up to 3 scripts a month selected for development and may be
referred to industry professionals; all winners become eligible for Discovery of the
Year Award: up to 3 scripts a year optioned by society for up to $10,000.
Guidelines: unproduced feature screenplay not under current option; write for
guidelines. **Submission procedure:** screenplay, completed application, release
form and $45 fee; screenplay will not be returned. **Deadline:** last day of each
month for monthly selection; 1 Dec each year for annual cycle.

CLAUDER COMPETITION FOR EXCELLENCE IN PLAYWRITING

Box 383259; Cambridge, MA 02238-3259; (617) 322-3187
Betsy Carpenter, *Director*

Types of material: full-length plays. **Frequency:** biennial. **Remuneration:** $3000 1st
prize; production by professional New England theatre; $500 prize and staged
reading for several runners-up. **Guidelines:** resident of or student attending
school or college in CT, MA, ME, NH, RI or VT; play not produced professionally
and minimum 45 minutes long; write for guidelines. **Submission procedure:** script
and production history, if any. **Deadline:** summer 1997; exact date TBA.
Notification: fall 1997.

COE COLLEGE NEW WORKS FOR THE STAGE COMPETITION

Department of Theatre Arts; 1220 First Ave NE; Cedar Rapids, IA 52402;
(319) 399-8689, FAX 399-8557; E-mail swolvert@coe.edu
Susan Wolverton, *Chair, Playwriting Festival*

Types of material: full-length plays, plays for young audiences. **Frequency:**
biennial, contingent on funding. **Remuneration:** $325; staged reading; travel,
room and board for 1-week residency during Jan term. **Guidelines:** unproduced,
unpublished play dealing with theme of Playwriting Festival and Symposia (theme
different each year); festival includes workshops and public discussions; no
translations, adaptations or musicals; send SASE for guidelines. **Submission
procedure:** script only. **Deadline:** 1 May 1998. **Notification:** 1 Nov 1998.

CONNECTIONS
Delaware Theatre Company; 200 Water St; Wilmington, DE 19801-5030
Cleveland Morris, *Artistic Director*

Types of material: full-length plays, musicals. **Frequency:** biennial. **Remuneration:** $10,000 1st prize; staged reading; possible full production with travel to rehearsals, housing and royalties; $500 each to 2nd and 3rd prize winners. **Guidelines:** full-length play, which has not received full professional production, that deals with interracial dynamics in America. **Submission procedure:** 3 copies of script with production history, if any, and brief bio. **Deadline:** 1 Apr 1998. **Notification:** Aug 1998.

THE CUNNINGHAM PRIZE FOR PLAYWRITING
Theatre School; DePaul University; 2135 North Kenmore;
      Chicago, IL 60614-4111; (312) 325-7938, FAX 325-7920
Lara Goetsch, *Public Relations Director*

Types of material: full-length plays, plays for young audiences, musicals, solo pieces. **Frequency:** annual. **Remuneration:** $5000. **Guidelines:** Chicago-area playwright; play which "affirms the centrality of religion, broadly defined, and the human quest for meaning, truth and community"; write for guidelines. **Submission procedure:** script and brief statement making connection to purpose of prize. **Deadline:** 1 Dec 1996. **Notification:** 1 Mar 1997.

DALE WASSERMAN DRAMA AWARD
Council for Wisconsin Writers; Box 55322; Madison, WI 53705; (608) 233-2484,
      FAX 833-8808
Russell King, *Treasurer*

Types of material: full-length plays, one-acts, translations, adaptations, plays for young audiences, musicals, solo pieces, operas. **Frequency:** annual. **Remuneration:** $1000. **Guidelines:** current or former WI resident; work produced during preceding calendar year. **Submission procedure:** completed entry form, script and $15 fee. **Deadline:** 1 Jan 1997.

DAVID JAMES ELLIS MEMORIAL AWARD
Theatre Americana; Box 245; Altadena, CA 91003; (818) 683-1740
Playreading Committee

Types of material: full-length plays. **Frequency:** annual. **Remuneration:** $500 to best of 4 plays selected for production; color videotape of produced play. **Guidelines:** unpublished original play, not more than 2 hours in length; prefers American writers and plays on the American scene; 2-submission limit; send SASE for guidelines. **Submission procedure:** script and resume. **Deadline:** 31 Jan 1997.

DAYTON PLAYHOUSE FUTUREFEST

1301 East Siebenthaler Ave; Dayton, OH 45414; (513) 277-0144, FAX 277-9539
Tina McPhearson, *Managing Director*

Types of material: full-length plays, solo pieces. **Frequency:** annual. **Remuneration:** 3 plays selected for full production, 3 for reading at Jul 1997 FutureFest weekend; travel and housing to attend rehearsals; judges view full productions and award $1000 1st prize, $500 to 5 runners-up. **Guidelines:** unproduced, unpublished play; send SASE for guidelines. **Submission procedure:** script and resume. **Deadline:** 30 Sep 1996. **Notification:** Apr 1997.

DEEP SOUTH WRITERS CONFERENCE

c/o English Department; Box 44691; University of Southwestern Louisiana;
        Lafayette, LA 70504-4691; FAX 482-6195; E-mail jwf4516@usl.edu
Jerry McGuire, *Director*

James H. Wilson Full-Length Play Award

Types of material: full-length plays, solo pieces. **Frequency:** annual. **Remuneration:** $300 1st prize, $100 2nd prize. **Guidelines:** original, unpublished play (no adaptations or musicals) not produced commercially; send SASE for guidelines. **Submission procedure:** script, brief bio and $15 fee per submission; script will not be returned. **Deadline:** 15 Jul 1997. **Notification:** Sep 1997.

Miller Award

Types of material: full-length plays, solo pieces. **Frequency:** biennial. **Remuneration:** not less than $500. **Guidelines:** unpublished play, readily adaptable for film or TV, dealing with some aspect of the English Renaissance and/or the life of Edward de Vere, Earl of Oxford; write for guidelines, which are subject to change. **Submission procedure:** script and brief bio; script will not be returned. **Deadline:** 15 Jul 1997. **Notification:** Sep 1997.

Paul T. Nolan One-Act Play Award

Types of material: one-acts, solo pieces. **Frequency:** annual. **Remuneration:** $200 1st prize, $100 2nd prize; possible publication in DSWC *Chapbook*. **Guidelines:** original, unpublished play (no adaptations or musicals) less than 50 pages long, not produced commercially; publication rights to winning plays reserved until 1 Jun 1998; send SASE for guidelines. **Submission procedure:** script, brief bio and $10 fee per submission; script will not be returned. **Deadline:** 15 Jul 1997. **Notification:** Sep 1997.

DOROTHY SILVER PLAYWRITING COMPETITION

Jewish Community Center of Cleveland; 3505 Mayfield Rd; *216 (area code)*
        Cleveland Heights, OH 44118; (216) 382-4000, ext 275, FAX 382-5401
Elaine Rembrandt, *Director of Cultural Arts*

Types of material: full-length plays. **Frequency:** annual. **Remuneration:** $1000 (including $500 to cover residency expenses); staged reading; possible production. **Guidelines:** unproduced play that provides fresh and significant perspective on the range of Jewish experience. **Submission procedure:** script only. **Deadline:** 15 Dec 1996. **Notification:** Aug 1997.

DRAMAFEST '98

Lodi Arts Commission; 125 South Hutchins St, Suite D; Lodi, CA 95240;
    (209) 333-6895
Cyndi Olagaray, *Arts Coordinator*

Types of material: full-length plays, plays for young audiences, musicals. **Frequency:** biennial. **Remuneration:** $1000 for full-length play or musical, $1000 for play for young audiences; production; travel, housing and board to attend rehearsals. **Guidelines:** unproduced, unpublished work; write for guidelines. **Submission procedure:** completed entry form and script. **Deadline:** 1 Apr 1997; no submission before 1 Jan 1997. **Notification:** fall 1997.

DRAMARAMA

The Playwrights' Center of San Francisco; Box 460466;
    San Francisco, CA 94146-0466; (415) 626-4603, FAX 863-0901;
    E-mail playctrsf@aol.com
Sheppard Kominers, *Chairman*

Long Play Contest

Types of material: full-length plays, solo pieces. **Frequency:** annual. **Remuneration:** up to 4 scripts given 4–5 rehearsals and staged readings at fall festival; $500 prize awarded on basis of readings. **Guidelines:** unproduced play minimum 60 minutes; send SASE for guidelines and application. **Submission procedure:** see guidelines; submission requirements include $25 fee. **Deadline:** 15 Mar 1997. **Dates:** Oct 1997.

Short Play Contest

Types of material: one-acts, solo pieces. **Frequency:** annual. **Remuneration:** up to 4 scripts given 4–5 rehearsals and staged readings at fall festival; $500 prize awarded on basis of readings. **Guidelines:** unproduced play maximum 60 minutes; send SASE for guidelines and application. **Submission procedure:** see guidelines; submission requirements include $25 fee. **Deadline:** 15 Mar 1997. **Dates:** Oct 1997.

DRURY COLLEGE ONE-ACT PLAY COMPETITION

Drury College; 900 North Benton Ave; Springfield, MO 65802; (417) 873-7430
Sandy Asher, *Writer-in-Residence*

Types of material: one-acts. **Frequency:** biennial. **Remuneration:** $300 1st prize, 2 runners-up receive $150; possible production; winners recommended to the Open Eye Theater (see entry in Production). **Guidelines:** unproduced, unpublished play 20–45 minutes long; prefers small cast, 1 set; 1 submission; send SASE for guidelines. **Submission procedure:** script only. **Deadline:** 1 Dec 1996. **Notification:** 1 Apr 1997.

DUBUQUE FINE ARTS PLAYERS
NATIONAL ONE-ACT PLAYWRITING CONTEST
1321 Tomahawk Dr; Dubuque, IA 52003; (319) 583-6748
Jennie G. Stabenow, *Coordinator*

Types of material: one-acts, one-act adaptations. **Frequency:** annual. **Remuneration:** $600 1st prize, $300 2nd prize, $200 3rd prize; possible production for all 3 plays. **Guidelines:** unproduced, unpublished play maximum 35 pages and 40 minutes long; prefers cast limit of 5, 1 set; no submission limit but playwright may not win more than 1 prize; only adaptations of material in public domain; send SASE for guidelines. **Submission procedure:** completed entry form, 2 copies of script, 1-paragraph synopsis and $10 fee per submission; SASP if acknowledgment of receipt is desired. **Deadline:** 31 Jan 1997; no submission before 1 Nov 1996. **Notification:** 30 Jun 1997.

EMERGING PLAYWRIGHT AWARD
Playwrights' Preview Productions; 17 East 47th St;
    New York, NY 10017; (212) 289-2168
Pamela Faith Jackson, *Literary Associate*

Types of material: full-length plays, one-acts. **Frequency:** annual. **Remuneration:** $500; production; travel to attend rehearsals. **Guidelines:** play unproduced in New York; submissions from minority playwrights and plays with ethnically diverse casts encouraged. **Submission procedure:** script, production history (if any) and bio. **Deadline:** ongoing; best submission time Jul–Aug and Dec.

FERNDALE REPERTORY THEATRE
NEW WORKS COMPETITION
Box 892; Ferndale, CA 95536-0892; (707) 725-2378, FAX 725-2378
Clinton Rebik, *Artistic Director*

Types of material: full-length plays, musicals, solo pieces. **Frequency:** annual. **Remuneration:** production with $250 royalty; set of all photos and promotional materials. **Guidelines:** unpublished work which has not received full production; minimal technical demands; write for guidelines. **Submission procedure:** script, cast list and synopsis; resume, SASP. **Deadline:** 15 Oct 1996. **Notification:** 1 Jun 1997.

THE FESTIVAL OF EMERGING AMERICAN THEATRE (FEAT) COMPETITION

The Phoenix Theatre; 749 North Park Ave; Indianapolis, IN 46202;
    (317) 635-7529, FAX 635-7529 (call first)
Bryan Fonseca, *Producing Director*

Types of material: full-length plays, one-acts, solo pieces. **Frequency:** annual. **Remuneration:** $750 for full-length play, $375 for one-act; 2 full-production slots will be filled, each with a full-length play or a bill of one-acts; housing to attend rehearsals. **Guidelines:** unpublished play not professionally produced and suitable for theatre with 150-seat and 75-seat houses that produces contemporary, issue-oriented works; moderate cast size and production demands; availability of playwright for rehearsals a consideration; 1 submission. **Submission procedure:** script, production history, 1- or 2-page synopsis, bio and $5 entry fee; optional SASE for critique. **Deadline:** 28 Feb 1997. **Notification:** May/Jun 1997.

FESTIVAL OF FIRSTS PLAYWRITING COMPETITION

Sunset Center; Box 1950; Carmel, CA 93921; (408) 624-3996
Director

Types of material: full-length plays. **Frequency:** annual. **Remuneration:** up to $1000; possible production. **Guidelines:** unproduced play; send SASE for guidelines. **Submission procedure:** completed entry form, script, cast list, synopsis and $15 entry fee. **Deadline:** 31 Aug 1997; no submission before 15 Jun 1996.

GEORGE HAWKINS PLAYWRITING CONTEST

The Ensemble Theatre; 3535 Main St; Houston, TX 77002; (713) 520-0055,
    FAX 520-1269
Eileen Morris, *Artistic Director*

Types of material: one-acts and musicals for young audiences. **Frequency:** annual. **Remuneration:** $500 1st prize; production; travel and housing to attend final week of rehearsals; 2nd and 3rd prizewinners receive staged reading. **Guidelines:** original work, not professionally produced, that illuminates the African-American experience for young people aged 6–18; prefers works maximum 45 minutes long with cast limit of 7 and simple set and props; write for guidelines. **Submission procedure:** completed entry form and script. **Deadline:** 20 Mar 1997; no submission before 1 Dec 1996. **Notification:** 20 May 1997.

GEORGE HOUSTON BASS PLAY-RITES FESTIVAL
AND MEMORIAL AWARD

Rites and Reason Theatre; Box 1148; Brown University; Providence, RI 02912;
    (401) 863-3558, FAX 863-3559
Elmo Terry-Morgan *Artistic Director*

Types of material: full-length plays, one-acts, musicals, solo pieces. **Frequency:** annual. **Remuneration:** 4 winners receive $250, staged reading at festival, travel and housing to attend rehearsals; winner of best play of festival receives $1000, workshop production, housing and travel to attend rehearsals. **Guidelines:** plays dealing with theme of cultural diversity; prefers long one-acts but will consider short full-length plays; writer must be willing to develop work further. **Submission procedure:** script only; include cassette for musicals. **Deadline:** 1 Apr 1997. **Notification:** Jun 1997. **Dates:** Oct 1997.

GEORGE R. KERNODLE PLAYWRITING CONTEST

Department of Drama; 619 Kimpel Hall; University of Arkansas;
    Fayetteville, AR 72701; (501) 575-2953
Director

Types of material: one-acts. **Frequency:** annual. **Remuneration:** $300 1st prize, $200 2nd prize, $100 3rd prize; possible staged reading or production. **Guidelines:** U.S. or Canadian playwright; unproduced, unpublished play, not more than 1 hour long; cast limit of 8; 3-submission limit; write for guidelines. **Submission procedure:** script with statement that play has not received full production, $3 fee per submission and optional SASE or SASP for acknowledgment of receipt. **Deadline:** 1 Jun 1997; no submission before 1 Jan 1997. **Notification:** 1 Nov 1997.

GILMAN AND GONZALEZ-FALLA THEATRE FOUNDATION MUSICAL THEATRE AWARD

109 East 64th St; New York, NY 10021; (212) 734-8011
Sarah Smith, *Coordinator*

Types of material: musicals. **Frequency:** annual. **Remuneration:** $25,000. **Guidelines:** writer(s) must have had a musical produced by commercial or nonprofit theatre; contact foundation for guidelines after 1 Jan 1996. **Submission procedure:** see guidelines. **Deadline:** Aug or Sep 1997; exact date TBA.

GILMORE CREEK PLAYWRITING COMPETITION

Campus Box 78; St. Mary's College of Minnesota; Winona, MN 55987;
    (507) 457-1606, FAX 457-1752; E-mail bpevitts@smumn.edu
Robert Pevitts, *Dean of School of Arts and Humanities*

Types of material: full-length plays, translations, adaptations, plays for young audiences, musicals, solo pieces. **Frequency:** biennial. **Remuneration:** $2500; production; stipend to cover travel, room and board for 2-week residency. **Guidelines:** full-length work not produced professionally. **Submission procedure:** completed application and script. **Deadline:** 15 Jan 1997. **Notification:** 15 May 1997.

GOSHEN COLLEGE PEACE PLAYWRITING CONTEST

Goshen College; 1700 South Main St; Goshen, IN 46526; (219) 535-7393,
    FAX 535-7618; E-mail laurendf@goshen.edu
Lauren Friesen, *Director of Theatre*

Types of material: one-acts. **Frequency:** biennial. **Remuneration:** $500; production; room and board to attend rehearsals and/or production. **Guidelines:** 1

unproduced submission, 30–50 minutes long, exploring a contemporary peace theme. **Submission procedure:** script only. **Deadline:** 31 Dec 1997. **Notification:** 1 May 1998.

GREAT PLATTE RIVER PLAYWRIGHTS' FESTIVAL

University of Nebraska-Kearney Theatre; Kearney, NE 68849-5260;
(308) 865-8406, FAX 865-8806; E-mail garrisonj@platte.unk.edu
Artistic Director

Types of material: full-length plays, one-acts, plays for young audiences, musicals. **Frequency:** annual. **Remuneration:** $500 1st prize, $300 2nd prize, $200 3rd prize; production; travel and housing to attend rehearsals. **Guidelines:** unproduced, unpublished original work; submission of works-in-progress for possible development encouraged. **Submission procedure:** script with cover letter; include cassette for musical. **Deadline:** 1 Apr 1997. **Notification:** 15 May 1997.

THE GREGORY KOLOVAKOS AWARD

PEN American Center; 568 Broadway; New York, NY 10012; (212) 334-1660,
FAX 334-2181; E-mail pen@echonyc.com
John Morrone, *Awards Coordinator*

Types of material: translations. **Frequency:** biennial. **Remuneration:** $2000. **Guidelines:** award to U.S. writer, critic or translator whose work has made a sustained contribution over time to the cause of Latin American literatures, as well as their Iberian counterparts, in English; primarily recognizes work from Spanish but contributions from other Hispanic languages also considered; candidate must be nominated by editor or colleague; write for guideline. **Submission procedure:** letter from nominator documenting candidate's qualifications with particular attention to depth and vision of his or her work; candidate's vita; supporting materials may be requested from finalists. **Deadline:** 1 Dec 1997. **Notification:** finalists mid-Dec 1997; winner mid-Mar 1998.

HAROLD MORTON LANDON TRANSLATION AWARD

The Academy of American Poets; 584 Broadway, Suite 1208;
New York, NY 10012; (212) 274-0343
Matthew Brogan, *Program Director*

Types of material: translations. **Frequency:** annual. **Remuneration:** $1000. **Guidelines:** U.S. citizen; published translation of verse, including verse drama, from any language into English verse; book published in 1996. **Submission procedure:** 3 copies of book (no manuscripts). **Deadline:** 31 Dec 1996.

HENRICO THEATRE COMPANY
ONE-ACT PLAYWRITING COMPETITION
The County of Henrico; Division of Recreation and Parks; Box 27032;
    Richmond, VA 23273; (804) 672-5115, FAX 672-5284
J. Larkin Brown, Cultural Arts Coordinator

Types of material: one-act plays, musicals, solo pieces. **Frequency:** annual.
Remuneration: $250 and production 1st prize; $125, possible production and
video for runner-up. **Guidelines:** unproduced, unpublished work; no controversial
themes; prefers small cast, simple set; write for guidelines. **Submission procedure:**
2 copies of script. **Deadline:** 1 Jul 1997. **Notification:** 31 Dec 1997.

HRC's ANNUAL PLAYWRITING CONTEST
Hudson River Classics, Inc; Box 940; Hudson, NY 12534; (518) 828-1329
W. Keith Hedrick, *President*

Types of material: full-length plays, one-acts, solo pieces. **Frequency:** annual.
Remuneration: $500; staged reading; room, board and travel to attend perfor-
mance. **Guidelines:** 60–90-minute unpublished play by New York State playwright.
Submission procedure: script and $5 fee. **Deadline:** 1 Jun 1997; no submission
before 15 Jan 1997. **Notification:** 15 Aug 1997.

INNER CITY CULTURAL CENTER COMPETITION
The Ivar Theater; 1605 North Ivar Ave; Los Angeles, CA 90028; (213) 962-2102,
    FAX 386-9017
C. Bernard Jackson, *Executive Director*

Types of material: one-acts, translations, adaptations, plays for young audiences,
musicals, solo pieces, operas. **Frequency:** annual. **Remuneration:** cash award
($1000 1st prize, $500 2nd prize, $250 3rd prize) or paid professional internship
with film studio to winner (past winners awarded internships with Warner
Brothers and Universal Studios). **Guidelines:** fully mounted productions compete
in series of elimination rounds; maximum 40 minutes running time; small cast,
minimal set; translations and adaptations must be of unpublished work; write for
guidelines. **Submission procedure:** completed application and $45 fee. **Deadline:**
21 Jul 1997. **Dates:** Jul–Oct 1997.

JACKIE WHITE MEMORIAL NATIONAL
CHILDREN'S PLAYWRITING CONTEST
309 Parkade Blvd; Columbia, MO 65202; (573) 874-5628
Betsy Phillips, *Chair*

Types of material: plays and musicals to be performed by young actors.
Frequency: annual. **Remuneration:** $250; production by Columbia Entertainment
Company Children's Theatre School; room, board and partial travel to attend
performance; all entrants receive written evaluation. **Guidelines:** unpublished
original work, 60–90 minutes in length, with 20–30 speaking characters of all
ages, at least 10 developed in some detail, to be played by students aged 10–15;

send SASE for guidelines. **Submission procedure:** completed entry form, script, character description, act/scene synopsis, resume and $10 fee; include cassette for musical. **Deadline:** 1 Jun 1997. **Notification:** 30 Aug 1997.

JAMES D. PHELAN AWARD IN LITERATURE

Intersection for the Arts/The San Francisco Foundation; 446 Valencia St;
    San Francisco, CA 94103; (415) 626-2787, FAX 626-1636
Awards Coordinator

Types of material: full-length plays, one-acts, plays for young audiences. **Frequency:** annual. **Remuneration:** $2000. **Guidelines:** unpublished play-in-progress; author CA born and aged 20–35 years as of 31 Jan 1997. **Submission procedure:** completed application and script. **Deadline:** 31 Jan 1997; no submission before 15 Nov 1996. **Notification:** 15 Jun 1997.

JANE CHAMBERS PLAYWRITING AWARD

English Department; Box 1852; Brown University; Providence, RI 02912;
    (401) 247-2911
Tori Haring-Smith, *Coordinator*

Types of material: full-length plays, one-acts, solo pieces, performance-art texts. **Frequency:** annual. **Remuneration:** $1000; student submissions eligible for $250 Student Award; both winners receive listing in mailing sent to all TCG theatres. **Guidelines:** work by a woman that reflects a feminist perspective and contains a majority of roles for women; special interest in works by and about women from a diversity of positions in respect to race, class, sexual preference, physical ability, age and geographical region; experimentation with dramatic form encouraged; 1-submission limit; send SASE for guidelines and application. **Submission procedure:** completed application form, script, synopsis and resume; if possible, letter of endorsement by theatre professional familiar with writer's work; optional SASP for acknowledgment of receipt. **Deadline:** 15 Feb 1997. **Notification:** 30 May 1997.

JEWEL BOX THEATRE PLAYWRIGHTING AWARD

3700 North Walker; Oklahoma City, OK 73118-7099; (405) 521-1786,
    FAX 525-6562
Charles Tweed, *Production Director*

Types of material: full-length plays, solo pieces. **Frequency:** annual. **Remuneration:** $500; possible production. **Guidelines:** unproduced full-length play of strong ensemble nature with emphasis on character rather than spectacle; send SASE for guidelines and forms. **Submission procedure:** completed entry form, playwright's agreement and 2 copies of script. **Deadline:** 15 Jan 1997. **Notification:** Apr 1997.

JOHN GASSNER MEMORIAL PLAYWRITING AWARD

The New England Theatre Conference; c/o Department of Theatre;
    Northeastern University; 306 Huntington Ave; Boston, MA 02115;
    (617) 424-9275, FAX 424-1057

Types of material: full-length plays, solo pieces. **Frequency:** annual. **Remuneration:** $500 1st prize, $250 2nd prize; staged reading at NETC annual convention; possible publication. **Guidelines:** New England resident or NETC member; unpublished play that has not had professional full production and is not under consideration for publication or professional production; 1 submission. **Submission procedure:** script with cover page, cast list with character descriptions, brief synopsis and statement that play has not been published or professionally produced and is not under consideration; SASP for acknowledgment of receipt; $10 fee, except for NETC members. **Deadline:** 15 Apr 1997. **Notification:** 1 Sep 1997 (winners only).

KATHERINE AND LEE CHILCOTE AWARD

Cleveland Public Theatre; 6415 Detroit Ave; Cleveland, OH 44102;
    (216) 631-2727, FAX 631-2575; E-mail cpt@en.com
Terence Cranendonk, *Director, New Plays Festival*

Types of material: full-length plays, one-acts. **Frequency:** annual. **Remuneration:** 10–12 plays receive staged reading at Jan festival; of those, 2 chosen to receive award of $2000; 1 given full production. **Guidelines:** unproduced play; to be eligible for award, play must be chosen for inclusion in New Plays Festival (see Cleveland Public Theatre in Production); write for guidelines. **Submission procedure:** script and $10 fee (waivable). **Deadline:** 1 Sep 1996. **Notification:** 1 Dec 1996 for festival; 1 Jan 1997 for award.

KENNEDY CENTER AMERICAN COLLEGE THEATER FESTIVAL: MICHAEL KANIN PLAYWRITING AWARDS PROGRAM

The John F. Kennedy Center for the Performing Arts;
    Washington, DC 20566-0001; (202) 416-8850, FAX 416-8802
John Lion, *Producing Director*

The Fourth Freedom Forum Playwriting Award

Types of material: full-length plays. **Remuneration:** 1st prize: for playwright, $5000 plus all-expense-paid 2-week residency at Sundance Playwrights Laboratory (see Development), which includes consultation with Sundance directors and dramaturgs and reading by Lab actors; $1500 to producing college or university; 2nd prize: $2500 to playwright; $1000 to producing college or university. **Guidelines:** play on themes of world peace and international disarmament; produced by an ACTF-participating college or university; writer enrolled as full-time student at college or university during year of production; write for KC/ACTF brochure. **Submission procedure:** college or university which has entered production of work in ACTF registers work for awards program. **Deadline:** 1 Dec 1996. **Dates:** 14–22 Apr 1997.

The KC/ACTF Musical Theater Award

Types of material: musicals. **Frequency:** annual. **Remuneration:** $1000 for lyrics; $1000 for music; $1000 for book; $1000 to producing college or university. **Guidelines:** original and copyrighted work produced by an ACTF-participating college or university; at least 50% of writing team must be enrolled as full-time student(s) at college or university during year of production or during either of the 2 years preceding the production; write for KC/ACTF brochure. **Submission procedure:** college or university which has entered production of work in ACTF registers work for awards program. **Deadline:** 1 Dec 1996. **Dates:** 14–22 Apr 1997.

The Lorraine Hansberry Playwriting Award

Types of material: full-length plays. **Frequency:** annual. **Remuneration:** 1st prize: $2500, all-expenses-paid fellowship to attend playwrights retreat and publication of play by Dramatic Publishing Company (see Publication); $750 to producing college or university; 2nd prize: $1000 to playwright; $500 to producing college or university. **Guidelines:** play dealing with the black experience produced by an ACTF-participating college or university; writer enrolled as full-time student at college or university during year of production or during either of the 2 years preceding the production; write for KC/ACTF brochure. **Submission procedure:** college or university which has entered production of work in ACTF registers work for awards program. **Deadline:** 1 Dec 1996. **Dates:** 14–22 Apr 1997.

The National AIDS Fund Award for Playwriting

Types of material: full-length plays, adaptations, musicals. **Frequency:** annual. **Remuneration:** $2500 plus fellowship to attend Bay Area Playwrights Festival (see Development). **Guidelines:** play concerning personal and social implications of HIV/AIDS produced by an ACTF-participating college or university; writer enrolled as full-time student at college or university during year of production or during either of the 2 years preceding the production; write for KC/ACTF brochure. **Submission procedure:** college or university which has entered production of work in ACTF registers work for awards program. **Deadline:** 1 Dec 1996. **Dates:** 14–22 Apr 1997.

The National Student Playwriting Award

Types of material: full-length plays, adaptations, musicals. **Frequency:** annual. **Remuneration:** $2500; production at Kennedy Center during festival; publication by Samuel French with royalties; offer of William Morris Agency management contract; fellowship to attend Mount Sequoyah New Play Retreat (see Development); Dramatists Guild membership (see Membership and Service Organizations). **Guidelines:** work must be produced by an ACTF-participating college or university; writer enrolled as full-time student at college or university during year of production or during either of the 2 years preceding the production; write for KC/ACTF brochure. **Submission procedure:** college or university which has entered production of work in ACTF registers work for awards program. **Deadline:** 1 Dec 1996. **Dates:** 14–22 Apr 1997.

The Short Play Awards Program

Types of material: one-acts, one-act adaptations. **Frequency:** annual. **Remuneration:** up to 3 awards: $1000; publication by Samuel French; Dramatists Guild membership (see Membership and Service Organizations). **Guidelines:** one-act must be produced by an ACTF-participating college or university; writer enrolled as full-time student at college or university during year of production or during either of the 2 years preceding the production; simple production demands (minimal setup and strike time); write for KC/ACTF brochure. **Submission procedure:** college or university which has entered production of work in ACTF registers work for awards program. **Deadline:** 1 Dec 1996. **Dates:** 14–22 Apr 1997.

KUMU KAHUA PLAYWRITING CONTEST
Department of Theatre and Dance; University of Hawaii at Manoa;
      1770 East-West Rd; Honolulu, HI 96822; (808) 956-2588, FAX 956-4234
Dennis Carroll, *Chair, Theatre and Dance*

Types of material: full-length plays, one-acts. **Frequency:** annual. **Remuneration:** *first category:* $500 for full-length play, $200 for one-act; *second category:* $250 for full-length play, $100 for one-act; reading and/or production if playwright present. **Guidelines:** unproduced play; previous entries ineligible; *first category:* play set in HI and dealing with some aspect of HI experience; *second category:* play not dealing with HI by HI resident only. **Submission procedure:** write for entry brochure. **Deadline:** 1 Jan 1997. **Notification:** 1 May 1997.

L. ARNOLD WEISSBERGER PLAYWRITING COMPETITION
New Dramatists; 424 West 44th St; New York, NY 10036; (212) 757-6960
Coordinator

Types of material: full-length plays. **Frequency:** annual. **Remuneration:** $5000. **Guidelines:** 1 unpublished submission; play not produced professionally; write for guidelines. **Submission procedure:** script must be nominated by theatre professional or college department head and then, at request of New Dramatists, submitted with optional SASP for acknowledgment of receipt. **Deadline:** 31 May 1997; no submission before 15 Sep 1996. **Notification:** May 1997.

LAMIA INK! INTERNATIONAL ONE-PAGE PLAY COMPETITION
Box 202, Prince St Station; New York, NY 10012
Cortland Jessup, *Editor*

Types of material: 1-page plays. **Frequency:** annual. **Remuneration:** $200; reading in New York City and publication in magazine (see entry in Publication) for winner and 11 other best plays. **Guidelines:** 3-submission limit; send SASE for guidelines. **Submission procedure:** completed application, script, SASE for response and $1 fee per submission. **Deadline:** 15 Mar 1997. **Notification:** 15 Apr 1997.

Lawrence S. Epstein Playwriting Award
115 Hatteras Rd; Barnegat, NJ 08005-2814
Lawrence S. Epstein, *Director*

Types of material: full-length plays, bills of related one-acts. **Frequency:** annual. **Remuneration:** $250. **Guidelines:** unproduced play. **Submission procedure:** script and optional $1 fee to help cover expenses. **Deadline:** 31 Mar 1997; no submission before 1 Jan 1997. **Notification:** Dec 1997.

The Lee Korf Playwriting Awards
The Original Theatre Works; Burnight Center; Cerritos College;
    11110 Alondra Blvd; Norwalk, CA 90650-6298;
    (310) 860-2451, ext 2638, FAX 467-5097
Gloria Manriquez, *Production Coordinator*

Types of material: full-length plays, musicals, theatre pieces, extravaganzas. **Frequency:** annual. **Remuneration:** $750; production. **Guidelines:** special interest in works with multicultural themes. **Submission procedure:** send SASE for guidelines and application. **Deadline:** 1 Sep 1996. **Notification:** 1 Apr 1997.

Lesbian Play Award

See LEND (Lesbian Exchange of New Drama) in Membership and Service Organizations.

Letras de Oro Spanish Literary Prize Competition
University of Miami; 1531 Brescia Ave; Coral Gables, FL 33124-3010;
    (305) 284-3266, FAX 284-4406
Joaquin Roy, *Graduate School of International Studies*

Types of material: full-length plays. **Frequency:** annual. **Remuneration:** $2500; publication. **Guidelines:** U.S. resident; unpublished play written in Spanish that has not won a previous award; 1 submission; write for rules. **Submission procedure:** 3 copies of script. **Deadline:** 12 Oct 1996. **Notification:** Mar 1997.

The Little Theatre of Alexandria
National One-Act Playwriting Competition
Little Theatre of Alexandria; 600 Wolfe St; Alexandria, VA 22314;
    (703) 683-5778
Chairman, Playwriting Competition

Types of material: one-acts. **Frequency:** annual. **Remuneration:** $350 1st prize, $250 2nd prize, $150 3rd prize; possible production. **Guidelines:** U.S. citizen; 1 unpublished, unproduced submission; prefers plays with running times of 20–60 minutes, few scenes and 1 set. **Submission procedure:** script, synopsis, character descriptions and $5 fee; send SASE for guidelines. **Deadline:** 28 Feb 1997; no submission before 1 Sep 1996. **Notification:** Sep 1997.

LIVE OAK THEATRE'S HARVEST FESTIVAL OF NEW AMERICAN PLAYS
200 Colorado St; Austin, TX 78701; (512) 472-5143, FAX 472-7199
Michael Hankin, *Associate Director*

Types of material: full-length plays, solo pieces. **Frequency:** annual. **Remuneration:** $1000 for best American play; $500 Larry L. King Playwriting Award for Outstanding Texas Playwright; $500 for University of Texas student "who makes outstanding contribution towards new play development"; staged reading in fall festival; possible full production. **Guidelines:** 1 submission, not produced professionally. **Submission procedure:** send SASE for guidelines. **Deadline:** 1 Apr 1997. **Notification:** summer 1997.

LOIS AND RICHARD ROSENTHAL NEW PLAY PRIZE
Cincinnati Playhouse in the Park; Box 6537; Cincinnati, OH 45206;
    (513) 345-2242
Artistic Associate

Types of material: full-length plays, musicals. **Frequency:** annual. **Remuneration:** $10,000; production; travel and housing to attend rehearsals. **Guidelines:** 1 unpublished submission, not produced professionally. **Submission procedure:** no scripts; 5 pages of dialogue, 2-page maximum abstract including synopsis, character breakdown and playwright's bio, submitted by playwright or agent. **Deadline:** 1 Feb 1997; no submission before 15 Oct 1996. **Notification:** 2 months; 6 months if script is requested.

LOS ANGELES DESIGNERS' THEATRE COMMISSIONS
Box 1883; Studio City, CA 91614-0883; (213) 650-9600 (voice),
    (818) 769-9000 (TDD), FAX 985-9200
Richard Niederberg, *Artistic Director*

Types of material: full-length plays, bills of related one-acts, translations, adaptations, plays for young audiences, musicals, solo pieces, operas. **Frequency:** ongoing. **Remuneration:** negotiable commissioning fee; possible travel to attend rehearsals if developmental work is needed. **Guidelines:** commissioning program for work with commercial potential which has not received professional full production, is not under option and is free of commitment to specific director, actors or other personnel; large casts and multiple sets welcome; prefers controversial material. **Submission procedure:** proposal or synopsis and resume; include cassette for musical; materials will not be returned. **Deadline:** ongoing. **Notification:** at least 4 months.

LOVE CREEK ANNUAL SHORT PLAY FESTIVAL
Love Creek Productions; c/o 79 Liberty Pl; Weehawken, NJ 07087-7014
Cynthia Granville-Callahan, *Festival Literary Manager/Chair, Reading Committee*

Types of material: one-acts. **Frequency:** annual. **Remuneration:** approximately 40 finalists receive mini-showcase production in New York City during festival; $300 prize for best play of festival. **Guidelines:** unpublished play featuring women in major roles, not produced in NYC area within past year; maximum length of 40 minutes; cast of 2 or more, simple sets and costumes; 2-submission limit; send SASE for guidelines. **Submission procedure:** script with letter giving theatre permission to produce play if chosen and specifying whether Equity showcase is acceptable. **Deadline:** 30 Sep 1996. **Dates:** Jan–Feb 1997.

THE MARC A. KLEIN PLAYWRITING AWARD

Department of Theater Arts; Case Western Reserve University; 10900 Euclid Ave; Cleveland, OH 44106-7077; (216) 368-4868, FAX 368-5184; E-mail ksg@po.cwru.edu
John Orlock, *Chair, Reading Committee*

Types of material: full-length plays, bills of related one-acts. **Frequency:** annual. **Remuneration:** $1000, including $500 to cover residency expenses; production. **Guidelines:** student currently enrolled at U.S. college or university; work, endorsed by faculty member of university theatre department, that has not received professional full production or trade-book publication. **Submission procedure:** completed entry form and script. **Deadline:** 15 May 1997. **Notification:** 1 Aug 1997.

MARGARET BARTLE PLAYWRITING AWARD

Community Children's Theatre; 8021 East 129th Terr; Grandview, MO 64030-2114; (816) 761-5775
Blanche Sellens, *Chairman, Playwriting Contest*

Types of material: plays and musicals for young audiences. **Frequency:** annual. **Remuneration:** $500. **Guidelines:** unpublished, unproduced work 55–60 minutes long, suitable for grades 1–6; 8-character limit; all parts played by adult women. **Submission procedure:** script only; include cassette for musical. **Deadline:** 31 Jan 1997. **Notification:** Apr 1997.

MARVIN TAYLOR PLAYWRITING AWARD

Sierra Repertory Theatre; Box 3030; Sonora, CA 95370; (209) 532-3120, FAX 532-7270
Dennis Jones, *Producing Director*

Types of material: full-length plays, adaptations, musicals, solo pieces. **Frequency:** annual. **Remuneration:** $500; possible production. **Guidelines:** 1 submission that has received no more than 2 productions or staged readings; cast limit of 15, prefers 6; not more than 2 sets. **Submission procedure:** script only. **Deadline:** 31 Aug 1997. **Notification:** Mar 1998.

MAXIM MAZUMDAR NEW PLAY COMPETITION

Alleyway Theatre; 1 Curtain Up Alley; Buffalo, NY 14202-1911; (716) 852-2600, FAX 852-2266
Joyce Stilson, *Dramaturg*

Types of material: full-length plays, one-acts, musicals. **Frequency:** annual.

Remuneration: $400, production with royalty, and travel and housing to attend rehearsals for full-length play or musical; $100 and production for one-act play or musical. **Guidelines:** unproduced full-length work minimum 90 minutes long with cast limit of 10 and unit set or simple set, or unproduced one-act work less than 60 minutes long with cast limit of 6 and simple set; prefers work with unconventional setting that explores the boundaries of theatricality; limit of 1 submission in each category. **Submission procedure:** script and resume; $5 fee per playwright. **Deadline:** 1 Jul 1997. **Notification:** 1 Jan 1998 for finalists; 1 Feb 1998 for winners.

MCLAREN MEMORIAL COMEDY PLAYWRITING COMPETITION

Midland Community Theatre; 2000 West Wadley Ave; Midland, TX 79705;
    (915) 682-2544, FAX 682-6136
Mary Lou Cassidy, *Coordinator*

Types of material: full-length plays, one-acts, translations, adaptations, plays for young audiences, musicals, solo pieces. **Frequency:** annual. **Remuneration:** $400; staged reading; housing while attending rehearsals. **Guidelines:** comedies only; prefers work that has not received professional full production but will consider work with 1 nonprofit-theatre production. **Submission procedure:** script and $5 fee. **Deadline:** 31 Jan 1997; no submission before 1 Dec 1996. **Notification:** 15 May 1997.

MIDWEST THEATRE NETWORK ORIGINAL PLAY COMPETITION/ ROCHESTER PLAYWRIGHT FESTIVAL

5031 Tongen Ave NW; Rochester, MN 55901; (507) 281-1472
Joan Sween, *Executive Director*

Types of material: full-length plays, collections of one-acts, plays for young audiences, musicals, full-length solo pieces, satirical revues. **Frequency:** annual. **Remuneration:** 4–8 awards of $1000 each (contingent on funding); full production at 1 of 7 cooperating theatres; possible travel, room and board to attend performance. **Guidelines:** unpublished work that has not received professional production; send SASE for guidelines and entry form. **Submission procedure:** 1 completed entry form with each script; first submission free, $5 fee for each additional script; include cassette for musical. **Deadline:** 30 Nov 1996. **Notification:** Feb 1997.

MIDWESTERN PLAYWRIGHTS FESTIVAL

The University of Toledo; Department of Theatre, Film and Dance;
    Toledo, OH 43606-3390; (419) 537-2202, FAX 530-8439
John S. Kuhn, *Playwriting Festival Coordinator*

Types of material: full-length plays, translations, adaptations, musicals. **Frequency:** annual. **Remuneration:** winner receives $1000, staged reading in fall 1997, production at Toledo Repertoire Theatre in spring 1998, and travel, room and board for reading and 2-week residency during production; 1st runner-up receives

$350 and staged reading; 2nd runner-up receives $150 and staged reading. **Guidelines:** resident of IL, IN, MI or OH; 1 full-length, 2-act submission not published or produced professionally; cast limit of 10; prefers 1 set; write for guidelines. **Submission procedure:** 2 copies of script, 1-page synopsis, resume and cover letter. **Deadline:** 1 May 1997. **Notification:** 1 Aug 1997.

MILDRED AND ALBERT PANOWSKI PLAYWRITING AWARD

Forest A. Roberts Theatre; Northern Michigan University; Marquette, MI 49855; (906) 227-2553, FAX 227-2567
James A. Panowski, *Director*

Types of material: full-length plays, adaptations, solo pieces. **Frequency:** annual. **Remuneration:** $2000; production; travel, room and board for 1-week residency. **Guidelines:** 1 unpublished, unproduced submission; rewrites of previous entries ineligible; production will be entered in Kennedy Center American College Theater Festival (see entry in this section) if playwright is eligible; write for guidelines. **Submission procedure:** completed entry form and script. **Deadline:** 15 Nov 1996. **Notification:** Apr 1997.

THE MILL MOUNTAIN THEATRE NEW PLAY COMPETITION: THE NORFOLK SOUTHERN FESTIVAL OF NEW WORKS

1 Market Square SE, 2nd Floor; Roanoke, VA 24011-1437; (540) 342-5730, FAX 342-5745
Jo Weinstein, *Literary Manager*

Types of material: full-length plays, one-acts, solo pieces. **Frequency:** annual. **Remuneration:** $1000; staged reading with possibility of production; travel stipend and housing for limited residency. **Guidelines:** U.S. resident; 1 unproduced, unpublished submission; cast limit of 10; no 10-minute plays; send SASE for guidelines. **Submission procedure:** agent submission or script with professional recommendation by director, literary manager or dramaturg. **Deadline:** 1 Jan 1997; no submission before 1 Oct 1996. **Notification:** Aug 1997.

MIXED BLOOD VERSUS AMERICA

Mixed Blood Theatre Company; 1501 South 4th St; Minneapolis, MN 55454; (612) 338-0937
David Kunz, *Script Czar*

Types of material: full-length plays, musicals, solo pieces. **Frequency:** annual. **Remuneration:** $2000; production. **Guidelines:** unproduced, unpublished work by U.S. citizen who has had at least 1 work produced or workshopped professionally or by educational institution; 2-submission limit; write for guidelines. **Submission procedure:** script and resume or other evidence of work produced or workshopped; include cassette of songs for musical; mark all contest submissions "Mixed Blood Versus America." **Deadline:** 15 Mar 1997. **Notification:** fall 1997.

MORTON R. SARETT NATIONAL PLAYWRITING COMPETITION

Department of Theatre Arts; University of Nevada, Las Vegas;
    4505 Maryland Pkwy, Box 455036; Las Vegas, NV 89154-5036;
    (702) 895-3666
Corrine A. Bonate, *Coordinator*

Types of material: full-length plays, musicals. **Frequency:** biennial. **Remuneration:** $3000; production; travel and housing to attend rehearsals and opening performance. **Guidelines:** unpublished, unproduced play or musical; send SASE for guidelines. **Submission procedure:** completed application, 2 copies of script and 50-word synopsis. **Deadline:** 15 Dec 1997; no submission before 1 Sep 1997. **Notification:** Jun 1998.

MRTW SCRIPT CONTEST

Midwest Radio Theatre Workshop; KOPN Radio; 915 East Broadway;
    Columbia, MO 65201; (573) 874-5676, FAX 499-1662;
    E-mail mrtw@mrtw.org; Web http://www.mrtw.org/mrtw
Steve Donofrio, *Director*

Types of material: short radio plays. **Frequency:** annual. **Remuneration:** $800 to be divided among 2–4 winners; possible radio production for local broadcast and national distribution via satellite and tape sales; scholarship to attend May 1997 Midwest Radio Theatre Workshop (see Development); publication in MRTW Scriptbook. **Guidelines:** original radio play 15–30 minutes long (no adaptations) by established or emerging writer; special interest in plays by women, gay and lesbian writers and writers of color and in issue-oriented plays on contemporary themes; 1 submission; write for guidelines. **Submission procedure:** 3 copies of script in radio format and cover letter indicating if play has been produced; $10 fee. **Deadline:** 15 Nov 1996. **Notification:** 1 Mar 1997.

NANTUCKET SHORT PLAY FESTIVAL AND COMPETITION

Nantucket Theatrical Productions; Box 2177; Nantucket, MA 02584;
    (508) 228-5002
Jim Patrick, *Literary Manager*

Types of material: one-acts, solo pieces. **Frequency:** annual. **Remuneration:** $200; 1 or more staged readings for winning play and selected additional plays as part of summer festival. **Guidelines:** unpublished play which has not received Equity production; maximum length of 1 hour; special interest in multiracial themes and plays by playwrights of color; simple production demands; send SASE for rules. **Submission procedure:** completed entry form, script and $5 fee. **Deadline:** 1 Mar 1997. **Notification:** 1 May 1997. **Dates:** Jul 1997.

NATIONAL CHILDREN'S THEATRE FESTIVAL

Actors' Playhouse at the Miracle Theatre; 280 Miracle Mile;
Coral Gables, FL 33134, FAX (305) 444-4181
Judy Buckland, *Education Director*

Types of material: works for young audiences. **Frequency:** annual. **Remuneration:** 3 awards in each of 2 categories (plays and musicals): $800–1200 1st prize plus production, travel and housing to attend fall festival. **Guidelines:** unpublished play for young people aged 12–17, 45–60 minutes long, with cast limit of 6 (may play multiple roles) and minimal sets suitable for touring; or unpublished musical for young people aged 5–12, 45–60 minutes long, with cast limit of 8 (may play multiple roles) and maximum of 2 major or 4 simple sets; translations and adaptations eligible only if writer owns copyright to material; special interest in works dealing with social issues including multiculturalism in today's society; write for guidelines. **Submission procedure:** completed entry form, script and $10 fee; include score and cassette for musical. **Deadline:** 1 Oct 1996. **Notification:** 1 Jan 1997. **Dates:** 5–10 May 1997.

NATIONAL HISPANIC PLAYWRITING CONTEST

Arizona Theatre Company; Box 1631; Tucson, AZ 85702; (602) 884-8210, FAX 628-9123
Rebecca Million, *Literary Manager*

Types of material: full-length plays, adaptations. **Frequency:** annual. **Remuneration:** $1000; staged reading; travel, room and board to attend rehearsals and performance. **Guidelines:** playwright of Hispanic heritage residing in U.S., territories or Mexico; 1 unproduced submission written in English or in Spanish with English translation with Hispanic-American themes or setting. **Submission procedure:** script (with English translation if original in Spanish), 1-page cover letter including production history, if any, and bio. **Deadline:** 1 Sep 1996. **Notification:** spring 1997.

NATIONAL PLAY AWARD

7080 Hollywood Blvd, Suite 908; Hollywood, CA 90028; (213) 465-9517, FAX 463-3170; E-mail nrtf@aol.com
Raul Espinoza, *Project Director*

Types of material: full-length plays. **Frequency:** annual. **Remuneration:** $5000. **Guidelines:** original unpublished play, not produced with paid Equity cast, that has not won major award or been previously submitted to NPA. **Submission procedure:** script and $20 fee (check payable to National Repertory Theatre Foundation). **Deadline:** 30 Sep 1996. **Notification:** spring 1997.

NATIONAL TEN-MINUTE PLAY CONTEST

Actors Theatre of Louisville; 316 West Main St; Louisville, KY 40202-4218;
    (502) 584-1265, FAX 584-1265
Michael Bigelow Dixon, *Literary Manager*
Michele Volansky, *Assistant Literary Manager*

Types of material: 10-minute plays and solo pieces. **Frequency:** annual. **Remuneration:** Heideman Award of $1000; possible production with royalty. **Guidelines:** U.S. citizen or resident; play 10 pages long or less which has not had Equity production; 2-submission limit; previous entries ineligible; write for guidelines. **Submission procedure:** script only. **Deadline:** 1 Dec 1996. **Notification:** fall 1997.

NEW AMERICAN COMEDY (NAC) FESTIVAL

Ukiah Players Theatre; 1041 Low Gap Rd; Ukiah, CA 95482; (707) 462-1210
Catherine Babcock Magruder, *NAC Producer*

Types of material: full-length plays. **Frequency:** biennial. **Remuneration:** 2 awards: $1000; staged reading; up to $400 travel, housing and $25 per diem to attend 2-week festival. **Guidelines:** unproduced, unpublished comedy; prefers small cast, simple set; playwright must be available to participate in 2-week developmental process during festival; write for guidelines. **Submission procedure:** completed application, script with 1-page summary of plot, scenic requirements, character breakdown and estimated running time; optional resume. **Deadline:** 31 Dec 1997. **Notification:** 1 Mar 1998. **Dates:** May 1998.

NEW CHRISTIAN PLAYS AWARD

Ensemble Theatre Company/Colorado Christian University;
    180 South Garrison St; Lakewood, CO 80226; (303) 238-5386, ext 131;
    E-mail prdorn@aol.com
Patrick Rainville Dorn, *Literary Manager*

Types of material: full-length plays, one-acts, adaptations, plays for young audiences, musicals, solo pieces. **Frequency:** annual. **Remuneration:** $200 1st prize; possible production and publication in *Christian Drama Magazine* or *Encore Performance Publishing* for winner and 3 finalists. **Guidelines:** unpublished play that is "good theatre with a Christian worldview and not preachy or didactic"; send SASE for guidelines. **Submission procedure:** script and $15 fee. **Deadline:** 1 Jun 1997. **Notification:** 1 Sep 1997.

NEW ENGLAND NEW PLAY COMPETITION

The Vineyard Playhouse; Box 2452; Vineyard Haven, MA 02568-2452;
    (508) 693-6450
(Ms.) M. J. Munafo, *Artistic Director*
Eileen Wilson, *Director of Competition*

Types of material: full-length plays. **Frequency:** annual. **Remuneration:** $500 grand prize; staged reading for grand prizewinner and 3 other finalists; travel and housing to attend rehearsals and reading. **Guidelines:** New England resident; 1 full-length, unpublished submission, not produced professionally; prefers cast of 10 or fewer, simple set suitable for small stage; guidelines subject to change; send SASE for information. **Submission procedure:** completed application, 2 copies of script and $5 fee. **Deadline:** 1 Jun 1997. **Notification:** Sep 1997. **Dates:** Oct 1997.

NEW PROFESSIONAL THEATRE WRITERS FESTIVAL
(formerly NPT Screenplay/Playwriting Festival)
424 West 42nd St, 3rd Floor; New York, NY 10036;
    (212) 290-8150, FAX 290-8202
Sherman Johnson, *Literary Manager*

Types of material: full-length plays. **Frequency:** annual. **Remuneration:** 3 awards of $2000 and professional staged reading. **Guidelines:** special interest in women writers. **Submission procedure:** script, resume and SASP for acknowledgment of receipt. **Deadline:** 1 Jun 1997. **Notification:** Sep 1997.

NEW WOMEN PLAYWRIGHT'S CONTEST
Off Center Theater; Tampa Bay Performing Arts Center; Box 518;
    Tampa, FL 33601-0518; (813) 222-1033, -1021, FAX 222-1057;
    E-mail tbpac@cent.com
Wendy Leigh, *Artistic Director*

Types of material: full-length plays, solo pieces. **Frequency:** annual. **Remuneration:** 1st prize $1000, full production, travel and housing to attend rehearsals and performance; 2nd prize $100, staged reading, possible travel and housing; 3rd prize $50, reading. **Guidelines:** comedies by and about women with casts at least 50% female; prefers unproduced plays with small casts depicting "strong, intelligent, contemporary women with keen senses of humor." **Submission procedure:** script, synopsis and $15 fee. **Deadline:** 15 Sep 1996. **Notification:** Dec 1996.

NEW YORK CITY HIGH SCHOOL PLAYWRITING CONTEST
Young Playwrights Inc; 321 West 44th St, Suite 906; New York, NY 10036;
    (212) 307-1140
Sheri M. Goldhirsch, *Artistic Director*

Types of material: full-length plays, one-acts. **Frequency:** annual. **Remuneration:** $500. **Guidelines:** New York City high school student; writers under 18 years of age automatically entered in Young Playwrights Festival National Playwriting Contest (see listing in this section); write for guidelines. **Submission procedure:** script with playwright's name, date of birth, home address, phone number, school and grade on title page. **Deadline:** 1 Apr 1997. **Notification:**

Off-Off Broadway Original Short Play Festival
45 West 25th St; New York, NY 10010-2751; (212) 206-8990, FAX 206-1429
William Talbot, *Festival Coordinator*

Types of material: one-acts, segments of full-length plays. **Frequency:** annual.
Remuneration: festival production hosted by Love Creek Productions on Theatre
Row in New York City; possible publication by Samuel French. **Guidelines:**
presentation less than 40 minutes long of work developed and produced by
theatre, professional school or college that has playwriting program. **Submission
procedure:** no submission by playwright; completed application submitted by
organization producing work. **Deadline:** Jan–Mar 1997; exact date TBA. **Notification:** within 2 weeks. **Dates:** late spring 1997.

Oglebay Institute Towngate Theatre Playwriting Contest
Oglebay Institute; Stifel Fine Arts Center; 1330 National Rd;
    Wheeling, WV 26003; (304) 242-7700, FAX 242-7700
Performing Arts Department

Types of material: full-length plays. **Frequency:** annual. **Remuneration:** $300;
production; partial travel to attend performances. **Guidelines:** unpublished, unproduced play; simple set. **Submission procedure:** script and resume. **Deadline:**
1 Jan 1997. **Notification:** 31 Mar 1997.

Pacific Northwest Writers Conference Literary Contest
2033 Sixth Ave, Suite 804; Seattle, WA 98121;
    (206) 443-3807, FAX 441-8262
Shirley Bishop, *Executive Director*

Types of material: one-acts. **Frequency:** annual. **Remuneration:** 3 prizes awarded
to writers chosen from 13 categories, 1 of which is playwriting; $300 1st prize,
$200 2nd prize, $150 3rd prize; all finalists receive written critiques; award-
winning play receives reading at summer conference. **Guidelines:** unpublished,
unproduced play; maximum 40 pages long and cast limit of 4; 1-submission limit
per category per writer; send SASE for guidelines and registration form.
Submission procedure: completed registration form, 2 copies of script submitted
anonymously with separate sheet giving 1-sentence plot summary and playwright's
name and contact information; $30 fee for nonmembers or $20 fee for members;
include SASE for critique and SASP for acknowledgment of receipt. **Deadline:** 15
Mar 1997. **Notification:** Jul 1997.

Paul Green Playwrights Prize
North Carolina Writers' Network; Box 954; Carrboro, NC 27510;
    FAX (919) 929-0535

Types of material: full-length plays, one-acts, solo pieces. **Frequency:** annual.
Remuneration: $500, possible production. **Guidelines:** unpublished, unproduced
play; send SASE for guidelines. **Submission procedure:** 2 copies of script, synopsis

and $10 fee for nonmembers or $7.50 fee for members; do not list name on manuscript, include separate cover sheet with title, name and contact information; include SASE for winners list. **Deadline:** 30 Sep 1996. **Notification:** Jan 1997.

PEN Center USA West Literary Awards
672 South Lafayette Park Pl, Suite 41; Los Angeles, CA 90057;
(213) 365-8500, FAX 365-9616
Rachel Hall, *Administrative Coordinator*

Types of material: full-length plays, screenplays, teleplays. **Frequency:** annual. **Remuneration:** $500 award in each of several categories, including drama, screenwriting and television writing. **Guidelines:** writer residing west of Mississippi River; only full-length (original or adapted) screenplays and teleplays; script first produced during 1996 calendar year. **Submission procedure:** 4 copies of script with cover letter giving title of work, author's name and state of residence, name of producer and production dates. **Deadline:** 31 Dec 1996.

PEN–Book-of-the-Month Club Translation Prize
PEN American Center; 568 Broadway; New York, NY 10012;
(212) 334-1660, FAX 334-2181; E-mail pen@echonyc.com
John Morrone, *Program Coordinator*

Types of material: translations. **Frequency:** annual. **Remuneration:** $3000. **Guidelines:** book-length translation from any language into English published in U.S. during current calendar year. **Submission procedure:** 3 copies of book. **Deadline:** 20 Dec 1996. **Notification:** spring 1997.

Perishable Theatre Women's Playwriting Festival
Box 23132; Providence, RI 02903; (401) 331-2695, FAX 331-2867
Kathleen Jenkins, *Festival Director*

Types of material: one-act plays and solo pieces. **Frequency:** annual. **Remuneration:** 3 awards of $200; production. **Guidelines:** unproduced one-act, less than 1 hour in length, by woman playwright. **Submission procedure:** script and resume. **Deadline:** 31 Dec 1996. **Notification:** 31 Mar 1997.

Playhouse on the Square New Play Competition
Playhouse on the Square; 51 South Cooper St; Memphis, TN 38104;
(901) 725-0776, 726-4498
Jackie Nichols, *Executive Director*

Types of material: full-length plays, musicals. **Frequency:** annual. **Remuneration:** $500; production. **Guidelines:** unproduced work; small cast; full arrangement for piano for musical; prefers southern playwrights. **Submission procedure:** script only. **Deadline:** 1 Apr 1997.

PLAYWRIGHTS FIRST AWARD

c\o The Players; 16 Gramercy Park South; New York, NY 10003;
(212) 249-6299, 677-1966

Types of material: full-length plays. **Frequency:** annual. **Remuneration:** $1000 for best play; reading for selected plays; useful introductions to theatre professionals. **Guidelines:** 1 unproduced play written within last 2 years (no adaptations or translations). **Submission procedure:** script and resume. **Deadline:** 15 Oct 1996. **Notification:** May 1997.

PLAYWRIGHTS' THEATER OF DENTON PLAYWRITING COMPETITION

Box 732; Denton, TX 76202-0732
Mark Pearce, *Artistic Director*

Types of material: full-length plays, one-acts, solo pieces. **Frequency:** annual. **Remuneration:** $1000. **Submission procedure:** script and $15 fee (check payable to Sigma Corporation). **Deadline:** 15 Dec 1996.

QRL POETRY SERIES AWARDS

Quarterly Review of Literature; Princeton University; 26 Haslet Ave;
Princeton, NJ 08540
Renée Weiss, *Co-Editor*

Types of material: full-length plays, one-acts, translations. **Frequency:** annual. **Remuneration:** $1000; publication in QRL Poetry Series; 100 complimentary paperback copies. **Guidelines:** up to 6 awards a year for poetry and poetic drama only; play 50–100 pages in length; send SASE for guidelines. **Submission procedure:** submissions accepted in Nov and May only; must be accompanied by $20 subscription for books published in series.

RENATO POGGIOLI AWARD

PEN American Center; 568 Broadway; New York, NY 10012; (212) 334-1660,
FAX 334-2181; E-mail pen@echonyc.com
John Morrone, *Program Coordinator*

Types of material: translations. **Frequency:** annual. **Remuneration:** $3000. **Guidelines:** book-length translation from Italian into English by promising young translator; work-in-progress eligible. **Submission procedure:** curriculum vitae, sample of translation and original Italian text. **Deadline:** 20 Dec 1996. **Notification:** May 1997.

REVA SHINER FULL-LENGTH PLAY CONTEST

Bloomington Playwrights Project; 308 South Washington St;
Bloomington, IN 47401; (812) 334-1188
Kathy Fletcher, *Artistic Director*

Types of material: full-length plays, musicals. **Frequency:** annual. **Remuneration:**

$500; staged reading; production. **Guidelines:** unpublished, unproduced work 75–150 minutes long, suitable for production in small 65-seat theatre; welcomes innovative works; simple set; write for guidelines. **Submission procedure:** script, cover letter and $5 fee; include cassette for musical. **Deadline:** 15 Jan 1997. **Notification:** Apr 1997.

ROBERT BONE MEMORIAL PLAYWRITING AWARD
The Playwrights' Project; Sammons Center for the Arts, #12;
    3630 Harry Hines Blvd; Dallas, TX 75219; (214) 497-1752
Rafael Parry, *Artistic Director*

Types of material: full-length plays, musicals. **Frequency:** annual. **Remuneration:** $500. **Guidelines:** resident of AR, AZ, CO, NM, OK or TX; 1 unproduced submission. **Submission procedure:** script, synopsis, bio and $15 fee; optional SASE for acknowledgment of receipt; include cassette for musical. **Deadline:** 1 May 1997. **Notification:** Aug 1997.

ROBERT J. PICKERING AWARD
FOR PLAYWRITING EXCELLENCE
Coldwater Community Theater; c/o 89 South Division; Coldwater, MI 49036;
    (517) 279-7963
J. Richard Colbeck, *Chairman, Play Selection Committee*

Types of material: full-length plays, plays for young audiences, musicals, solo pieces. **Frequency:** annual. **Remuneration:** 1st prize $300, production and housing to attend performance; 2nd prize $100; 3rd prize $50. **Guidelines:** unproduced play. **Submission procedure:** script only. **Deadline:** 31 Dec 1996. **Notification:** 1 Feb 1997.

SAM EDWARDS DEAF PLAYWRIGHTS COMPETITION
New York Deaf Theatre; 305 Seventh Ave, 11th Floor;
    New York, NY 10001-6008; (212) 924-9491 (voice), -9535 (teletypewriter)
Tony Allicino, *General Manager*

Types of material: full-length plays, one-acts. **Frequency:** annual. **Remuneration:** $400 for full-length play, $200 for one-act; possible full or workshop production or staged reading. **Guidelines:** unproduced play by deaf playwright; write for guidelines. **Submission procedure:** completed application, script, short synopsis and bio; fee of $10 for U.S. playwright, $15 for non-U.S. playwright. **Deadline:** 31 Jan 1997. **Notification:** Apr 1997.

SCHOLASTIC WRITING AWARDS
555 Broadway; New York, NY 10012; (212) 343-6892

Types of material: for high school seniors only, portfolios of 3–8 pieces (fiction, poetry, drama, etc.); for students grades 7–12, individual pieces in various categories, including drama (stage, film, television and radio scripts). **Frequency:** annual. **Remuneration:** $5000 scholarship towards college tuition for author of each of 5 best portfolios; $1000 merit award, to be applied toward tuition for New York University's Tisch School of the Arts dramatic writing program, for best work in any category by high school senior; cash prizes totaling $14,000 awarded to several top students in each category, including dramatic writing. **Guidelines:** portfolio totaling not more than 50 pages; for dramatic category, unpublished script not more than 30 minutes long; write for further information by 1 Nov 1996. **Submission procedure:** completed application and portfolio or script. **Deadline:** mid-Jan 1997; exact date TBA. **Notification:** May 1997.

SHORT GRAIN CONTEST

Grain Magazine; Box 1154; Regina, SK S4P 3B4; Canada; (306) 244-2828, FAX 665-7707; E-mail grain@bailey2.unibase.com
Greg Nelson, *Business Manager*

Types of material: monologues. **Frequency:** annual. **Remuneration:** $500 1st prize, $300 2nd prize, $200 3rd prize (Canadian dollars); winners and honorable mentions receive payment for publication in magazine. **Guidelines:** unpublished, unproduced monologue not submitted elsewhere; 500-word maximum; write for guidelines. **Submission procedure:** entry form and $20 fee for first 2 entries (fee includes 1-year subscription). **Deadline:** 31 Jan 1997. **Notification:** 30 Apr 1997.

SHUBERT FENDRICH MEMORIAL PLAYWRITING CONTEST

Pioneer Drama Service; Box 4267; Englewood, CO 80155-4267; (303) 779-4035, FAX 779-4315; E-mail piodrama@aol.com
Lynne Zborowski, *Editor*

Types of material: full-length plays, one-acts, translations, adaptations, plays for young audiences, musicals. **Frequency:** annual. **Remuneration:** publication with $1000 advance on royalties (10% book royalty, 50% performance royalty). **Guidelines:** produced, unpublished work not more than 90 minutes long; subject matter and language appropriate for schools and community theatres; prefers works with a preponderance of female roles and minimal set requirements; all entries considered for publication; send SASE for guidelines. **Submission procedure:** script with proof of production (e.g., program, reviews); include score or cassette for musical. **Deadline:** 1 Mar 1997 (scripts received after deadline will be considered for 1998 contest).

SIENA COLLEGE INTERNATIONAL PLAYWRIGHTS COMPETITION

Department of Creative Arts; Siena College; 515 Loudon Rd; Loudonville, NY 12211-1462; (518) 783-2381, FAX 783-4293; E-mail maciag@siena.edu
Gary Maciag, *Director of Theatre*

Types of material: full-length plays. **Frequency:** biennial. **Remuneration:** $2000; production; $1000 to cover residency expenses. **Guidelines:** play that has had no previous workshop or full production; prefers play suitable for college audience and featuring characters suitable for college-age performers; prefers small cast;

playwright must be available for 6-week residency in Jan/Feb 1999. **Submission procedure:** send SASE for application form and guidelines after 1 Nov 1997; mail completed application with letter-size SASE in advance of script. **Deadline:** 30 Jun 1998; no submission before 1 Feb 1998. **Notification:** 30 Sep 1998.

SOURCE THEATRE COMPANY
1997 LITERARY PRIZE
1835 14th St NW; Washington, DC 20009; (202) 462-1073
Keith Parker, *Literary Manager*

Types of material: full-length plays, one-acts, musicals, solo pieces. **Frequency:** annual. **Remuneration:** $250; workshop production in Washington Theatre Festival (see theatre's entry in Production). **Guidelines:** work not produced professionally. **Submission procedure:** script, synopsis, resume and letter-size SASE for response; materials will not be returned. **Deadline:** 15 Jan 1997. **Notification:** 15 May 1997.

SOUTH CAROLINA PLAYWRIGHTS' FESTIVAL
Trustus Theatre; Box 11721; Columbia, SC 29211; (803) 771-9153,
        FAX 771-9153
Jayce T. Tromsness, *Literary Manager*

Types of material: full-length plays, one-acts, solo pieces. **Frequency:** annual. **Remuneration:** 1st prize of $500 and production with travel and housing to attend rehearsals and opening; 2nd prize of $250 and staged reading; one-acts eligible only for $50 prize and reading as part of Late Night series. **Guidelines:** play not produced professionally; cast limit of 8; prefers 1 set; full-length play not less than 80 minutes long; send SASE for guidelines and application. **Submission procedure:** completed application and $5 fee. **Deadline:** 1 Mar 1997; no submission before 1 Jan 1997. **Notification:** 1 Jun 1997.

SOUTHEASTERN THEATRE CONFERENCE NEW PLAY PROJECT
Box 9868; Greensboro, NC 27429-0868; (910) 272-3645
James I. Schempp, *Coordinator*

Types of material: full-length plays, bills of 2 related one-acts. **Frequency:** annual. **Remuneration:** $1000; staged reading at SETC Annual Convention; travel, room and board to attend convention; submission of work by SETC to O'Neill Center for favored consideration for National Playwrights Conference (see Development). **Guidelines:** resident of state in SETC region (AL, FL, GA, KY, MS, NC, SC, TN, VA, WV); unproduced work; bills of one-acts bound in 1 cover; limit of 1 full-length submission or bill of 2 one-acts. **Submission procedure:** completed application and script. **Deadline:** 1 Jun 1997; no submission before 1 Mar 1997. **Notification:** Nov 1997.

Southern Playwrights Competition

Center for Southern Studies; 228 Stone Center; Jacksonville State University;
Jacksonville, AL 36265; (205) 782-5411, FAX 782-5689
Steven J. Whitton, *Coordinator*

Types of material: full-length plays, solo pieces. **Frequency:** annual. **Remuneration:** $1000; production; housing to attend rehearsals. **Guidelines:** native or resident of AL, AR, FL, GA, KY, LA, MS, NC, SC, TN, TX, VA or WV; 1 unpublished original submission that deals with the southern experience and has not received Equity production; write for guidelines. **Submission procedure:** completed entry form, script and synopsis. **Deadline:** 15 Feb 1997. **Notification:** 1 May 1997.

Summerfield G. Roberts Award

The Sons of the Republic of Texas; 1717 8th St; Bay City, TX 77414;
(409) 245-6644, FAX 245-6644
Melinda Williams

Types of material: full-length plays. **Frequency:** annual. **Remuneration:** $2500 given to work from 1 of several genres, including playwriting. **Guidelines:** play about living in the Republic of Texas, completed during calendar year preceding deadline. **Submission procedure:** 5 copies of script; scripts will not be returned. **Deadline:** 15 Jan 1997. **Notification:** early Apr 1997.

The Susan Smith Blackburn Prize

3239 Avalon Pl; Houston, TX 77019; (713) 522-8529
Emilie S. Kilgore, *Board of Directors*

Types of material: full-length plays. **Frequency:** annual. **Remuneration:** $5000 1st prize plus signed Willem de Kooning print, made especially for Blackburn Prize; $2000 2nd prize; $500 to each of 8–10 other finalists. **Guidelines:** woman playwright of any nationality writing in English; unproduced play or play produced within one year of deadline. **Submission procedure:** no submission by playwright; professional artistic director, literary manager or dramaturg invited to submit play and submits 2 copies of script; playwright may bring script to attention of eligible nominator; send 55¢-postage SASE for guidelines and list of theatres eligible to nominate. **Deadline:** 20 Sep 1996. **Notification:** Jan 1997 for finalists; Feb 1997 for winners.

SWTA Annual New Play Contest

Southwest Theatre Association; University of Oklahoma School of Drama;
563 Elm Ave; Norman, OK 73019-0310; (405) 325-4021, FAX 325-0400
Ray Paolino, *New Plays Committee*

Types of material: full-length plays, one-acts, adaptations. **Frequency:** annual. **Remuneration:** $200 1st prize; staged reading at SWTA convention in Nov 1997; publication in SWTA journal, *Theatre Southwest.* **Guidelines:** unproduced, unpublished play. **Submission procedure:** script, brief synopsis, character breakdown and $10 fee (check payable to SWTA); letter of recommendation helpful. **Deadline:** 1 Mar 1997.

TADA! SPRING STAGED READING SERIES/NEW PLAY PROJECT
120 West 28th St; New York, NY 10001; (212) 627-1732, FAX 243-6736
Janine Nina Trevens, *Artistic Director*

Types of material: plays and musicals for young audiences. **Frequency:** annual. **Remuneration:** 1 award of $400 and workshop production; 3 awards of $200 and staged reading. **Guidelines:** unproduced play or musical by professional or student playwright; majority of roles must be for child actors who do not play adult characters; prefers works with human characters, as opposed to "animal" plays. **Submission procedure:** script and character breakdown; include cassette for musical. **Deadline:** 15 Jan 1996. **Notification:** 15 Mar 1997.

TENNESSEE WILLIAMS/NEW ORLEANS LITERARY FESTIVAL
ONE-ACT PLAY COMPETITION
Metro College Conference Services, ED 122; University of New Orleans;
    New Orleans, LA 70148; (504) 286-6680

Types of material: one-acts. **Frequency:** annual. **Remuneration:** $1000; reading in spring 1997 festival; production in spring 1998 festival. **Guidelines:** unpublished play on an American subject, not more than 1 hour long and not produced professionally. **Submission procedure:** script with SASE for notification and $15 fee (check payable to University of New Orleans); script will not be returned; write for guidelines before submitting work. **Deadline:** 15 Dec 1996.

THEATER AT LIME KILN REGIONAL PLAYWRITING CONTEST
Lime Kiln Arts; 14 South Randolph St; Lexington, VA 24450; (540) 463-7088,
    FAX 463-1082; E-mail limekiln@cfw.com
Eleanor Connor, *Community Liaison/Dramaturg*

Types of material: full-length plays, one-acts, musicals. **Frequency:** annual. **Remuneration:** $1000 1st prize, $500 2nd prize; possible staged reading. **Guidelines:** unproduced, unpublished work relating to the Appalachian region; plays with music encouraged; write for guidelines. **Submission procedure:** completed entry form, script, short synopsis, history of play and bio; include letter-size SASE if notification is desired. **Deadline:** 30 Sep 1996. **Notification:** 1 Mar 1997 (if SASE is enclosed).

THEATRE MEMPHIS NEW PLAY COMPETITION
630 Perkins St Extended; Memphis, TN 38117-4799; (901) 682-8323,
    FAX 763-4096
Chair, New Play Competition

Types of material: full-length plays. **Frequency:** triennial. **Remuneration:** cash award, exact amount TBA ($1500 in 1996); award may be split between 2 winners; possible production with travel and housing to attend performance. **Guidelines:**

original work not produced with royalty payment prior to deadline date; send SASE for guidelines. **Submission procedure:** script submitted anonymously with detached title page giving playwright's name and address; resume. **Deadline:** 1 Jul 1999. **Notification:** Dec 1999.

THEATREWORKS/USA COMMISSIONING PROGRAM
Theatreworks/USA; 890 Broadway; New York, NY 10003; (212) 677-5959,
    FAX 353-1632
Barbara Pasternack, *Associate Artistic Director*

Types of material: plays with music and musicals for young and family audiences. **Frequency:** ongoing. **Remuneration:** step commissioning process; 2-week developmental workshop and production. **Guidelines:** works dealing with issues relevant to target audiences; special interest in historical/biographical subject matter and musical adaptations of fairy tales and traditional or contemporary classics; 1 hour long; cast of 5 actors, set suitable for touring. **Submission procedure:** prefers treatment with sample scenes, lyric sheets and cassette of music preferred; will accept script only. **Deadline:** ongoing.

THEODORE WARD PRIZE FOR AFRICAN-AMERICAN PLAYWRIGHTS
Columbia College Chicago Theater/Music Center; 72 East 11th St;
    Chicago, IL 60605; (312) 663-1600, ext 6136, FAX 663-9591;
    E-mail chuck.smith@mail.colum.edu
Chuck Smith, *Facilitator*

Types of material: full-length plays, translations, adaptations, full-length solo pieces. **Frequency:** annual. **Remuneration:** 1st prize $2000, production, travel and housing to attend rehearsals; 2nd prize $500, staged reading; 3rd prize, staged reading at Goodman Theatre. **Guidelines:** U.S. resident of African-American descent; 1 full-length submission not professionally produced; translations and adaptations of material in public domain only; write for guidelines. **Submission procedure:** script, short synopsis, production history and brief resume. **Deadline:** 1 Aug 1997; no submission before 1 May 1997. **Notification:** Nov 1997.

THRESHOLD THEATER METAPHYSICAL PLAY CONTEST
1907 Cannonwood Ln; Austin, TX 78745; (512) 448-4373
Jennifer Mellett, *Executive Director*

Types of material: full-length plays. **Frequency:** annual. **Remuneration:** $200. **Guidelines:** play, not professionally produced, whose theme involves two contrasting levels of theatrical reality (e.g. the dead and the living, waking and dreaming, body and soul, material and nonmaterial) and the crossing of the "threshold" between them; 100–135 minutes long; must have at least 3 substantial speaking roles and maximum cast of 8; prefers 1 set; write for guidelines by 1 Jan 1997. **Submission procedure:** script, synopsis, resume and $15 fee. **Deadline:** 1 Apr 1997. **Notification:** 31 Mar 1998.

TOWNGATE THEATRE PLAYWRITING CONTEST

Oglebay Institute Stifel Fine Arts Center; 1330 National Rd;
Wheeling, WV 26003, FAX 242-7700

Types of material: full-length plays. **Frequency:** annual. **Remuneration:** $300;
production; partial travel expenses. **Guidelines:** unproduced, unpublished play;
no submission limit. **Submission procedure:** script only. **Deadline:** 1 Jan 1997.
Notification: 1 May 1997.

TOWSON STATE UNIVERSITY PRIZE FOR LITERATURE

Towson State University; Towson, MD 21204-7097; (410) 830-2128
Dean, College of Liberal Arts

Types of material: book or book-length manuscript; all literary genres eligible,
including plays. **Frequency:** annual. **Remuneration:** $1000. **Guidelines:** work
published within 3 years prior to submission or scheduled for publication within
the year; author no more than 40 years of age, MD resident for 3 years and at
time prize awarded. **Submission procedure:** publisher or playwright submits
completed application and 5 copies of work; write for guidelines. **Deadline:** 15
May 1997. **Notification:** 1 Dec 1997.

UNICORN THEATRE NATIONAL PLAYWRIGHTS' AWARD

3820 Main St; Kansas City, MO 64111; (816) 531-7529
Literary Manager

Types of material: full-length plays. **Frequency:** no set dates. **Remuneration:**
$1000; production; possible travel and residency. **Guidelines:** unpublished play
not produced professionally; special interest in social issues; contemporary (post-
1950) themes and settings only; cast limit of 10; 2-submission limit. **Submission
procedure:** no scripts; send synopsis, at least 10 pages of dialogue, resume, letter
of inquiry and SASE for response. **Deadline:** ongoing. **Notification:** 4 weeks; 4–6
months if script is requested.

UNIVERSITY OF LOUISVILLE GRAWEMEYER AWARD
FOR MUSIC COMPOSITION

Grawemeyer Music Award Committee; School of Music; University of Louisville;
Louisville, KY 40292; (502) 852-6907, FAX 852-0520;
E-mail mlgreeoi@ulkyum.louisville.edu
Paul Brink, *Executive Secretary*

Types of material: works in major musical genres, including music-theatre works
and operas. **Frequency:** annual. **Remuneration:** $150,000 (paid in 5 annual
installments of $30,000). **Guidelines:** work premiered during previous 5 years;
entry must be sponsored by professional music organization or individual; write
for guidelines. **Submission procedure:** completed application, score, cassette,
supporting materials and $50 fee submitted jointly by composer and sponsor.
Deadline: 27 Jan 1997. **Notification:** late spring 1997.

URBAN STAGES AWARD
17 East 47th St; New York, NY 10017; (212) 289-2168

Types of material: one-acts. **Frequency:** annual. **Remuneration:** $200, 4–6 "radio style" staged readings in libraries throughout New York City's boroughs. **Guidelines:** play no more than 1 hour long with cast limit of 5 which has not been produced in New York; special interest in minority playwrights and ethnically diverse casts; send SASE for guidelines. **Submission procedure:** script, production history and author bio. **Deadline:** 15 Jun 1997.

UTAH PLAYFEST
Theatre Arts Department; Utah State University; Logan, UT 84322-4025;
    (801) 797-3021
Roger Held, *Director*

Types of material: full-length plays, bills of related one-acts. **Frequency:** annual. **Remuneration:** $100–500; possible publication and production; if produced, writer receives travel and housing; $5000 royalty for produced full-length play. **Guidelines:** submission limit of 1 full-length play or bill of related one-acts. **Submission procedure:** playwright sends name of artistic director of theatre where their work has been previously produced. **Deadline:** 30 Nov 1996. **Notification:** 1 Apr 1997.

VERMONT PLAYWRIGHTS AWARD
The Valley Players; Box 441; Waitsfield, VT 05673-0441; (802) 496-3751
Jennifer Howard, *Coordinator*

Types of material: full-length plays. **Frequency:** annual. **Remuneration:** $1000; probable production. **Guidelines:** resident of ME, NH or VT; unproduced, unpublished play, suitable for community group, that has not won playwriting competition; moderate production demands; send SASE for guidelines. **Submission procedure:** completed entry form and 2 copies of script. **Deadline:** 1 Feb 1997.

VERY SPECIAL ARTS YOUNG PLAYWRIGHTS PROGRAM
Education Office; The John F. Kennedy Center for the Performing Arts;
    Washington, DC 20566; (800) 933-8721 (voice), 737-0645 (TDD),
    FAX 737-0725
Elena Widder, *Assistant Director, National Programs*

Types of material: full-length plays, one-acts. **Frequency:** annual. **Remuneration:** professional production at Kennedy Center; travel, room and board to attend performance. **Guidelines:** play dealing with some aspect of disability by writer aged 12–18 years; write for guidelines. **Submission procedure:** 2 copies of script and short bio. **Deadline:** Apr 1997; exact date TBA.

WALDO M. AND GRACE C. BONDERMAN IUPUI PLAYWRITING COMPETITION FOR YOUNG AUDIENCES

IUPUI University Theatre; 525 North Blackford St; Indianapolis, IN 46202-3120; (317) 274-2095; E-mail dwebb@iupui.edu
Mark McCreary, *Literary Manager*

Types of material: plays for young audiences. **Frequency:** biennial. **Remuneration:** 4 prizes of $1000; 1 week of developmental work culminating in showcase reading at National Youth Theatre Playwriting Symposium; travel, room and board for residency. **Guidelines:** well-crafted play with strong storyline, compelling characters and careful attention to language; unpublished play at least 45 minutes long and not previously produced by Equity company; writer must be available for week-long residency. **Submission procedure:** send SASE for entry form and guidelines. **Deadline:** 1 Sep 1996. **Notification:** Dec 1996. **Dates:** 24–28 Apr 1997.

WAREHOUSE THEATRE COMPANY ONE-ACT COMPETITION

Stephens College; Columbia, MO 65215; (314) 876-7194
Artistic Director

Types of material: one-acts. **Frequency:** annual. **Remuneration:** $200; production as part of company's Evening of One-Acts. **Guidelines:** unpublished, unproduced script by undergraduate or graduate student; special interest in scripts by, for or about women; write for guidelines. **Submission procedure:** script with $10 fee. **Deadline:** 31 Dec 1996. **Notification:** 1 Feb 1997.

WEST COAST ENSEMBLE CONTESTS

Box 38728; Los Angeles, CA 90038; (213) 871-8673
Les Hanson, *Artistic Director*

West Coast Ensemble Full-Length Play Competition

Types of material: full-length plays. **Frequency:** annual. **Remuneration:** $500; production; royalty on any performances beyond 8-week run. **Guidelines:** 1 submission not produced in southern CA; cast limit of 12. **Submission procedure:** script with SASE or SASP for acknowledgment of receipt. **Deadline:** 31 Dec 1996. **Notification:** within 6 months of deadline.

West Coast Ensemble Musical Stairs

Types of material: musical theatre works. **Frequency:** annual. **Remuneration:** $500; production; royalty on any performances beyond 8-week run. **Guidelines:** 1 unpublished musical submission not produced in southern CA; all genres and styles eligible, including pop, rock, country and western, etc.; cast limit of 12. **Submission procedure:** script, cassette of music (include score and lead sheets if available). **Deadline:** 30 Jun 1997. **Notification:** within 6 months.

WESTERN GREAT LAKES PLAYWRITING COMPETITION

South Bend Civic Theatre; Box 11375; South Bend, IN 46634; (219) 234-1112
Tom Vander Ven, *Competition Chair*

Types of material: full-length plays. **Frequency:** annual. **Remuneration:** $300; staged reading; possible production; travel, room and board to attend reading or production. **Guidelines:** resident of IL, IN, MI, MN, OH or WI; play not produced professionally; send SASE for guidelines. **Submission procedure:** script and signed statement that play has not been professionally produced. **Deadline:** 30 Aug 1996.

WHITE BIRD ANNUAL PLAYWRITING CONTEST

White Bird Productions; Box 20233, Columbus Circle Station;
New York, NY 10023; (718) 788-5984
Kathryn Dickinson, *Artistic Director*

Types of material: full-length plays, one-acts. **Frequency:** annual. **Remuneration:** $200; staged reading; possible travel to attend rehearsals. **Guidelines:** play whose theme, plot and/or central idea deals in a general or specific way with the environment; 2-submission limit. **Submission procedure:** script and resume. **Deadline:** 15 Feb 1997. **Notification:** Jun 1997.

THE WHITE-WILLIS NEW PLAYWRIGHTS CONTEST

The White-Willis Theatre; 5266 Gate Lake Rd; Fort Lauderdale, FL 33319;
(305) 722-4371
Ann White, *Founder/Executive Director*

Types of material: full-length plays. **Frequency:** annual. **Remuneration:** $500; production. **Guidelines:** unpublished, unproduced play; small cast, simple set preferred; after closing of Fort Lauderdale production, theatre retains option to produce first-class production for 120 days and requires 5% of all playwright's earnings from play for 3 years; send SASE for guidelines. **Submission procedure:** script and $10 fee. **Deadline:** 1 Oct 1996. **Notification:** Jan 1997.

WICHITA STATE UNIVERSITY PLAYWRITING CONTEST

University Theatre; Wichita State University; Wichita, KS 67260-0153;
(316) 689-3368, FAX 689-3951
Leroy Clark, *Contest Director*

Types of material: full-length plays, bills of related one-acts. **Frequency:** annual. **Remuneration:** production; expenses for playwright to attend production. **Guidelines:** unpublished, unproduced work at least 90 minutes long by student currently enrolled at U.S. college or university; write for guidelines. **Submission procedure:** script only. **Deadline:** 15 Feb 1997. **Notification:** 15 Apr 1997.

WRITER'S DIGEST WRITING COMPETITION
1507 Dana Ave; Cincinnati, OH 45207-1005; (513) 531-2690, ext 580
Competition Coordinator

Types of materials: full-length plays, screenplays, teleplays. **Frequency:** annual. **Remuneration:** Grand Prize: Apple PowerBook computer, expenses-paid trip to New York City to meet with editors and agents; $500 1st prize, $250 2nd prize, $100 3rd prize, each with $100 worth of Writer's Digest books; $50 4th prize with current *Writer's Market* and 1-year subscription to *Writer's Digest* magazine; $25 5th prize with 1-year subscription to *Writer's Digest* magazine. **Guidelines:** unproduced, unpublished work, not accepted by publisher or producer at time of submission; previous entries ineligible; send SASE for guidelines. **Submission procedure:** completed entry form, first 15 pages of script, 1-page synopsis and indication of projected market for work, and $8 fee. **Deadline:** 31 May 1997. **Notification:** fall 1997.

YEAR-END-SERIES (Y.E.S.) NEW PLAY FESTIVAL
Department of Theatre; Northern Kentucky University;
Highland Heights, KY 41099; (606) 572-6362, FAX 572-5566;
E-mail mking@nku.edu
Michael King, *Project Director*

Types of material: full-length plays, adaptations, musicals. **Frequency:** biennial. **Remuneration:** 3 awards of $400; production; travel and expenses to attend late rehearsals and performance; 1 award of $100; staged reading; travel and expenses to attend reading. **Guidelines:** unproduced work in which majority of roles can be handled by students; small orchestra for musicals; 1 submission; playwright available for visit in Apr 1997. **Submission procedure:** completed application and script. **Deadline:** 15 Oct 1996. **Notification:** Jan 1997. **Dates:** 17–27 Apr 1997.

YOUNG PLAYWRIGHTS FESTIVAL NATIONAL PLAYWRITING CONTEST
Young Playwrights Inc.; 321 West 44th St, Suite 906; New York, NY 10036;
(212) 307-1140
Sheri M. Goldhirsch, *Artistic Director*

Types of material: full-length plays, one-acts. **Frequency:** annual. **Remuneration:** staged reading or production with royalty; travel and residency; 1-year Dramatists Guild membership (see Membership and Service Organizations). **Guidelines:** playwright 18 years of age or younger as of 15 Oct 1996; submissions from minority playwrights encouraged; write for guidelines. **Submission procedure:** script with playwright's name, date of birth, home address and phone number on title page. **Deadline:** 15 Oct 1996.

Publication

What is listed in this section?

Those who are primarily or exclusively play publishers and who consider work of unpublished writers. In addition, we list literary magazines and other small presses which have indicated they publish plays.

How can I determine the best places to submit my play?

Think of these publishers as highly individual people looking for very particular kinds of material, which means you should find out as much as possible about their operations before submitting scripts. One of the best ways to do research is by contacting the Council of Literary Magazines and Presses: 154 Christopher St, Suite 3C; New York, NY 10014-2839; (212) 741-9110. Ask for *The 1996-97 Directory of Literary Magazines* ($12.95 paper, plus $3.05 for 1st-class postage and handling), a descriptive listing of hundreds of magazines, including many which say they publish plays. You may be able to look at copies of some of these in a local library or bookstore. Other leads may be found in the *1996-97 International Directory of Little Magazines and Small Presses* (Dustbooks; Box 100; Paradise, CA 95967; (916) 877-6110; $30.95 paper, $46.95 cloth, plus $6.00 shipping and handling). You can also write to individual publishers listed here and ask for style sheets, catalogues, sample copies, etc. Don't forget that when publishers say they accept unsolicited scripts, they *always* require you to enclose an SASE for return of the manuscript.

ALABAMA LITERARY REVIEW
253 Smith Hall; Troy State University; Troy, AL 36082; (334) 670-3307
FAX 670-3519
Theron Montgomery, *Chief Editor*

Types of material: full-length plays, one-acts, translations, adaptations, solo pieces. **Remuneration:** 3 complimentary copies (more on request); $5–10 a page when funds are available. **Guidelines:** biannual literary journal publishing 1 play a year; plays less than 50 pages long, less than 30 pages preferred. **Submission procedure:** accepts unsolicited scripts. **Response time:** 2–3 months.

AMELIA MAGAZINE
329 "E" St; Bakersfield, CA 93304; (805) 323-4064
Frederick A. Raborg, Jr., *Editor*

Types of material: one-acts, including translations and solo pieces. **Remuneration:** $150 prize; 10 complimentary copies. **Guidelines:** winner of annual Frank McClure One-Act Play Award published in magazine Oct 1997; unpublished play maximum 45 minutes long. **Submission procedure:** submit script, including note of any productions, and $15 fee. **Deadline:** 15 May 1997. **Notification:** 15 Jul 1997.

AMERICAN THEATRE
Theatre Communications Group; 355 Lexington Ave; New York, NY 10017-0217;
(212) 697-5230
Jim O'Quinn, *Editor*
Wendy Weiner, *Play Editor*

Types of material: full-length plays, one-acts, translations, adaptations, plays for young audiences. **Remuneration:** fee for one-time serial rights; 25 complimentary copies. **Guidelines:** national magazine publishing 6 plays a year; significant works from the contemporary world theatre. **Submission procedure:** no unsolicited scripts; submissions at play editor's request only.

AMERICAN WRITING: A MAGAZINE
4343 Manayunk Ave; Philadelphia, PA 19128
Alexandra Grilikhes, *Editor*

Types of material: translations, solo pieces, short experimental theatre pieces, performance pieces, performance artists' in-process notes and diaries. **Remuneration:** 3 complimentary copies. **Guidelines:** biannual literary/arts journal publishing 1 or 2 theatrical works a year; seeks new writing that takes risks and explores new forms; interested in "the voice of the loner"; 10,000 words maximum. **Submission procedure:** accepts unsolicited scripts. **Response time:** 3–6 months.

THE AMERICAS REVIEW

Arte Público Press; University of Houston; Houston, TX 77204-2090;
(713) 743-2841
Nicolás Kanellos, *Publisher*
Lauro Flores, *Editor*

Types of material: one-acts, excerpts from full-length plays. **Remuneration:** fee; 2 complimentary copies. **Guidelines:** unpublished works in English or Spanish by Hispanic writers only. **Submission procedure:** accepts unsolicited scripts. **Response time:** 3 months.

ANCHORAGE PRESS

Box 8067; New Orleans, LA 70182; (504) 283-8868, FAX 866-0502
Orlin Corey, *Editor*

Types of material: works for young audiences, including full-length plays, one-acts, translations, adaptations and musicals. **Remuneration:** negotiated royalty. **Guidelines:** specialty house publishing quality works for young audiences only; works produced at least 3 times. **Submission procedure:** accepts unsolicited scripts with proof of production. **Response time:** 45–90 days.

ARAN PRESS

1320 South 3rd St; Louisville, KY 40208-2306; (502) 636-0115
Tom Eagan, *Editor and Publisher*

Types of material: full-length plays, one-acts, translations, adaptations, solo pieces. **Remuneration:** 10% book royalty, 50% production royalty; playwright contributes to publishing costs: $300 for full-length play, $150 for one-act. **Guidelines:** plays suitable for marketing to community, college and university, summer stock, dinner and professional theatres. **Submission procedure:** accepts unsolicited scripts; prefers letter of inquiry with SASE for response. **Response time:** 2 weeks.

ART CRAFT PUBLISHING COMPANY

Box 1058; Cedar Rapids, IA 52406; (319) 364-6311, FAX 364-1771
C. Emmett McMullen, *Editor and Publisher*

Types of material: plays for young audiences, including full-length plays, one-acts and musicals. **Remuneration:** outright purchase or performance royalty; complimentary copies. **Guidelines:** works suitable for middle school and junior and senior high school market. **Submission procedure:** accepts unsolicited scripts. **Response time:** 1–2 months.

ARTE PÚBLICO PRESS

University of Houston; Houston, TX 77204-2090; (713) 743-2841, FAX 743-2847
Nicolás Kanellos, *Publisher*

Types of material: full-length plays, one-acts, adaptations, plays for young audiences, musicals. **Remuneration:** negotiated royalty; complimentary copies.

Guidelines: unpublished works in English or Spanish by Hispanic writers only; usually writers whose work has previously been published in *The Americas Review* (see entry in this section). **Submission procedure:** accepts unsolicited scripts. **Response time:** 6 months.

Asian Pacific American Journal

37 Saint Marks Pl, Suite B; New York, NY 10003-7801; (212) 228-6718, FAX 228-7718; E-mail aaww@panix.com; Web http://www.panix.com./~aaww
Editors

Types of material: one-acts. **Remuneration:** 2 complimentary copies. **Guidelines:** biannual literary journal devoted to the work of Asian-American writers; plays maximum 4000 words. **Submission procedure:** accepts unsolicited scripts; send 2 copies of script. **Response time:** 3 months.

Audrey Skirball-Kenis Play Collection

630 West 5th St.; Los Angeles, CA 90071; (213) 228-7327, FAX 228-7339
Tom Harris, *Project Director*

Types of material: full-length plays, one-acts, translations, adaptations, plays for young audiences, musicals, solo pieces, performance-art texts. **Remuneration:** descriptive listing of work in Southern California Unpublished Plays Collection, catalogue of plays housed in Central Library in downtown Los Angeles. **Guidelines:** plays must be unpublished and professionally produced in Southern California; all scripts meeting criteria are accepted. **Submission procedure:** accepts unsolicited scripts.

Baker's Plays

100 Chauncy St; Boston, MA 02111; (617) 482-1280, FAX 482-7613
Raymond Pape, *Associate Editor*

Types of material: full-length plays, one-acts, plays for young audiences, musicals, chancel dramas. **Remuneration:** negotiated book and production royalty. **Guidelines:** prefers produced plays; prefers plays suitable for high school, community and regional theatres; "Plays from Young Authors" division features plays by high school playwrights. **Submission procedure:** accepts unsolicited scripts with resume; include press clippings if play has been produced. **Response time:** 2–6 months. **Special programs:** Baker's Plays High School Playwriting Contest (see Prizes).

The Bellingham Review

The Signpost Press; Mail Stop 9053; Western Washington University; Bellingham, WA 98225
Robin Hemley, *Editor*

Types of material: one-acts, solo pieces. **Remuneration:** 1 complimentary copy; 1-year subscription. **Guidelines:** biannual small-press periodical featuring short plays, fiction, poetry and creative nonfiction; unpublished plays less than 10,000 words long. **Submission procedure:** accepts unsolicited scripts; submit 1 Sep–1 May only. **Response time:** 4 months.

BLIZZARD PUBLISHING

73 Furby St; Winnipeg, MB R3C 2A2; Canada;
    (204) 775-2923, (800) 694-9256, FAX (204) 775-2947;
    E-mail atwood@blizzard.mb.ca
Anna Synenko, *Marketing Manager*

Types of material: full-length plays, one-acts, translations, adaptations, plays for young audiences. **Remuneration:** advance against royalties; 10% book royalty; complimentary copies. **Guidelines:** publishes 11 plays a year and critical literature on theatre; special interest in contemporary or provocative themes and educational works; write for guidelines. **Submission procedure:** no unsolicited scripts; synopsis and letter of inquiry; submit Mar–Nov only. **Response time:** 4 months.

BROADWAY PLAY PUBLISHING

56 East 81st St; New York, NY 10028; (212) 772-8334, FAX 772-8358;
    E-mail BroadwayPl@aol.com

Types of material: full-length plays. **Remuneration:** 10% book royalty, 80% amateur royalty, 90% stock royalty; 10 complimentary copies. **Guidelines:** major interest is in original, innovative work by American playwrights; no historical or autobiographical plays. **Submission procedure:** no unsolicited scripts; letter of inquiry. **Response time:** 3 months.

CALLALOO

Department of English; University of Virginia; Bryan Hall;
    Charlottesville, VA 22903; (804) 924-6637, FAX 924-1478
Charles H. Rowell, *Editor*

Types of material: one-acts, including translations. **Remuneration:** complimentary copies and offprints; payment when grant money is available. **Guidelines:** journal of Afro-American and African arts and letters published by Johns Hopkins University Press. **Submission procedure:** accepts unsolicited scripts. **Response time:** 6 months.

CHICAGO PLAYS

2632 North Lincoln; Chicago, IL 60614; (312) 348-4658, FAX 348-5561
Jill Murray

Types of material: full-length plays, one-acts, adaptations, plays for young audiences, musicals. **Remuneration:** book and performance royalties; complimentary copies (usually 10). **Guidelines:** publishes for professional and amateur market. **Submission procedure:** accepts unsolicited scripts with proof of or notice of application for copyright, programs, reviews and publicity material; write or call for guidelines. **Response time:** 3 months.

COLLAGES & BRICOLAGES
Box 86; Clarion, PA 16214; (814) 226-5799; E-mail fortis@vaxa.clarion.edu
Marie-José Fortis, *Editor*

Types of material: one-acts. **Remuneration:** 2 complimentary copies. **Guidelines:** annual journal of international writing publishing poetry, fiction, drama and criticism, including 1–5 plays a year; minimalist plays; avant-garde and feminist work; innovative plays less than 30 pages long reflecting philosophical and social concerns. **Submission procedure:** accepts unsolicited scripts; submit only 1 Aug–1 Dec for following year's issue. **Response time:** 2 weeks–3 months.

CONFRONTATION
English Department; C.W. Post College of Long Island University;
    Greenvale, NY 11548; (516) 299-2391, FAX 299-2735;
    E-mail mtucker@eagle.liunet.edu
Martin Tucker, *Editor*

Types of material: one-acts. **Remuneration:** $15–75; 1 complimentary copy. **Guidelines:** general magazine for literate audience; unpublished plays. **Submission procedure:** accepts unsolicited scripts. **Response time:** 8–10 weeks.

CONTEMPORARY DRAMA SERVICE
Meriwether Publishing, Ltd; 885 Elkton Dr; Colorado Springs, CO 80907
    (719) 594-4422, FAX 594-9916
Arthur L. Zapel, *Executive Editor*

Types of material: full-length plays, one-acts, adaptations, plays for young audiences, musicals, readers' theatre, monologues. **Remuneration:** book royalties or payment for amateur and professional performance rights. **Guidelines:** publishes works suitable for teenage, high school and college market, as well as collections of scenes and practical books on theatre arts; no works for preteen audiences; prefers comedies; prefers produced works; special interest in works by authors with name recognition. **Submission procedure:** accepts unsolicited scripts; send $2 for sample catalogue and guidelines. **Response time:** 2 months.

CRAZYQUILT QUARTERLY
Box 632729; San Diego, CA 92163-2729; (619) 688-1023, FAX 688-1753
Marsh Cassady, *Drama Editor*

Types of material: one-acts, including solo pieces. **Remuneration:** 2 complimentary copies. **Guidelines:** quarterly literary journal publishing 4–6 plays a year. **Submission procedure:** accepts unsolicited scripts. **Response time:** 2 months.

DESCANT
Box 314, Station P; Toronto, Ontario; Canada M5S 2S8; (416) 593-2557
Tracy Jenkins, *Managing Editor*

Types of material: full-length plays, one-acts, performance-art texts. **Remunera-

tion: $100 honorarium; 1 complimentary copy (additional copies at 40% discount). **Guidelines:** quarterly literary magazine publishing an average of 2 plays a year; unpublished plays. **Submission procedure:** accepts unsolicited scripts. **Response time:** 6 months.

THE DRAMATIC PUBLISHING COMPANY

311 Washington St; Box 129; Woodstock, IL 60098; (815) 338-7170,
    FAX 338-8981; E-mail 75712.3621@compuserve.com;
    Web: http://ourworld.compuserve.com/homepages/DramaticPublishing;
    Bulletin Board: (815) 338-7212 (by modem)
Julie Kunzie, *Editor*

Types of material: full-length plays, one-acts, translations, adaptations, plays for young audiences, musicals, solo pieces. **Remuneration:** standard royalty; 10 complimentary copies (30% discount on additional copies). **Guidelines:** works for stock and amateur market; at least 10 minutes long; prefers produced plays. **Submission procedure:** accepts unsolicited scripts. **Response time:** 4–12 months.

DRAMATICS MAGAZINE

3368 Central Pkwy; Cincinnati, OH 45225; (513) 559-1996, FAX 559-0012
Don Corathers, *Editor*

Types of material: full-length plays, one-acts, solo pieces. **Remuneration:** payment for 1-time publication rights; complimentary copies. **Guidelines:** educational theatre magazine; plays suitable for high school production; prefers produced plays. **Submission procedure:** accepts unsolicited scripts. **Response time:** 2–3 months.

DRAMATISTS PLAY SERVICE

440 Park Ave South; New York, NY 10016; (212) 683-8960, FAX 213-1539;
    E-mail postmaster@dramatists.com
Stephen Sultan, *President*

Types of material: full-length plays, one-acts, translations, adaptations, plays for young audiences, musicals. **Remuneration:** usually advance against royalties; 10% book royalty, 80% amateur royalty, 90% stock royalty; 10 complimentary copies. **Guidelines:** works for stock and amateur market; prefers works produced in New York City. **Submission procedure:** no unsolicited scripts; letter of inquiry. **Response time:** 2–4 months.

EARTH'S DAUGHTERS

Box 41, Central Park Station; Buffalo, NY 14215; (716) 837-7778

Types of material: full-length plays, one-acts, translations, adaptations, plays for young audiences, solo pieces. **Remuneration:** 2 complimentary copies. **Guidelines:** triannual feminist literary and art periodical with focus on experience and creative expression of women; frequently publishes play excerpts with occasional issue devoted to complete text of play. **Submission procedure:** accepts unsolicited scripts. **Response time:** 2 months.

ELDRIDGE PUBLISHING COMPANY
Box 1595; Venice, FL 34284-1595; (800) HI-STAGE
Nancy S. Vorhis, *Editor*

Types of material: full-length plays, one-acts, musicals. **Remuneration:** outright purchase of religious material only; all other works, 10% book royalty, 50% amateur and educational royalty; complimentary copies (50% discount on additional copies). **Guidelines:** publishes 50–75 plays and musicals a year for school, church and community theatre; comedies, mysteries or serious drama. **Submission procedure:** accepts unsolicited scripts; if possible, include cassette for musicals. **Response time:** 2 months.

ENCORE PERFORMANCE PUBLISHING
Box 692; Orem, UT 84057; (801) 225-0605
Michael C. Perry, *President*

Types of material: full-length plays, one-acts, translations, adaptations, plays for young audiences, musicals, solo pieces. **Remuneration:** 10% book royalty, 50% performance royalty; 10 complimentary copies (discount on additional copies). **Guidelines:** publishes 10–30 plays and musicals a year; works must have had at least 2 amateur or professional productions; special interest in works with strong family or Judeo-Christian message and in Christmas, Halloween and other holiday plays. **Sub-mission procedure:** no unsolicited scripts; synopsis, production information and letter of inquiry; best submission time May–Aug. **Response time:** 2–4 weeks letter; 2–3 months script.

THE FOUR DIRECTIONS
AMERICAN INDIAN LITERARY QUARTERLY
Snowbird Publishing Company; Box 729; Tellico Plains, TN 37385;
    (423) 253-3680
William Meyer, *Publisher*

Types of material: one-acts, including translations, adaptations, plays for young audiences, and solo pieces. **Remuneration:** 1.5¢ a word; 4 complimentary copies. **Guidelines:** quarterly magazine publishing fiction, poetry, plays and articles by and of interest to Native Americans; one-acts by Native American playwrights only. **Submission procedure:** accepts unsolicited scripts with statement of tribal affiliation and brief bio listing any other publications in which playwright's work appears. **Response time:** 4–6 weeks.

FREELANCE PRESS
Box 548; Dover, MA 02030; (508) 785-1260, FAX 785-1260
Narcissa Campion, *Managing Editor*

Types of material: musicals. **Remuneration:** 10% book royalty, 70% performance royalty; 1 complimentary copy. **Guidelines:** unpublished issue-oriented musicals and musical adaptations of classics; approximately 1 hour long, suitable for performing by young people only. **Submission procedure:** accepts unsolicited scripts. **Response time:** 3 months.

HAWAI'I REVIEW

c/o UH Mānoa Department of English; 1733 Donaghho Rd; Honolulu, HI 96822; (808) 956-3030
Malia Gellert, *Editor-in-Chief*

Types of material: one-acts, translations, adaptations, solo pieces. **Remuneration:** 2 complimentary copies. **Guidelines:** triquarterly literary journal; submit up to 28 double-spaced pages. **Submission procedure:** accepts unsolicited scripts with SASE for response. **Response time:** 2 months.

HEUER PUBLISHING COMPANY

Box 248; Cedar Rapids, IA 52406; (319) 364-6311, FAX 364-1771
C. Emmett McMullen, *Editor and Publisher*

Types of material: works for young audiences, including full-length plays, one-acts and musicals. **Remuneration:** outright purchase or performance royalty; complimentary copies. **Guidelines:** works suitable for middle school and junior and senior high school markets. **Submission procedure:** accepts unsolicited scripts. **Response time:** 1–2 months.

HOLVOE BOOKS

Box 62; Hewlett, NY 11557-0062; (800) 536-0099; E-mail holvoe@aol.com
Steven Fisch, *Associate Editor*

Types of material: full-length plays, one-acts, translations, adaptations, plays for young audiences, libretti, solo pieces. **Remuneration:** complimentary copies; possible advance and royalties. **Guidelines:** publishes play anthologies for libraries and colleges and limited trade distribution; publishes *This Month ON STAGE* (see entry this section). **Submission procedure:** accepts unsolicited scripts with resume and cover letter with SASE for response; send SASE for guidelines. **Response time:** 12–18 months.

I. E. CLARK PUBLICATIONS

Box 246; Schulenburg, TX 78956-0246; (409) 743-3232
Donna Cozzaglio, *Editorial Department*

Types of material: full-length plays, one-acts, translations, adaptations, plays for young audiences, musicals. **Remuneration:** book and performance royalties. **Guidelines:** publishes for worldwide professional, amateur and educational market; prefers produced works. **Submission procedure:** accepts unsolicited scripts; cassette or videotape must accompany musical; include proof of production with reviews and photos for produced works; send $3 for catalogue; send SASE for submission guidelines. **Response time:** 2–6 months.

KALLIOPE, A JOURNAL OF WOMEN'S ART
Florida Community College; 3939 Roosevelt Blvd; Jacksonville, FL 32205;
  (904) 381-3511
Mary Sue Koeppel, *Editor*

Types of material: one-acts, including solo pieces. **Remuneration:** 3 complimentary copies or free 1-year subscription. **Guidelines:** triannual journal of women's art publishing short fiction, poetry, artwork, photography, interviews, reviews and an average of 1 play a year; unpublished plays, less than 25 pages long, by women only; no trite themes or erotica. **Submission procedure:** accepts unsolicited scripts. **Response time:** 3–6 months.

THE KENYON REVIEW
Kenyon College; Gambier, OH 43022; (614) 427-5202, FAX 427-5417;
  E-mail kenyonreview@kenyon.edu
David H. Lynn, *Editor*

Types of material: one-acts (including solo pieces), excerpts from full-length plays. **Remuneration:** cash payment; 2 complimentary copies. **Guidelines:** literary journal publishing an average of 2 plays a year; unproduced, unpublished works maximum 30 pages long. **Submission procedure:** accepts unsolicited scripts (typed and double-spaced only) with SASE for response. **Response time:** 3 months.

LAMIA INK!
Box 202, Prince St Station; New York, NY 10012
Cortland Jessup, *Editor*

Types of material: very short monologues and performance pieces; 1-page plays for contest (see below). **Remuneration:** 4 complimentary copies. **Guidelines:** triannual "art rag" magazine; experimental theatre pieces maximum 5 pages long, prefers 2–3 pages; special interest in Japanese, Pacific Rim and Native American writers, and poets' theatre, performance poems, theatre manifestos and essays. **Submission procedure:** accepts unsolicited scripts with SASE for response. **Deadline:** 30 Sep for Dec issue; 30 Dec for Feb issue; 30 Mar for May issue. **Response time:** 2–3 weeks after deadline. **Special programs:** Lamia Ink! International One-Page Play Competition (see Prizes).

LIBRETO/AS
The Presbyter's Peartree; 15 Alta Vista Dr; Princeton, NJ 08540-7416;
  (609) 737-7065
Laurence M. Leive, *Publisher*

Types of material: full-length plays, one-acts, translations, adaptations, plays for young audiences, musicals, solo pieces. **Remuneration:** royalty; complimentary copies. **Guidelines:** theatre press publishing an average of 5 works a year by writers of Cuban origin. **Submission procedure:** accepts unsolicited scripts; prefers synopsis and letter of inquiry. **Response time:** 1 week letter; 1 month script.

LILLENAS DRAMA RESOURCES

Lillenas Publishing Company; Box 419527; Kansas City, MO 64141;
   (816) 931-1900, FAX 753-4071
Paul M. Miller, *Consultant/Editor*

Types of material: full-length plays, one-acts, musicals, collections of sketches, skits, playlets, recitations. **Remuneration:** outright purchase or royalty. **Guidelines:** unpublished "creatively conceived and practically producible scripts and outlines that provide church and school with an opportunity to glorify God and his creation in drama." **Submission procedure:** accepts unsolicited scripts; send SASE for contributor's guidelines and current need sheet. **Response time:** 3 months.

MODERN INTERNATIONAL DRAMA

Theatre Department; State University of New York–Binghamton; Box 6000;
   Binghamton, NY 13902-6000; (607) 777-2704
George E. Wellwarth and Anthony M. Pasquariello, *Editors*

Types of material: translations. **Remuneration:** 3 complimentary copies. **Guidelines:** biannual journal; unpublished translations of plays not previously translated only; style guide sent on request. **Submission procedure:** accepts unsolicited scripts. **Response time:** 1 month.

NEW PLAYS

Box 5074; Charlottesville, VA 22905; (804) 979-2777
Patricia Whitton, *Publisher*

Types of material: plays for young audiences. **Remuneration:** 10% book royalty, 50% performance royalty. **Guidelines:** innovative material not duplicated by other sources of plays for young audiences; produced plays, directed by someone other than author. **Submission procedure:** accepts unsolicited scripts. **Response time:** at least 1–2 months.

PACIFIC REVIEW

English Department; California State University; 5500 University Pkwy;
   San Bernardino, CA 92407-2397; (909) 880-5894
James Brown and Juan Delgado, *Faculty Editors*

Types of material: one-acts, including solo pieces. **Remuneration:** 2 complimentary copies. **Guidelines:** annual literary journal; plays maximum 25 pages long. **Submission procedure:** accepts unsolicited scripts; submit 1 Sep–1 Feb only. **Response time:** 2 months.

PAJ BOOKS

Box 260, Village Station; New York, NY 10014-0260; (212) 243-3885,
   FAX 243-3885; E-mail pajpub@aol.com
Bonnie Marranca and Gautam Dasgupta, *Editors*

Types of material: full-length plays, one-acts, translations, solo pieces. **Remu-

neration: royalty and/or fee. **Guidelines:** plays and critical literature on the performing arts from the international repertoire published by John Hopkins University Press; special interest in translations. **Submission procedure:** no unsolicited scripts; synopsis and letter of inquiry. **Response time:** 1–2 months.

PERFORMING ARTS JOURNAL

Box 260, Village Station; New York, NY 10014-0260; (212) 243-3885,
    FAX 243-3885; E-mail pajpub@aol.com
Bonnie Marranca and Gautam Dasgupta, *Co-Publishers and Editors*

Types of material: short full-length plays, one-acts, translations, solo pieces. **Remuneration:** fee. **Guidelines:** publishes plays and critical essays on the performing arts from the international repertoire; special interest in translations; plays less than 40 pages long. **Submission procedure:** no unsolicited scripts; synopsis and letter of inquiry. **Response time:** 1–2 months.

PIONEER DRAMA SERVICE

Box 4267; Englewood, CO 80155-4267; (303) 779-4035, FAX 779-4315;
    E-mail piodrama@aol.com

Types of material: full-length plays, one-acts, plays for young audiences, musicals. **Remuneration:** outright purchase or royalty. **Guidelines:** produced work suitable for educational theatre, including melodramas and Christmas plays. **Submission procedure:** accepts unsolicited scripts; prefers synopsis and letter of inquiry. **Response time:** 2 weeks letter; 3 months script. **Special programs:** Shubert Fendrich Memorial Playwriting Contest (see Prizes).

PLAYERS PRESS

Box 1132; Studio City, CA 91614-0132; (818) 789-4980
Robert W. Gordon, *Senior Editor*

Types of material: full-length plays, one-acts, translations, adaptations, plays for young audiences, musicals, solo pieces, monologues, scenes, teleplays, screenplays. **Remuneration:** cash option and/or outright purchase or royalty; complimentary copies (additional copies at 20% discount). **Guidelines:** theatre press publishing technical and reference books and scripts; produced works for professional, amateur and educational markets. **Submission procedure:** accepts unsolicited scripts with proof of production, resume and 2 business-size SASEs; prefers synopsis, proof of production, resume and letter of inquiry with SASE for response. **Response time:** 1–6 weeks letter; 1–6 months script.

PLAYS ON TAPE

Box 5789; Bend, OR 97708-5789; (541) 923-6246, FAX 923-6246;
    E-mail PlaysOnTap@aol.com;
    Web http://www.transport.com/~playsont/playsontape.index.html
Literary Dept.

Types of material: full-length plays, one-acts, plays for young audiences, solo pieces. **Remuneration:** $1000 plus 1% royalty for full-length plays; negotiable fee and royalty for shorter works; 10 complimentary copies of audiotape. **Guidelines:** audiobook company marketing primarily to bookstores; "works that do not diminish in quality due to restrictions of audiotape" only; prefers plays that take risks and have contemporary themes; special interest in works by women and minorities. **Submission procedure:** accepts unsolicited scripts; prefers synopsis, letter of inquiry and up to 10 pages of dialogue with SASE or e-mail address for response. **Response time:** 3 months.

PLAYS, THE DRAMA MAGAZINE FOR YOUNG PEOPLE
120 Boylston St; Boston, MA 02116-4615; (617) 423-3157
Elizabeth Preston, *Managing Editor*

Types of material: one-act plays for young audiences, including adaptations of material in the public domain. **Remuneration:** payment on acceptance. **Guidelines:** publishes about 70 plays and programs a year; prefers work 20–30 minutes long for junior and senior high, 15–20 minutes for middle grades, 8–15 minutes for lower grades; no religious plays. **Submission procedure:** accepts unsolicited original scripts; letter of inquiry for adaptations; prefers format used in magazine (send SASE for style sheet). **Response time:** 2 weeks.

PLAYSOURCE
Theatre Communications Group; 355 Lexington Ave; New York, NY 10017-0217;
      (212) 697-5230, FAX 983-4847
Wendy Weiner, *Editor*

Types of material: full-length plays, one-acts, translations, adaptations, plays for young audiences, musicals, solo pieces. **Remuneration:** brief descriptive listing of work circulated in quarterly bulletin to potential producers; 1 complimentary copy. **Guidelines:** works that have received full production at TCG Constituent or Associate theatre, or workshop or staged reading as part of major developmental program; bulletin mailed Oct, Jan, Apr and Jul to 300-plus TCG theatres and to subscribers, including other nonprofit theatres, college and university theatres and libraries, and some film and television production companies. **Submission procedure:** TCG Constituent and Associate theatres or developmental organizations supply TCG with list of new works they have produced or developed in their current or most recent season; TCG sends playwright listing form to complete. **Deadline:** ongoing.

POEMS & PLAYS
English Department; Middle Tennessee State University; Murfreesboro, TN 37132;
      (615) 898-2712, -2573, FAX 898-5098
Gay Brewer, *Editor*

Types of material: one-acts and short plays, including solo pieces. **Remuneration:** 1 complimentary copy. **Guidelines:** annual magazine of poetry and short plays published Apr and including an average of 2–3 plays in each issue; unpublished works; prefers works not more than 10 pages long. **Submission procedure:** accepts unsolicited scripts; submissions read 1 Oct–15 Jan only. **Response time:** 1–2 months. **Special programs:** Tennessee Chapbook Prize: annual award for one-act (or combination of short plays) maximum 24–30 pages long; winning script published as interior chapbook in magazine; playwright receives 50 complimentary copies; submit script and $10 for reading fee and copy of next issue; *deadline:* 15 Jan 1997; no submissions before 1 Oct 1996.

PORTLAND REVIEW
Box 751-SD; Portland, OR 97207; (503) 725-4533, FAX 725-5860
Editor

Types of material: short plays. **Remuneration:** 1 complimentary copy. **Guidelines:** triannual journal of the arts published Sep, Jan and May; plays less than 4000 words long. **Submission procedure:** accepts unsolicited scripts. **Response time:** 2 months.

PRISM INTERNATIONAL
Department of Creative Writing; University of British Columbia;
    Buch E462–1866 Main Mall; Vancouver, BC; Canada V6T 1Z1;
    (604) 822-2514, FAX 822-3616; E-mail prism@unixg.ubc.ca;
    Web http://www.arts.ubc.ca/crwr/prism/prism.html
Sara O'Leary, *Editor*

Types of material: one-acts (including translations and solo pieces), excerpts from full-length plays. **Remuneration:** $20–30 per printed page; 1-year subscription. **Guidelines:** quarterly literary magazine; unpublished plays, maximum 40 pages long; send SASE for guidelines. **Submission procedure:** accepts unsolicited scripts, include copy or original with translations. **Response time:** 2–4 months.

PROVINCETOWN ARTS/PROVINCETOWN ARTS PRESS
650 Commercial St; Provincetown, MA 02657; (508) 487-3167, FAX 487-8634
Christopher Busa, *Editor and Publisher*

Types of material: one-acts, translations, solo pieces, performance-art texts. **Remuneration:** $50–300; 2 complimentary copies. **Guidelines:** annual magazine focusing broadly on artists and writers who inhabit or visit the tip of Cape Cod, and publishing an average of 1 play a year; also small press publishing 1 play or collection of plays a year; especially interested in performance-art texts; unpublished plays not more than 30 pages long. **Submission procedure:** accepts unsolicited scripts; submissions read Sep–Mar. **Response time:** 2 months.

RAG MAG
Box 12; Goodhue, MN 55027; (612) 923-4590
Beverly Voldseth, *Editor and Publisher*

Types of material: full-length plays, one-acts, solo pieces. **Remuneration:** 1 complimentary copy. **Guidelines:** biannual small-press literary magazine publishing artwork, prose and poetry, and interested in receiving play submissions; for Oct issue, works on theme "families" only; innovative character plays; prefers short one-acts but will consider longer plays with a view to publishing extracts or scenes. **Submission procedure:** accepts unsolicited short one-acts; send maximum 10-page sample, bio and letter of inquiry for longer plays; submit Apr-Jun for Oct issue. **Response time:** 1–2 months.

RESOURCE PUBLICATIONS

160 East Virginia St, #290; San Jose, CA 95112-5848; (408) 286-8505,
        FAX 287-8748; E-mail mdrnlitrgy@aol.com; Web http://www.rpinet.com
Nick Wagner, *Editorial Director*

Types of material: plays 7–15 minutes long. **Remuneration:** royalty. **Guidelines:** unpublished plays or collections of plays suitable for celebrations, religious education classes, youth ministry, and education, counseling and therapy. **Submission procedure:** accepts unsolicited scripts. **Response time:** 2 months.

ROCKFORD REVIEW

Box 858; Rockford, IL 61105
David Ross, *Editor*

Types of material: one-acts, including solo pieces. **Remuneration:** one-acts selected for publication eligible for quarterly "Editor's Choice" prize of $25 (winner invited to reading and reception as guest of honor in Jun); 1 complimentary copy. **Guidelines:** quarterly journal publishing poetry, fiction, satire, artwork and an average of 4–5 plays a year; one-acts not more than 10 pages long, preferably of a satirical nature; interested in work that provides new insight into the human dilemma ("to cope or not to cope"). **Submission procedure:** accepts unsolicited scripts; sample copy $5. **Response time:** 1–2 months.

SAMUEL FRENCH

45 West 25th St; New York, NY 10010-2751; (212) 206-8990
Lawrence Harbison and William Talbot, *Editors*

Types of material: full-length plays, one-acts, plays for young audiences, musicals, solo pieces. **Remuneration:** 10% book royalty; 10 complimentary copies (40% discount on additional copies). **Guidelines:** "Many of our publications have never been produced in New York; these are generally comprised of light comedies, mysteries, mystery-comedies, a handful of one-acts and plays for young audiences, and plays with a preponderance of female roles; however, do not hesitate to send in your Future Pulitzer Prize Winner." **Submission procedure:** accepts unsolicited scripts. **Response time:** 2–4 months.

SCRIPTS AND SCRIBBLES

141 Wooster St; New York, NY 10012-3163; (212) 473-6695, FAX 473-6695
Daryl Chin, *Consulting Editor*

Types of material: full-length plays, one-acts, solo pieces, performance-art texts or scenarios. **Remuneration:** 25 complimentary copies. **Guidelines:** series initiated to publish texts for nontraditional theatre work and works produced outside New York City. **Submission procedure:** no unsolicited scripts; synopsis and letter of inquiry. **Response time:** 6 months.

SINISTER WISDOM
Box 3252; Berkeley, CA 94703
Akiba Onada-Sikwoia, *Editor*

Types of material: one-acts, excerpts from full-length plays (3000 words maximum). **Remuneration:** 2 complimentary copies. **Guidelines:** lesbian quarterly of art and literature; works by lesbians reflecting the diversity of lesbians; no heterosexual themes; send SASE for current themes. **Submission procedure:** accepts unsolicited scripts. **Response time:** 2–9 months.

SMITH AND KRAUS
Box 127; Lyme, NH 03768; (603) 795-4331, FAX 795-4427
Marisa Smith, *President*

Types of material: full-length plays, one-acts, translations, adaptations, plays for young audiences, solo pieces, monologues. **Remuneration:** usually fee or royalty; at least 10 complimentary copies. **Guidelines:** theatre press publishing works of interest to theatrical community, especially to actors, including collections of monologues and an average of 50 full-length plays a year. **Submission procedure:** no unsolicited scripts; synopsis and letter of inquiry. **Response time:** 2–4 months.

STET MAGAZINE
Box 75; Cambridge, MA 02238-0075; (508) 264-4938, FAX 264-4938
Cassandra Oxley, *Editor and Publisher*

Types of material: one-acts, solo pieces, performance-art texts. **Remuneration:** 2 complimentary copies. **Guidelines:** quarterly literary magazine publishing an average of 2 plays a year; unpublished works maximum 20 pages long; special interest in short pieces and in innovative, experimental work. **Submission procedure:** accepts unsolicited scripts with bio; sample copy $4. **Response time:** 2–3 months.

SUN & MOON PRESS
6026 Wilshire Blvd; Los Angeles, CA 90036; (213) 857-1115;
     E-mail djmess@sunmoon.com; Web www.sunmoon.com
American Theater and Literature Program (ATL)

Types of material: full-length plays, one-acts, translations. **Remuneration:** royalty; 10 complimentary copies. **Guidelines:** press publishing average of 10 single-play volumes a year including 2 winners of *American Theater and Literature Program Contest*; unpublished plays. **Submission procedure:** accepts unsolicited script for prize only, submit with $25 fee. **Response time:** 2–6 months.

THEATER

222 York St; New Haven, CT 06520; (203) 432-1568, FAX 432-8336;
    E-mail theater.magazine@quickmail.yale.edu
Erika Munk, *Editor*

Types of material: full-length plays, one-acts, translations, adaptations, solo pieces. **Remuneration:** minimum fee of $150; complimentary copies. **Guidelines:** triannual theatre journal publishing an average of 2 plays in each issue; special interest in experimental, innovative work; "no standard psychological realism or TV-script clones." **Submission procedure:** accepts unsolicited scripts with resume. **Response time:** 3–6 months.

THEATREFORUM

Theatre Department; University of California–San Diego;
    9500 Gilman Dr; La Jolla, CA 92093-0344; (619) 534-6598, FAX 534-1080;
    E-mail theatreforum@ucsd.edu
Jim Carmody, Adele Edling Shank and Theodore Shank, *Editors*

Types of material: full-length plays, translations, adaptations, solo pieces. **Remuneration:** varies by length; 10 complimentary copies. **Guidelines:** biannual international journal focusing on innovative work. **Submission procedure:** no unsolicited scripts; professional recommendation. **Response time:** 3 months.

THIS MONTH ON STAGE

Box 62; Hewlett, NY 11557-0062; (800) 536-0099; E-mail tmonstage@aol.com
Editorial Department

Types of material: full-length plays, one-acts, translations, adaptations, libretti, solo pieces. **Remuneration:** $1; 2 complimentary copies. **Guidelines:** monthly theatre magazine; special interest in short plays and one-acts. **Submission procedure:** accepts unsolicited scripts with resume, cover letter and SASE for response; send SASE for guidelines. **Response time:** 12–18 months.

TOMORROW MAGAZINE

Box 148486; Chicago, IL 60614; (312) 984-6092; E-mail audrelv@tezcat.com
Tim W. Brown, *Editor*

Types of material: one-acts, monologues, solo pieces, performance-art texts. **Remuneration:** 1 complimentary copy. **Guidelines:** biannual magazine publishing all literary genres, including an average of 1–2 plays a year; works maximum 15 pages long; special interest in comedy. **Submission procedure:** accepts unsolicited scripts; sample copy $5. **Response time:** 3 weeks–3 months.

TWANAT

The Museum at Warm Springs, Box C; Warm Springs, OR 97701;
(541) 553-3331, FAX 553-3338
Lori Edmo-Suppah, *Editor*

Types of material: full-length plays, one-acts, translations, adaptations, plays for young audiences, solo pieces, performance-art texts. **Remuneration:** fee; 10 complimentary copies. **Guidelines:** quarterly newsletter of the American Indian confederate tribes; works by Native American writers or containing Native American characters or subject matter only. **Submission procedure:** accepts unsolicited scripts. **Response time:** 3 months.

UBU REPERTORY THEATER PUBLICATIONS

See Membership and Service Organizations.

UNITED ARTS

141 Wooster St; New York, NY 10012-3163; (212) 473-6695, FAX 473-6695
Daryl Chin, *Editor*

Types of material: one-acts, translations, solo pieces, performance-art texts, scenarios, manifestos. **Remuneration:** complimentary copies. **Guidelines:** journal of analysis and opinion covering visual arts, film, video, theatre and dance, published 3–4 times a year by University Arts Resources; nontraditional, avant-garde plays. **Submission pro-cedure:** accepts unsolicited scripts; prefers synopsis and letter of inquiry. **Re-sponse time:** 6 months.

VENTANA PRODUCTIONS/PUBLICATIONS

Box 191973; San Francisco, CA 94119; (415) 522-8989
Vicky Simmons, *Literary Manager*

Types of material: full-length plays, one-acts, monologues. **Remuneration:** 10% book royalty, 90% production royalty; 10 complimentary copies. **Guidelines:** independent production company and small press publishing original single- and multiple-play volumes; prefers produced plays or plays with significant accomplishments. **Submission procedure:** no unsolicited scripts; synopsis and letter of inquiry. **Response time:** 3 months. **Special programs:** Ventana Publications Play Award: annual award for full-length or one-act play with significant accomplishments; winning script receives publication and public reading, playwright receives book and performance royalties and 10 complimentary copies; submit script with proof of production/accomplishments and $10 fee; send SASE for guidelines; *deadline:* 15 Feb 1997.

Development

What's in this section?

Conferences, festivals, workshops and programs whose primary purpose is to develop plays and playwrights, including a substantial number devoted to music-theatre. Also listed are some playwright groups and membership organizations whose main activity is play development. Developmental organizations such as New Dramatists whose many programs cannot be adequately described in the brief format used in this section are listed in Membership and Service Organizations. Some programs listed in Prizes also include a developmental element.

How can I get into these programs?

Keep applying to those for which you are convinced your work is suited. If you're turned down one year, you may be accepted the next on the strength of your latest piece. If you're required to submit a script with your application, don't forget your SASE!

146

ACADEMY THEATRE NEW PLAY DEVELOPMENT PROGRAM

501 Means St NW; Atlanta, GA 30318; (404) 525-4111, FAX 688-8009
Robert Waterhouse, *Artistic Education Director*

Open to: playwrights. **Description:** year-round program of 6–8 week workshops; 8–10 plays developed each workshop in collaboration with actors, directors and dramaturgs, culminating in readings and staged readings; playwright receives access to theatre's studio spaces and conference room for independent rehearsals and readings. **Financial arrangement:** $100–160 fee per workshop. **Guidelines:** resident of metro-Atlanta area or Southeast region. **Application procedure:** 10-page dialogue sample of work-in-progress, synopsis, bio and letter of inquiry. **Deadline:** ongoing.

ALCAZAR SCRIPTS IN PROGRESS

650 Geary St; San Francisco, CA 94102; (415) 441-6655, FAX 441-9567
Alan Ramos, *Script Supervisor*

Open to: playwrights, composers, solo performers, screenwriters. **Description:** 1 play developed through 3-month process, including 2 staged readings; possible full production with 4 weeks of rehearsal. **Financial arrangement:** room and board; royalties, if produced. **Guidelines:** unproduced play. **Application procedure:** script and resume. **Deadline:** 31 Dec 1996. **Notification date:** 28 Feb 1997. **Dates:** Jun–Sep 1997.

AMERICAN PLAYWRIGHT PROGRAM

Westbeth Theatre Center; 151 Bank St; New York, NY 10014; (212) 691-2272
Steven Bloom, *Literary Manager*

Open to: playwrights, solo performers. **Description:** program to develop full-length plays through critiques, story conferences and staged readings; possible production by Westbeth Theatre Center or through referral to other producing organizations. **Financial arrangement:** free. **Guidelines:** contemporary themes; cast limit of 8, minimal set; welcomes work by minority playwrights; send SASE for guidelines. **Application procedure:** script only. **Deadline:** ongoing. **Notification:** 4–6 months.

ASCAP MUSICAL THEATRE WORKSHOP

1 Lincoln Plaza; New York, NY 10023; (212) 621-6234
Michael A. Kerker, *Director of Musical Theatre*

Open to: composers, lyricists. **Description:** 10-week workshop meeting once a week for 3 hours under the direction of Stephen Schwartz; works presented to panels of musical theatre professionals. **Financial arrangement:** free; $500 Bernice Cohen Musical Theatre Fund Award given to most promising participating individual or team. **Guidelines:** write for press release. **Application procedure:** resume and cassette of 4 theatrical songs (no pop songs). **Deadline:** 1 Oct 1996. **Notification:** Oct 1996. **Dates:** workshop begins Jan 1997.

ASIAN AMERICAN THEATER COMPANY
NEW PLAYS & PLAYWRIGHTS DEVELOPMENT PROGRAM

403 Arguello Blvd; San Francisco, CA 94118; (415) 751-2600, FAX 751-3842
Karen Amano, *Artistic Director*

Open to: playwrights. **Description:** developmental workshop for 2–4 plays, leading to staged reading or production; plays not selected for workshop considered for inclusion in series of 8–10 readings presented each season. **Financial arrangement:** free. **Guidelines:** American, Canadian or U.K. playwright of Asian-Pacific descent writing in English; prefers plays depicting Asian-Pacific American perspective. **Application procedure:** script and letter of inquiry. **Deadline:** ongoing. **Dates:** TBA.

THE AUDREY SKIRBALL-KENIS THEATRE

9478 West Olympic Blvd, Suite 304; Beverly Hills, CA 90212; (310) 284-8965,
    FAX 203-8067; E-mail askplay@primenet.com;
    Web http://www.primenet.com/~askplay
Mead K. Hunter, *Director of Literary Programs*

Open to: playwrights, solo performers. **Description:** 15–20 plays receive staged readings; of those, 2–3 selected for workshop production. **Financial arrangement:** playwright receives $150 for staged reading, $1000 for workshop production. **Guidelines:** full-length play-in-progress not produced or scheduled for production. **Application procedure:** script submissions accepted only from agents or with professional recommendation; playwrights may submit synopsis, sample pages and resume. **Deadline:** ongoing. **Notification:** 4–6 months.

BAY AREA PLAYWRIGHTS FESTIVAL

The Playwrights Foundation; Box 460357; San Francisco, CA 94114;
    (415) 263-3986
Jayne Wenger, *Artistic Director*

Open to: playwrights. **Description:** 6–9 scripts given dramaturgical attention and 2 rehearsed readings separated by 5–6 days for rewrites during 2-week festival at Magic Theatre; prefestival weekend retreat for initial brainstorming with directors and dramaturgs. **Financial arrangement:** small stipend, travel. **Guidelines:** unproduced original full-length play only. **Application procedure:** script and resume. **Deadline:** 1 Feb 1997. **Notification:** May 1997. **Dates:** prefestival weekend Jul 1997; festival Sep 1997.

BMI–LEHMAN ENGEL MUSICAL THEATRE WORKSHOP

Broadcast Music, Inc.; 320 West 57th St; New York, NY 10019; (212) 830-2515,
    FAX 262-2824
Norma Grossman, *Director, Musical Theatre*

Open to: composers, librettists, lyricists. **Description:** 2-year program of weekly workshop meetings; showcase presentation to invited members of entertainment industry each year. **Financial arrangement:** free. **Application procedure:** completed application and work samples. **Deadline:** 1 May 1996 for librettists; 1 Aug 1996 for composers and lyricists.

BORDER PLAYWRIGHTS PROJECT

Borderlands Theater; Box 2791; Tucson, AZ 85702; (520) 882-8607,
FAX 882-7406 (call first)

Open to: playwrights. **Description:** 2–3 plays developed over 7–10 day residency with actors, director and dramaturg, culminating in staged reading. **Financial arrangement:** small stipend, travel, housing. **Guidelines:** unproduced full-length play which reflects the culturally diverse realities of the border region, or uses the border as metaphor; English, Spanish and bilingual scripts accepted; special interest in works by writers of color; write for information. **Application procedure:** 3 copies of script. **Deadline:** 30 Mar 1997. **Notification:** Jun 1997. **Dates:** Sep 1997.

BROADWAY TOMORROW

191 Claremont Ave, Suite 53; New York, NY 10027; (212) 864-4736
Elyse Curtis, *Artistic Director*

Open to: composers, librettists, lyricists. **Description:** new musicals presented in concert with writers' involvement. **Financial arrangement:** free. **Guidelines:** resident of NY metropolitan area. **Application procedure:** submissions accepted with professional recommendation from past participant only; cassette of 3 songs with description of 3 scenes in which they occur, synopsis, resume, reviews if available and SASE for response. **Deadline:** 31 Aug 1997.

CAC PLAYWRIGHT'S UNIT

Contemporary Arts Center; Box 30498; New Orleans, LA 70190; (504) 523-1216, FAX 528-3828
Pamela Marquis, *Theatre Coordinator*

Open to: playwrights. **Description:** 9-month workshop for 8–10 writers; participants' works developed and given staged readings. **Financial arrangement:** write or call for information. **Guidelines:** writer living in New Orleans area. **Application procedure:** script only. **Deadline:** ongoing. **Dates:** Sep–May.

CARNEGIE MELLON DRAMA'S SHOWCASE OF NEW PLAYS

Carnegie Mellon Drama; College of Fine Arts; Pittsburgh, PA 15213;
(412) 268-3284, FAX 621-0281; E-mail mc1f@andrew.cmu.edu
Frank Gagliano, *Artistic Director* (submissions)
Mary Lou Chlipala, *Managing and Literary Director* (phone inquiries)

Open to: playwrights, translators, solo performers. **Description:** 5 playwrights each brought in for 1 week to work on play with director and Equity company of actors, culminating in 2 public script-in-hand performances. **Financial arrangement:** $1000 stipend, travel and housing. **Guidelines:** full-length play, bill of related one-acts, or one-act which writer is developing into full-length play;

program seeks "plays of risk; no subjects are taboo; all forms are acceptable; the more audacious and the richer the language, the better." **Application procedure:** script with resume of past productions and readings; submissions accepted only from agents or when accompanied by a letter of recommendation from literary manager of a major theatre. **Deadline:** 1 Dec 1996. **Notification:** Apr 1997. **Dates:** Jul 1997.

CHARLOTTE FESTIVAL/NEW PLAYS IN AMERICA

Charlotte Repertory Theatre; 2040 Charlotte Plaza; Charlotte, NC 28244;
(704) 375-4796
Claudia Carter Covington, *Literary Manager*
Carol Bellamy, *Literary Associate*

Open to: playrights, translators. **Description:** 4 plays each given 12–16 hours of rehearsal with Equity company, culminating in 2 public staged readings, during week-long festival; some scripts subsequently receive full production as part of theatre's regular season. **Financial arrangement:** honorarium, travel, housing. **Guidelines:** only full-length plays and translations that have not received professional production. **Application procedure:** script only. **Deadline:** ongoing.

THE CHESTERFIELD FILM COMPANY/WRITER'S FILM PROJECT

8205 Santa Monica Blvd, #200; Los Angeles, CA 90046; (213) 683-3977,
FAX 960-3466

Open to: playwrights, screenwriters. **Description:** up to 10 writers annually chosen for year-long screenwriting workshop meeting 3–5 times a week; writer creates 2 feature-length screenplays; company intends to produce best of year's work. **Financial arrangement:** $20,000 stipend. **Guidelines:** current and former writing-program students encouraged to apply; write or call for information. **Application procedure:** 2 copies of completed application, writing samples and $39.50 fee. **Deadline:** 1 Jun 1997. **Notification:** Sep 1997. **Dates:** Oct 1997–Sep 1998.

CORNERSTONE DRAMATURGY AND DEVELOPMENT PROJECT

Penumbra Theatre Company; 270 North Kent St; St. Paul, MN 55102-1794;
(612) 224-4601, FAX 224-7074
Lou Bellamy, *Artistic Director*

Open to: playwrights. **Description:** 1 playwright a year offered mainstage production with possible 3–4 week residency; 1 playwright offered 4-week workshop-residency culminating in staged reading; 3 playwrights offered staged reading. **Financial arrangement:** varies according to needs of project. **Guidelines:** full-length play dealing with the African-American and/or Pan African experience which has not received professional full production; one-acts considered; write for guidelines. **Application procedure:** script and resume. **Deadline:** ongoing.

DENVER CENTER THEATRE COMPANY
U S WEST WORKSHOPS
1050 13th St; Denver, CO 80204; (303) 893-4000
Tom Szentgyorgyi, *Associate Artistic Director/New Play Development*

Open to: playwrights. **Description:** new plays receive workshops and rehearsed readings throughout company's season; most plays given 15–30 hours of rehearsal, culminating in 1 public presentation. **Financial arrangement:** stipend, travel, housing. **Guidelines:** unproduced full-length play only; no plays for young audiences, musicals or 1-person shows. **Application procedure:** write for guidelines. **Deadline:** ongoing. **Dates:** Sep–Jun.

DIAMOND HEAD THEATRE DEVELOPMENTAL PROGRAMS
520 Makapuu Ave; Honolulu, HI 96816; (808) 734-8763, FAX 735-1250
John Rampage, *Artistic Director*

Originals

Open to: playwrights. **Description:** ongoing playwrights' workshop led by Jim Hutchison in which playwrights meet regularly to develop their scripts through reading and discussion; monthly public readings of works-in-progress. **Financial arrangement:** participant pays $5 a session. **Application procedure:** attend workshop session; check date and time of sessions (currently every other Wednesday 7–10 p.m.).

Pacific Rim Play Festival

Open to: playwrights. **Description:** 2 plays each rehearsed with participation of playwright and given 2 staged readings a week apart, followed by discussion with audience (playwright has opportunity to revise script between readings). **Financial arrangement:** free. **Guidelines:** current HI resident. **Application procedure:** script and cover letter indicating that submission is for festival. **Deadline:** 30 Apr 1997. **Dates:** Aug 1997.

DRAMA LEAGUE NEW DIRECTORS–NEW WORKS SERIES
The Drama League of New York; 165 West 46th St, Suite 601;
New York, NY 10036; (212) 302-2100, FAX 302-2254;
E-mail dlny@echonyc.com
Roger T. Danforth, *Artistic Director*

Open to: playwright-director teams. **Description:** 3 projects each summer receive 4 weeks of rehearsal space in New York City; development ranges from exploratory rehearsals to workshop production according to needs of collaborative team. **Financial arrangement:** $1000 for each team. **Application procedure:** proposal describing project submitted jointly by playwright and director; bios; write or call for guidelines. **Deadline:** 15 Feb 1997.

FAIRCHESTER PLAYWRIGHTS
24 Spruce Dr; Wilton, CT 06897; (203) 762-8343
Sherman K. Poultney, *Director*

Open to: playwrights, screenwriters, television writers. **Description:** Sep–Jun workshop meets monthly for public staged readings of members' works by professional actors. **Financial arrangement:** writer receiving reading pays for room rental and refreshments for public and fellow writers. **Guidelines:** writer must be able to attend regular meetings; unproduced work; plays may be full-length or one-act; adaptations eligible. **Application procedure:** write or call for guidelines, or to arrange to attend a reading. **Deadline:** ongoing.

FIRST STAGE
Box 38280; Los Angeles, CA 90038; (213) 850-6271
Dennis Safren, *Literary Manager*

Open to: playwrights, solo performers, screenwriters. **Description:** organization providing year-round developmental services using professional actors, directors and dramaturgs; weekly staged readings of plays and screenplays followed by discussions; bimonthly playwriting and screenwriting workshops; periodic dramaturgy workshops; annual short-play marathon. **Financial arrangement:** subscription of $115 a year or $35 a quarter for resident of Los Angeles, Orange or Ventura counties; $58 annual subscription for nonresident; nonmember may submit script for reading. **Application procedure:** script only. **Deadline:** ongoing.

THE FRANK SILVERA WRITERS' WORKSHOP
Box 1791; Manhattanville Station; New York, NY 10027; (212) 662-8463,
    FAX 662-8469 (call first); E-mail playrite@tmn.com
Garland Lee Thompson, *Founding Executive Director*

Open to: playwrights. **Description:** program includes Monday series of readings of new plays by new and established writers, followed by critiques; Wednesday seminars conducted by master playwrights; staged readings and 2–3 Equity showcase productions a year. **Financial arrangement:** $35 annual fee plus $10 per Wednesday class; Monday-night readings free. **Guidelines:** interested in new plays by writers of all colors and backgrounds. **Application procedure:** Sep open house; submitting script and attending a Monday-night session encouraged; call for information.

FREDERICK DOUGLASS CREATIVE ARTS CENTER
WRITING WORKSHOPS
270 West 96th St; New York, NY 10025; (212) 864-3375,
    FAX 864-3474 (call first)
Fred Hudson, *Artistic Director*

Open to: playwrights, screenwriters, television writers. **Description:** 4 cycles a year of 8-week workshops; beginning and advanced playwriting; latter includes readings and possible productions; also film and television writing workshops;

weekly meetings. **Financial arrangement:** $125 fee per workshop; author of play given staged reading receives $50, author of produced play receives $500. **Application procedure:** contact FDCAC for information. **Deadline:** Sep 1996 for 1st cycle; Jan 1997 for 2nd cycle; May 1997 for 3rd cycle; Jul 1997 for 4th cycle; call for exact dates. **Dates:** Oct–Dec 1996; Jan–Mar 1997; Apr–Jun 1997; Jul–Sep 1997.

FREE PLAY READING SERIES AND PLAYWRIGHT DEVELOPMENT WORKSHOP

American Renaissance Theatre of Dramatic Arts; 10 West 15th St, Suite 325; New York, NY 10011; (212) 924-6862, FAX 255-2598
Rich Stone, *Artistic Director*

Open to: playwrights, solo performers. **Description:** up to 5 plays-in-progress given 2 rehearsals and a public reading, followed by audience critique; some scripts may subsequently receive full production; playwright also attends workshop about "business" of playwriting. **Financial arrangement:** free. **Guidelines:** unproduced play; resident of New York city area. **Application procedure:** synopsis, 10 sample pages, letter of recommendation and SASE for response. **Deadline:** 15 Jan 1997. **Notification:** 30 Mar 1997. **Dates:** May/June 1997 (exact dates TBA).

FULL MOON PLAYWRIGHTS EXCHANGE

160 West 71st St, PHA; New York, NY 10023; (212) 787-1945
Stuart Warmflash, *Managing Director*

Open to: playwrights. **Description:** members meet weekly to develop their scripts through supportive critical process. **Financial arrangement:** free. **Application procedure:** full-length script, resume and SASE for response. **Deadline:** ongoing. **Notification:** 3 months.

HAROLD PRINCE MUSICAL THEATRE PROGRAM

The Directors Company; 311 West 43rd St, Suite 206; New York, NY 10036; (212) 246-5877, FAX 265-7482
HPMTP Selection Committee

Open to: playwrights, composers, librettists, lyricists, screenwriters. **Description:** program supports creation, development and production of new musicals; writers and composers work collaboratively with director under guidance of TDC Artistic Staff and Harold Prince; process includes monthly meetings, reading series, 4 weeks of rehearsal, presentation for invited audience in New York City, and possible future full production at Denver Center Theatre Company. **Financial arrangement:** writer paid fee for option on first production; commissioning fees, residencies and fellowships available. **Guidelines:** full-length musical or operetta that has not received professional New York production. **Application procedure:** script with at least 1 complete act, tape of score, synopsis, resume, 3 letters of recommendation and letter of interest. **Deadline:** ongoing. **Notification date:** Oct 1996. **Dates:** fall 1996–Jun 1997.

HISPANIC PLAYWRIGHTS PROJECT

South Coast Repertory; Box 2197; Costa Mesa, CA 92628-2197;
    (714) 957-2602, ext. 215
José Cruz González, *Project Director*

Open to: playwrights. **Description:** up to 3 scripts given 6-day workshop with director, dramaturg and professional cast, culminating in public reading and discussion; playwright meets with director and dramaturg prior to workshop. **Financial arrangement:** honorarium, travel, housing. **Guidelines:** Hispanic-American playwright; unproduced play preferred but produced play which would benefit from further development will be considered; play must not be written entirely in Spanish; no musicals. **Application procedure:** script, synopsis and bio. **Deadline:** 28 Mar 1997. **Notification:** 9 May 1997. **Dates:** preworkshop meeting weekend of 14 Jun 1997; workshop 23 Jul–2 Aug 1997.

THE ISIDORA AGUIRRE PLAYWRIGHTING LAB

El Teatro de la Esperanza; Box 40578; San Francisco, CA 94140-0578;
    (415) 255-2320, FAX 255-8031
Program Manager

Open to: playwrights. **Description:** 1–3 plays developed through individual sessions and weekly seminars with professional dramaturg over 6-week period, culminating in public staged reading; possible future full production for 1 or more plays. **Financial arrangement:** stipend to cover room and board. **Guidelines:** Chicano/Latino playwright; full-length play-in-progress reflective of or adaptable to the Chicano experience; prefers bilingual plays, but accepts monolingual plays in Spanish or English; prefers cast limit of 6 (doubling allowed) and set suitable for touring, but will consider larger-cast plays with nontourable sets; write for guidelines. **Application procedure:** 3 copies of script and resume (material will not be returned). **Deadline:** 15 Mar 1997. **Notification:** 15 May 1997. **Dates:** Jun–Jul 1997.

KEY WEST THEATRE FESTIVAL

Box 992; Key West, FL 33041; (302) 292-3725, FAX 293-0845;
    E-mail theatrekw@aol.com
Joan McGillis, *Artistic Director*

Open to: playwrights, translators, solo performers. **Description:** 8 plays given staged readings and 5 plays given full productions during 10-day festival, which also includes workshops and seminars. **Financial arrangement:** travel and housing. **Guidelines:** unproduced full-length play, one-act, musical, work for young audiences. **Application procedure:** script, resume and letter of recommendation. **Deadline:** ongoing. **Dates:** early fall.

L. A. Black Playwrights

Box 191535; Los Angeles, CA 90019; (213) 292-9438
James Graham Bronson, *President*

Open to: playwrights, librettists, lyricists. **Description:** group meets every second Sunday for guest speakers, private and public readings, and showcases. **Financial arrangement:** free. **Guidelines:** resident of Los Angeles area; members mainly but not exclusively black; prefers produced playwright. **Application procedure:** submit full-length play. **Deadline:** ongoing. **Dates:** year-round.

The Lehman Engel Musical Theatre Workshop

6425 Hollywood Blvd; Hollywood, CA 90028; (213) 465-9142;
      E-mail jsparksco@aol.com
John Sparks, *Co-Director*

Open to: composers, librettists, lyricists. **Description:** Sep–Jun workshop; in-house staged readings; skeletal productions (Equity contract). **Financial arrangement:** 1st-year workshop members pay dues of $500, which include nonrefundable application fee (see below); in subsequent years, members pay dues of $300. **Application procedure:** completed application; 1-page resume; cassette of 3 songs or equivalent for composer; 3 lyrics for lyricist; short scene for librettist; nonrefundable $25 fee. **Deadline:** 1 Aug 1997. **Notification:** Sep 1997. **Dates:** Sep 1997–Jun 1998.

The Loft Fest '97—Festival of Shorts

1441 East Fletcher Ave; Tampa, FL 33612; (813) 972-1200, FAX 977-8485
Kelly Smith, *Artistic Director*

Open to: playwrights, solo performers. **Description:** 10 10-minute plays and/or monologues and 4–6 one-acts each given full production during 6-week festival. **Financial arrangement:** $100 honorarium for one-act, $50 for 10-minute play or monologue. **Guidelines:** unproduced one-act, 10-minute play or monologue. **Application procedure:** script, synopsis, letter of interest and $5 fee per submission (material will not be returned). **Deadline:** 30 Apr 1997. **Notification:** 31 May 1997. **Dates:** 25 Jul–31 Aug 1997.

Long Wharf Theatre Stage II Workshops

222 Sargent Dr; New Haven, CT 06511; (203) 787-4284, FAX 776-2287
Sari Bodi, *Literary Analyst*

Open to: playwrights, translators, composers, librettists, lyricists. **Description:** 2 scripts given 3 weeks of rehearsal, 3 weeks of performance with playwright in residence; optional discussion after performance with audience members, who complete comment sheets (no critics); unit set, costumes and props from stock. **Financial arrangement:** stipend. **Application procedure:** script and professional recommendation, or agent submission. **Deadline:** ongoing. **Notification:** 6 months. **Dates:** Sep–May.

MANHATTAN PLAYWRIGHTS UNIT
338 West 19th St, #6B; New York, NY 10011-3982; (212) 989-0948
Saul Zachary, *Artistic Director*

Open to: playwrights, screenwriters. **Description:** developmental workshop meeting weekly for in-house readings and discussions of members' works-in-progress; end-of-season series of staged readings of new plays. **Financial arrangement:** free. **Guidelines:** produced or published writer. **Application procedure:** letter of inquiry, resume and SASE for response. **Deadline:** ongoing.

MARK TAPER FORUM DEVELOPMENTAL PROGRAMS
135 North Grand Ave; Los Angeles, CA 90012; (213) 972-7574
Oliver Mayer, *Associate Literary Manager*

Asian-Pacific American Friends of the Center Theater Group (APAF-CTG) Reading Series

Open to: playwrights, solo performers. **Description:** 3–5 plays a year each given 2–4 days of rehearsal and reading followed by discussion with audience. **Financial arrangement:** honorarium. **Guidelines:** Asian-Pacific playwright; program designed to bring Asian-Pacific artists and audiences into CTG on an ongoing basis; scripts selected by APAF-CTG and Taper staff. **Application procedure:** script and resume. **Deadline:** call for information.

New Work Festival

Open to: playwrights, solo performers. **Description:** 16–18 plays given workshops (2 weeks of rehearsal, 2 public presentations) or rehearsed readings. **Financial arrangement:** remuneration varies. **Guidelines:** unproduced, unpublished play. **Application procedure:** call for information. **Deadline:** TBA.

THE MAXWELL ANDERSON PLAYWRIGHTS SERIES
Box 671; West Redding, CT 06896; (203) 938-2770
Bruce Post, *Dramaturg*

Open to: playwrights. **Description:** 10 new plays a year each given staged reading with professional director and actors, followed by audience discussion. **Financial arrangement:** stipend. **Guidelines:** unproduced play. **Application procedure:** script only. **Deadline:** ongoing.

MERELY PLAYERS
49 Murray St, #1; New York, NY 10007; (212) 349-0369, FAX 349-1335;
    E-mail hayesmon@aol.com
Monica M. Hayes, *Artistic Director*

Open to: playwrights. **Description:** nonprofit theatre organization with a membership of more than 65 actors, directors and writers develops new scripts through Directors Lab, bimonthly readings and critiques, Second Step staged readings and full productions. **Financial arrangement:** members pay annual dues of $80; initial free participation for playwright not yet enrolled as member. **Guidelines:** playwrights willing to participate in development of their plays may submit scripts; playwright who has had at least 1 full-length script developed through the group's process may be invited to become a member. **Application procedure:** script only. **Deadline:** ongoing.

MIDWEST RADIO THEATRE WORKSHOP

KOPN Radio; 915 East Broadway; Columbia, MO 65201; (573) 874-5676,
     FAX 499-1662; E-mail mrtw@mrtw.org; Web http://www.mrtw.org/mrtw
Director

Open to: playwrights, radio writers. **Description:** annual program of 6-day radio-theatre workshops for writers, actors, directors and sound designers: 55 participants of all disciplines take workshops in production, direction, acting, writing and engineering; commissioned plays or scripts selected through MRTW Script Contest (see Prizes) produced for radio broadcast and live performance with audience. **Financial arrangement:** $200–300 fee for each workshop; some partial and full scholarships available based on financial need and experience, with priority given to women and people of color; possibility of free housing in community. **Application procedure:** completed registration form with deposit; write for information. **Deadline:** 1 Jan 1997 for scholarship applications; most workshops filled at least 1 month before starting date. **Dates:** May 1997.

MOUNT SEQUOYAH NEW PLAY RETREAT

c/o Department of Drama; Kimpel Hall 619; The University of Arkansas;
     Fayetteville, AR 72701; (501) 575-2953, FAX 575-7602;
     E-mail rdgross@comp.uark.edu
Roger Gross, *Director*

Open to: playwrights. **Description:** 3-week developmental workshop for 6 playwrights; personal writing time combined with workshop sessions in which plays are developed with participating directors and resident acting company under supervision of retreat's staff of directors and produced playwrights; each play receives public staged reading. **Financial arrangement:** workshop free; playwright pays travel; fellowships cover room and board. **Application procedure:** previously completed one-act or full-length play; draft or partial draft of play to be worked on at retreat, resume, and names and phone numbers of 3 theatre professionals who have worked with applicant. **Deadline:** 1 Feb 1997. **Notification:** 1 Apr 1997. **Dates:** 18 May–8 Jun 1997.

MUSICAL THEATRE WORKS

440 Lafayette St; New York, NY 10003; (212) 677-0040, FAX 598-0105
Anthony J. Stimac, *Artistic Director*

Open to: composers, librettists, lyricists. **Description:** new composers, librettists and lyricists work with established musical-theatre professionals to develop projects through meetings, informal readings, staged readings and full Off

Broadway productions. **Financial arrangement:** free. **Guidelines:** completed unproduced work. **Application procedure:** script and cassette of music. **Deadline:** ongoing.

NATIONAL MUSIC THEATER CONFERENCE

O'Neill Theater Center; 234 West 44th St, Suite 901;
      New York, NY 10036-3909; (212) 382-2790, FAX 921-5538
Paulette Haupt, *Artistic Director*
Michael E. Nassar, *Administrator*

Open to: composers, librettists, lyricists. **Description:** development period of 2–4 weeks at O'Neill Center, Waterford, CT for new music-theatre works of all genres, traditional and nontraditional; some works developed privately, others presented as staged readings. **Financial arrangement:** stipend, round-trip travel from NYC, room and board. **Guidelines:** U.S. citizen; unproduced work; adaptations acceptable if rights have been obtained. **Application procedure:** send SASE for guidelines and application form after 15 Sep 1996. **Deadline:** 1 Mar 1997; no submission before 1 Nov 1996. **Dates:** Aug 1997.

NATIONAL MUSIC THEATER NETWORK

1697 Broadway, Suite 902; New York, NY 10019; (212) 664-0979,
      FAX 664-0978
Timothy Jerome, *President*

Open to: composers, librettists, lyricists. **Description:** national screening of submitted musical theatre works; written evaluations sent to all writers; descriptive listings of recommended works published in catalogue distributed to producers/ theatres and 12 of these given staged readings in annual "Broadway Dozen," a showcase for potential producers. **Financial arrangement:** free. **Guidelines:** completed work with original music which has not received a major production. **Application procedure:** completed application and $45 fee; write for details. **Deadline:** ongoing.

NATIONAL PLAYWRIGHTS CONFERENCE

O'Neill Theater Center; 234 West 44th St, Suite 902; New York, NY 10036-3909;
      (212) 382-2790, FAX 921-5538
Lloyd Richards, *Artistic Director*
Mary F. McCabe, *Conference Administrator*

Open to: playwrights, screenwriters, television writers. **Description:** 4-week conference at O'Neill Center, Waterford, CT; 9–12 plays developed and presented as staged readings; 1–3 screenplays/teleplays developed and read; preconference weekend for initial reading and planning. **Financial arrangement:** stipend, travel, room and board. **Guidelines:** U.S. citizen or resident; unoptioned and unproduced work; no adaptations or translations. **Application procedure:** send SASE for guidelines after 15 Sep 1996. **Deadline:** 1 Dec 1996. **Notification:** Apr 1996. **Dates:** preconference weekend TBA; conference Jul 1997.

THE NEW HARMONY PROJECT CONFERENCE/LABORATORY
613 North East St; Indianapolis, IN 46202; (317) 464-9405, FAX 635-4201
Jeffrey L. Sparks, *Executive Director*
Andrew Tsao, *Artistic Director*

Open to: playwrights, composers, librettists, screenwriters, television writers. **Description:** 4–6 scripts given up to 2 weeks of intensive development with professional community of directors, actors, producers, dramaturgs and musical directors. **Financial arrangement:** stipend of $200–400, depending on length of stay; travel, room and board. **Guidelines:** narrative works that "emphasize the dignity of the human spirit and the worth of the human experience." **Application procedure:** 10-page writing sample, project proposal and statement of artistic purpose. **Deadline:** 15 Nov 1996. **Notification:** 15 Mar 1997. **Dates:** 14 May–2 Jun 1997.

NEW VOICES PLAY DEVELOPMENT PROGRAM
Plowshares Theatre Company; Fisher Building Station; Box 11399;
    Detroit, MI 48211; (313) 862-4386, FAX (810) 353-1274;
    E-mail garydarnel@aol.com
Gary Anderson, *Producing Artistic Director*

Open to: playwrights, translators, solo performers. **Description:** up to 6 plays-in-progress given 2 weeks of rehearsal with professional company of actors, directors and dramaturgs, culminating in 2 staged readings followed by audience discussion; program provides marketing assistance following development; possible future full production. **Financial arrangement:** free; some travel stipends available. **Guidelines:** African-American playwright; unproduced play addressing the African-American experience. **Application procedure:** completed application, synopsis and resume. **Deadline:** 31 Oct 1996. **Notification date:** Mar 1997. **Dates:** 10–27 Jul 1997.

NEW YORK FOUNDATION FOR THE ARTS
SPONSORSHIP PROGRAM
155 Ave of the Americas, 14th Floor; New York, NY 10013-1507;
    (212) 366-6900, FAX 366-1778; E-mail nyfaafp@artswire.org
Kevin Duggan, *Assistant Director of Artists' Services*

Open to: playwrights, translators, composers, librettists, lyricists, solo performers, screenwriters, radio and television writers. **Description:** program supports development, production and distribution of creative new projects by individual artists, both emerging talents and established professionals, with strong emphasis on independent film and video but also including radio, literature, performance art, theatre, music, dance and visual arts; as sponsoring organization for nonprofit status, NYFA provides fiscal management assistance and proposal reviews with focus on fundraising counsel; program does not offer grants. **Financial arrangement:** as a service fee, NYFA retains 8% of grants and contributions it receives on behalf of a project; $50 contract fee payable on signing. **Guidelines:** majority of sponsored artists located in NY metropolitan area; solid project proposal with realistic budget (most selected projects budgeted at not less than $25,000); selection based on artistic excellence, uniqueness and fundability of project, and on artist's previous work and proven ability to complete proposed work. **Application procedure:** write for application form and further information. **Deadline:** 18 Oct 1996; 17 Jan 1997; 18 Apr 1997; 18 Jul 1997. **Notification:** 3 months.

NEWGATE THEATRE NEW PLAY DEVELOPMENT
134 Mathewson St; Providence, RI 02906; E-mail djlima@ids.net
David J. Lima, *Literary Manager*

Open to: playwrights, solo performers. **Description:** organization providing year-round developmental services; bimonthly meetings for local playwrights; 4–8 scripts each season receive staged reading, in some cases leading to workshop production; at least 1 play receives mainstage production; 2–6 plays receive workshop productions in annual Short Play Festival. **Financial arrangement:** free; small stipend and possible housing for main stage production. **Guidelines:** resident of southern New England. **Application procedure:** script, resume and SASE for response. **Deadline:** 1 Feb 1997 for reading; 1 Jun 1997 for festival. **Dates:** Short Play Festival Sep 1997.

THE NEXT STAGE
The Cleveland Play House; Box 1989; Cleveland, OH 44106-0189;
    (216) 795-7010, ext 207, FAX 795-7005; E-mail skryt@aol.com
Scott Kanoff, *Literary Manager/Dramaturg*

Open to: playwrights. **Description:** 3-tier developmental program: Stage One: The Playwrights Unit, ongoing playwrights' workshop; new plays developed through discussion and readings; members allowed to attend rehearsals, performances and all other theatre programming. Stage Two: in Oct, 4–8 plays each given 1 week of rehearsal with Play House company, culminating in public reading. Stage Three: at least 1 play developed in Stages One or Two offered main stage production. **Financial arrangement:** for Stage One: free; possible small stipend; for Stage Two: stipend, transportation and housing; for Stage Three: royalties, transportation and housing. **Guidelines:** for Stage One, resident of Northern Ohio area, produced or unproduced full-length play; for Stage Two, unproduced full-length play. **Application procedure:** script, resume and letter of inquiry. **Deadline:** for Stage One, submit 1–30 Apr only; for Stage Two, submit 15 May–30 Jun only.

PLAYFORMERS
20 Waterside Plaza, Apt 11G; New York, NY 10010; (212) 213-9835
John Fritz, *Executive Director*

Open to: playwrights. **Description:** playwrights' support group meeting 1 or 2 times a month Sep–Jun for readings of works-in-progress and critiques. **Financial arrangement:** $15 initiation fee on acceptance; $90 annual dues. **Guidelines:**

playwright invited to attend meetings as guest before applying for membership. **Application procedure:** script and resume. **Deadline:** ongoing.

PLAYLABS

The Playwrights' Center; 2301 Franklin Ave East; Minneapolis, MN 55406-1099; (612) 332-7481
Elissa Adams, *Artistic Director*

Open to: playwrights, solo performers. **Description:** 4–6 new works given 2 weeks of development with playwright's choice of professional director, dramaturg and Twin Cities actors, culminating in staged reading followed by audience discussion. **Financial arrangement:** travel, housing and per diem. **Guidelines:** U.S. citizen or permanent resident; unproduced, unpublished play, solo performance piece or mixed-media piece; full-length works preferred; writer must be available to attend entire conference and preconference weekend. **Application procedure:** completed application and script; send SASE for application after 16 Oct 1996. **Deadline:** 15 Dec 1996. **Notification:** 1 May 1997. **Dates:** preconference weekend May/June 1997 (exact dates TBA); conference Jul–Aug 1997.

PLAYQUEST

(formerly New Voices for a New America)
Arena Stage; 6th & Maine Ave, SW; Washington, DC 20024; (202) 554-9066, FAX 488-4056
Cathy Madison, *Literary Manager*

Open to: playwrights. **Description:** 2–5 plays each year developed in text-intensive workshop with playwright in residence, culminating in a mini-season of minimally staged public performances. **Financial arrangement:** varies. **Guidelines:** unproduced full-length play, translation, adaptation or musical; special interest in works for a multicultural company and works by writers of color. **Submission procedure:** synopsis, 10-page dialogue sample, bio and letter of inquiry. **Deadline:** ongoing (early summer best time to submit). **Notification:** 1–2 weeks; 6 months to respond to script, if requested.

PLAYS-IN-PROGRESS FESTIVALS OF NEW WORKS

615 4th St; Eureka, CA 95501; (707) 443-3724
Susan Bigelow-Marsh, *Executive Director*

Open to: playwrights. **Description:** 5 scripts each given full production and 8–10 scripts each given 3–4 weeks of development with actors and directors, culminating in staged reading followed by discussion, in spring or fall festival of new work; ongoing development and Monday night reading series for local writers. **Financial arrangement:** negotiable; housing. **Guidelines:** primarily CA writers; 1 out-of-state writer selected for each festival; unproduced, unpublished play. **Application procedure:** script and resume. **Deadline:** 1 Mar 1997; 1 Jul 1997. **Dates:** Sep 1997; May 1998.

PlayWorks Festival

Theatre Department; Fox Fine Arts Center; University of Texas at El Paso;
El Paso, TX 79968-0549; (915) 747-5146, -7854, FAX 747-5438;
E-mail mwright@utep.edu
Michael Wright, *Head of Playwriting and Directing*

Open to: playwrights, solo performers. **Description:** 3 playwrights each given 3-week residencies to write new play, culminating in public presentation of work-in-progress followed by critique; possible future full production. **Financial arrangement:** stipend TBA (amount contingent on funding); travel and housing. **Guidelines:** student playwright enrolled in college or university in AR, AZ, LA, NM, NV, OK or TX; submissions from Latin-American and Native American playwrights especially encouraged. **Submission procedure:** work sample, proposal for script to be developed in residence and names of at least two faculty references. **Deadline:** 31 Jan 1997. **Notification:** 1 Apr 1997. **Dates:** Jun 1997.

Playwrights' Center of San Francisco Staged Readings

Box 460466; San Francisco, CA 94146-0466; (415) 626-4603, FAX 863-0901;
E-mail playctrsf@aol.com
Sheppard B. Kominers, *Chairman of the Board*

Open to: playwrights. **Description:** developmental program meeting weekly for 1 staged reading, monthly for reading and discussion of works-in-progress. **Financial arrangement:** $45 annual fee plus $3 per reading and $3–5 per works-in-progress meeting; non-members can attend meetings for higher fees. **Application procedure:** completed application. **Deadline:** ongoing.

Playwrights Forum

Box 11488; Washington, DC 20008-0688; (301) 816-0569, FAX 816-0569;
E-mail playforum@aol.com
Ernest Joselovitz, *President*

Open to: playwrights. **Description:** ongoing developmental program including 3-tier range of membership options: Forum 2, professional playwriting groups meeting biweekly; Forum 1, workshop program offering three 3-month sessions a year for apprentice playwrights; and Associate membership offering participation in many of Forum's auxiliary programs but not in workshops; depending on type of membership, members variously eligible for in-house and public readings, Musical Theatre Wing, special classes including Rewrites and screenwriting, production observerships, free theatre tickets, annual conference, organization's newsletter and handbook, and new published series of members' scripts. **Financial arrangement:** for Forum 2, $90 every 4 months; for Forum 1, $90 per 15-week session; Associate membership $25 a year. **Guidelines:** resident of mid-Atlantic area only; for Forum 2, prefers produced playwright or former Forum 1 participant, willing to make long-term commitment; send SASE for further information. **Application procedure:** for Forum 2, script and bio; for Forum 1, send SASE or call for information; for Associate membership, send annual fee. **Deadline:** for Forum 2, ongoing; for Forum 1, 10 Sep 1996, 10 Jan 1997, 10 May 1997. **Notification:** 4 weeks.

THE PLAYWRIGHTS' KITCHEN ENSEMBLE
8621 Hayden Pl; Culver City, CA 90232; FAX (310) 838-8430
Dan Lauria, *Artistic Director*

Open to: playwrights. **Description:** 1 play per week given staged reading by celebrity actors and directors for audience including theatre, film and TV professionals; 4–6 plays selected for production. **Financial arrangement:** free. **Guidelines:** play unproduced in Los Angeles. **Application procedure:** script only. **Deadline:** submit 31 Dec–1 Aug only.

PLAYWRIGHTS' PLATFORM
164 Brayton Rd; Boston, MA 02135; (617) 254-4482
Beverly Creasey, *President*

Open to: playwrights. **Description:** ongoing developmental program including weekly workshop held at Massachusetts College of Art, staged readings, summer festival of full productions, dramaturgical and referral services. **Financial arrangement:** playwright receives percentage of gate for festival productions; participants encouraged to become members of organization ($15 annual dues). **Guidelines:** MA resident only; unpublished, unproduced play; write for membership information. **Application procedure:** letter of inquiry only. **Deadline:** ongoing.

PLAYWRIGHTS' PREVIEW PRODUCTIONS
17 East 47th St; New York, NY 10017; (212) 289-2168
Frances Hill, *Artistic Director*
Pamela Faith Jackson, *Literary Associate*

Open to: playwrights. **Description:** 8–12 plays receive staged readings, some chosen for full production or further development; see also Urban Stages Award and Emerging Playwright Award in Prizes. **Financial arrangement:** free. **Guidelines:** play not produced in NY metropolitan area. **Application procedure:** script, production history, bio and SASE for response. **Deadline:** ongoing; best submission times Jul, Aug, Dec. **Dates:** Oct–Nov, Feb–Mar.

PLAYWRIGHTS THEATRE OF NEW JERSEY
NEW PLAY DEVELOPMENT PROGRAM
33 Green Village Rd; Madison, NJ 07940; (201) 514-1787
Kate McAteer, *Literary Manager*

Open to: playwrights. **Description:** new plays developed through sit-down readings, staged readings and productions; liaison with other producing theatres provided. **Financial arrangement:** playwright receives royalty. **Guidelines:** unproduced play by American playwright; write for brochure. **Application procedure:** script and developmental history, if any; resume and SASP for acknowledgment of receipt. **Deadline:** submit 1 Sep–30 Apr only.

PLAYWRIGHTS WEEK
The Lark Theatre Company; 395 Riverside Dr, Suite 12B;
    New York, NY 10025; (212) 727-3626
Marjorie Wampole, Literary Manager

Open to: playwrights, solo performers. **Description:** 8 plays-in-progress given up to 15 hours of rehearsal, culminating in staged reading followed by optional audience discussion or critique; at least 1 script receives subsequent full production. **Financial arrangement:** free; possible travel and housing. **Application procedure:** script only. **Deadline:** 1 Dec 1996. **Notification date:** 15 Mar 1997. **Dates:** 4–9 Jun 1997.

PRIMARY STAGES COMPANY
584 Ninth Ave; New York, NY 10036; (212) 333-7471, FAX 333-2025
Andrew Leynse, *Literary Manager*

Open to: playwrights, solo performers. **Description:** organization committed to developing new plays through readings and full productions. **Financial arrangement:** varies. **Guidelines:** play or musical, not produced in New York City, by American playwright. **Application procedure:** script or synopsis, 10-page dialogue sample, letter of inquiry and SASE for response. **Deadline:** ongoing.

PUERTO RICAN TRAVELING THEATRE
PLAYWRIGHTS' WORKSHOP
141 West 94th St; New York, NY 10025; (212) 354-1293, FAX 307-6769
Allen Davis III, *Director*

Open to: playwrights, solo performers. **Description:** 3 units, 1 for professional playwrights, 2 for beginners; weekly meetings; spring staged reading series; City "In Sight" showcase production series. **Financial arrangement:** free. **Guidelines:** resident of New York City area; Latino or other minority playwright or playwright interested in multicultural theatre. **Application procedure:** for professional unit, submit full-length play; beginners contact director. **Deadline:** 30 Sep 1996. **Notification:** within 2 weeks. **Dates:** Oct 1996–Jul 1997.

RED OCTOPUS THEATRE COMPANY
ORIGINAL SCRIPTS WORKSHOP
Box 1403; Newport, OR 97365; FAX (541) 265-9464
Attn: Original Scripts

Open to: playwrights, solo performers. **Description:** short plays or excerpts from plays developed over period of 3 weeks in collaboration with director and actors, culminating in staged reading. **Financial arrangement:** free housing. **Guidelines:** unproduced, unpublished work-in-progress, approximately 30 minutes long; cast limit of 6; 1 submission; previous submissions ineligible. **Application procedure:** script only; playwright's name on cover page only (not on script). **Deadline:** 1 Dec 1996. **Notification:** 1 Apr 1997. **Dates:** spring 1997.

REMEMBRANCE THROUGH THE PERFORMING ARTS
NEW PLAY DEVELOPMENT
3300 Bee Caves Rd, Suite 650; Austin, TX 78746; (512) 329-9118,
    FAX 329-9118
Marla Macdonald, *Director of New Play Development*

Open to: playwrights, solo performers. **Description:** 8 playwrights chosen biannually for winter and spring developmental workshops, culminating in work-in-progress productions in fall; plays subsequently given referral to nationally recognized theatres for world premieres. **Financial arrangement:** free. **Guidelines:** resident of central TX; full-length play that has not received Equity production. **Application procedure:** script, synopsis and resume. **Deadline:** ongoing.

THE RICHARD RODGERS AWARDS
American Academy of Arts and Letters; 633 West 155th St;
    New York, NY 10032-7599; (212) 368-5900, FAX 491-4615
Attn: Richard Rodgers Awards

Open to: playwrights, composers, librettists, lyricists. **Description:** 1 or more works a year given full production, studio/lab production or staged reading by nonprofit theatre in New York City; writer(s) participate in rehearsal process. **Financial arrangement:** free. **Guidelines:** U.S. citizen or permanent resident; new work by writer/composer not already established in musical theatre; innovative, experimental works encouraged; 1 submission; previous submissions ineligible. **Application procedure:** send SASE for application and information. **Deadline:** 1 Nov 1996. **Notification:** Mar 1997.

THE SCHOOLHOUSE
Owens Rd; Croton Falls, NY 10519; (914) 234-7232, FAX 234-4196
Douglas Michael, *Literary Manager*

Open to: playwrights. **Description:** about 6 plays a year receive development with director and actors, culminating in public reading and possible full production; ongoing weekly writer's group. **Financial arrangement:** small fee to help offset costs. **Guidelines:** resident of Westchester or Putnam counties, NY or Fairfield County, CT, who can participate in program; prefers full-length plays. **Application procedure:** script or excerpt (at least 10 pages) and letter of inquiry. **Deadline:** ongoing. **Notification:** 1 month.

THE SCRIPTEASERS
3404 Hawk St; San Diego, CA 92103-3862; (619) 295-4040, FAX 299-2084
Jonathan Dunn-Rankin, *Corresponding Secretary*

Open to: playwrights, screenwriters, television writers. **Description:** writers, directors and actors meet every other Friday evening in private home for cold readings of new scripts, followed by period of constructive criticism and light refreshments; 1 or 2 rehearsed staged readings a year presented at local theatres as showcases. **Financial arrangement:** donations of $1 accepted at each reading.

Guidelines: membership by invitation only; guest writer must attend at least 2 readings before submitting script; unproduced script by new or established writer who is resident of San Diego County; write or call for guidelines. **Submission procedure:** see guidelines. **Deadline:** ongoing.

SHENANDOAH INTERNATIONAL PLAYWRIGHTS RETREAT
ShenanArts; Rt 5, Box 167-F; Staunton, VA 24401; (540) 248-1868,
   FAX 248-7728
Robert Graham Small, *Director*
Kathleen Tosco, *Managing Director*

Open to: playwrights, screenwriters. **Description:** 7-week retreat for 4–6 American writers and 6 international writers at Pennyroyal farm in Shenandoah Valley; program geared to facilitate major rewrite or new draft of existing script; personal writing balanced by workshops and staged readings with professional company of dramaturgs, directors and actors. **Financial arrangement:** fellowships cover costs. **Guidelines:** competitive admission based on submitted work. **Application procedure:** 2 copies of completed draft of script to be worked on at retreat; personal statement of applicant's background as a writer; SASP for acknowledgment of receipt; call or write for guidelines. **Deadline:** 1 Feb 1997. **Notification:** after 10 Jun 1997. **Dates:** Aug–Sep 1997.

SOUTHERN APPALACHIAN PLAYWRIGHTS' CONFERENCE
Southern Appalachian Repertory Theatre; Box 620; Mars Hill, NC 28754-0620;
   (704) 689-1384, FAX 689-1474; E-mail sart@mhc.edu
Gaynelle M. Caldwell, Jr., *Assistant Managing Director*

Open to: playwrights. **Description:** up to 5 writers selected to participate in annual 3-day conference at which 1 work by each writer is given informal reading and critiqued by panel of theatre professionals; 1 work selected for production as part of summer 1998 season. **Financial arrangement:** room and board; writer of work selected for production receives $500 honorarium. **Guidelines:** unproduced, unpublished play. **Application procedure:** script with cast list and synopsis; resume. **Deadline:** 1 Oct 1996. **Dates:** Apr 1997.

STAGES REPERTORY THEATRE
3201 Allen Pkwy, #101; Houston, TX 77019; (713) 527-0240,
   FAX 527-8669
Beth Sanford, *Associate Artistic Director*

Texas Playwrights Festival

Open to: playwrights. **Description:** 2 plays chosen for development with dramaturg, director and actors over period of 7–30 days, culminating in staged readings. **Financial arrangement:** small stipend, contingent on funding. **Guidelines:** TX native or resident or non-TX playwright writing on TX theme; play not produced professionally; prefers small cast. **Application procedure:** script only. **Deadline:** 31 Jan 1997. **Notification:** May 1997. **Dates:** Jun 1997.

Women's Repertory Project

Open to: playwrights. **Description:** 6 plays chosen for development with professional actors and director over period of 1 week, culminating in presentation of scenes. **Financial arrangement:** stipend. **Guidelines:** woman playwright. **Application procedure:** script only. **Deadline:** 31 Dec 1996; no submission before 1 Oct 1996. **Dates:** Mar 1997.

SUMMERNITE, NEW PLAY STUDIO

Stevens Bldg; Northern Illinois University; DeKalb, IL 60115-2854;
    (815) 753-8258, FAX 753-8415
Gene Terruso, *Artistic Director*

Open to: playwrights. **Description:** up to 10 plays receive staged readings during 15-week program; 2 plays chosen for subsequent full production. **Financial arrangement:** free; royalties for plays chosen for production. **Guidelines:** full-length play or one-act not previously produced in Chicago area. **Application procedure:** synopsis. **Deadline:** 1 Mar 1997. **Notification date:** 1 Dec 1997. **Dates:** May–Aug 1998.

THE SUNDANCE INSTITUTE
INDEPENDENT FEATURE FILM PROGRAM

225 Santa Monica Blvd, 8th Floor; Santa Monica, CA 90401; (310) 394-4662,
    FAX 394-8353; E-mail sundance@deltanet.com

Open to: playwrights, screenwriters, filmmaking teams (e.g., writer/director, writer/producer). **Description:** program includes 5-day Screenwriters Labs each Jan and Jun offering participants one-on-one problem-solving sessions with professional screenwriters; 3-week Filmmakers Lab in Jun in which projects are explored through work with directors, writers, actors, cinematographers, producers, editors and other resource personnel; network/advisory service offers practical and creative assistance to selected projects. **Financial arrangement:** travel, room and board for at least 1 writer/filmmaker per project; possible room and board for additional members of team. **Guidelines:** "compelling, original narrative scripts (they can be based on a true story or be adaptations of plays, novels, short stories, etc.) which represent the unique vision of the writer and/or director"; special interest in supporting new talent and artists in transition (e.g., theatre artist who wants to work in film, writer who wants to direct); send SASE for guidelines. **Submission procedure:** completed application, cover letter, first 5 pages of screenplay, synopsis, bios of project participants and $25 fee; after review process, applicants who pass 1st round of selection will be asked to send full screenplay. **Deadline:** Nov 1996 for Jun 1997 Screenwriters Lab and Filmmakers Lab; Jun 1997 for Jan 1998 Screenwriters Lab (exact dates TBA).

THE SUNDANCE PLAYWRIGHTS LABORATORY

Box 16450; Salt Lake City, UT 84116; (801) 328-3456, FAX 575-5175
David Kirk Chambers, *Managing Director*

Open to: playwrights. **Description:** 10–18 days of intensive developmental workshops and readings of 8–12 scripts; each assigned cast, director and dramaturg. **Financial arrangement:** travel, room and board. **Guidelines:** unproduced play for young or adult audiences; playwright and script must be nominated by nonprofit theatre. **Application procedure:** letter of nomination from theatre, script and playwright's resume. **Deadline:** 15 Dec 1996. **Notification:** Apr 1997. **Dates:** Jul 1997.

THE TEN-MINUTE MUSICALS PROJECT

Box 461194; West Hollywood, CA 90046; (213) 656-8751
Michael Koppy, *Producer*

Open to: composers, librettists, lyricists, solo performers. **Description:** up to 10 brief pieces selected during annual cycle for possible inclusion in full-length anthology-musicals to be produced at Equity theatres in U.S. and Canada; occasionally some pieces workshopped using professional actors and director. **Financial arrangement:** $250 royalty advance with equal share of licensing royalties when produced. **Guidelines:** complete work with a definite beginning, middle and end, 7–14 minutes long, in any musical style or genre; adaptations of strongly structured material in the public domain, or for which rights have been obtained, are encouraged; cast of 2–9, prefers 6–9; write for guidelines. **Application procedure:** script, lead sheets and cassette of sung material. **Deadline:** 31 Aug 1997. **Notification:** 2 months.

THEATRE ARTISTS WORKSHOP OF WESTPORT

17 Morningside Dr S; Westport, CT 06880; (203) 227-5836
Admissions Committee

Open to: playwrights, composers, librettists, lyricists. **Description:** laboratory where professional writers can exercise their craft and develop projects in collaboration with member directors, actors and allied theatre artists; ongoing workshop meetings; work presented for peer evaluation. **Financial arrangement:** annual membership dues and contributions of $220; $50 initiation fee. **Guidelines:** serious, theatre-oriented writer of professional caliber. **Application procedure:** completed application and 3 copies of script. **Deadline:** ongoing.

THE THEATRE-STUDIO PLAYTIME SERIES

750 Eighth Ave, #200; New York, NY 10036; (212) 719-0500
A. M. Raychel, *Artistic Director/Producer*

Open to: playwrights, solo performers. **Description:** program to develop plays through staged readings and full productions; playwright receives free rehearsal and performance space. **Financial arrangement:** free. **Application procedure:** script only. **Deadline:** ongoing.

UNIVERSITY OF ALABAMA NEW PLAYWRIGHTS' PROGRAM

Department of Theatre and Dance; University of Alabama; Box 870239;
Tuscaloosa, AL 35487-0239; (205) 348-9032, FAX 348-9048;
E-mail pcastagn@woodsquad.as.ua.edu
Paul C. Castagno, *Director and Dramaturg*

Open to: playwrights, composers, librettists, lyricists, solo performers. **Description:** opportunity for writer to develop unproduced script or to pursue further development of produced work, culminating in full production; writer may visit campus several times during rehearsal process and required to offer limited playwriting workshops during visit(s); recent MFA playwrights encouraged to apply; production considered for entry in the Kennedy Center American College Theater Festival (see Prizes). **Financial arrangement:** substantial stipend, travel and expenses. **Guidelines:** writer with some previous experience and script that has had some development; special interest in works with southern themes. **Application procedure:** script or synopsis and cover letter. **Deadline:** ongoing. **Notification:** 6 months. **Dates:** fall–spring. **Other programs:** department will also consider one-acts for festival by its directing students and writers' proposals for workshops with its playwriting and acting students.

VOICE AND VISION
RETREAT FOR WOMEN THEATRE ARTISTS

Box 021529; Brooklyn, NY 11202; (212) 502-1151, FAX 475-9506
Marya Mazor and Jean Wagner, *Artistic Directors*

Open to: playwrights, translators, composers, librettists, lyricists, solo performers. **Description:** up to 5 works-in-progress given 1 week of rehearsal and workshop performance or staged reading at Smith College in Northampton, MA; projects chosen to reflect broad range of aesthetics, ethnic backgrounds, artistic experiences and age groups. **Financial arrangement:** travel, housing, some meals. **Guidelines:** project initiator must be a woman; emerging or established artist; submission of dance-theatre, multimedia and performance-art projects encouraged. **Application procedure:** script or project description; resumes of project's main participants; statement of goals to be accomplished during retreat, number of project participants, whether additional participants will be needed (director, actors, etc.) and any special equipment needs. **Deadline:** 15 Jan 1997 for retreat. **Dates:** summer 1997. **Other programs:** Play With Your Food reading series; year-round developmental services in New York City; *deadline:* ongoing.

WHETSTONE THEATRE COMPANY PLAYWRIGHTS PROGRAM

Box 1580; Brattleboro, VT 05302; (802) 257-2600
Bill Hickok, *Artistic Director*

Open to: playwrights, translators. **Description:** selected plays, translations and adaptations enter program of public workshop sessions, staged readings and discussions aimed at assisting development of writer's work, providing new opportunities for the company and informing audience about the playwriting process; possibility of selection for full production (1 new play produced each season). **Financial arrangement:** stipend of $100–500, depending on project; possible travel and housing. **Guidelines:** play not produced professionally; prefers small cast and simple technical requirements. **Application procedure:** script and resume. **Deadline:** ongoing.

WORDSMITHS
City of Los Angeles Cultural Affairs Dept/
    Performing Arts Division; Los Angeles Theatre Center;
    514 South Spring St; Los Angeles, CA 91030; (213) 485-1624, ext 220
Melody Archer Moore, *Project Coordinator*

Open to: playwrights. **Description:** 10–12 playwrights chosen 4 times a year for 12-week developmental workshop offering script analysis and critique. **Financial arrangement:** free. **Guidelines:** resident of Los Angeles area; full-length play, one-act or play-in-progress; no cowritten material. **Application procedure:** script with cover sheet listing title and playwright. **Deadline:** 20 Sep 1996; 20 Dec 1996; 24 Mar 1997; Jul 1997 (exact date TBA). **Notification:** 2 weeks. **Dates:** year-round.

Career Opportunities

- Agents
- Fellowships and Grants
- Emergency Funds
- State Arts Agencies
- Colonies and Residencies
- Membership and Service Organizations

Agents

I'm wondering whether or not I should have an agent. Where can I get information to help me decide?

Write to the Association of Authors' Representatives at 10 Astor Pl, 3rd Floor; New York, NY 10003. Send a check or money order for $5 and a 55¢ SASE to receive the AAR's brochure describing the role of the literary agent and how to find an agent, and its membership list and canon of ethics. See Useful Publications for books you can consult on the subject. Ask fellow playwrights what they think.

How do I select the names of appropriate agents to contact?

All of the agents listed here represent playwrights. (In some cases, the name of the agency contains the name of the agent.) The Dramatists Guild also has a list of agents available to its members, and provides advice on relationships with agents (see Membership and Service Organizations). You may come across names that appear on none of these lists, but be wary, especially if someone tries to charge you a fee to read your script. Again, talk to other playwrights about their experiences. Look at copies of scripts for the names of agents representing specific playwrights. See what kinds of plays various agents handle in order to make an intelligent guess as to whether they would be interested in representing you and your work.

How do I approach an agent?

Do not telephone, do not drop in, do not send manuscripts. Write a brief letter describing your work and asking if the agent would like to see a script. Enclose your professional resume; it should show that you have had work produced or published and make clear that you look at writing as an ongoing career, not an occasional hobby. If you're a beginning writer who's just finished your first play, you'd probably do better to work on getting a production rather than an agent.

ABE NEWBORN ASSOCIATES
1365 York Ave, #25G; New York, NY 10021; (212) 861-4635
Abe Newborn, Joyce Newborn, *Agents*

THE AGENCY
1800 Ave of the Stars, Suite 400; Los Angeles, CA 90067; (310) 551-3000
Dino Carlaftes, Emile Gladstone, Nick Mechanic, Walter Morgan, James Scott, Michael Van Dyck, Jerome Zeitman, *Agents*

AGENCY FOR THE PERFORMING ARTS
888 Seventh Ave, Suite 602; New York, NY 10106; (212) 582-1500
Leo Bookman, *Agent*

ANN ELMO AGENCY
60 East 42nd St; New York, NY 10165; (212) 661-2880
Mari Cronin, Letti Lee, *Agents*

THE BARBARA HOGENSON AGENCY, INC.
19 West 44th St, Suite 1000; New York, NY 10036; (212) 730-7306

BERMAN, BOALS & FLYNN
225 Lafayette St, Suite 1207; New York, NY 10012; (212) 966-0339
Lois Berman, Judy Boals, Jim Flynn, *Agents*

BERTHA KLAUSNER INTERNATIONAL LITERARY AGENCY
71 Park Ave; New York, NY 10016; (212) 685-2642

THE BETHEL AGENCY
360 West 53rd St, Suite BA; New York, NY 10019; (212) 664-0455
Lewis Chambers, *Agent*

BRET ADAMS LTD.
448 West 44th St; New York, NY 10036; (212) 765-5630
Bret Adams, Bruce Ostler, *Agents*

DON BUCHWALD & ASSOCIATES

10 East 44th St; New York, NY 10017; (212) 867-1200
Traci Ching Weinstein, *Agent*

THE DRAMATIC PUBLISHING COMPANY

311 Washington St; Box 129; Woodstock, IL 60098; (815) 338-7170
Julie Kunzie, Dana Wolworth (musicals), *Agents*

ELISABETH MARTON AGENCY

1 Union Square, Room 612; New York, NY 10003-3303; (212) 255-1908
Tonda Marton, *Agent*

FIFI OSCARD ASSOCIATES

24 West 40th St, 17th Floor; New York, NY 10018; (212) 764-1100
Carmen LaVia, Kevin McShane, Fifi Oscard, *Agents*

FLORA ROBERTS

157 West 57th St; New York, NY 10019; (212) 355-4165
Sarah Douglas, Flora Roberts, *Agents*

FREIDA FISHBEIN, LTD.

2556 Hubbard St; Brooklyn, NY 11235; (212) 247-4398
Janice Fishbein, Douglas Michael, *Agents*

THE GERSH AGENCY

130 West 42nd St; New York, NY 10036; (212) 997-1818
Elyse Kroll, Scott Yoselow, *Agents*

GRAHAM AGENCY

311 West 43rd St; New York, NY 10036; (212) 489-7730
Earl Graham, *Agent*

HARDEN-CURTIS ASSOCIATES

850 Seventh Ave, Suite 405; New York, NY 10019; (212) 977-8502
Mary Harden, *Agent*

HELEN MERRILL

435 West 23rd St, Suite 1A; New York, NY 10011; (212) 691-5326
Clyde Kuemmerle, Helen Merrill, *Agents*

INTERNATIONAL CREATIVE MANAGEMENT

40 West 57th St; New York, NY 10019; (212) 556-5600
Bridget Aschenberg, Mitch Douglas, *Agents*

THE JOYCE KETAY AGENCY
1501 Broadway, Suite 1908; New York, NY 10036; (212) 354-6825
Joyce P. Ketay, Carl Mulert, *Agents*

THE KOPALOFF COMPANY
6440 West Olympic Blvd; Los Angeles, CA 90048; (213) 782-1854
Don Kopaloff, *Agent*

LANTZ-HARRIS LITERARY AGENCY
888 Seventh Ave, Suite 2500; New York, NY 10106; (212) 586-0200
Robert Lantz, *Agent*
156 Fifth Ave, Suite 617; New York, NY 10010; (212) 924-6269
Joy Harris, *Agent*
In association with: The Roberts Company; 10345 West Olympic Blvd,
Penthouse; Los Angeles, CA 90064; (310) 552-7800
Nancy Roberts, *Agent*

MICHAEL IMISON PLAYWRIGHTS
28 Almeida St; London N1 1TD; England; 441-71-354-3174

PARAMUSE ARTISTS ASSOCIATES
1414 Ave of the Americas; New York, NY 10019; (212) 758-5055
Shirley Bernstein, *Agent*

THE PARNESS AGENCY
1424 4th St, Suite 404; Santa Monica, CA 90401; (310) 319-1664
Leslie Parness, *Agent*

PEREGRINE WHITTLESEY AGENCY
345 East 80th St, #31F; New York, NY 10021; (212) 737-0153

ROBERT A. FREEDMAN DRAMATIC AGENCY
1501 Broadway, Suite 2310; New York, NY 10036; (212) 840-5760
Robert A. Freedman, Selma Luttinger, *Agents*

ROSENSTONE/WENDER
3 East 48th St, 4th Floor; New York, NY 10017; (212) 832-8330
Ronald Gwiazda, Howard Rosenstone, *Agents*

SAMUEL FRENCH
45 West 25th St; New York, NY 10010-2751; (212) 206-8990
Lawrence Harbison, *Editor*

SHUKAT COMPANY, LTD.
340 West 55th St, Suite 1A; New York, NY 10019; (212) 582-7614
Scott Shukat, Patricia McLaughlin, *Agents*

STEPHEN PEVNER, INC.
248 West 73rd St, 2nd Floor; New York, NY 10023; (212) 496-0474

THE SUSAN GURMAN AGENCY
865 West End Ave, #15A; New York, NY 10025; (212) 864-5243

SUSAN SCHULMAN LITERARY AGENCY
454 West 44th St; New York, NY 10036; (212) 713-1633

THE TANTLEFF OFFICE
375 Greenwich St, Suite 603; New York, NY 10013; (212) 941-3939
John B. Santoianni, Jack Tantleff, *Agents*

WILLIAM MORRIS AGENCY
1325 Ave of the Americas; New York, NY 10019; (212) 586-5100
Peter Franklin, George Lane, Owen Laster, Biff Liff, Mary Meagher,
Gilbert Parker, *Agents*

WRITERS & ARTISTS AGENCY
19 West 44th St, Suite 1000; New York, NY 10036; (212) 391-1112
William Craver, Peter Hagan, Phyllis Kaufman, Greg Wagner, *Agents*

Fellowships and Grants

Can I apply directly to all the programs listed in this section?

No. You will see that a number of the grant programs we list must be applied to by a producing or presenting organization. However, you should be aware that these programs exist so that you can bring them to the attention of organizations with which you have a working relationship. All or most of the funds disbursed directly benefit the individual artist since they go to cover commissioning fees, residencies and other expenses related to the creation of new works.

How can I enhance my chances of winning an award?

Start early. This is so important that we give full listings to the increasing number of awards offered in alternate years, even when the deadline falls outside the period this *Sourcebook* covers. Use the Submission Calendar in the back of this book to help you plan your campaign. In the case of all awards for which you can apply directly, write for guidelines and application forms months ahead. Study the guidelines carefully and follow them meticulously. Don't hesitate to ask for advice and assistance from the organization to which you are applying. Submit a well thought-out, excellently written, neatly typed application—and make sure it arrives in the organization's office by the deadline. (Never assume, without checking, that the deadline is the postmark date.) Apply for as many awards as you qualify for; once you have written the first grant proposal, you can often, with little additional work, adapt it to fit others' guidelines.

THE ALFRED HODDER FELLOWSHIP

The Council of the Humanities; 122 East Pyne; Princeton University; Princeton, NJ 08544-5264; (609) 258-4717, FAX 258-2783

Open to: playwrights, translators. **Frequency:** annual. **Remuneration:** $42,000 fellowship. **Guidelines:** writer spends academic year at Princeton pursuing independent project; prefers writer who has published 1 critically acclaimed book. **Application procedure:** maximum 10-page work sample, 2–3 page project proposal, resume and SASE for response. **Deadline:** 15 Nov 1996.

THE AMERICAN-SCANDINAVIAN FOUNDATION

725 Park Ave; New York, NY 10021; (212) 879-9779, FAX 249-3444; E-mail grants@amscan.org
Exchange Division

Open to: playwrights, translators, composers, librettists, lyricists. **Frequency:** annual. **Remuneration:** $3000–15,000. **Guidelines:** grants and fellowships for research and study in Scandinavian countries; U.S. citizen or permanent resident with undergraduate degree; prefers artist with Scandinavian language competence. **Application procedure:** completed application, supplementary materials and $10 fee. **Deadline:** 1 Nov 1996. **Notification:** Mar 1997.

ARTIST TRUST

1402 Third Ave, Suite 404; Seattle, WA 98101-2118; (206) 467-8734, FAX 467-9633; E-mail arttrust@artswire.org
Marschel Paul, *Director*

Fellowships

Open to: playwrights, composers, librettists, lyricists, screenwriters, radio and television writers. **Frequency:** awards rotate among disciplines. **Remuneration:** $5000 award. **Guidelines:** WA resident only; practicing professional artist of exceptional talent and demonstrated ability; award based on creative excellence and continuing dedication to an artistic discipline; send SASE for guidelines. **Application procedure:** completed application and work sample. **Deadline:** late spring 1997 for composers, librettists, lyricists, screenwriters, radio and television writers; late spring 1998 for playwrights; exact dates TBA (14 Jun in 1996).

GAP (Grants for Artist Projects)

Open to: playwrights, composers, librettists, lyricists, screenwriters, radio and television writers. **Frequency:** annual. **Remuneration:** grant of up to $1000. **Guidelines:** WA resident only; grant for the initiation, continuation or completion of specific creative project undertaken by individual artist; award based on quality of work as represented by supporting material and on creativity and feasibility of proposed project; write for guidelines. **Application procedure:** completed application and work sample. **Deadline:** 28 Feb 1997.

ARTISTS-IN-BERLIN PROGRAMME
German Academic Exchange Service (DAAD); 950 Third Ave, 19th Floor;
New York, NY 10022; (212) 758-3223

Open to: playwrights, composers. **Frequency:** annual. **Remuneration:** monthly grant to cover living costs and rent during 1-year residency in Berlin (6 months in exceptional cases); workspace provided or paid for; travel for writer and any members of immediate family who will be staying in Berlin for period of residency; health and accident insurance; in some cases specific projects such as readings or publications can be subsidized. **Guidelines:** to enable 15–20 internationally known and qualified young artists to pursue own work while participating in the cultural life of the city and making contact with local artists; must reside in Berlin for period of grant; German nationals and foreign writers who are resident in Germany ineligible; write for guidelines. **Application procedure:** completed application; samples of published work, preferably in German, otherwise in English or French, (no manuscripts) for playwrights; scores, records, tapes or published work for composers. **Deadline:** 31 Dec 1996. **Notification:** May 1997. **Dates:** residency begins between 1 Jan and 30 Jun 1998.

ARTS INTERNATIONAL
Institute of International Education; 809 United Nations Plaza;
New York, NY 10017-3580; (212) 984-5370, FAX 984-5574

Cintas
Miriam González Acosta, *Program Officer*
E-mail macosta@iie.org

This fellowship program has been temporarily suspended. All inquiries will be added to mailing list and information will be sent on 1997 activity.

Fund for U.S. Artist at International Festivals and Exhibitions
(see also NEA International Program in this section)
Laura Moore, *Program Officer*
E-mail thefund@iie.org

Open to: performing artists and groups, including solo performers and theatre companies. **Frequency:** triannual. **Remuneration:** grants of up to $25,000 (most grants $500–10,000) to cover foreign travel, housing, per diem and production costs. **Guidelines:** U.S. citizen or permanent resident who has been invited to international festival. **Application procedure:** completed application; copy of invitation from festival; full budget showing all costs of participation in festival and festival's contribution to these costs; work sample; bio. **Deadline:** 2 Sep 1996; 15 Jan 1997; 1 May 1997.

Inroads
Miriam González Acosta, *Program Officer*
E-mail macosta@iie.org

Open to: performing artists and organizations. **Frequency:** annual. **Remuneration:** grants of up to $20,000. **Guidelines:** funds to be used for short-term planning residencies for partnership between artists in different disciplines; 1 artist must be U.S. resident, 1 must be resident of Africa, Asia, Latin America, the Middle East, the Pacific Islands or the Caribbean; project must be under umbrella of U.S. host organization. **Application procedure:** write for guidelines and application. **Deadline:** Jan 1997 (exact date TBA).

ASIAN CULTURAL COUNCIL
1290 Ave of the Americas; New York, NY 10104; (212) 373-4300

ACC Residency Program in Asia

Open to: playwrights, composers, librettists, lyricists. **Frequency:** annual. **Remuneration:** amount varies. **Guidelines:** to support American artists, scholars, and specialists undertaking collaborative research, teaching or creative residencies at cultural and educational institutions in East and Southeast Asia. **Application procedure:** write describing project and requesting application. **Deadline:** 1 Feb 1997.

Japan-United States Arts Programs

Open to: playwrights, composers, librettists, lyricists. **Frequency:** annual. **Remuneration:** amount varies. **Guidelines:** to support residencies in Japan for American artists for a variety of purposes, including creative activities (other than performances), research projects, professional observation tours and specialized training. **Application procedure:** write describing project and requesting application. **Deadline:** 1 Feb 1997.

ATLANTA BUREAU OF CULTURAL AFFAIRS
675 Ponce de Leon Ave; Atlanta, GA 30308; (404) 817-6815, FAX 817-6827
Sophia Lyman, *Project Adminstrator*

Artists Project

Open to: playwrights, composers, librettists, lyricists. **Frequency:** annual. **Remuneration:** grant of up to $3000. **Guidelines:** practicing professional artist resident in city of Atlanta for at least 1 year prior to deadline. **Application procedure:** write for guidelines and application. **Deadline:** Nov 1996; exact date TBA. **Notification:** 3 months.

Mayor's Fellowships in the Arts

Open to: playwrights, composers, librettists, lyricists. **Frequency:** awards rotate among disciplines. **Remuneration:** $6600 award. **Guidelines:** practicing professional artist resident in city of Atlanta for at least 3 consecutive years prior to deadline; playwright may apply under literary or theatre arts; composer, librettist, lyricist applies under music. **Application procedure:** write for guidelines and application. **Deadline:** Feb 1997 for playwrights (exact date TBA); subsequent rotation not yet set. **Notification:** 3 months.

BRODY ARTS FUND

California Community Foundation; 606 South Olive St, Suite 2400;
    Los Angeles, CA 90014-1526; (213) 413-4042
Program Officer, Arts

Open to: playwrights, composers, librettists, lyricists, solo performers, screenwriters, radio and television writers. **Frequency:** awards rotate among disciplines. **Remuneration:** fellowship of $5000. **Guidelines:** L.A. county resident; emerging artist; prefers artist in "expansion arts" field (minority, inner-city, rural and tribal arts); write for guidelines; application available in Jan of application year. **Application procedure:** completed application and supporting materials. **Deadline:** Mar 1997 for playwrights, screenwriters, radio and television writers; Mar 1999 for composers, librettists, lyricists; exact dates TBA. **Notification:** Jun.

BUNTING FELLOWSHIP PROGRAM

The Mary Ingraham Bunting Institute of Radcliffe College; 34 Concord Ave;
    Cambridge, MA 02138; (617) 495-8212, FAX 495-8136
Fellowships Coordinator

Open to: playwrights, composers, librettists. **Frequency:** annual. **Remuneration:** $33,000 1-year fellowship. **Guidelines:** to provide opportunity and support for professional woman of demonstrated accomplishment and exceptional promise to complete substantial project in her field; full-time appointment; fellow required to reside in Boston area and expected to present work-in-progress in public colloquia during year; office or studio space, auditing privileges and access to libraries and other resources of Radcliffe and Harvard provided. **Application procedure:** completed application with $45 fee. **Deadline:** 15 Oct 1996. **Notification:** Apr 1997. **Dates:** 15 Sep 1997–15 Aug 1998.

BUSH ARTIST FELLOWSHIPS

The Bush Foundation; E-900 First National Bank Bldg; 332 Minnesota St;
    St. Paul, MN 55101; (612) 227-5222
Sally Dixon, *Program Director*

Open to: playwrights, composers, screenwriters. **Frequency:** awards rotate biennially among disciplines. **Remuneration:** $36,000 in equal monthly installments for 12–18 months. **Guidelines:** MN, ND, SD or western WI resident at least 25 years old; playwright must have had at least 1 play given full production or workshop production by professional (not necessarily Equity) theatre; screenwriter must have had 1 public staged reading, professional workshop production, or screenplay sale or option. **Application procedure:** write for guidelines and application. **Deadline:** next deadline for playwrights, composers and screenwriters late Oct 1998; exact date TBA. **Notification:** late Mar 1999.

DOBIE-PAISANO FELLOWSHIP

University of Texas at Austin; Main Bldg 101; Austin, TX 78712;
  (512) 471-7213, FAX 471-7620; E-mail gsans@utxbp.bp.utexas.edu
Audrey Slate, *Coordinator*

Open to: playwrights. **Frequency:** annual. **Remuneration:** $7200 stipend to cover 6-month residency at 265-acre ranch; free housing; families welcome. **Guidelines:** native Texan, or playwright who has lived in TX for at least 2 years or has published work about TX; ordinarily 2 writers selected each year. **Application procedure:** write for application after 1 Oct 1996. **Deadline:** 24 Jan 1997. **Notification:** May 1997.

THE DON AND GEE NICHOLL
FELLOWSHIPS IN SCREENWRITING

Academy of Motion Picture Arts and Sciences; 8949 Wilshire Blvd;
  Beverly Hills, CA 90211-1972; (310) 247-3059; Web http://www.oscars.org/
Greg Beal, *Program Coordinator*

Open to: playwrights, screenwriters. **Frequency:** annual. **Remuneration:** up to 5 fellowships of $25,000. **Guidelines:** playwright, screenwriter or fiction writer who has not worked as a professional screenwriter for theatrical films or television or sold screen or television rights to any original story, treatment, stage play, screenplay or teleplay; 1st-round selection based on submission of original screenplay or screen adaptation of writer's own original work, 100–130 pages, written in standard screenplay format; send SASE for guidelines after 1 Jan 1997. **Application procedure:** completed application, screenplay and $30 application fee. **Deadline:** 1 May 1997. **Notification:** 1st-round selection Aug 1997; winners late Oct 1997.

ELECTRONIC ARTS GRANT PROGRAM

  Experimental Television Center; 109 Lower Fairfield Rd;
  Newark Valley, NY 13811; (607) 687-4341, FAX 687-4341
Sherry Miller Hocking, *Program Director*

Finishing Funds

Open to: media artists, including writers and composers, involved in creation of film, audio, video or computer-generated time-based works. **Frequency:** annual. **Remuneration:** 20–25 grants of up to $500. **Guidelines:** resident of NY State; funds to be used to assist completion of work which is time-based in conception and execution and is to be presented as tape or installation; work must be completed before 30 Sep 1997; write for guidelines. **Application procedure:** 3 copies of completed application, project description, work samples and resume. **Deadline:** 15 Mar 1997. **Notification:** 6 weeks.

Presentation Funds

Open to: nonprofit organizations presenting audio, film, video or computer-generated time-based works. **Frequency:** ongoing. **Remuneration:** grant of approximately $150–300 to assist presentation of work and artist's involvement in activities related to presentation. **Guidelines:** New York State organization; event must be open to public and should emphasize work of NY State artist(s); write for guidelines. **Application procedure:** individual may not apply; completed application and supporting materials submitted by organization well in advance of event. **Notification:** 15th of month following month of submission.

FULBRIGHT SCHOLAR AWARDS
Council for International Exchange of Scholars (CIES); 3007 Tilden St NW, Suite 5M, Box FEL; Washington, DC 20008-3009; (202) 686-7877, FAX 362-3442; E-mail cies1@ciesnet.cies.org

Open to: scholars and professionals in all areas of theatre and the arts, including playwrights, translators, composers, librettists and lyricists. **Frequency:** annual. **Remuneration:** grant for university lecturing or research in one of more than 100 countries for 2–9 months; amount varies with country of award; travel; maintenance allowance for living costs of grantee and possibly family. **Guidelines:** U.S. citizen; MFA, Ph.D. or comparable professional qualifications; university or college teaching experience for lecturing awards; for selected countries, proficiency in a foreign language. **Application procedure:** completed application. **Deadline:** 1 Aug 1997. **Notification:** up to 11 months, depending on country; average 8 months.

FUND FOR NEW AMERICAN PLAYS
The John F. Kennedy Center for the Performing Arts; 2700 F St NW; Washington, DC 20566; (202) 416-8024, FAX 416-8026
Sophy Burnham, *Manager*

Open to: nonprofit professional theatres. **Frequency:** annual. **Remuneration:** $10,000 grant to playwright whose work theatre is producing, plus grant (amount dependent on quality of proposal and need) to theatre (4 in 1995); $2,500 Roger L. Stevens award to playwright whose work shows "extraordinary promise" (5 in 1995). **Guidelines:** $10,000 playwright grant to cover living and travel expenses during minimum of 4 weeks of rehearsal and during any necessary additional rehearsals and rewrites in course of run; theatre grant to cover expenses exceeding theatre's budget allocation for hiring of director, designer and guest actors; limit of 1 proposal per theatre; translations and musicals ineligible; write for guidelines. **Application procedure:** playwright may not apply; proposal and supporting materials submitted by theatre. **Deadline:** 15 Mar 1997.

GEORGE BENNETT FELLOWSHIP
Phillips Exeter Academy; Exeter, NH 03833-1104
Charles Pratt, *Coordinator, Selection Committee*

Open to: playwrights. **Frequency:** annual. **Remuneration:** academic-year stipend of $5000; free room and board for fellow and family. **Guidelines:** individual who is seriously contemplating or pursuing a career as a writer and who needs time and freedom from material considerations to complete a project in progress;

fellow expected to make self and talents available in informal and unofficial way to students interested in writing; send SASE for guidelines and application (no phone inquiries). **Application procedure:** completed application, work sample, statement concerning work-in-progress, names of 2 references and $5 fee. **Deadline:** 1 Dec 1996. **Notification:** 15 Mar 1997. **Dates:** Sep 1997–Jun 1998.

INSTITUTE OF INTERNATIONAL EDUCATION
809 United Nations Plaza; New York, NY 10017-3580; (212) 984-5330
U.S. Student Programs Division

Open to: playwrights, translators, composers, librettists, lyricists. **Frequency:** annual. **Remuneration:** fellowship or grant; amount varies with country of award. **Guidelines:** specific opportunities for study abroad in the arts; write for brochure. **Application procedure:** completed application and supporting materials. **Deadline:** 23 Oct 1996. **Notification:** Jan 1997.

THE JAPAN FOUNDATION
152 West 57th St, 39th Floor; New York, NY 10019; (212) 489-0299,
    FAX 489-0409
Artists Fellowship Program

Open to: specialists in the fields of fine arts, performing arts, music, journalism and creative writing, including playwrights, composers, librettists, lyricists and screenwriters. **Frequency:** annual. **Remuneration:** monthly stipend of ¥370,000 (about $3500) or ¥430,000 (about $4000), depending on grantee's professional career; travel; other allowances. **Guidelines:** U.S. citizen or permanent resident; fellowship of 2–6 months, not to be held concurrently with another major grant, to support project substantially related to Japan. **Application procedure:** write for guidelines and application, stating theme of project, present position and citizenship. **Deadline:** 1 Dec 1996. **Notification:** late Mar/early Apr 1997. **Dates:** between 1 Apr 1997 and 31 Mar 1998.

JOHN SIMON GUGGENHEIM MEMORIAL FOUNDATION
90 Park Ave; New York, NY 10016; (212) 687-4470, FAX 697-3248;
    E-mail fellowships@gf.org

Open to: playwrights, composers. **Frequency:** annual. **Remuneration:** 1-year fellowship (in 1995 152 fellowships with average grant of $28,105). **Guidelines:** citizen or permanent resident of U.S. or Canada; recipient must demonstrate exceptional creative ability; grant to support research in any field of knowledge or creation in any of the arts under the freest possible conditions. **Application procedure:** write for information. **Deadline:** 1 Oct 1996. **Notification:** Mar 1997.

The Kleban Award

c/o Zissu, Stein & Mosher; 270 Madison Ave, Suite 1410; New York, NY 10016;
    (212) 683-5320
Alan J. Stein, *Secretary*

Open to: TBA (librettists and/or lyricists). **Frequency:** annual. **Remuneration:** TBA ($100,000 each to lyricist and librettist, payable in installments of $50,000 a year, in 1996-97). **Guidelines:** applicant whose work has received a full or workshop production, or who has been a member or associate of a professional musical workshop or theatre group (e.g., ASCAP or BMI workshop or Dramatists Guild Musical Theater Development Program); writer whose work has been performed on the Broadway stage for a cumulative period of 2 years ineligible; write for guidelines. **Application procedure:** completed application and work sample. **Deadline:** TBA (16 Oct in 1995).

Manhattan Theatre Club Playwriting Fellowships

453 West 16th St; New York, NY 10011; (212) 645-5590, FAX 691-9106;
    E-mail 76735,3316@compuserve.com
Jordan Schildcrout, *Literary Assistant*

Open to: playwrights. **Frequency:** annual. **Remuneration:** $10,000 fellowship. **Guidelines:** New York-based playwright who has completed formal education and can demonstrate financial need; writers from diverse cultural groups encouraged to apply; fellowship includes commission for new play, production assistantship, 1-year residency at MTC; send SASE for further information. **Application procedure:** sample script, resume, statement of purpose and letter of recommendation from theatre professional or professor. **Deadline:** spring 1997; exact date TBA.

Mary Flagler Cary Charitable Trust Commissioning Program

122 East 42nd St, Room 3505; New York, NY 10168; (212) 953-7705,
    FAX 953-7720
Gayle Morgan, *Music Program Director*

Open to: performance institutions including theatre and opera companies. **Frequency:** biennial. **Remuneration:** grant to help nonprofit professional organization commission new musical work from established or emerging composer; amount varies (total of $300,000 available for 1995 grants). **Guidelines:** New York City organization only; funds to be used to compensate composer and librettist for creative work and to cover copying costs; write for guidelines. **Application procedure:** individual may not apply; letter of application and representative audiotape of composer's music submitted by organization. **Deadline:** 30 Jun 1997.

THE MARY ROBERTS RINEHART AWARDS

English Department; MSN 3E4; George Mason University;
    Fairfax, VA 22030-4444; (703) 993-1185
Director, Writing Program

Open to: playwrights. **Frequency:** biennial. **Remuneration:** grant; amount varies with fund's income (currently around $900). **Guidelines:** playwright who lacks financial means to complete a definitely projected work; playwrights who have had a play professionally produced or published, or who have previously received a Rinehart Fund Grant, are ineligible. **Application procedure:** playwright may not apply; nominations accepted from established authors, editors, agents or writing program faculty members. **Deadline:** 30 Nov 1996. **Notification:** Mar 1997.

MATURE WOMEN SCHOLARSHIP AWARD

The National League of American Pen Women; 1300 17th St NW;
    Washington, DC 20036-1973; (202) 785-1997
National Scholarship Chairman

Open to: playwrights, composers, librettists, lyricists. **Frequency:** biennial. **Remuneration:** $1000 grant. **Guidelines:** American woman aged over 35; 3 awards (1 in art, 1 in music, 1 in letters) to further creative goals of women at age when encouragement can lead to realization of long-term purposes; NLAPW members ineligible; send SASE after 1 Aug 1997 for guidelines. **Application procedure:** work sample; statement of purpose for which money will be used; statement that applicant is over age 35 and is not a member of NLAPW; and $8 fee. **Deadline:** 15 Jan 1998. **Notification:** Jun 1998.

THE MCKNIGHT INTERDISCIPLINARY FELLOWSHIP GRANT

Intermedia Arts, Minnesota; 2822 Lyndale Ave. South; Minneapolis, MN 55408;
    (612) 871-4444, FAX 871-6927
Sandy Agustin, *Community Programs Manager*

Open to: interdisciplinary artists. **Frequency:** annual. **Remuneration:** $12,000 fellowship; some travel. **Guidelines:** resident of MN for 1 year before application; mid-career interdisciplinary artists; fellowship and technical support to pursue educational/presentational activity during 18-month fellowship period; send SASE for guidelines after Oct 1996. **Application procedure:** completed application, 1-page maximum artist statement, 10-page maximum work sample, resume and optional SASP for acknowledgment of receipt. **Deadline:** TBA (1 Dec in 1995). **Notification:** spring 1997.

MEET THE COMPOSER GRANT PROGRAMS

2112 Broadway, Suite 505; New York, NY 10023; (212) 787-3601

International Creative Collaboration
Pablo Martinez, *Program Manager*

Open to: opera, theatre and music-theatre companies, arts presenters and musical organizations. **Frequency:** annual. **Remuneration:** up to $75,000 for com-missioning, residency and travel costs. **Guidelines:** U.S. organizations apply for funds to support collaborations up to 3 years in length between U.S.-based composers, librettists or playwrights in Africa, Middle East, Asia, Pacific Islands, Latin America or Caribbean; priority given to projects involving composers; call or write for guidelines. **Application procedure:** individual may not apply; performing organization submits letter of intent before making formal application. **Deadline:** spring 1997 for letter of intent; exact date TBA (15 Mar in 1996). **Notification:** summer 1997.

Meet the Composer/Arts Endowment Commissioning Music/USA
Theodore Wiprud, *Program Manager*

Open to: opera, theatre and music-theatre companies, arts presenters, musical organizations, TV production companies and radio stations. **Frequency:** annual. **Remuneration:** commissioning grant of up to $30,000 to cover composer, librettist, TV writer and/or radio writer fees for opera or music-theatre work (amount dependent on scope and length of work). **Guidelines:** organizations that have been producing or presenting for at least 3 years; application may be from single organization for grants up to $10,000, or from consortium of organizations for grants up to $30,000; plans must involve full production of work and at least 4 performances for a single organization, or at least 6 for a consortium; write for guidelines. **Application procedure:** individual may not apply; 1 host organization submits completed application and supporting materials. **Deadline:** 14 Jun 1997. **Notification:** Aug 1997.

New Residencies
Theodore Wiprud, *Program Manager*

Open to: opera, theatre and music-theatre companies, arts presenters and musical organizations. **Frequency:** annual. **Remuneration:** grant for composer's salary ($40,000 per annum for 2 years; $20,000 towards 3rd-year salary, to be matched by host organizations); $15,000 toward institutional partnership building activities; possible $1500 for composer's relocation costs. **Guidelines:** 3–5 organizations, including at least 2 producing or presenting organizations and at least 1 human service or community organization, form Residency Partnership to sponsor 3-year composer residency; composer writes pieces for all host organizations and works at least 60 hours per month "making music a positive force in community life" through teaching, organizing cultural events, recruiting other composers to community work, etc; host organizations produce residency works, provide office space and logistical support and provide health insurance; write for guidelines. **Application procedure:** individual may not apply; performing organizations in Residency Partnership submit letter of intent with composer work samples before making formal application. **Deadline:** 15 Mar 1997 for letter of intent; 15 Jun 1997 for formal application. **Notification:** Sep 1997. **Dates:** residencies begin Oct 1997.

National Endowment for the Arts
International Program
1100 Pennsylvania Ave NW, Room 618; Washington, DC 20506;
    (202) 682-5429, FAX 682-5602
Merianne Liteman, *Director*

ArtsLink Collaborative Projects
All applications and inquiries to Citizen Exchange Council; 12 West 31st St; New York, NY 10001-4415; (212) 643-1985, FAX 643-1996; E-mail cecny@igc.apc.org

Open to: creative, interpretive and traditional artists, including playwrights, translators, composers, librettists, lyricists and solo performers. **Frequency:** annual. **Remuneration:** grant of up to $6000 (most grants $1500–3500). **Guidelines:** U.S. citizen or permanent resident; to enable individual artists or groups of up to 5 artists to work with their counterparts in Central or Eastern Europe, the former Soviet Union or the Baltics; mutually beneficial collaborative project that will enrich artists' work and/or create new work that draws inspiration from knowledge and experience gained in country visited; write for guidelines. **Application procedure:** completed application and supporting materials. **Deadline:** 18 Mar 1997. **Notification:** 15 Jun 1997.

The Fund for U.S. Artists at International Festivals and Exhibitions
(see also Arts International in this section)
All applications and inquiries to: Arts International; Institute of International Education; 809 United Nations Plaza; New York, NY 10017-3580;
    (212) 984-5370, FAX 984-5574

Open to: performing artists and groups, including solo performers and theatre companies. **Frequency:** triannual. **Remuneration:** grants of up to $25,000 (most grants $500–10,000) to cover foreign travel, housing, per diem and production costs. **Guidelines:** U.S. citizen or permanent resident who has been invited to international festival. **Application procedure:** completed application; copy of invitation from festival; full budget showing all costs of participation in festival and festival's contribution to these costs; work sample; bio. **Deadline:** 2 Sep 1996; 15 Jan 1997; 1 May 1997.

United States/Japan Creative Artists' Fellowships

Open to: creative, interpretive or traditional artists, including playwrights, translators, composers, librettists and lyricists. **Frequency:** annual. **Remuneration:** monthly stipend to cover housing, living expenses and modest professional support services; roundtrip transportation for artist and family members; stipend to study Japanese language in U.S., if necessary. **Guidelines:** U.S. citizen or permanent resident; to enable established artist to pursue discipline in Japan for 6 consecutive months; artists who have spent more than 3 months in Japan ineligible. **Application procedure:** write or call for guidelines and application materials. **Deadline:** TBA (Feb in 1996).

NATIONAL ENDOWMENT FOR THE ARTS
LITERATURE PROGRAM
1100 Pennsylvania Ave NW, Room 722; Washington, DC 20506;
(202) 682-5451
Gigi Bradford, *Director*

Fellowships for Translators

Next deadline for dramatic writers May 1997; guidelines available Mar 1997.

NATIONAL ENDOWMENT FOR THE ARTS,
THEATER
1100 Pennsylvania Ave NW; Washington, DC 20008; (202) 682-5509,
FAX 682-5669
Eleanor Denegre, *Theater and Musical Theater Specialist*

Theater Residency Program for Playwrights

Open to: playwrights. **Frequency:** annual (contingent on funding). **Remuneration:** $25,000 grant. **Guidelines:** U.S. citizen; applicant must have had play published or produced by professional theatre within last 5 years. **Application procedure:** completed application and supporting materials; write for guidelines after 30 Sep 1996. **Deadline:** TBA.

NATIONAL ENDOWMENT FOR THE HUMANITIES
PUBLIC PROGRAMS
1100 Pennsylvania Ave NW; Washington, DC 20506; (202) 606-8267
Nancy Rogers, *Director*

Humanities Projects in Media
James J. Dougherty, *Assistant Director* (202) 606-8278

Open to: independent producers, radio and television writers. **Frequency:** annual. **Remuneration:** varies. **Guidelines:** support for planning, writing and/or production of television and radio projects focused on subjects and issues central to the humanities, and aimed at an adult national or broad regional audience; eligible projects include dramatizations; no adaptations of literary works; write for guidelines. **Application procedure:** submit draft proposal before making formal application. **Deadline:** 6 Dec 1996. **Notification:** Jul 1997.

NATIONAL ENDOWMENT FOR THE HUMANITIES
RESEARCH AND EDUCATION PROGRAMS
1100 Pennsylvania Ave NW; Washington, DC 20506; (202) 606-8200
James Herbert, *Director*

Collaborative Research
Margot Backas (202) 606-8207: E-mail: mbackas@neh.fed.us

Open to: translators. **Frequency:** annual. **Remuneration:** grant; amount varies according to project. **Guidelines:** U.S. citizen or resident for 3 years; money to support individual or collaborative projects to translate into English works that provide insight into the history, literature, philosophy and artistic achievements of other cultures and that make available to scholars, students, teachers and the public the thought and learning of those civilizations. **Application procedure:** completed application and supporting materials; write for guidelines. **Deadline:** 1 Sep 1996. **Notification:** Apr 1997.

NEW PLAY COMMISSIONS IN JEWISH THEATRE
National Foundation for Jewish Culture; 330 Seventh Ave, 21st Floor;
    New York, NY 10001; (212) 629-0500
Rachel Novick, *Grants Administrator*

Open to: North American nonprofit theatres. **Frequency:** annual. **Remuneration:** grant of $1000–5000. **Guidelines:** 1 award a year to theatre that has completed at least 2 seasons of public performances and is commissioning new full-length play, adaptation, work for young audiences, musical or opera dealing substantively with issues of Jewish history, tradition, values or contemporary life; theatre must commit to presenting at least a public workshop production and/or staged reading of work, followed by discussion with audience; funds may be applied to commissioning fee, playwright's residency expenses or workshop costs; write for guidelines. **Application procedure:** completed proposal cover sheet and supporting materials, submitted by theatre. **Deadline:** Sep 1996; exact date TBA. **Notification:** spring 1997.

NEW YORK FOUNDATION FOR THE ARTS
ARTISTS' FELLOWSHIPS
155 Ave of the Americas, 14th Floor; New York, NY 10013-1507;
    (212) 366-6900, FAX 366-1778; E-mail nyfaafp@artswire.org
Penelope Dannenberg, *Director, Artists' Programs and Services*

Open to: playwrights, composers, screenwriters. **Frequency:** awards alternate biennially among disciplines. **Remuneration:** $7000 fellowship. **Guidelines:** NY State resident for 2 years prior to deadline; students ineligible. **Application procedure:** completed application and supporting materials; application seminars held each Sep. **Deadline:** next deadline for playwrights, composers and screenwriters fall 1997; exact date TBA.

PILGRIM PROJECT

156 Fifth Ave, Suite 400; New York, NY 10010; (212) 627-2288, FAX 627-2184
Davida Goldman, *Secretary*

Open to: playwrights, solo performers, individual producers and theatre companies. **Frequency:** ongoing. **Remuneration:** grant of $1000–7000. **Guidelines:** grant towards cost of reading, workshop production or full production of play that deals with questions of moral significance; write for further information. **Application procedure:** script only. **Deadline:** ongoing.

THE PLAYWRIGHTS' CENTER GRANT PROGRAMS

2301 Franklin Ave East; Minneapolis, MN 55406-1099; (612) 332-7481
Carlos Cuesta, *Executive Director*

Jerome Playwright-in-Residence Fellowships

Open to: playwrights, solo performers. **Frequency:** annual. **Remuneration:** 5 1-year fellowships of $7000. **Guidelines:** U.S. citizen or permanent resident; emerging playwright whose work has not received more than 2 professional full productions; fellow must spend year in residence at Center, where fellow has access to developmental workshops, readings and other services; send SASE for guidelines. **Application procedure:** completed application and supporting materials. **Deadline:** 16 Sep 1996. **Notification:** 15 Jan 1997. **Dates:** 1 Jul 1997–30 Jun 1998.

Many Voices Multicultural Collaboration Grants

Open to: playwrights, translators, composers, librettists, solo performers, screenwriters. **Frequency:** annual, contingent on funding. **Remuneration:** $200–2000 grant to each of 2–4 teams. **Guidelines:** team of 2 or more artists of differing cultural backgrounds with commitment from MN organization to produce proposed collaborative work; team's lead artist must be MN playwright of color. **Application procedure:** send SASE for guidelines. **Deadline:** 16 Sep 1996. **Notification:** 18 Nov 1996. **Dates:** 1 Jan 1997–1 Jan 1998.

Many Voices Playwriting Residency Awards

Open to: playwrights, solo performers. **Frequency:** annual, contingent on funding. **Remuneration:** 8 awards: $750 stipend, playwriting-class scholarship, 1-year Playwrights' Center membership, opportunity to participate in culturally focused playwriting roundtables, dramaturgical assistance, workshop and public reading. **Guidelines:** MN resident of color. **Application procedure:** send SASE for guidelines. **Deadline:** 16 Sep 1996. **Notification:** 2 Dec 1996. **Dates:** 1 Jan 1996–1 Jan 1997.

McKnight Advancement Grants

Open to: playwrights, solo performers. **Frequency:** annual. **Remuneration:** 3 grants of $8500; up to $1500 per fellow for workshops and staged readings using center's developmental program or for allocation to partner organization for joint development and/or production. **Guidelines:** U.S. citizen or permanent resident and legal MN resident since 1 May 1995; playwright of exceptional merit and potential who has had at least 2 plays fully produced by professional theatres; funds intended to significantly advance fellow's art and/or career and may be used to cover a variety of expenses, including writing time, residency at theatre or other arts organization, travel/study, production or presentation; fellow must participate actively in Center's outreach or educational programming (at least 20 hours), and must designate 2 months of grant year during which he or she plans to participate actively in Center's programs, including weekly attendance at and critical participation in readings and workshops of other members' work; send SASE for guidelines after 1 Dec 1996. **Application procedure:** completed application and supporting materials. **Deadline:** 3 Feb 1997. **Notification:** 1 May 1997. **Dates:** 1 Jul 1997–30 Jun 1998.

McKnight Fellowships

Open to: playwrights, solo performers. **Frequency:** annual. **Remuneration:** 2 fellowships of $10,000; up to $2000 program allocation to cover reading/workshop expenses; possible partial travel and living expenses for fellows living outside 150-mile radius of Twin Cities. **Guidelines:** U.S. citizen or permanent resident whose work has made significant impact on contemporary theatre and who has had at least 2 plays fully produced by professional theatres; fellow must spend 1 month in residence at Center, where fellow has access to developmental workshops, readings and other services; send SASE for guidelines after 15 Nov 1995. **Application procedure:** completed application and supporting materials. **Deadline:** 16 Jan 1997. **Notification:** 15 Apr 1997. **Dates:** 1 Jul 1997–30 Jun 1998.

PRINCESS GRACE AWARDS: PLAYWRIGHT FELLOWSHIP
Princess Grace Foundation–USA; 150 East 58th St, 21st Floor;
New York, NY 10155; (212) 317-1470, FAX 317-1473
(Ms.) Toby Boshak, *Executive Director*

Open to: playwrights. **Frequency:** annual. **Remuneration:** $7500 grant; 10-week residency with travel at New Dramatists, New York City (see entry in Membership and Service Organizations); inclusion of submitted script in New Dramatists' lending library and in its ScriptShare national script-distribution program for 1 year. **Guidelines:** U.S. citizen or permanent resident; under ordinary circumstances, playwright not more than 30 years of age at time of application; award based primarily on artistic quality of submitted play and potential of fellowship to assist writer's growth; original, unproduced, unpublished play (no adaptations); eligibility requirements and application procedures currently under review; write for guidelines. **Application procedures:** see guidelines. **Deadline:** 31 Mar 1997.

TCG Grant Programs

Theatre Communications Group; 355 Lexington Ave;
New York, NY 10017-0217; (212) 697-5230, FAX 983-4847
Fran Kumin, *Director of Artistic Programs*

Extended Collaboration Grants

E-mail grants@tcg.org

Open to: nonprofit theatres, in collaboration with playwrights. **Frequency:** annual, contingent on funding. **Remuneration:** grant of $5000 (4 awarded in 1995–96). **Guidelines:** augments normal development resources of TCG Constituent theatre by enabling playwright to develop work over an extended period of time in collaboration with director, designer, choreographer, composer and/or artist from another discipline; period of collaboration must exceed that which theatre would normally support; funds cover inter-city transportation within the U.S. and Canada and other expenses related to research and meetings among the collaborators. **Application procedure:** playwright may not apply; completed application submitted by artistic director of theatre. **Deadline:** late fall 1996 (contingent on funding).

National Theatre Artist Residency Program

E-mail ntarp@tcg.org

Category I: Residency Grants

Open to: playwrights, translators, composers, librettists, lyricists and other theatre artists in association with nonprofit professional theatres. **Frequency:** annual. **Remuneration:** approximately 10–14 grants of $50,000 or $100,000. **Guidelines:** experienced theatre artists who have created significant body of work and theatres with high artistic standards and organizational capacity to provide substantial support services to artists; funds cover compensation and residency expenses of 1 or 2 resident artists, working singly or in collaboration, during discrete periods used exclusively for residency-related activities that total at least 6 full months over 2-year period; proposals must be developed jointly by artists and institutions; theatres applying for $100,000 grant must have minimum operating budget of $500,000 in most recently completed fiscal year; theatres applying for $50,000 grant must have minimum operating budget of $250,000 in most recently completed fiscal year; write for guidelines. **Application procedure:** 2 copies of completed application and supporting materials. **Deadline:** write for 1997 deadlines.

Category II: Matching Grants to Continue Existing Residencies

Open to: previous Category I grant recipients. **Frequency:** annual, contingent on funding. **Remuneration:** $50,000 in matching funds. **Guidelines:** matching funds to support the continuation of particularly fruitful partnerships; to be considered, applicants must meet Category I eligibility requirements. **Application procedure:** 2 copies of completed application and supporting materials. **Deadline:** write for 1997 deadlines.

TRAVEL AND STUDY GRANT PROGRAM

c/o Jerome Foundation; West 1050, First National Bank Bldg; 332 Minnesota St;
St. Paul, MN 55101-1312; (612) 224-9431, FAX 224-3439
Cynthia Gehrig, *President*

Open to: theatre artists and administrators, including playwrights, composers, librettists and lyricists. **Frequency:** annual. **Remuneration:** grant of up to $5000 for foreign or domestic travel. **Guidelines:** resident of Twin Cities metropolitan area; program funded by Dayton-Hudson, General Mills and Jerome Foundation to support short-term travel or period of significant professional development through travel and study for independent professional artist or staff member of nonprofit organization; write for guidelines. **Application procedure:** completed application, work sample and resume. **Deadline:** TBA (2 Oct in 1995).

U.S.-MEXICO FUND FOR CULTURE

Londres 16 P.B.; Col. Juárez México, DF; Mexico 06600; 52-5-592-5386,
FAX 52-5-208-8943; E-mail cssport@servidor.unam.mx;
Web http://www.la#neta.apc.org/usmexcult/intro.html
Beatriz Nava, *Assistant to the Coordinator*

Open to: playwrights, translators, librettists, lyricists, screenwriters, TV and radio writers, and producing organizations. **Frequency:** annual. **Remuneration:** grants of $2000-25,000. **Guidelines:** Mexican and North American artists and cultural institutions; program sponsored by Bancomer Cultural Foundation, the Rockefeller Foundation and Mexico's National Fund for Culture and the Arts to fund performing arts projects of excellence that reflect artistic and cultural diversity of Mexico and U.S. and encourage mutual collaboration between artists of both countries; in media arts, script translation and adaptation of fiction, drama and poetry also considered; for brochure and application materials, send 78¢-postage SASE to U.S. Mexico Fund for Culture, c/o Benjamin Franklin Library, Laredo, TX 78044-3087. **Application procedure:** write for guidelines and application or see Web page. **Deadline:** 31 Mar 1996. **Notification:** Aug 1997.

THE WALT DISNEY STUDIOS FELLOWSHIP PROGRAM

500 South Buena Vista St; Burbank, CA 91521-0880; (818) 560-6894
Brenda Hathaway, *Program Administrator*

Open to: playwrights, screenwriters, television writers. **Frequency:** annual. **Remuneration:** 1-year salary of $30,000 for 10–15 writers; travel and 1 month's housing for fellows from outside Los Angeles area. **Guidelines:** to enable writers to work full-time at developing their craft in Disney Studios features or television division; no previous film or TV writing experience necessary; writer with Writers Guild of America credits eligible but should apply through the Guild's Employment Access at (213) 782-4648; call for guidelines. **Application procedure:** completed application and notarized standard letter agreement with resume and writing sample (for feature division: screenplay approximately 120 pages long or full-length play; for TV division: 30-minute TV script approximately 45 pages long, full-length play, or one-act more than 24 pages long). **Deadline:** TBA (spring in 1996 with no submission before 1 Apr 1996); call for exact date. **Notification:** Aug 1997. **Dates:** fellowship year begins Oct 1997.

Emergency Funds

How do emergency funds differ from other sources of financial aid?

Emergency funds are for writers in severe *temporary* financial difficulties. Some funds give outright grants, others make interest-free loans. For support for anything other than a genuine emergency, turn to Fellowships and Grants.

THE AUTHORS LEAGUE FUND

330 West 42nd St, 29th Floor; New York, NY 10036; (212) 268-1208,
    FAX 564-8363
Susan Drury, *Administrator*

Open to: playwrights. **Type of assistance:** interest-free loan; no restriction on amount but request should be limited to immediate needs. **Guidelines:** published or produced working professional; must demonstrate real need. **Application procedure:** completed application and supporting materials. **Notification:** 2–4 weeks.

CARNEGIE FUND FOR AUTHORS
1 Old Country Rd, Suite 113; Carle Place, NY 11514

Open to: playwrights. **Type of assistance:** emergency grant. **Guidelines:** playwright who has had at least 1 play or collection of plays published commercially in book form (anthologies excluded); emergency which has placed applicant in substantial verifiable financial need. **Application procedure:** write for application form.

CHANGE
Box 705, Cooper Station; New York, NY 10276; (212) 473-3742

Open to: playwrights, composers, librettists, lyricists. **Type of assistance:** grant of up to $1000. **Guidelines:** to assist in emergency financial situation such as overdue medical bills, utility turnoffs, eviction or fire damage; applicant must verify professional status and financial need; students ineligible; write or call for fact sheet. **Application procedure:** apply by letter only, detailing financial emergency and explaining its causes; enclose copies of outstanding bills or eviction notices, resume, reviews, production announcements and at least 2 letters from theatre professionals verifying applicant's professional status.

THE DRAMATISTS GUILD FUND
330 West 42nd St, 29th Floor; New York, NY 10036; (212) 268-1208
        FAX 564-8363
Susan Drury, *Administrator*

Open to: playwrights, composers, librettists, lyricists. **Type of assistance:** interest-free loan; no restriction on amount but request should be limited to immediate needs. **Guidelines:** published or produced working professional; must demonstrate real need. **Application procedure:** completed application and supporting materials. **Notification:** 2–4 weeks.

PEN FUND FOR WRITERS & EDITORS WITH AIDS
PEN American Center; 568 Broadway; New York, NY 10012; (212) 334-1660,
        FAX 334-2181; E-mail pen@echonyc.com
India Amos, *Program Coordinator*

Open to: playwrights, translators. **Type of assistance:** grant or interest-free loan of up to $500. **Guidelines:** emergency assistance for published or produced writer in financial difficulties due to HIV or AIDS-related illness. **Application procedure:** completed application, work sample, documentation of financial emergency and resume. **Notification:** within 6–8 weeks.

PEN Writers Fund

PEN American Center; 568 Broadway; New York, NY 10012; (212) 334-1660,
FAX 334-2181; E-mail pen@echonyc.com
India Amos, *Program Coordinator*

Open to: playwrights, translators. **Type of assistance:** grant or interest-free loan of up to $500. **Guidelines:** emergency assistance for published or produced writer in financial difficulties. **Application procedure:** completed application, work sample, documentation of financial emergency and resume. **Notification:** within 6–8 weeks.

State Arts Agencies

What can my state arts agency do for me?

Possibly quite a bit—the only way to find out is to ask your agency for guidelines and study them carefully. State programs vary greatly and change frequently. Most have some sort of residency requirement, but eligibility is not always restricted to current residents, and may include people who were born in, raised in, attended school in or had some other association with the state in question.

What if my state doesn't give grants to individual artists?

A number of state arts agencies are restricted in this way. However, those with such restrictions, by and large, are eager to help artists locate nonprofit organizations that channel funds to individuals; you should ask specifically about this.

The New York State Council on the Arts, for example, is prohibited from funding individuals directly, and must contract with a sponsoring nonprofit organization when it awards grants to individual artists. Yet NYSCA has a number of ways of supporting the work of theatre writers. The Literature Program funds, in alternate years, translations, and writers' residencies in communities. The Individual Artists Program assists nonprofit organizations in commissioning works, including plays, music-theatre pieces; theatre and composers' commissions are also granted in alternate years. Moreover, NYSCA subgrants funds to the New York Foundation for the Arts, which in turn provides project development assistance for individual artists and creative teams (see NYFA Sponsorship

Program in Development) and funds fellowships (see Fellowships and Grants). NYFA also assists residencies (see Artists in Residence Program in Colonies and Residencies).

At the least, every state has some kind of Artist-in-Education program; if you are able and willing to function in an educational setting you should certainly investigate this possibility.

ALABAMA STATE COUNCIL ON THE ARTS
1 Dexter Ave; Montgomery, AL 36130-1800; (334) 242-4076, FAX 240-3269
Al Head, *Executive Director*

ALASKA STATE COUNCIL ON THE ARTS
411 West 4th Ave, Suite 1E; Anchorage, AK 99501-2343; (907) 269-6610,
FAX 269-6601; E-mail tjwasca@tmn.com
Timothy Wilson, *Executive Director*

AMERICAN SAMOA COUNCIL ON CULTURE, ARTS AND HUMANITIES
Box 1540; Office of the Governor; Pago Pago, AS 96799; 684-633-4347,
FAX 684-633-2059
(Mrs.) Fa'ailoilo Lauvao, *Executive Director*

ARIZONA COMMISSION ON THE ARTS
417 West Roosevelt St; Phoenix, AZ 85003; (602) 255-5882, FAX 256-0282
Shelley Cohn, *Executive Director*

ARKANSAS ARTS COUNCIL
1500 Tower Bldg; 323 Center St; Little Rock, AR 72201; (501) 324-9766,
FAX 324-9154; E-mail jim@dah.state.ar.us
Jim Mitchell, *Executive Director*

CALIFORNIA ARTS COUNCIL
1300 I St; Sacramento, CA 95814; (916) 322-6555, FAX 322-6575;
E-mail calartcl@tmn.com
Barbara Pieper, *Executive Director*

COLORADO COUNCIL ON THE ARTS
750 Pennsylvania St; Denver, CO 80203; (303) 894-2617, FAX 894-2615;
E-mail coarts@tmn.com
Fran Holden, *Executive Director*

CONNECTICUT COMMISSION ON THE ARTS
Gold Building; 755 Main St; Hartford, CT 06103; (860) 566-4770,
FAX 566-6462
John Ostrout, *Executive Director*

DELAWARE DIVISION OF THE ARTS

Carvel State Office Bldg; 820 North French St; Wilmington, DE 19801;
(302) 577-3540, FAX 577-6561; E-mail delarts@tmn.com
Peggy Amsterdam, *Director*

DISTRICT OF COLUMBIA (DC) COMMISSION
ON THE ARTS AND HUMANITIES

410 8th St NW, 5th Floor; Washington, DC 20004; (202) 724-5613,
FAX 727-4135
Pamela Holt, *Executive Director*

FLORIDA DIVISION OF CULTURAL AFFAIRS

Department of State, The Capitol; Tallahassee, FL 32399-0250; (904) 487-2980,
FAX 922-5259
(Ms.) Peyton C. Fearington, *Executive Director*

GEORGIA COUNCIL FOR THE ARTS

530 Means St NW, Suite 115; Atlanta, GA 30318; (404) 651-7920,
FAX 651-7922
Caroline Ballard Leake, *Executive Director*

GUAM COUNCIL ON THE ARTS & HUMANITIES AGENCY

Office of the Governor; Box 2950; Agana, GU 96910; 671-475-CAHA,
FAX 671-472-ART1
Deborah Bordallo, *Executive Director*

STATE FOUNDATION ON CULTURE
AND THE ARTS (HAWAII)

44 Merchant St; Honolulu, HI 96813; (808) 586-0306, FAX 586-0308;
E-mail 44sfca@tmn.com
Wendell Silva, *Executive Director*

IDAHO COMMISSION ON THE ARTS

Box 83720; Boise, ID 83720-0008; (208) 334-2119, FAX 334-2488;
E-mail idarts@tmn.com
Margot H. Knight, *Executive Director*

ILLINOIS ARTS COUNCIL

State of Illinois Center; 100 West Randolph St, Suite 10-500; Chicago, IL 60601;
(312) 814-6750, FAX 814-1471; E-mail brose@tmn.com
Lori Spear Montana, *Executive Director*

INDIANA ARTS COMMISSION

402 West Washington St, Room 072; Indianapolis, IN 46204; (317) 232-1268, FAX 232-5595
Dorothy Ilgen, *Executive Director*

IOWA ARTS COUNCIL

Capitol Complex; 600 East Locust; Des Moines, IA 50319; (515) 281-4451, FAX 242-6498
William H. Jackson, *Executive Director*

KANSAS ARTS COMMISSION

Jayhawk Tower; 700 Southwest Jackson, Suite 1004; Topeka, KS 66603; (913) 296-3335, FAX 296-4989
Eric Hayashi, *Executive Director*

KENTUCKY ARTS COUNCIL

31 Fountain Pl; Frankfort, KY 40601; (502) 564-3757, FAX 564-2839
Dennis Horn, *Acting Director*

LOUISIANA DIVISION OF THE ARTS

Box 44247; Baton Rouge, LA 70804; (504) 342-8180, FAX 342-8173
James Borders, *Executive Director*

MAINE ARTS COMMISSION

55 Capitol St; State House Station 25; Augusta, ME 04333; (207) 287-2724, FAX 287-2335
Alden C. Wilson, *Executive Director*

MARYLAND STATE ARTS COUNCIL

601 North Howard St, 1st Floor; Baltimore, MD 21201; (410) 333-8232, FAX 333-1062
Jim Backas, *Executive Director*

MASSACHUSETTS CULTURAL COUNCIL

120 Boylston St, 2nd Floor; Boston, MA 02116-4600; (617) 727-3668, FAX 727-0044
Mary Kelley, *Executive Director*

MICHIGAN COUNCIL FOR THE ARTS & CULTURAL AFFAIRS

1200 6th Ave, Executive Plaza; Detroit, MI 48226-2461; (313) 256-3731, FAX 256-3781; E-mail mcacal@tmn.com
Betty Boone, *Executive Director*

MINNESOTA STATE ARTS BOARD
Park Square Court; 400 Sibley St, Suite 200; St. Paul, MN 55102;
(612) 215-1600, FAX 215-1602; E-mail casey@tmn.com
Sam Grabarski, *Executive Director*

MISSISSIPPI ARTS COMMISSION
239 North Lamar St, 2nd Floor; Jackson, MS 39201; (601) 359-6030, -6040,
FAX 359-6008; E-mail msarts@tmn.com
Betsy Bradley, *Executive Director*

MISSOURI ARTS COUNCIL
111 North 7th St, Suite 105; St. Louis, MO 63101; (314) 340-6845,
FAX 340-7215
Anthony Radich, *Executive Director*

MONTANA ARTS COUNCIL
316 North Park Ave, Room 252; Box 202201; Helena, MT 59620-2201;
(406) 444-6430, FAX 444-6548; E-mail montana@tmn.com
Arlynn Fishbaugh, *Executive Director*

NEBRASKA ARTS COUNCIL
Joslyn Castle Carriage House; 3838 Davenport; Omaha, NE 68131-2329;
(402) 595-2122, FAX 595-2334; E-mail lindanac@tmn.com
Jennifer Severin Clark, *Executive Director*

NEVADA STATE COUNCIL ON THE ARTS
Capitol Complex; 602 North Curry St; Carson City, NV 89710; (702) 687-6680,
FAX 687-6688
Susan Boskoff, *Executive Director*

NEW HAMPSHIRE STATE COUNCIL ON THE ARTS
40 North Main St, Phenix Hall; Concord, NH 03301; (603) 271-2789,
FAX 271-3584
Rebecca Lawrence, *Acting Director*

NEW JERSEY STATE COUNCIL ON THE ARTS
20 West State St, 3rd Floor, CN 306; Trenton, NJ 08625-0306; (609) 292-6130,
FAX 989-1440; E-mail njscaaah@tmn.com
Barbara Russo, *Executive Director*

NEW MEXICO ARTS DIVISION
228 East Palace Ave; Santa Fe, NM 87501; (505) 827-6490, FAX 827-6043
Lara Morrow, *Director*

NEW YORK STATE COUNCIL ON THE ARTS
915 Broadway; New York, NY 10010; (212) 387-7000, FAX 387-7164;
E-mail nysca@tmn.com
Al Berr, *Acting Executive Director*

NORTH CAROLINA ARTS COUNCIL
Department of Cultural Resources; Raleigh, NC 27611; (919) 733-2821,
FAX 733-4834; E-mail ncartscl@tmn.com
Mary Regan, *Executive Director*

NORTH DAKOTA COUNCIL ON THE ARTS
418 East Broadway, Suite 70; Bismarck, ND 58501-4086; (701) 328-3954,
FAX 328-3963; E-mail ndca@tmn.com
Patsy Thompson, *Executive Director*

COMMONWEALTH COUNCIL FOR ARTS AND CULTURE (NORTHERN MARIANA ISLANDS)
Box 5553, CHRB; Saipan, MP 96950; 670-322-9982, -9983, FAX 670-322-9028
Margarita De Leon Guerrero Wonenberg, *Executive Director*

OHIO ARTS COUNCIL
727 East Main St; Columbus, OH 43205; (614) 466-2613, FAX 466-4494;
E-mail wlawson@mail.oac.ohio.gov
Wayne Lawson, *Executive Director*

STATE ARTS COUNCIL OF OKLAHOMA
Jim Thorpe Bldg; Box 52001-2001; Oklahoma City, OK 73152-2001;
(405) 521-2931, FAX 521-6418; E-mail okarts@tmn.com
Betty Price, *Executive Director*

OREGON ARTS COMMISSION
775 Summer St, NE; Salem, OR 97310; (503) 986-0082, FAX 986-0260;
E-mail christine.t.darcy@state.or.us
Christine D'Arcy, *Executive Director*

PENNSYLVANIA COUNCIL ON THE ARTS
Finance Bldg, Room 216; Harrisburg, PA 17120; (717) 787-6883, FAX 783-2538
Philip Horn, *Executive Director*

INSTITUTE OF PUERTO RICAN CULTURE
Box 4184; San Juan, PR 00902-4184; (809) 723-2115, FAX 722-2033
Dr. Luis Diaz Hernandez, *Executive Director*

RHODE ISLAND STATE COUNCIL ON THE ARTS
95 Cedar St, Suite 103; Providence, RI 02903-1034; (401) 277-3880,
FAX 521-1351; E-mail ae418@osfn.rhilinet.gov
Randall Rosenbaum, *Executive Director*

SOUTH CAROLINA ARTS COMMISSION
1800 Gervais St; Columbia, SC 29201; (803) 734-8696, FAX 734-8526;
E-mail kenmay@tmn.com
Suzette Surkamer, *Executive Director*

SOUTH DAKOTA ARTS COUNCIL
Office of the Arts; 800 Governors Dr; Pierre, SD 57501-2294; (605) 733-3131,
FAX 773-6962; E-mail dennish@deca.state.sd.us
Dennis Holub, *Executive Director*

TENNESSEE ARTS COMMISSION
404 James Robertson Pkwy; Parkway Towers, Suite 160;
Nashville, TN 37243-0780; (615) 741-1701, FAX 741-8559;
E-mail btarleton@mail.state.tn.us
Bennett Tarleton, *Executive Director*

TEXAS COMMISSION ON THE ARTS
Box 13406, Capitol Station; Austin, TX 78711; (512) 463-5535, FAX 475-2699
John Paul Batiste, *Executive Director*

UTAH ARTS COUNCIL
617 East South Temple St; Salt Lake City, UT 84102; (801) 533-5895,
FAX 533-6196; E-mail jeanirwi@tmn.com
Bonnie Stephens, *Executive Director*

VERMONT COUNCIL ON THE ARTS
136 State St, Drawer 33; Montpelier, VT 05633-6001; (802) 828-3291,
FAX 828-3363
Nicolette Clarke, *Executive Director*

VIRGIN ISLANDS COUNCIL ON THE ARTS
41-42 Norre Gade; Box 103; St. Thomas, VI 00804; (809) 774-5984,
FAX 774-6206
John Jowers, *Executive Director*

VIRGINIA COMMISSION FOR THE ARTS
223 Governor St; Richmond VA 23219; (804) 225-3132, FAX 225-4327;
E-mail vacomm@tmn.com
Peggy Baggett, *Executive Director*

WASHINGTON STATE ARTS COMMISSION

Box 42675; Olympia, WA 98504-2675; (360) 753-3860, FAX 586-5351;
E-mail wsac@tmn.com
Karen Kamara Gose, *Executive Director*

ARTS & HUMANITIES SECTION
WEST VIRGINIA DIVISION OF CULTURE & HISTORY

1900 Kanawha Blvd E; Charleston, WV 25305; (304) 558-0240, FAX 558-2779
Lakin Ray Cook, *Executive Director*

WISCONSIN ARTS BOARD

101 East Wilson St, 1st Floor; Madison, WI 53702; (608) 266-0190,
FAX 267-0380
Dean Amhaus, *Executive Director*

WYOMING ARTS COUNCIL

2320 Capitol Ave; Cheyenne, WY 82002; (307) 777-7742, FAX 777-5499;
E-mail wyoarts@tmn.com
John G. Coe, *Executive Director*

Colonies and Residencies

What entries make up this section?

Though artist colonies that admit theatre writers constitute the majority of the listings, there are other kinds of residencies, such as artist-in-residence positions at universities, listed here as well. You can also find listings in the Development and Fellowships and Grants sections that could be considered residencies. Finally, we have included several "writers' rooms" where playwrights in need of a quiet place for uninterrupted work are welcome.

Note: you should assume that each deadline listed in this section is the date application materials must be *received*, unless you have ascertained that it is the postmark date.

THE ADAMANT PROGRAM

Box 73; Adamant, VT 05640-0073; (802) 223-2324, -3347, FAX 223-0915
Patricia Hutchinson, *Resident Manager*

Open to: playwrights, composers, screenwriters. **Description:** residencies of 2–8 weeks for artists, including writers, composers and visual artists, at retreat in small VT village of Adamant, near Montpelier; small individual studio in woods and private bedroom in 1 of 2 main houses; experimental theatre for the use of playwrights, grand pianos available for composers; lunch and dinner provided, residents make own breakfast and share housekeeping chores. **Financial**

arrangement: resident pays $25 a day towards cost of room, board and studio; very limited number of fellowships available for those who show genuine need. **Guidelines:** creative artist with professional standing in field; less established artists of recognized ability also considered; write for guidelines. **Application procedure:** completed application, work sample, 3 references and $10 fee. **Deadline:** 30 May 1997. **Dates:** Sep–Oct.

ALDEN B. DOW CREATIVITY CENTER
Northwood University; 3225 Cook Road; Midland, MI 48640-2398;
(517) 837-4478, FAX 837-4468
Carol B. Coppage, *Executive Director*

Open to: playwrights, translators, composers, librettists, lyricists, screenwriters. **Description:** 4 "Creativity Fellowships" each year for individuals working in any field, including the arts; 8-week summer residency at Northwood University, which provides environment for intense independent study; program includes interaction among fellows and formal presentation of work in Aug. **Financial arrangement:** travel, room, board, $750 for personal expenses and project materials. **Guidelines:** projects that are creative, original and have potential for impact on applicant's field; prefers 1 applicant per project; no accommodation for spouses or children. **Application procedure:** completed application, brief project description, budget, work sample, resume and $10 application fee. **Deadline:** 31 Dec 1996. **Notification:** 1 Apr 1997. **Dates:** Jun–Aug 1997.

ALTOS DE CHAVON
c/o Parsons School of Design; 2 West 13th St, Room 707; New York, NY 10011;
(212) 229-5370, FAX 229-5370; E-mail altos@spacelab.net
Stephen D. Kaplan, *Arts/Education Director*

Open to: playwrights, composers, screenwriters. **Description:** residencies of 3½ months for 15 artists a year, 1–2 of whom may be writers or composers, at nonprofit arts center located in tropical Caribbean surroundings 8 miles from town of La Romana in the Dominican Republic; efficiency studios or apartments with kitchenettes; small individual studios nearby; small visual-arts-oriented library; no typewriters for writers. **Financial arrangement:** $100 nonreturnable reservation fee; resident pays rent of $300 a month and provides own meals (estimated cost $20 a day). **Guidelines:** prefers Spanish-speaking artists who can use talents to benefit community, and whose work relates to Dominican or Latin American context; residents may teach workshops and are expected to contribute to group exhibition/performance at end of stay; write for further information. **Application procedure:** letter explaining applicant's interest in program, work sample and resume. **Deadline:** 1 Jul 1997. **Notification:** 15 Aug 1997. **Dates:** residencies start 1 Feb 1998, 1 Jun 1998, 1 Sep 1998.

APOSTLE ISLANDS NATIONAL LAKESHORE

Route 1, Box 4; Bayfield, WI 54814; (715) 779-3397, FAX 779-3049
Kate L. Miller, *Chief, Resources Education*

Open to: playwrights, composers, lyricists, solo performers. **Description:** 1 writer, poet, visual artist or choreographer at a time housed for 2–3 weeks on island in national park; cabin near beach and forest; no running water or electricity; resident must bring 2–3 week supply of food. **Financial arrangement:** free housing. **Guidelines:** writer with accomplishment, artistic integrity and ability to relate to park through their work; must donate 1 work to colony and communicate experience of residency through 1 program for public. **Application procedure:** completed application, project description, work sample, resume and cover letter. **Deadline:** 31 Dec 1996; no submission before 1 Oct 1996. **Notification:** 15 Feb 1997. **Dates:** Jun–Sep.

ATLANTIC CENTER FOR THE ARTS

1414 Art Center Ave; New Smyrna Beach, FL 32168; (904) 427-6975;
    (800) 393-6975, FAX (904) 427-5669; E-mail acansb@aol.com
Suzanne Fetscher, *Executive Director*
Nicholas Conroy, *Program Director*

Open to: playwrights, composers. **Description:** 6 1–3-week workshops each year offering writers and visual and performing artists opportunity of concentrated study with internationally known Master Artists-in-Residence. **Financial arrangement:** resident pays $100 a week for tuition, $25 a day for private room with bath; limited scholarships available. **Application procedure:** Master Artist specifies submission materials and selects participants; write or call for brochure. **Deadline:** 4 months before residency. **Notification:** 3 months before residency. **Dates:** TBA; see brochure.

BLUE MOUNTAIN CENTER

Blue Mountain Lake, NY 12812; (518) 352-7391
Harriet Barlow, *Director*

Open to: playwrights, composers, librettists, lyricists, solo performers. **Description:** 4-week residencies for 14 writers, composers and visual artists at center in Adirondack Mountains. **Financial arrangement:** free room and board; voluntary contribution requested. **Guidelines:** artist whose work is aimed at a general audience and reflects social concerns. **Application procedure:** statement of plan for work at center, including preference for early or late summer or fall residency; 10-page work sample, bio, reviews and list of previous BMC residents whom you know, if any; $20 fee. **Deadline:** 1 Feb 1997. **Notification:** early Apr 1997. **Dates:** mid-Jun–mid-Oct 1997.

BYRDCLIFFE ART COLONY
The Woodstock Guild; 34 Tinker St; Woodstock, NY 12498; (914) 679-2079,
    FAX 679-4529
Artists Residency Program

Open to: playwrights, translators, librettists, lyricists, solo performers, screenwriters. **Description:** 10 concurrent summer residencies of 1–4 4-week sessions for artists in all disciplines at historic 600-acre colony in the Catskill Mountains, 1½ miles from Woodstock village center, 90 miles north of New York City; private room and separate individual studio space in Villetta Inn, spacious turn-of-the-century mountain lodge; common dining room and living room; residents provide own meals, using community kitchen. **Financial arrangement:** resident pays fee of $400 for Jun session, $500 for Jul session, $500 for Aug session, $400 for Sep session; reductions offered to residents staying more than 1 session; limited scholarships available to eligible applicants. **Guidelines:** proof of serious commitment to field of endeavor is major criterion for acceptance; professional recognition helpful but not essential; send SASE for further information. **Application procedure:** completed application, work sample, project description, resume, reviews and articles if available, contact information for 2 references and $5 fee. **Deadline:** 15 Apr (applications received after deadline considered for any space still available). **Dates:** Jun–Sep.

CAMARGO FOUNDATION
B.P. 75; 13260 Cassis; France; 33-42-01-1157, -1311
Michael Pretina, *Director*
U.S. Office:
W1050 First National Bank Bldg; 332 Minnesota St; St. Paul, MN 55101

Open to: playwrights, translators, composers. **Description:** 11 concurrent residencies, most for scholars and teachers pursuing projects relative to Francophone culture, but also including 1 for writer, 1 for composer and 1 for visual artist, at estate in ancient Mediterranean fishing port 30 minutes from Marseilles; furnished apartments; music studio available for composer. **Financial arrangement:** free housing; residents provide own meals. **Guidelines:** resident outlines project to fellow colony members during stay and writes final report; families welcome when space available; write to U.S. office for guidelines. **Application procedure:** completed application, project description, bio and 3 letters of recommendation. **Deadline:** 1 Feb 1997. **Notification:** 5 Apr 1997. **Dates:** Sep–Dec; Jan–May.

CENTRUM ARTIST-IN-RESIDENCY PROGRAM
Fort Worden State Park; Box 1158; Port Townsend, WA 98368; (360) 385-3102,
    FAX 385-2470
Marlene Bennett, *Residency Coordinator*

Open to: playwrights, translators, composers, librettists, lyricists, solo performers, television and screenwriters. **Description:** 1-month residencies for writers, composers, poets, visual artists and choreographers at center near Victorian seaport in 440-acre Fort Worden State Park; self-contained cottages near beach and hiking trails; separate studio space. **Financial arrangement:** $300 stipend. **Guidelines:** artist who has clear direction and substantial accomplishment in field. **Application procedure:** completed application, project description, work sample, resume and $10 fee. **Deadline:** 1 Oct 1996. **Notification:** 1 Nov 1996. **Dates:** Sep–May.

CHATEAU DE LESVAULT
58370 Onlay; Villapourçon; France; 33-86-843291, FAX -843578
Bibbi Lee, *Director*

Open to: playwrights, translators, librettists. **Description:** 5 concurrent winter residencies at 19th-century French château located in "le Morvan," a national park in western Burgundy 3½ hours from Paris, 3 hours from Geneva; large bedroom/studio with private bath; use of salon, library and grounds. **Financial arrangement:** resident pays Fr. 4500 (about $900) a month or Fr. 2500 (about $500) for 2 weeks, which covers room, utilities, and meals 7 days a week. **Application procedure:** brief description of project, maximum 3-page work sample, list of publications (if any) and 2 references; 50% deposit required 30 days before start of residency. **Deadline:** 90 days before proposed residency. **Dates:** Oct–Apr.

DJERASSI RESIDENT ARTISTS PROGRAM
2325 Bear Gulch Rd; Woodside, CA 94062-4405; (415) 747-1250,
     FAX 747-0105; E-mail djerassi@artswire.com
Charles Amirkhanian, *Executive Director*
Carol Law, *General Manager*

Open to: playwrights, translators, composers, librettists, lyricists, solo performers, screenwriters. **Description:** 1-month residencies for writers; choreographers; composers; media, visual and interdisciplinary artists and performers concurrently at 600-acre ranch in Santa Cruz mountains 1 hour south of San Francisco; interdisciplinary projects encouraged; collaborative projects considered. **Financial arrangement:** free room and board. **Guidelines:** emerging or established artist whose work has clear direction; send SASE for application. **Application procedure:** completed application, sample of published work or work-in-progress, resume and $25 fee. **Deadline:** 15 Feb 1997 for 1998 residencies. **Dates:** Apr–Oct.

DORLAND MOUNTAIN ARTS COLONY
Box 6; Temecula, CA 92593; (909) 676-5039
Admissions

Open to: playwrights, composers, lyricists. **Description:** 1-month residencies for 6 writers, composers and visual artists concurrently in individual studios on 300-acre nature preserve 50 miles northeast of San Diego; no electricity. **Financial arrangement:** $50 processing fee on acceptance; resident pays rent of $300 a month. **Guidelines:** artist must demonstrate clear direction and accomplishment in field. **Application procedure:** send SASE for application and information. **Deadline:** 1 Sep 1996; 1 Mar 1997. **Notification:** 2 months.

DORSET COLONY FOR WRITERS

Box 519; Dorset, VT 05251; (802) 867-2223, FAX 867-0144
John Nassivera, *Executive Director*

Open to: playwrights, composers, librettists, lyricists and collaborative teams.
Description: residencies of 1 week–1 month at house located in historic village in
southern VT. **Financial arrangement:** resident pays fee for housing according to
means (suggested fee $95 a week); meals not provided; large, fully equipped
kitchen. **Guidelines:** artist must demonstrate seriousness of purpose and have
record of professional achievement (readings or productions of works); work
sample may be requested from less established artist. **Application procedure:** letter
of inquiry with description of proposed project and desired length and dates of
stay; resume. **Deadline:** open. **Dates:** 1 Oct–1 Jun.

FINE ARTS WORK CENTER IN PROVINCETOWN

24 Pearl St; Provincetown, MA 02657; (508) 487-9960, FAX 487-8873
Michael Wilkerson, *Executive Director*

Open to: playwrights. **Description:** 21 concurrent residencies of 7 months for
writers, poets and visual artists, including 1 playwright, at 6-building complex on
tip of Cape Cod; studio/living spaces with kitchens; residents provide own meals.
Financial arrangement: $375 monthly stipend. **Guidelines:** emerging artists.
Application procedure: completed application form, work sample and $35
application fee. **Deadline:** 1 Feb 1997. **Dates:** 1 Oct–1 May.

THE HAMBIDGE CENTER FOR CREATIVE ARTS AND SCIENCES

Box 339; Rabun Gap, GA 30568; (706) 746-5718, FAX 746-9933;
    E-mail jbarber@purple.tmn.com
Judith Barber, *Executive Director*

Open to: playwrights, translators, composers, librettists, lyricists. **Description:**
residencies of 2 weeks–2 months for professionals in all areas of arts and
humanities on 600 acres in northeast GA mountains; 7 private cottages with
bedroom, kitchen, bathroom and studio/work area; evening meal provided
Mon–Fri, May–Oct only; send SASE for guidelines. **Financial arrangement:**
resident pays $125 a week toward total cost. **Application procedure:** completed
application, work sample, resume, reviews and 3 letters of recommendation from
professionals in applicant's field. **Deadline:** 31 Jan 1997; 31 Aug 1997. **Notification:** 2–3 months. **Dates:** year-round; most residencies May–Oct.

HAWTHORNDEN CASTLE
INTERNATIONAL RETREAT FOR WRITERS

Lasswade, Midlothian; Scotland EH18 1EG; 441-31-440-2180
Administrator

Open to: playwrights. **Description:** spring, summer and fall residencies of 4 weeks
at medieval castle on secluded crag overlooking valley of the River Esk 8 miles
south of Edinburgh; 5 writers in residence at any one time; fully furnished study-

bedroom; communal breakfast and dinner, lunch brought to writer's room; typewriter rental and use of excellent libraries in Edinburgh can be arranged. **Financial arrangement:** free room and board. **Guidelines:** author of at least 1 published work. **Application procedure:** write for application and further information. **Deadline:** 30 Sep 1996. **Notification:** mid-Jan 1997. **Dates:** Feb–Dec 1997.

HEADLANDS CENTER FOR THE ARTS
944 Fort Barry; Sausalito, CA 94965; (415) 331-2787, FAX 331-3857
Kathryn Reasoner, *Executive Director*

Open to: playwrights, composers, librettists, lyricists, screenwriters, television writers. **Description:** residencies of 1–3 months for artists in all disciplines at center in national park on 13,000 acres of coastal wilderness across the bay from San Francisco; accommodation in 4-bedroom house with communal kitchen; evening meal provided in mess hall Sun–Thur; 11-month "live-out" residencies available for Bay Area artists only, providing studio space, 2 meals a week and access to center's facilities but no housing; all residents encouraged to interact with fellow artists in other media and with the environment. **Financial arrangement:** stipend of $500 a month, travel and free housing for artist from outside Bay Area; $2500 stipend and studio space for Bay Area artist. **Guidelines:** CA, NC or OH residents only; students ineligible. **Application procedure:** call or write for information (applications available Apr 1997). **Deadline:** Jun 1997 (exact date TBA). **Dates:** Feb–Dec 1998.

HEDGEBROOK
2197 East Millman Rd; Langley, WA 98260; (360) 321-4786
Linda Bowers, *Director*

Open to: playwrights, librettists, solo performers. **Description:** residencies of 1 week–3 months for women writers of diverse cultural backgrounds working in all literary genres; 6 individual cottages on 30 wooded acres on Whidbey Island, near Seattle; writer furnishes own typewriter or computer. **Financial arrangement:** free room and board. **Guidelines:** woman writer of any age, published or unpublished; women of color encouraged to apply. **Application procedure:** send SASE for application; submit completed application, project description and work sample. **Deadline:** 1 Oct 1996 for winter–spring 1997; 1 Apr 1997 for summer–fall 1997. **Notification:** 2 months.

HELENE WURLITZER FOUNDATION OF NEW MEXICO
Box 545; Taos, NM 87571; (505) 758-2413, FAX 758-2559

Open to: playwrights, composers, librettists, lyricists, screenwriters, television and radio writers. **Description:** 12 studio/apartments available to creative artists working in all media (performing artists ineligible); length of residency flexible, usually 3 months. **Financial arrangement:** free housing and utilities; resident provides own meals; no financial aid. **Application procedure:** completed application with project description, work sample and resume. **Deadline:** open. **Dates:** 1 Apr–30 Sep.

ISLE ROYALE NATIONAL PARK ARTIST-IN-RESIDENCE

800 East Lakeshore Dr; Haughton, MI 49931; (906) 482-7860 or 487-7150, FAX 487-7170
Gayle Pekkala or Greg Blust, *Coordinators*

Open to: playwrights, composers, lyricists, solo performers. **Description:** 1 writer or visual artist at a time housed for 2–3 weeks on remote island in national park; cabin near Lake Superior; no electricity; resident must bring 2–3 week supply of food. **Financial arrangement:** free housing. **Guidelines:** writer with artistic integrity and ability to relate to park through their work; must donate 1 work to colony and communicate experience of residency through programs for public. **Application procedure:** completed application form, project description, work sample and resume. **Deadline:** 15 Feb 1997. **Notification:** 15 Apr 1997. **Dates:** Jun–Sep.

THE JAMES THURBER WRITER-IN-RESIDENCE

The Thurber House; 77 Jefferson Ave; Columbus, OH 43215; (614) 464-1032, FAX 228-7445
Michael J. Rosen, *Literary Director*

Open to: playwrights. **Description:** 4 residencies a year, each for 1 academic quarter (2 for journalists, 1 for playwright, 1 for poet or fiction writer); writer teaches course at Ohio State University. **Financial arrangement:** $5000 stipend; 2-bedroom apartment provided. **Guidelines:** playwright who has had at least 1 play produced by a major theatre; teaching experience helpful; write or call for further information. **Application procedure:** letter of interest and curriculum vita. **Deadline:** 15 Dec 1996. **Notification:** within 2 months. **Dates:** winter or spring 1998.

JENNY MCKEAN MOORE VISITING WRITER IN WASHINGTON

Department of English; The George Washington University; Washington, DC 20052; (202) 994-6180
Christopher Sten, *English Department*

Open to: writers of poetic drama. **Description:** 1-year fellowship/teaching position for creative writers (residency rotates among disciplines); fellow gives public reading of own work in fall and teaches a community writing workshop and 1 class for GWU students each semester. **Financial arrangement:** minimum salary of $40,000, benefits, moving allowance. **Guidelines:** practicing writer with experience of and commitment to teaching; conventional academic credentials not necessary; must reside in Washington area Sep–May of residency year. **Application procedure:** work sample, resume and letters of recommendation; write for details. **Deadline:** TBA for playwrights (15 Nov in 1995).

THE JOHN STEINBECK WRITER'S ROOM

Long Island University–Southampton Campus Library; Southampton, NY 11968;
 (516) 287-8382, FAX 287-4049; E-mail sclibrary@sunburn.liunet.edu
Robert Gerbereux, *Library Director*

Open to: playwrights. **Description:** small room, space for 4 writers; carrel, storage space, access to reference material in room and to library. **Financial arrangement:** free. **Guidelines:** writer working under contract or with specific commitment. **Application procedure:** completed application.

LEIGHTON STUDIOS

The Banff Centre for the Arts; Box 1020, Station 28; 107 Tunnel Mountain Dr;
 Banff, Alberta; Canada T0L 0C0; (403) 762-6180 or (800) 565-9989,
 FAX (403) 762-6345; E-mail arts_info@banffcentre.ab.ca;
 Web http://www.banffcentre.ab.ca/
Office of the Registrar

Open to: playwrights, composers, solo performers. **Description:** residencies of 1 week–3 months for writers, composers, musicians and visual artists at studios situated in mountains of Banff National Park; 8 specially designed studios, each with washroom and kitchenette; living accommodation (single room with bath) on Centre's main campus; nearby access to all amenities of Centre, including communal cafeteria, library and recreation complex. **Financial arrangement:** resident pays for studio, room and optional meals; discount on studio cost only available for those who demonstrate need. **Guidelines:** artist who can demonstrate sustained contribution to own field and show evidence of significant achievement. **Application procedure:** write for application and further information. **Deadline:** open; apply at least 6 months before desired residency. **Dates:** year-round.

THE MacDOWELL COLONY

100 High St; Peterborough, NH 03458-2485; (603) 924-3886 or (212) 535-9690,
 FAX (603) 924-9142
Mary Carswell, *Executive Director*

Open to: playwrights, composers, film and video writers. **Description:** residencies of up to 2 months for writers, composers, visual artists, video/filmmakers, architects and interdisciplinary artists at 450-acre estate; studios and common areas accessible for those with mobility impairments. **Financial arrangement:** voluntary contributions accepted; travel grants available. **Guidelines:** admission based on talent. **Application procedure:** send SASE or call for application; submit completed application, work samples, names of 2 professional references and $20 fee; collaborating artists must apply separately. **Deadline:** 15 Sep 1996 for Jan–Apr 1997; 15 Jan 1997 for May–Aug 1997; 15 Apr 1997 for Sep–Dec 1997. **Notification:** 2 months.

MARY ANDERSON CENTER FOR THE ARTS

101 St. Francis Dr; Mount St. Francis, IN 47146; (812) 923-8602, FAX 923-3200
Sarah Roberson Yates, *Executive Director*

Open to: playwrights, translators, composers, librettists, lyricists. **Description:** residencies of 2 weeks–3 months for 6 writers and visual artists concurrently at center on beautiful 400-acre wooded site with lake, 15 minutes from Louisville, KY; private studio/bedroom, communal kitchen and dining room. **Financial arrangement:** resident pays suggested minimum fee of $210 a week for room and board; possibility of funded residencies; write for information. **Guidelines:** formal education and production credits are not requirements but will be taken into consideration when applications are reviewed. **Application procedure:** completed application, project description, work sample, resume and 2 references. **Deadline:** open. **Dates:** year-round.

THE MILLAY COLONY FOR THE ARTS

East Hill Rd; Box 3; Austerlitz, NY 12017-0003; (518) 392-3103;
        E-mail director@millay.colony.org
Gail Giles, *Assistant Director*

Open to: playwrights, composers, screenwriters. **Description:** 1-month residencies for up to 5 writers, composers and visual artists concurrently at 600-acre estate in upstate NY; studio space and separate bedroom. **Financial arrangement:** free room, board and studio space. **Application procedure:** send SASE or e-mail application@millaycolony.org for application; submit completed application and supporting materials. **Deadline:** 1 Sep for Feb–May; 1 Feb for Jun–Sep; 1 May for Oct–Jan. **Notification:** 10–12 weeks after deadline.

NANTUCKET PLAYWRIGHTS RETREAT

Box 2177; Nantucket MA 02584; (508) 228-5002
Jim Patrick, *Director*

Open to: playwrights. **Description:** new project of Nantucket Theatrical Productions (see also Nantucket Short Play Festival in Prizes) planned to start in winter of 1996–97; residencies of 1 week or longer will probably be offered with opportunity to have work-in-progress read and discussed with directors, actors and peers during stay; accommodation in guest house with kitchen privileges. **Financial arrangement:** TBA; playwright will probably pay $150 workshop fee plus $250 a week for housing. **Application procedure:** write for information. **Deadline:** open. **Dates:** probably Nov–Mar.

NEW YORK FOUNDATION FOR THE ARTS—ARTISTS IN RESIDENCE PROGRAM

155 Ave of the Americas, 14th Floor; New York, NY 10013-1507;
        (212) 366-6900, ext 222, FAX 366-1778
Greg McCaslin, *Director, Education and Information*

Open to: schools and cultural organizations. **Description:** matching grants to assist schools and organizations bring in artists, including playwrights, composers, librettists and lyricists, for residencies of 12 days–10 months; residency activities include artist-conducted student or teacher workshops, lecture-demonstrations, readings and performances. **Financial arrangement:** artist is paid by school or organization; recommended minimum fee of $250 a day. **Guidelines:** artist must be NY State resident. **Application procedure:** completed application from school or organization; individual artists may not apply but are encouraged to write for guidelines and to collaborate with eligible sponsors to set up residencies; artists may also contact program for information and for help in finding sponsors. **Deadline:** 2 Apr 1997; subsidiary deadlines for smaller grants in Oct, Nov, Feb and Jun each year. **Dates:** Sep 1997–Jun 1998.

NEW YORK MILLS ARTS RETREAT
24 North Main Ave, Box 246; New York Mills, MN 56567; (218) 385-3339, FAX 385-3366
Kent Scheer, *Coordinator*

Open to: playwrights, translators, composers, librettists, lyricists, solo performers, screenwriters. **Description:** 1 artist at a time housed for 2–4 weeks in small farming community in north central Minnesota; housing ranges from bed and breakfast to private home; some meals provided. **Financial arrangement:** $750 stipend for 2 weeks, $1500 stipend for 4 weeks. **Guidelines:** emerging artist of demonstrated ability; must donate 8 hours per week during residency to community outreach. **Application procedure:** completed application form, project description, work sample, resume and 2 letters of recommendation. **Deadline:** 1 Oct 1996; 1 Apr 1997. **Notification:** 6 weeks after deadline. **Dates:** year-round.

NORCROFT
32 East First St. #330; Duluth, MN 55802; (218) 727-5199, FAX 727-3119
Jean Sramek, *Administrator*

Open to: playwrights. **Description:** 4 concurrent residencies of 1–4 weeks for writers of drama, fiction and poetry at remote lodge on shores of Lake Superior; private bedroom and separate individual "writing shed." **Financial arrangement:** free housing; groceries provided, resident does own cooking. **Guidelines:** women only; artist whose work demonstrates an understanding of and commitment to feminist change. **Application procedure:** completed application, five-page writing sample and description of project to be pursued at colony. **Deadline:** Sep or Oct 1996; exact date TBA. **Dates:** May–Oct.

RAGDALE FOUNDATION
1260 North Green Bay Rd; Lake Forest, IL 60045; (708) 234-1063, FAX 234-1075
Sonja Carlborg, *Director*

Open to: playwrights, composers, librettists, lyricists. **Description:** residencies of 2 weeks–2 months for writers and visual artists from all over the U.S. and abroad at estate situated on edge of prairie, 1 mile from center of town. **Financial arrangement:** resident pays $105 a week for room and board; partial or full fee waivers awarded on basis of financial need. **Guidelines:** admission based on quality of work submitted. **Application procedure:** send SASE for application; submit completed application, description of work-in-progress, work sample, resume, 3 references and $20 fee. **Deadline:** 15 Jan for Jun–Dec; 1 Jun for Jan–Apr. **Dates:** year-round except for May and last 2 weeks in Dec.

SAMUEL BECKETT PLAYWRITING INTERNSHIP

Gloucester Stage Company; 267 East Main St; Gloucester, MA 01930;
    (508) 281-4099, FAX 283-5150
Israel Horovitz, *Artistic Director*

Open to: playwrights. **Description:** 10-week residency for 1–2 playwrights at Gloucester Stage Company, a nonprofit professional theatre located in small working-class seaport on the Atlantic coast; intern, who is expected to start and complete new play under artistic director's guidance during residency, works on own writing each morning (word processor not provided), assists artistic director in afternoon and works as crew member on theatre's current production at night. **Financial arrangement:** $1000 stipend; free housing. **Guidelines:** early-career playwright. **Application procedure:** 20-page writing sample; detailed cover letter describing playwright's goals; resume and references; program contingent on funding (call before submitting). **Deadline:** 1 Mar 1997. **Notification:** May 1997. **Dates:** summer 1997.

SNUG HARBOR CULTURAL CENTER

1000 Richmond Terr; Staten Island, NY 10301-9926; (718) 448-2500,
    FAX 442-8534
Rental Coordinator

Open to: playwrights, composers. **Description:** studio workspace in performing and visual arts center with theatre, art galleries, shops, museum, meeting rooms and banquet hall, located in 80-acre historic park. **Financial arrangement:** current monthly rental approximately $10 per sq. ft.; renewable 1-year lease; tenant must carry own insurance. **Guidelines:** professional artist. **Application procedure:** work sample with resume.

STUDIO FOR CREATIVE INQUIRY

Carnegie Mellon University; College of Fine Arts; Pittsburgh, PA 15213-3890;
    (412) 268-3454, FAX 268-2829; E-mail mmbm@andrew.cmu.edu
Marge Myers, *Assistant Director*

Open to: playwrights, translators, composers, librettists, lyricists, solo performers, television and screenwriters. **Description:** 25 short-term residencies of 2 weeks–3 months and 2 long-term residencies of 6 months–3 years concurrently for artists in all disciplines; residency provides studio facility located in Carnegie Mellon's College of Fine Arts building, including office and meeting space, work area, computers, sound and video editing equipment; fellows may also use resources of university, including library. **Financial arrangement:** stipend; assistance in finding housing in community. **Guidelines:** admission based on quality of work, clear statement of intention, experience with collaboration, and project feasibility. **Application procedure:** work sample, resume and letter of application. **Deadline:** open. **Notification:** 2 months. **Dates:** year-round.

THE TYRONE GUTHRIE CENTRE

Annaghmakerrig; Newbliss; County Monaghan; Ireland; 353-47-54003,
    FAX -54380; E-mail 101450.3652@compuserve.com
Bernard Loughlin, *Resident Director*

Open to: playwrights, composers, librettists, lyricists, screenwriters, television writers. **Description:** residencies of 3 weeks–3 months for artists in all disciplines from Ireland and abroad at former country home of Tyrone Guthrie, set amid 400 acres of forested estate overlooking large lake; private apartments; music room, rehearsal/performance space and extensive library. **Financial arrangement:** non-Irish artists pay about Irish £1600 (about $2550) a month May–Aug, £1200 (about $1900) a month the rest of the year for housing and meals; self-catering houses also available at reasonable rents. **Guidelines:** artist must show evidence of sustained dedication and a significant level of achievement; prefers artists with clearly defined projects; artist teams (e.g. writer/director, composer/librettist) welcome; several weeks reserved each year for development of projects. **Application procedure:** write for application and further information.

UCROSS FOUNDATION RESIDENCY PROGRAM

2836 U.S. Hwy 14-16 East; Clearmont, WY 82835; (307) 737-2291,
    FAX 737-2322
Elizabeth Guheen, *Executive Director*

Open to: playwrights, translators, composers, librettists, lyricists. **Description:** residency of 2 weeks–2 months at "Big Red," restored historic site in the foothills of the Big Horn Mountains; 8 concurrent residencies for writers, composers and visual artists; opportunity to concentrate on own work without distraction and to present work to local communities, if desired. **Financial arrangement:** free room, board and studio space. **Guidelines:** criteria are quality of work and commitment. **Admission procedure:** completed application, project description and work sample; send SASE for application and further information. **Deadline:** 1 Oct for Feb–Jun; 1 Mar for Aug–Dec. **Notification:** 8 weeks.

VERMONT STUDIO CENTER

Box 613NW; Johnson, VT 05656; (802) 635-2727, FAX 635-2730

Open to: playwrights, translators, screenwriters. **Description:** residencies of 2 or 4 weeks for up to 25 writers and visual artists "who, together with the year-round VSC staff artists, form a dynamic working community" in Green Mountains of northern VT; opportunity for as much solitude or interchange and support as each resident wishes; private workspace and housing for writers in village residencies within walking distance of Red Mill complex containing dining room, lounge, offices and galleries; Johnson State College also within walking distance. **Financial arrangement:** resident pays $1400 for room and board for 4 weeks, $750 for 2 weeks; work-exchange fellowships awarded, based on financial need, to cover up to 50% of costs; write for information. **Guidelines:** established writer or one who shows promise. **Application procedure:** completed application, project description, 3 copies of script, resume, names of 3 references and $25 fee. **Deadline:** open. **Notification:** 2–3 weeks. **Dates:** year-round.

VILLA MONTALVO ARTIST RESIDENCY PROGRAM
Box 158; Saratoga, CA 95071-0158; (408) 741-3421
Judy Moran, *Artist Residency Program Director*

Open to: playwrights, composers, screenwriters. **Description:** residencies of 1–3 months for 5 writers, musicians and visual artists concurrently at Mediterranean-style villa on 175 acres; rural setting close to major urban center. **Financial arrangement:** free housing; resident provides own meals, transportation; 4 fellowships available. **Guidelines:** spouses welcome; no children or pets. **Application procedure:** send SASE for application and guidelines. **Deadline:** 1 Sep for Apr–Sep; 1 Mar for Oct–Mar.

VIRGINIA CENTER FOR THE CREATIVE ARTS
Box VCCA, Mt. San Angelo; Sweet Briar, VA 24595; (804) 946-7236
William Smart, *Director*

Open to: playwrights, translators, composers, librettists, lyricists, solo performers, screenwriters. **Description:** residencies of 2 weeks–2 months for writers, composers, and visual and performance artists at 450-acre estate in Blue Ridge Mountains; separate studios and bedrooms; all meals provided. **Financial arrangement:** resident pays suggested minimum of $30 a day for room and board or as means allow; financial status not a factor in selection process. **Guidelines:** admission based on achievement or promise of achievement. **Application procedure:** completed application with work sample, resume and 2 recommendations. **Deadline:** 15 Sep for Jan–Apr; 15 Jan for May–Aug; 15 May for Sep–Dec. **Notification:** 2 months. **Dates:** year-round.

WALDEN RESIDENCY PROGRAM
Extended Campus Programs; Southern Oregon State College; 1250 Siskiyou Blvd; Ashland, OR 97520; (541) 552-6331, FAX 552-6047; E-mail stevens@wpo.sosc.osshe.edu
Celeste Stevens, *Special Programs Coordinator*

Open to: playwrights. **Description:** 3 6-week residencies for writers of drama, fiction, poetry and creative nonfiction at farm near Ashland, OR; 1 writer at a time housed in cabin with kitchen facilities, which opens onto meadow surrounded by forest. **Financial arrangement:** free; no meals provided. **Guidelines:** OR resident only; send SASE in fall for application. **Application procedure:** completed application, project description, work sample and list of publications or productions. **Deadline:** 29 Nov 1996. **Notification:** mid-Dec 1996. **Dates:** Mar–Sep 1997.

WILLIAM FLANAGAN MEMORIAL CREATIVE PERSONS CENTER

Edward F. Albee Foundation; 14 Harrison St; New York, NY 10013;
   (212) 226-2020

Open to: playwrights, translators, composers, librettists, screenwriters. **Description:** 1-month residencies for up to 6 writers, composers and visual artists concurrently at "The Barn" in Montauk, Long Island. **Financial arrangement:** free housing. **Guidelines:** admission based on talent and need. **Application procedure:** completed application, script (recording for composers) and supporting materials; write for information. **Deadline:** 1 Apr 1997; no submission before 1 Jan 1997. **Notification:** May 1997. **Dates:** 1 Jun–1 Oct 1997.

THE WRITERS ROOM

10 Astor Pl, 6th Floor; New York, NY 10003; FAX (212) 533-6059
Donna Brodie, *Executive Director*

Open to: playwrights, translators, composers, librettists, lyricists. **Description:** large room with 35 desks separated by partitions, space for 180 writers each quarter; open 24 hours a day year-round; kitchen, lounge and bathrooms, storage for files and typewriters, small reference library; monthly readings. **Financial arrangement:** $50 initiation fee; fee for 3-month period: $350 for assigned project desk, $165 for "floater" desk. **Guidelines:** writer, emerging or established, must show seriousness of intent. **Application procedure:** completed application and references; all inquiries by mail (no visits without appointment).

THE WRITERS' STUDIO

The Mercantile Library Association; 17 East 47th St; New York, NY 10017;
   (212) 755-6710, FAX 758-1387; E-mail mercanlib@aol.com
Harold Augenbraum, *Director*

Open to: playwrights, composers. **Description:** carrel space for 17 writers (3 reserved for writers of children's literature) in nonprofit, private lending library of 175,000 volumes; storage for personal computers or typewriters, library membership, access to special reference collection and rare collection of 19th-century American and British literature. **Financial arrangement:** $200 fee for 3 months, renewal possible for up to 1 year. **Guidelines:** open to all writers; unpublished writer must submit evidence of serious intent. **Application procedure:** completed application and work sample or project outline.

YADDO

Box 395; Saratoga Springs, NY 12866-0395; (518) 584-0746, FAX 584-1312
Admissions Committee

Open to: playwrights, composers, performance artists, screenwriters. **Description:** residencies of 2 weeks–2 months for artists in all genres, working individually or as collaborative teams of up to 3 persons, at 19th-century estate on 400 acres; approximate total of 200 residents a year (15 concurrently Sep–May, 35 concurrently May–Labor Day). **Financial arrangement:** free room, board and studio space; contribution suggested to help underwrite cost of program. **Guidelines:** admission based on review by judging panels composed of artists in each genre; quality of work submitted is major criterion; send SASE for application and further information. **Application procedure:** completed application with work sample, resume, 2 letters of support, $20 fee and SASP for acknowledgment of receipt. **Deadline:** 15 Jan 1997 for mid-May 1997–Feb 1998; 1 Aug 1997 for 1 Nov 1997–mid-May 1998. **Notification:** 1 Apr 1997 for Jan deadline; 15 Oct 1997 for Aug deadline. **Dates:** year-round except early Sep.

Membership and Service Organizations

What's included here?

A number of organizations that exist to serve either the American playwright or a wider constituency of writers, composers and arts professionals. Some have a particular regional or special-interest orientation; some provide links to theatres in other countries. Taken together, these organizations represent an enormous range of services available to those who write for the theatre, and it is worth getting to know them.

THE ALLIANCE OF LOS ANGELES PLAYWRIGHTS

7510 Sunset Blvd, Suite 1050; Los Angeles, CA 90046-3418;
(213) 957-4752
Hollis Evans, Monique Friedman and Michael Van Duzer, *Co-Chairs*

Founded in 1993, ALAP is a support and service organization dedicated to addressing the professional needs of the diverse Los Angeles playwriting community by facilitating creative programs nurturing the critical analysis of the theory and craft of playwriting, administering grants and fellowships, documenting and publishing the work of L.A. playwrights, creating an archive, and providing continuing advocacy for the playwright's voice in society. ALAP's programs and activities include general membership meetings; a voice-mail service which announces members' play readings, productions and other projects and provides information and referrals; a database of plays by L.A. playwrights to be made available to theatres and producers; a lab series; a community outreach program; and a quarterly newsletter. Dues are $29.95 a year (this sum is a donation and no playwright is turned away for lack of funds).

THE ALLIANCE OF RESIDENT THEATRES/NEW YORK

131 Varick St, Room 904; New York, NY 10013-1410; (212) 989-5257,
FAX 989-4880
Virginia P. Louloudes, *Executive Director*
Mary Harpster, *Deputy Director*

A.R.T./New York is the trade and service organization for the New York City nonprofit professional theatre, serving more than 250 New York theatre companies and professional affiliates (theatres outside NY, colleges and universities, and organizations providing services to the theatre field). Publications of interest include *Hot Seats*, which lists current productions in NYC, *Member Directory* ($5), and Rehearsal and Performance Space Guide ($15), which provides information on various theatre spaces currently available for rent.

ALTERNATE ROOTS

1083 Austin Ave; Atlanta, GA 30307; (404) 577-1079, FAX 577-7991
Kathie deNobriga, *Development and Planning Director*

Alternate ROOTS is a service organization run by and for southeastern artists. Its mission is to support the creation and presentation of original performing art that is rooted in a particular community of place, tradition or spirit. It is committed to social and economic justice and the protection of the natural world and addresses these concerns through its programs and services. Founded in 1976, ROOTS now has more than 260 individual members across the 13 states of the Southeast, including playwrights, directors, choreographers, musicians, storytellers, clowns and new vaudevillians—both solo artists and representatives of 65 performing and presenting organizations. ROOTS aims to make artistic resources available to its members through workshops; to create appropriate distribution networks for the new work being generated in the region via touring, publications and liaison activity; and to provide opportunities for enhanced visibility and financial stability via publications and periodic performance festivals. Opportunities for member playwrights include readings and peer critiques of works-in-progress at the organization's annual meeting. Artists who are residents of the Southeast and whose work is consistent with the goals of ROOTS are accepted as new members after a year's provisional status. Annual membership dues are $50. The organization's meetings and workshops are open to the public and its triannual newsletter is available free to the public.

THE AMERICAN ALLIANCE FOR THEATRE & EDUCATION (AATE)

c/o Department of Theatre; Arizona State University; Box 873411;
Tempe, AZ 85287-3411; (602) 965-6064 (Mon–Fri, 8:30–2:30),
FAX 965-5351
Barbara Salisbury Wills, *Executive Director*
Julie DeChurch, *Administrative Director*

AATE is a membership organization created in 1987 with the merger of the

American Association of Theatre for Youth and the American Association for Theatre in Secondary Education. AATE provides a variety of services to support the work of theatre artists and educators who work with young people and to promote theatre and drama/theatre education in elementary and secondary schools. To encourage the development and production of plays for young audiences the AATE Unpublished Play Reading Project annually selects and publicizes promising new plays in this field. AATE also sponsors annual awards for the best play for young people and the outstanding book relating to any aspect of the field published in the past calendar year; only the play or book's publisher may nominate a candidate for these awards. AATE's publications, which are free to members, include a quarterly newsletter with a Playwright's Page; the yearly *Youth Theatre Journal;* and the quarterly *STAGE of the Art.* Membership is open to all and costs $100 for organizations, $75 for individuals, $55 for retirees and $45 for students; please add $20 (U.S. funds) for foreign members (outside the U.S. and Canada).

THE AMERICAN FILM INSTITUTE

2021 North Western Ave; Box 27999; Los Angeles, CA 90027; (213) 856-7600,
    FAX 464-5217; E-mail www.afionline.org
Jean Picker Firstenberg, *Director*
James Hindman, *Co-Director*

East Coast Office:
The John F. Kennedy Center for the Performing Arts; Washington, DC 20566;
    (202) 828-4000

The American Film Institute is an independent nonprofit organization established by the National Endowment for the Arts in 1967 to advance and preserve the art of the moving image and to encourage and develop new talent in the field. In pursuit of these goals, the AFI runs the Center for Advanced Film and Television Studies at its L.A. campus, coordinates the preservation of the nation's moving-image heritage through its National Center for Film and Video Preservation, and maintains the AFI National Theater at the Kennedy Center. AFI also sponsors festivals and touring programs and conducts workshops such as the Directing Workshop for Women. Of special interest to writers is AFI's annual Television Writers Summer Workshop, held in L.A., which provides 2–4 weeks of intensive advanced training for 10–12 competitively selected writers who have no major commercial television writing credits; participants pay a fee of $475; 3 full-tuition scholarships are available; interested writers should call (213) 856-7690 for guidelines and application information.

AMERICAN INDIAN COMMUNITY HOUSE

404 Lafayette St; New York, NY 10003; (212) 598-0100, FAX 598-4909
Rosemary Richmond, *Executive Director*
Jim Cyrus, *Director of Theatre*

American Indian Community House was founded in 1969 to encourage the interest of all U.S. ethnic groups in the cultural contributions of the American Indian, as well as to foster intercultural exchanges. The organization now serves the Native American population of the New York City region through a variety of social, economic and educational programs, and through cultural programs which include theatre events, an art gallery and a newsletter. Native Americans in the Arts, the performing arts component of the Community House, is committed to the development and production of works by Indian authors, and presents staged readings, workshop productions and full productions. The Community House also sponsors several other performing groups, including Spiderwoman Theatre, Coatlicue Theatre Company, the actors' group Off the Beaten Path, the Thunderbird American Indian Dancers, and the jazz-fusion and traditional singing group Ulali (formerly known as Pura Fe). A showcase for Native American artists is presented to agents and casting directors once or twice a year.

AMERICAN MUSIC CENTER

30 West 26th St, Suite 1001; New York, NY 10010-2011; (212) 366-5260,
    FAX 366-5265; E-mail center@amc.net
Nancy S. Clarke, *Executive Director*

The American Music Center provides numerous programs and services for composers, performers and others interested in contemporary American music. The Jory Copying Assistance Program helps composers pay for copying music and extracting performance materials. The center's library contains more than 50,000 scores and recordings available for perusal by interested performers. The AMC provides information on competitions, publishers, performing ensembles, composers and other areas of interest in new music, and its publication *Opportunities in New Music* is updated annually. Membership is open to any person or organization wishing to support the center's promotion of the creation, performance and appreciation of American music. Annual dues are $55 for individuals ($35 for students and senior citizens). Members receive discounts on AMC publications, monthly "Opportunity Updates" and the option of participating in group health insurance. New members receive a free packet of information and articles of interest to the American composer. All members may vote in the annual board elections and attend the annual meeting.

AMERICAN TRANSLATORS ASSOCIATION (ATA)

1800 Diagonal Rd, Suite 220; Alexandria, VA 22314-2840;
    (703) 683-6100, FAX (703) 683-6122; E-mail 73564.2032@compuserve.com
Walter W. Bacak, Jr., *Executive Director*

Founded in 1959, the ATA is a national not-for-profit association which seeks to promote recognition of the translation profession; disseminate information for the benefit of translators and those who use their services; define and maintain professional standards; foster and support the training of translators and interpreters; and provide a medium of cooperation with persons in allied professions. Active membership is open to U.S. citizens and permanent residents who have professionally engaged in translating or closely related work and have passed an ATA accreditation examination or demonstrated professional attainment by other prescribed means. Those who meet these professional standards but are not U.S. citizens or residents may hold Corresponding membership; other interested persons may be Associate members. All members receive the monthly *ATA Chronicle* and a membership directory. Other publications include a *Translation Services Directory* containing professional profiles of Active members. ATA holds an annual conference and sponsors several honors and awards (see American Translators Association Awards in Prizes). Interested persons should write for a membership application. Annual dues are $95 for Active, Corresponding and Associate members; $40 for Associate-Students; $120 for institutions; and $175 for corporations.

ASCAP (AMERICAN SOCIETY OF COMPOSERS, AUTHORS AND PUBLISHERS)

1 Lincoln Plaza; New York, NY 10023; (212) 621-6234, FAX 724-9064
Michael A. Kerker, *Director of Musical Theatre*

ASCAP is a nonprofit organization whose members are writers and publishers of musical works. It operates as a clearinghouse for performing rights, offering licenses that authorize the public performance of all the music of its composer, lyricist and music publishing members, and collecting license fees for these members. ASCAP also sponsors workshops for member and nonmember theatre writers (see ASCAP Musical Theatre Workshop in Development). Membership in ASCAP is open to any composer or lyricist who has been commercially recorded or "regularly published." Annual dues are $10 for individuals.

ASIAN AMERICAN ARTS ALLIANCE

74 Varick St, Suite 302; New York, NY 10013-1914; (212) 941-9208,
        FAX 941-7978; E-mail aaaajc@pipeline.com
June Choi, *Executive Director*

Formed in 1983, Asian American Arts Alliance is a nonprofit organization dedicated to increasing the support, recognition and appreciation of Asian-American arts. Alliance activities focus on relaying information, networking, providing advocacy services and pursuing related special projects. Ongoing services include information referrals; a resource library of books, journals, periodicals, files and other unique information on Asian-American culture and arts; and publications such as a directory of *Asian American Arts Organizations in New York & New Jersey* and *Beyond Boundaries National Resource Book*. Current initiatives include a 3-year Technical Assistance and Regrant Initiative (TARI) to help New York City Asian-American arts groups strengthen and grow; a 2-year Presenting Opportunities Pilot (POP) to cultivate presenting opportunities for Asian-American artists; and a national research project culminating in a report on the state of Asian Pacific American arts. Interested individuals may call to be included on the mailing list. There are 6 membership levels: artist/student/senior, $20; friend, $35; nonprofit organization, $50; patron, $100; benefactor, $250 and corporate, $500. Contributing members receive free library borrowing privileges, and are sent the monthlies *Asian American Arts Calendar* and *Asian American Arts Resources and Opportunities* as well as the quarterly magazine *Dialogue*. Members also receive discounts on advertising, special publications and events;

additional services and savings are provided to patron, benefactor and corporate members.

ASSITEJ/USA (INTERNATIONAL ASSOCIATION OF THEATRE FOR CHILDREN AND YOUNG PEOPLE)

Box 22365; Seattle, WA 98122-0365; (206) 392-2147, FAX 443-0442
Jen Marlowe, *Membership Coordinator*

ASSITEJ/USA is a nonprofit theatre agency which advocates the development of professional theatre for young audiences in the USA and facilitates interchange among theatre artists and scholars of the 60 member countries of ASSITEJ. ASSITEJ/USA sponsors festivals and seminars, operates an international playscript exchange and, with ASSITEJ/Japan, is founder of the Pacific-Asia Exchange program. Members are theatres, institutions and individuals concerned for the theatre, young audiences and international goodwill. Members receive *Theatre for Young Audiences Today* and priority consideration for participation in national and international events. Membership costs $50 a year for individuals, $25 for students and retirees, $100–300 for organizations, depending on size of budget, and $30 for libraries. Write for membership application.

THE ASSOCIATED WRITING PROGRAMS

Tallwood House, Mail Stop 1E3; George Mason University; Fairfax, VA 22030;
(703) 993-4301, FAX 993-4302
David Fenza, *Executive Director*

Founded in 1967, AWP serves the needs of writers, college and university writing programs, and students of writing by providing information services, job placement assistance, publishing opportunities, literary arts advocacy, and forums on all aspects of writing and its instruction. Writers not affiliated with colleges and universities but who support collective efforts to improve opportunities are also represented by AWP. The *AWP Chronicle*, published 6 times annually and available for $20 a year, includes listings of publishing opportunities, grants, awards and fellowships; interviews with writers; and essays on teaching creative writing. *The AWP Official Guide to Writing Programs* (7th edition, $23.95 postpaid) offers a comprehensive listing of writing programs and an expanded section on writing conferences, colonies and centers. Write or call AWP for information on membership requirements.

THE ASSOCIATION OF HISPANIC ARTS

173 East 116th St; New York, NY 10029; (212) 860-5445, FAX 427-2787;
E-mail aha1@artswire.com
Sandra Perez, *Executive Director of Programs*

A nonprofit organization founded in 1975, AHA promotes the Latin American arts as an integral part of this country's cultural life. It acts as a clearinghouse for information on all the arts, including theatre, and 9 times a year publishes a newsletter, *Hispanic Arts News*, that provides information on playwriting contests, workshops, forums and other items of interest to Latin American artists. AHA also provides technical assistance to Latin American artists seeking funding.

ASSOCIATION OF INDEPENDENT VIDEO AND FILMMAKERS

304 Hudson St, 6th Floor; New York, NY 10013; (212) 807-1400,
    FAX 463-8519; E-mail aivffivf@aol.com
Ruby Lerner, *Executive Director*

The association is a national trade organization of 5000 independent film and video makers. The independent producer's advocate in Washington and within the entertainment industry, AIVF offers members a subscription to *The Independent Film & Video Monthly* magazine; group insurance for health, disability, production liability and equipment; and other benefits. AIVF's educational arm, the Foundation for Independent Video and Film (FIVF), publishes *The Independent* as well as books related to the field, runs a festival bureau and conducts public events on independent production issues.

THE AUDREY SKIRBALL-KENIS THEATRE

9478 West Olympic Blvd, Suite 304; Beverly Hills, CA 90212; (310) 284-8965,
    FAX 203-8067; E-mail askplay@primenet.com;
    Web http://www.primenet.com/~askplay
Mead Hunter, *Director of Literary Programs*

Since 1989, the Audrey Skirball-Kenis Theatre has been an arts service organization dedicated to playwrights and new playwriting. Each year A.S.K. presents 15–20 rehearsed readings, out of which 2–3 plays are selected for workshop productions (see the theatre's entry in Development). Allied programs supported by A.S.K. include: the A.S.K. Unpublished Plays Project, a repository of plays that premiered in southern California, housed in the L.A. Central Library; the international playwriting program at London's Royal Court Theatre; 3 playwright exchange programs, one each with the Playwrights' Center, the Royal Court and New Dramatists; the Audrey Skirball-Kenis Playwrights Program at Lincoln Center; the Mark Taper Forum's New Work Festival; the UCLA Playwriting Award and the UCLA Playwriting Fellowship; the Los Angeles Drama Critics Circle Ted Schmitt Award; the playscript publication in TCG's *American Theatre* magazine; and the *L.A. Weekly* Playwriting Award. A.S.K. sponsors symposiums, caucuses and playwriting labs, which serve as forums wherein issues may be explored or practical approaches to writing shared. In addition, the theatre offers playwrights various services, the latest of which is the Electronic Library, a computer bulletin-board system that enables potential producers to search on-line for plays meeting specific criteria, and that provides writers with interactive opportunities for information-sharing and networking. A.S.K.'s publications include summary booklets of the symposium series entitled *Inventing the Future*; the *Directory of Los Angeles Playwright Groups*; the texts of plays given workshop productions; and *Parabasis*, a news magazine for, by and about playwrights. For additional information about A.S.K.'s programs and publications, contact the theatre.

BALTIMORE THEATRE PROJECT, INC.

45 West Preston St; Baltimore, MD 21201; (410) 539-3091, FAX 539-2137
Philip Arnoult, *Artistic Director*

Founded in 1971, Baltimore Theatre Project is a presenting theatre of new and innovative works, with special focus on Baltimore-area theatre companies. Additional services include workshops, roundtables, seminars, open auditions and a shared database of Balitmore-area affiliated artists. Membership is $25 and includes discounted tickets to participating Baltimore Theatre Project theatres and the monthly newsletter *Theatre Project Newsletter.*

BLACK THEATRE NETWORK

Box 11502, Fisher Bldg Station; Detroit, MI 48211; (352) 392-2038,
335-1757 (Membership Services), FAX 392-5114
Mikell Pinkney, *President*

Black Theatre Network (BTN) is a national network of professional artists, scholars and community groups founded in 1986 to provide an opportunity for the interchange of ideas; to collect and disseminate through its publications information regarding black theatre activity; to provide an annual national forum for the viewing and discussing of black theatre; and to encourage and promote black dramatists and the production of plays about the black experience. BTN members attend national conferences and workshops and receive complimentary copies of all BTN publications, which include the quarterly *BTN News*, listing conferences, contests, employment opportunities, BTN business matters and other items of interest from across the country; *Black Theatre Directory*, which contains over 800 listings of black theatre artists, scholars, companies, higher education programs and service organizations; *Dissertations Concerning Black Theatre: 1900–1994*, a listing of Ph.D. theses on black theatre; and *Minority Job Bulletin*, a quarterly listing of jobs in educational and professional theatre. *Black Voices*, a catalogue of works by black playwrights, is available from BTN for $20. Annual dues are $95 for organizations, $60 for individuals, $25 for retirees and students.

BMI (BROADCAST MUSIC INCORPORATED)

320 West 57th St; New York, NY 10019; (212) 586-2000, FAX 262-2824
Jean Banks, *Senior Director, Musical Theater and Jazz*

BMI, founded in 1940, is a performing rights organization which acts as steward for the public performance of the music of its writers and publishers, offering licenses to music users. BMI monitors music performances and distributes royalties to those whose music has been used. Any writer whose songs have been published and are likely to be performed can join BMI at no cost. BMI also sponsors a musical theatre workshop (see BMI-Lehman Engel Musical Theatre Workshop in Development).

The BMI Foundation (President, Theodora Zavin) was established in 1984 to provide support for individuals in furthering their musical education and to assist organizations involved in the performance of music and music training.

British American Arts Association

116 Commercial St; London E1 6NF; England; 44-171-247-5385,
    FAX 44-171-247-5256
Jennifer Williams, *Executive Director*

A nonprofit organization working in the field of arts and education, BAAA conducts research, organizes conferences, produces a quarterly newsletter and is part of an international network of arts and education organizations. As well as a specialized arts and education library, BAAA has a more general library which houses information on opportunities for artists and performers both in the UK and abroad. BAAA is not a grant-giving organization.

Broadway on Sunset

10800 Hesby St; North Hollywood, CA 91601; (818) 508-9270
Kevin Kaufman, *Executive Director*

Broadway on Sunset, a nonprofit organization established in 1981, is sponsored by the National Academy of Songwriters (N.A.S.) (see entry in this section). The organization provides a structured developmental program for musical theatre writers (composers, lyricists, librettists) of all skill levels, which emphasize a full understanding of the principles and standards of Broadway-level musical theatre craft, and provides writers opportunities to test their material at each level. Since its inception, Broadway on Sunset has presented more than 100 original musicals. There are no membership dues but writers may pay a nominal fee to participate in classes, readings and workshops. Writers and composers need to have access to the Los Angeles area to benefit fully from the workshops.

Carolina Playwrights Center

Box 1705; Pinehurst, NC 28374; (910) 295-6896, FAX 295-1203
Carolyn Cole Montgomery, *Playwright-in-Residence*

Founded in 1989, CPC is a service organization for native or resident North/ South Carolina member playwrights. CPC provides staff to conduct research during play development, investigate production opportunities and provide administrative support. Additional services include a monthly play development program, and a playwright-producer program in which playwrights produce and market their plays from informal readings through to full production. Programs run from Sep–May. Basic membership services are available year-round. Non-resident guest memberships are available space permitting. Annual dues are $100. Write or call for information.

Chicago Alliance for Playwrights (CAP)

Theatre Building; 1225 West Belmont; Chicago, IL 60657-3205;
    (312) 929-7367, ext 17, FAX 327-1404
Allan Chambers, *Board Member*

The Chicago Alliance for Playwrights is a service organization founded in 1990 to establish a network for Chicago-area playwrights and others committed to the development of new work for the stage. Members of the coalition include Columbia College New Musicals Project, Music/Theatre Workshop, New Tuners Theatre/Workshop, Studio Z, Voices, Women's Theatre Alliance (see this section), Writers Bloc and Zebra Crossing. The alliance sponsors forums of interest to writers and publishes an annual directory of Chicago-area playwrights and their principal works. Write or call for membership details; annual dues are $25 for individuals and $100 for groups.

CHICAGO DRAMATISTS WORKSHOP
1105 West Chicago Ave; Chicago, IL 60622; (312) 633-0630, FAX 633-0610
Russ Tutterow, *Artistic Director*

Founded in 1980, Chicago Dramatists Workshop is dedicated to the development and advancement of playwriting and new plays. It employs a variety of programs to nurture the artistic and career development of both established and emerging playwrights. These programs include play readings, classes, workshops, symposiums, discussions, panels, productions, festivals, talent coordination, marketing services, collaborative projects with other theatres, national playwright exchanges and referrals to producers.

The Resident Playwright program seeks to nurture and promote the work and careers of dramatists who will make potentially significant contributions to the national theatre repertory. At no charge, Resident Playwrights benefit from the Workshop's fullest and longest-term support (a 3-year, renewable term), with full access to all of the Workshop's programs and services. Admittance to the program is selective, with emphasis on artistic and professional accomplishment or potential. While most Resident Playwrights are from the Chicago area, dramatists from around the country who are able to spend substantial time in Chicago may also apply. Interested playwrights should contact the Workshop for full information and details of the application procedure, which includes the submission of 2 plays, a resume and letters of recommendation and intent. *Deadline:* 1 Jun each year (no submission before 1 Apr).

The Playwrights' Network provides any U.S. playwright the opportunity to form an association with the Workshop. For an annual fee of $95, Network Playwrights receive written script critiques, consideration for all Workshop programs (including the annual New Voices Festival), class discounts, free admittance to Workshop events and other benefits.

Classes, Script Consultancies, the bimonthly 10-Minute Workshop and the biannual Deadline Workshop are open to all playwrights. A quarterly newsletter announces the Workshop's events and programs, and includes application procedures.

COLORADO DRAMATISTS
Box 101405; Denver, CO 80250; (303) 595-5600
Wesley Webb, *President*

Founded in 1981, Colorado Dramatists, with chapters in Denver and Boulder, is a service organization for playwrights at all levels of development. In addition to bimonthly public readings, the organization sponsors private developmental readings, workshops and group nights at the theatre. Members receive a monthly newsletter, *The Colorado Theatre Guide*, and access to rehearsal space, and make photocopies at a discount. Annual membership dues are $30 a year.

CORPORATION FOR PUBLIC BROADCASTING
901 E St NW; Washington, DC 20004-2037; (202) 879-9600, FAX 783-1019;
   E-mail rmadden@cpb.org
Rick Madden, *Director, Radio Program Fund*
Don Marbury, *Director, Television Program Fund*

The Corporation for Public Broadcasting, a private nonprofit organization funded by Congress and by private sources, promotes and helps finance public television and radio. CPB provides grants to local public television and radio stations; conducts research in audience development, new broadcasting technologies and other areas. The corporation helped establish the Public Broadcasting Service and National Public Radio (see entries in this section). It supports public radio programming through programming grants to stations and other producers, and television programming by funding proposals made by stations and independent producers.

THE DRAMATISTS GUILD
1501 Broadway, Suite 701; New York, NY 10036; (212) 398-9366
   FAX 944-0420
Peter Stone, *President*
Richard Garmise, *Executive Director*

Now in its 75th year, the Dramatists Guild is a professional association established to advance the rights of playwrights, composers and lyricists. The Guild has more than 6000 members worldwide, from beginning writers to Broadway veterans. The Guild has 4 levels of membership: 1. Active ($125 a year): writers who have been produced on Broadway, Off-Broadway or on the main stage of a LORT theatre; 2. Associate ($75 a year): theatrical writers who have not been produced or published; 3. Student ($35 a year): full-time students enrolled in an accredited writing degree program; 4. Estate ($125 a year): representatives of the estates of deceased members. Membership benefits include a business affairs toll-free hotline, which offers advice on all theatre-related topics, including options, commissions, copyright procedures and contract reviews; model production contracts, which provide the best protection for the writer at all levels of production; collaboration, commission and licensing agreements; free seminars led by experienced professionals concerning pressing topics for today's dramatist; access to 2 national health insurance programs and a group term life insurance plan; free/discounted tickets to Off-Broadway/Broadway performances; and a meeting room that can accommodate up to 50 people for readings and backers auditions, available exclusively to members for a nominal rental fee.

The Guild publishes *The Dramatists Guild Newsletter*, issued 8 times a year with up-to-date business affairs articles and script opportunities; *The Dramatists Guild Quarterly*, a journal that contains interviews as well as articles on all aspects of theatre; *The Dramatists Guild Resource Directory*, an annual collection of contact information on producers, agents, contests, workshops and production companies. The periodicals are available to nonwriters on a subscription basis: Individual Subscribers ($50 a year): theatre-related individuals receive the *Quarterly* only; Institutional Subscribers ($135 a year): educational institutions, libraries and educational theatres receive all 3 periodicals and have access to audio tapes of Guild seminars; Professional Subscribers ($200 a year) receive all 3 periodicals. For further information contact Douglas Green, Membership Coordinator.

THE FIELD
161 Sixth Ave; New York, NY 10013; (212) 691-6969, FAX 255-2053;
    E-mail thefield@aol.com
Katherine Lougstreth, *Executive Director*

The Field is a not-for-profit organization dedicated to helping independent performing artists and groups develop artistically and professionally through a variety of performance opportunities, workshops, services and publications. The Field does not engage in curatorial activity; all artists are eligible to participate in its programs. Of special interest to New York metropolitan area playwrights wishing to produce their own work are programs such as the 90 Plays in 9 Days festival; marathon performances of 12-minute works; and Fieldwork, 10-week group developmental workshops for works-in-progress, culminating in performances. The Field assists artists with all aspects of producing their work, including grant writing, fund raising, project management, securing performance and rehearsal space, and cooperative promotional efforts. Publications include *Self-Production Guide; Funding Guide for Independent Artists; Space Chase*, a listing of performance opportunities in New York City as well as out-of-town festivals, residencies and artist colonies; and *Dealing with Healing*, a listing of healing practitioners who have artists' budgets in mind. All programs are available to members and non-members; members receive publications free, discounts on programs and may use the Field as an umbrella organization, falling under its nonprofit status. Annual membership costs $75; individual programs range in cost from $15–65. Striving to bring its programs to locations outside New York, the Field has initiated project sites in Atlanta, Chicago, Houston, Miami, Philadelphia, San Francisco, Seattle, Toronto and Washington D.C.

FIRST STAGE
Box 38280; Los Angeles, CA 90038; (213) 850-6271
Dennis Safren, *Literary Manager*

Founded in 1983, First Stage is a service organization for playwrights that holds staged readings, which are videotaped for the author's archival purposes; conducts workshops; provides referral services for playwrights; and publishes *First Stage Newsletter*. Services are free to nonmembers, except for workshops, which are available to members only. Membership dues are $35 per quarter or $115 per year.

THE FOUNDATION CENTER

National Libraries:
1001 Connecticut Ave NW; Washington, DC 20036; (202) 331-1400
79 Fifth Ave; New York, NY 10003; (212) 620-4230, FAX 807-3677
Judith Margolin, *Director of Public Services, New York Library*

Field Offices:
312 Sutter St; San Francisco, CA 94108; (415) 397-0902
Hurt Bldg, Suite 150, Grand Lobby; 50 Hurt Plaza; Atlanta, GA 30303;
    (404) 880-0094
1422 Euclid, Suite 1356; Cleveland, OH 44115; (216) 861-1934

The Foundation Center is a nationwide service organization established and supported by foundations to provide a single authoritative source of information on foundation giving. It disseminates information on foundations through a public service program and through such publications as *The Foundation Directory* and *The Foundation Grants Index.* Of special interest is *Foundation Grants to Individuals,* which lists scholarships, fellowships, residencies, internships, grants, loans, awards, prizes and other forms of assistance available to individuals from approximately 2600 grantmakers (1995 edition $65). The center maintains 5 libraries and a national network of more than 205 cooperating collections. For the name of the collection nearest you or for more information about the center's programs, call toll free (800) 424-9836.

HATCH-BILLOPS COLLECTION

491 Broadway, 7th Floor; New York, NY 10012-4412; (212) 966-3231
James V. Hatch, *Executive Secretary*

The Hatch-Billops Collection is a nonprofit research library specializing in black American art and theatre history. It was founded in 1975 to collect and preserve primary and secondary resource materials in the black cultural arts; to provide tools and access to these materials for artists and scholars, as well as the general public; and to develop programs in the arts which use the collection's resources. The library's holdings include 1800 oral-history tapes; theatre programs; approximately 300 unpublished plays by black American writers from 1858 to the present; files of clippings, letters, announcements and brochures on theatre, art and film; slides, photographs and posters; and more than 4000 books and 400 periodicals. The collection also presents a number of salon interviews and films, which are open to the public; and publishes transcriptions of its annual "Artist and Influence" series of salon interviews, many of which are with playwrights. The collection is open to artists, scholars and the public by appointment only.

HISPANIC ORGANIZATION OF LATIN ACTORS (HOLA)

250 West 65th St; New York, NY 10023-6403; (212) 595-8286, FAX 799-6718;
    E-mail holagram@aol.com
Manuel Alfaro, *Executive Director*

Founded in 1975, HOLA is a nonprofit arts service organization for Hispanic performers and related artists. HOLA provides information, a 24-hour hotline, casting referral services, professional seminars and workshops. The organization publishes a biennial *Directory of Hispanic Talent* and a newsletter, *La Nueva Ola*, that lists job opportunities, grants and contests of interest to Hispanic artists. Members pay annual dues of $45.

INDEPENDENT FEATURE PROJECT

104 West 29th St, 12th Floor; New York, NY 10001-5310;
(212) 465-8200, FAX (212) 465-8525
Catherine Tait, *Executive Director*

The Independent Feature Project (IFP), a nonprofit membership-supported organization, was founded in 1979 to encourage creativity and diversity in films produced outside the established studio system. The IFP produces the Independent Feature Film Market (IFFM), the premiere film event for U.S. independent cinema. The IFFM features 400 independent features, shorts, works-in-progress, documentaries and feature scripts. The IFP and IFP/West publish *Filmmaker*, a quarterly magazine. IFP also sponsors a series of screenings, professional seminars and industry showcases, including a conference on screenplay development. Group health insurance, a production insurance package, a Resource Program, publications, and a series of audiotapes of previous seminars and workshops are available to members. Membership dues start at $100 a year ($65 for students).

INSTITUTE FOR CONTEMPORARY EAST EUROPEAN AND SLAVIC DRAMA AND THEATRE

Graduate Center of the City University of New York; Box 355;
33 West 42nd St; New York, NY 10036-8099; (212) 642-2231, -2235
Daniel C. Gerould, *Director*

The Institute for Contemporary East European and Slavic Drama and Theatre, under the auspices of the Center for Advanced Study in Theatre Arts (CASTA), publishes a triquarterly journal, *Slavic and East European Performance: Drama, Theatre, Film*, which is available by subscription ($10 a year, $15 foreign) and includes articles about current events in the East European and Slavic theatre, as well as reviews of productions and interviews with playwrights, directors and other theatre artists. The Institute also has available 2 annotated bibliographies of English translations of Eastern European plays written since 1945: *Soviet Plays in Translation* and *Polish Plays in Translation* ($5 each, $6 foreign). The institute is interested in hearing of published or unpublished translations for possible listing in updated editions of these bibliographies; translators may submit descriptive letters or scripts.

INSTITUTE OF OUTDOOR DRAMA

CB #3240; Nations Bank Plaza; University of North Carolina;
Chapel Hill, NC 27599-3240; (919) 962-1328, FAX 962-4212;
E-mail iod.fpgnb3@mhs.unc.edu
Scott J. Parker, *Director*

The Institute of Outdoor Drama, founded in 1963, is a research and advisory agency of the University of North Carolina. It serves as a communications link between producers of existing outdoor dramas and is a resource for groups, agencies or individuals who wish to create new outdoor dramas or who are seeking information on the field. The institute provides professional consultation and conducts feasibility studies; holds annual auditions for summer employment in outdoor drama; sponsors conferences, lectures and symposiums; and publishes a quarterly newsletter, as well as information bulletins. Writers should note that the institute maintains a roster of available artists and production personnel, including playwrights and composers. It seeks to interest established playwrights and composers in participating in the creation of new outdoor dramas, and to encourage and advise new playwrights who wish to write for this specialized form of theatre.

INTERNATIONAL CENTER FOR WOMEN PLAYWRIGHTS

819 Forest Ave; Buffalo, NY 14209; (716) 882-9238, FAX (716) 883-6300
Deborah Kane and Camille Kazmierczak, *Co-Directors*

The ICWP supports women playwrights around the world, continuing the work begun with the First International Women Playwrights Conference, held in Buffalo in 1988. (The next triennial conference will take place 2 Jun 1997 in Galway, Ireland.) The center solicits new work at intervals, presents readings and channels work to production venues; it welcomes contact with theatre organizations seeking new plays by women. The center also publishes a periodical and newsletter which provide information about upcoming International Women Playwrights Conferences, and it handles communications for the International Advisory Committee, which determines sites and policies for these conferences. Basic membership dues are $20 (larger contributions are welcome); checks should be made out to the U.B. Foundation-ICWP.

INTERNATIONAL THEATRE INSTITUTE
OF THE UNITED STATES (ITI/US)

47 Great Jones St; New York, NY 10012; (212) 254-4141, FAX (212) 254-6814
Martha W. Coigney, *Director*
Adam Thorburn, *Assistant Director*
Louis A. Rachow, *Library Director*

Now operating centers in 90 countries, ITI was founded in 1948 by UNESCO "to promote the exchange of knowledge and practice in the theatre arts." ITI assists foreign theatre visitors in the U.S. and American theatre representatives traveling abroad. The ITI International Theatre Collection is a reference library which documents theatrical activity in 146 countries and houses over 12,700 plays from 97 countries. American playwrights, as well as other theatre professionals, frequently use the collection to make international connections; to consult foreign theatre directories for names of producers, directors or companies with a view to submitting plays abroad; and to research the programs and policies of theatres or managements. ITI answers numerous requests from abroad about American plays and also provides information on rights to foreign plays to American producers, directors and literary managers. Building upon its commitment to theatre professionals, ITI recently began the University and Theatre Partner Programs in order to work more closely with institutions interested in international exchange.

THE INTERNATIONAL WOMEN'S WRITING GUILD

Box 810, Gracie Station; New York, NY 10028-0082; (212) 737-7536;
E-mail iwwg@iwwg.com; Web http://www.iwwg.com7
Hannelore Hahn, *Executive Director*

The International Women's Writing Guild, founded in 1976, is a network of women writers in the U.S., Canada and abroad. Playwrights, television and film writers, songwriters, producers and other women involved in the performing arts are included in its membership. Workshops are offered throughout the U.S. and annually at a week-long writing conference/retreat at Skidmore College in Saratoga Springs, NY. Members may also submit playscripts to theatres who have offered to read, critique and possibly produce IWWG members' works. *Network*, a 32-page newsletter published 6 times a year, provides a forum for members to share views and to learn about playwriting contests and awards, and theatre- and TV-related opportunities. The guild offers contacts with literary agents, group health and life insurance and other services to its members. Annual dues are $35 ($45 for foreign membership).

LA TELARAÑA

(formerly conmoción's latina lesbian writers' telaraña)
2626 North Mesa, #273; El Paso, TX 79902
tatiana de la tierra, *Director*

La telaraña supports Latina lesbian writers by providing information, referrals, access to resources and a connection to each other through *el telarañazo*, a newsletter that includes current news and information on contests, calls for writing submissions and retreats; and a networking/support list of members for members. Annual membership is $13.

LATIN AMERICAN THEATER ARTISTS

30 Grant Ave; San Francisco, CA 94108; (415) 439-2425, FAX 834-3360
Luis Oropeza, *Artistic Director*

Latin American Theater Artists is a performing and support organization. As a theatre, LATA "embraces Latino theatre from its indigenous roots in Spain and the Americas through its classical development and its contemporary expression." LATA annually produces one full production, a reading series of both new and traditional Latin American plays and a children's show; LATA accepts new plays year-round. As an organization, LATA offers a casting and referral service to its dues-paying members, training workshops and a newsletter. LATA primarily serves Bay Area Latinos and Latinas, but is open for membership nationally. Annual dues are $25; checks should be made out to LATA.

LEAGUE OF CHICAGO THEATRES/
LEAGUE OF CHICAGO THEATRES FOUNDATION

67 East Madison, Suite 2116; Chicago, IL 60603-3013; (312) 977-1730,
FAX 977-1661

Founded in 1979, the League of Chicago Theatres/League of Chicago Theatres Foundation is a trade and service organization for Chicago theatre companies, theatre personnel and freelance artists. It provides marketing, advocacy and membership services; and acts as an information clearinghouse, maintains resource files and publishes a bimonthly newsletter. The League's HOTTIX program sells half-price day-of-performance theatre tickets as well as full-price theatre and concert tickets.

LEAGUE OF PROFESSIONAL THEATRE WOMEN/NEW YORK

c/o Shari Upbin; 45 East 89th St, 19F; New York, NY 10128; (212) 534-7983,
FAX 876-6212
Shari Upbin, *President*

Founded in 1979, the league is a not-for-profit organization of theatre professionals providing programs and services which promote women in all areas of professional theatre, create industry-related opportunities for women, and highlight contributions of theatre women, past and present. Through its seminars, educational programs, social events, awards and festivals, the league links professional, university and community theatres with theatre women nationally and internationally and provides an ongoing forum for ideas, methods and issues of concern to the theatrical community and its audiences. Programs include the Lee Reynolds Award, given annually to a woman or women whose work for, in, about or through the medium of theatre has helped to illuminate the possibilities for social, cultural or political change; the League Scholarship, given to a girl of high school age to study theatre in a professional setting during the summer; the annual Short Plays festival; the Oral History Project, which seeks to chronicle and document the contribution of significant theatre women; a Careers Committee; a membership directory; and panels discussing topics of interest to women theatre professionals with well-known experts in the field. Regular monthly meetings enable members to network, initiate programs and serve on committees. To be eligible for membership in the league, playwrights, composers, librettists and lyricists must have had a work presented in a First Class production in the U.S. or Canada; or in a New York City theatre under Equity's Basic Minimum Contract, excluding showcases; or at least 2 productions presented in a resident theatre, as defined under Equity's Minimum Basic Contract for Resident Theatres. Annual dues are $75. For further details of membership eligibility and application procedure, write or call for Membership Information brochure.

LEND (LESBIAN EXCHANGE OF NEW DRAMA)
559 Third St; Brooklyn, NY 11215; (212) 874-7900, ext 1103;
    E-mail anneharris@email.bony.com
Anne Harris, *Artistic Director*

Founded in 1993, LEND is a service organization for lesbian playwrights. Programs include LENDlist, a script-sharing catalog of lesbian-themed plays; PlayREADs, a developmental monthly reading series (playwright must be present); a quarterly newsletter; LENDFest!, an annual festival of staged readings; and the LOLAs, lesbian theatre arts awards, which include the Dyke Drama Award for most promising new lesbian play, which carries a $200 prize and staged reading; send script and bio; *deadline:* 31 Jan 1997; and the Eva Le Gallienne Award, which carries a $500 prize and tribute for outstanding contribution to lesbian theatre arts. LEND also offers the International Lesbian Playwright Exchange Program with Vitalstatistix Theatre in Adelaide, Australia, a two-week residency that gives an American lesbian playwright the opportunity to develop and present a new work in Australia; work need not be lesbian in content; playwright pays airfare; LEND provides housing and stipend, hires director and produces staged reading; send script, bio and letter of inquiry; *deadline:* 1 Dec 1996.

LITERARY MANAGERS AND DRAMATURGS
OF THE AMERICAS
Box 355–CASTA; CUNY Graduate Center; 33 West 42nd St;
    New York, NY 10036; (212) 642-2657, FAX 642-2642;
    E-mail ltimmel@email.gc.cuny.edu

LMDA is the professional service organization for American and Canadian literary managers and dramaturgs, founded in 1985 to affirm, examine and encourage these professions. Among the programs and services it offers are a free 800-number telephone job line; insurance coverage; the quarterly *LMDA Review*; the LMDA Script Exchange; the Production Diaries project; New Dramaturgs, which identifies and encourages new members of the profession and works to establish them in productive professional affiliations; and the University Program, which provides a liaison between training programs and the profession. Activities include public panels, symposiums and workshops, as well as membership-only meetings and an annual conference. Associate membership is open to playwrights, artistic directors, literary agents and other theatre professionals interested in dramaturgy. Dues are $45 for voting members, $35 for associates, $20 for students and $100 for institutional memberships.

LUMINOUS VISIONS
267 West 89th St; New York, NY 10024; (212) 581-7455, FAX 581-3964
Carla Pinza, *Co-Founder and Artistic Director*

Founded in 1976, Luminous Visions is a multicultural, nonprofit organization dedicated to developing the creative skills and culture of film and television writers, directors and actors seeking employment within the English-speaking film and television mainstream. The organization sponsors a weekly workshop for writers, an annual Writers Forum and a spring Stage Reading Festival.

MARY ANDERSON CENTER FOR THE ARTS

101 St. Francis Dr; Mount Saint Francis, IN 47146; (812) 923-8602,
FAX 923-8602
Sarah Roberson Yates, *Executive Director*

The Mary Anderson Center, founded in 1989, is a nonprofit organization dedicated to providing artists with a quiet place where they can concentrate and work on their craft. Named after the 19th-century actress from Louisville who rose to become an international celebrity, the center is located on 400 acres in southern Indiana. The center's goal is to provide retreats and residencies for artists in many disciplines (see the organization's entry in Colonies and Residencies). As part of its outreach effort to the Midwest and the nation, the center sponsors symposiums, conferences and other gatherings which explore, in a multidisciplinary mode, topics of major interest to society and to artists. Contributors to the center receive a quarterly newsletter featuring center activities and news of area artists.

MEET THE COMPOSER

2112 Broadway, Suite 505; New York, NY 10023; (212) 787-3601,
FAX 787-3601
John Duffy, *Director*

Meet The Composer, a national composer service organization, was founded in 1974 to foster the creation, performance and dissemination of music by American composers and to broaden audiences for music of our time. A nonprofit organization, Meet The Composer raises money from foundations, corporations, individual patrons and government sources, and designs programs that support all styles and genres of music—from folk, ethnic, jazz, electronic, symphonic and chamber to choral, music theatre, opera and dance. MTC provides composer fees to nonprofit organizations that perform, present or commission original works. Its programs include Commissioning Music/USA, Composer/Choreographer Project, International Creative Collaborations, New Residencies (see Meet The Composer Grant Programs in Fellowships and Grants), the Meet the Composer Fund and Affiliate Network, New Music for Schools and NYC Composers AIDS Fund.

MIDWEST RADIO THEATRE WORKSHOP

KOPN; 915 East Broadway; Columbia, MO 65201; (573) 874-5676,
FAX 499-1662; E-mail mrtw@mrtw.org; Web http://www.mrtw.org/mrtw
Director

MRTW is a national resource center for radio theatre in the areas of writing, directing, acting and sound design. Founded in 1979, it is a project of KOPN Radio/New Wave Corporation, a nonprofit community radio station serving central Missouri. MRTW holds an annual script contest (see MRTW Script Contest in Prizes) to identify and promote emerging and established radio writers. Winning scripts may be produced during one of a series of radio-theatre workshops held each year (see the organization's entry in Development). MRTW provides information and referral services and technical assistance to interested individuals and groups, distributes educational tapes and publishes an annual Scriptbook.

MISSOURI ASSOCIATION OF PLAYWRIGHTS
830 Spoede Rd; St. Louis, MO 63141; (314) 567-6341
Jo Lovins, *President*

Missouri Association of Playwrights (M.A.P.) was founded in 1976 to help playwrights develop their skills. The association's activities include monthly meetings at which members' scripts are presented as staged readings, periodic workshops, visits from guest speakers from the theatrical arena, seminars on writing for the theatre and an annual full production of one-act plays. Through its affiliation with the Theatre Guild of Webster Groves, M.A.P. submits one-act plays by its members to the theatre to be included in a program of one-acts that opens its season each year. Membership in M.A.P. is open to playrights living in the greater St. Louis area (including southwest IL). Annual dues are $20.

NATIONAL ACADEMY OF SONGWRITERS
6255 Sunset Blvd, Suite 1023; Hollywood, CA 90028; (213) 463-7178 (in CA),
    (800) 826-7287 (outside CA), FAX (213) 463-2146;
    E-mail nassong@aol.com; Web http://i-site.com/~nas/nashome.html
Brett W. Perkins, *Executive Director*

Founded in 1973, NAS is a nonprofit organization dedicated to educating, assisting and protecting songwriters. Members may call a toll-free number for answers to questions about the music business, have songs evaluated by industry professionals and, as proof of authorship, deposit songs in the academy's SongBank. NAS sponsors seminars and workshops. Members receive the newspaper *SongTalk* and a listing of publishers and producers looking for new songs. Annual dues are $200 for Gold Membership (those who have a certified gold single or album), $125 for Pro Membership (those who have had at least 1 song commercially released and distributed) and $95 for General Membership.

NATIONAL ALLIANCE FOR MUSICAL THEATRE
330 West 45th St, Lobby B; New York, NY 10036-3854; (212) 265-5376,
    FAX 582-8730; E-mail namtheatre@aol.com
Jim Thesing, *Executive Director*

The National Alliance for Musical Theatre is a service organization dedicated to supporting professional companies in their efforts to preserve and extend the American musical theatre as an art form. As part of its services, the Alliance annually publishes a Membership Directory with profiles of each member company, including details on those companies which develop and produce new works. The Alliance also produces an annual Festival of New Musicals in New

York City, which aims to encourage further productions of the showcased works. Works to be considered for the festival should be submitted to member theatres, not to the Alliance.

THE NATIONAL FOUNDATION FOR JEWISH CULTURE

330 Seventh Ave, 21st Floor; New York, NY 10001; (212) 629-0500,
    FAX 629-0508; E-mail nfjc@aol.com
Richard A. Siegel, *Executive Director*

The National Foundation for Jewish Culture (NFJC) is the central cultural agency of the American Jewish community. Founded in 1960, the NFJC has been dedicated to the enhancement of Jewish life in America through the support and promotion of the arts and humanities. Rooted in the principle that memory, knowledge and creativity are essential to Jewish continuity, the NFJC encourages innovation and excellence in artistic, scholarly and communal expression of Jewish culture. For the past 30 years, the NFJC has been a leader in advancing Jewish scholarship and preserving the Jewish cultural heritage in America. In recent years, the NFJC's program has expanded to include supporting new creativity in the arts, as well as bringing Jewish culture to local communities throughout North America.

The NFJC provides programs and services to cultural institutions, local communities and individual artists and scholars in every region of the country. It serves as: advocate and coordinator for the fields of Jewish culture through its Council of American Jewish Museums, Council of Jewish Theatres, and Council of Archives and Research Libraries in Jewish Studies; sponsor of grants and awards to artists, scholars and major cultural institutions such as YIVO, Leo Baeck Institute, American Jewish Historical Society, Histadrut Ivrit and the Jewish Publication Society of America; cultural innovator through conferences, symposia, publications, media productions, traveling exhibitions, residencies and performances which promote an understanding and appreciation of contemporary Jewish life and culture; and presenter of the annual Jewish Cultural Achievement Awards recognizing outstanding contributions to Jewish life in America through the arts and scholarship.

THE NATIONAL LEAGUE OF AMERICAN PEN WOMEN, INC.

1300 17th St NW; Washington, DC 20036-1973; (202) 785-1997
Frances J. Carter, *National President*

Founded in 1897, NLAPW is a national membership organization for professional women writers, composers and visual artists. Its local branches meet monthly. It holds annual State Association meetings, a National Biennial Convention and a National Art Show, and sponsors the biennial NLAPW Scholarships for Mature Women (see Fellowships and Grants). Members, who receive a bimonthly magazine, *The Pen Woman*, and a National Roster, pay dues of $30 a year.

NATIONAL PUBLIC RADIO

635 Massachusetts Ave NW; Washington, DC 20001-3753; (202) 414-2399,
    FAX 414-3032; E-mail atrudeau@npr.org
Andy Trudeau, *Director, Program Acquisition and Production*

National Public Radio is a private nonprofit membership organization which
provides a national program service to its over 400 member noncommercial radio
stations. It is funded by its member stations, the Corporation for Public
Broadcasting and corporate grants. Among the programs available to member
stations is *NPR Playhouse*, which presents 29-minute dramatic programs, series and
serials. Writers should note that NPR does not itself read or produce plays. It
acquires broadcast rights to produced packages. It will consider fully produced
programs or works-in-progress on tape only.

NATIONAL THEATRE WORKSHOP OF THE HANDICAPPED

354 Broome St, Loft 5-F; New York, NY 10013; (212) 941-9511, FAX 941-9486
Rick Curry, *Founder and Artistic Director*

Founded in 1977, the National Theatre Workshop of the Handicapped (NTWH)
is a training, production and advocacy organization serving physically disabled
adults who are talented in the performing arts. It is one of the very few places in
the country where new dramatic literature on themes of disability is regularly
tested and produced. In addition to offering professional instruction in acting,
music, voice and movement, and playwriting, NTWH maintains a professional
repertory theatre company which showcases the talents of its students. To help
serve the interests of the 43 million disabled Americans, NTWH solicits the
participation of both playwrights with disabilities and the playwriting community
at large in its annual Festival of Short Works. Playwrights wishing to submit scripts
to the festival should write for guidelines; submissions are accepted throughout
the year. Artists with disabilities who are interested in participating in NTWH's
training programs should contact the workshop for information.

NEW DRAMATISTS

424 West 44th St; New York, NY 10036; (212) 757-6960, FAX 265-4738;
    E-mail newdram@aol.com;
    Web html://www.itp.tsoa.nyu.edu/~diana/ndintro.html
Paul Alexander Slee, *Executive Director*
Elana Greenfield, *Director of Artistic Programs*

New Dramatists is a service organization for member playwrights, which is
designed to meet the varying needs of a large number of writers of diverse styles.
Rather than producing plays, New Dramatists serves as a laboratory where writers
can develop their craft through a comprehensive program which includes script-
in-hand readings followed by panel discussions; a loan fund; a library; free tickets
to Broadway and Off-Broadway productions; a monthly bulletin for members
detailing grants, contests and opportunities; a biannual newsletter, *The New
Dramatist*, whose subscribers include 5000 theatre professionals; exchanges with
theatres in other countries; a national script distribution service, ScriptShare; and
the Composer/Librettist Studio, a workshop exploring the composer/librettist

relationship. Annual New Dramatists awards for which members are eligible include the Joe A. Callaway Award, the Frederick Loewe Award in Music Theatre and the Clara Rotter Fellowship.

Membership is open to all playwrights living in the greater New York area, and to those living elsewhere who are able to spend sufficient time in the city to use membership to their advantage. To apply for membership submit 2 copies of 2 full-length plays (no screenplays or adaptations), 2 large SASEs, a resume, a bio and a statement outlining what you wish to accomplish over the next few years and how New Dramatists would serve that purpose; inclusion of letters of recommendation and reviews is optional. If admitted, a playwright is eligible for all the organization's services for 7 years. Scripts are accepted 15 Jul–15 Sep only. *Deadline:* 15 Sep 1996; *notification:* May 1997. Write or call for further information.

New Dramatists administers the L. Arnold Weissberger Playwriting Competition (see Prizes); and selects, and hosts a residency for, the winner of the Princess Grace Awards: Playwright Fellowship (see Fellowships and Grants).

NEW ENGLAND THEATRE CONFERENCE

Department of Theatre, Northeastern University; 360 Huntington Ave; Boston, MA 02115; (617) 424-9275, FAX 424-9275 *51
Corey Boniface, *Manager of Operations*

Founded in 1952, New England Theatre Conference is a membership organization primarily but not exclusively for New England theatre people, including playwrights, teachers, students and theatre professionals. Services include an annual conference, publication of a member directory and annual summer theatre auditions. NETC also administers the John Gassner Memorial Playwriting Award (see Prizes). The organization publishes *New England Theatre Journal* and *NETC News*. Membership dues are $80 for groups, $30 for individuals and $20 for students.

NEW GEORGES

90 Hudson St, Suite 2E; New York, NY 10013; (212) 620-0113
Susan Bernfield, *Artistic Director*

New Georges is a professional theatre organization that produces and develops new works by women and supports the creative efforts of emerging women theatre artists. The group's programs revolve around The Room, New Georges's workspace, and involve a loose network of affiliated artists. These include informal readings of works-in-progress and workshop presentations of pieces developed in The Room, as well as an annual season of new plays and performance pieces by women. Women playwrights interested in working with New Georges may submit a completed script or work-in-progress, together with a resume and cover letter.

NEW PLAYWRIGHTS FOUNDATION

c/o 608 San Vicente Blvd, #18; Santa Monica, CA 90402; (310) 393-3682
Jeffrey Lee Bergquist, *Artistic Director*

Founded in 1968, New Playwrights Foundation is a service organization for writers working in theatre, film, television and video. The foundation runs developmental workshops, holds readings, occcassionally coproduces video and film projects and assists members in furthering their careers. Membership in NPF is limited to a maximum of 15 writers who must be able to attend meetings in Santa Monica every other Monday. Applicants for membership attend meetings before submitting materials to be reviewed by the group.

THE NEW YORK PUBLIC LIBRARY
FOR THE PERFORMING ARTS

40 Lincoln Center Plaza; New York, NY 10023-7498; (212) 870-1639,
       FAX 787-3852; E-mail rtaylor@nypl.org
Bob Taylor, *Curator, The Billy Rose Theatre Collection*

The Billy Rose Theatre Collection, a division of the Library for the Performing Arts, is open to the public (aged 18 and over) and contains material on all aspects of theatrical art and the entertainment world, including stage, film, radio, television, circus, vaudeville and burlesque. The Theatre on Film and Tape Project (TOFT) is a special collection of films and videotapes of theatrical productions recorded during performance, as well as informal dialogues with important theatrical personalities. Tapes are available for viewing by appointment (call 870-1641) to students, theatre professionals and researchers.

NON-TRADITIONAL CASTING PROJECT

1560 Broadway, Suite 1600; New York, NY 10036;
       (212) 730-4750 (voice), -4913 (TDD), FAX 730-4820
Sharon Jensen, *Executive Director*

Founded in 1986, the Non-Traditional Casting Project is a nonprofit organization which exists to address and seek solutions to the problems of racism and exclusion in the theatre and related media, particularly as they relate to creative personnel: including, but not limited to, actors, directors, writers, designers and producers. The project works to advance the creative participation of artists of color and artists with disabilities through both advocacy and specific projects. Key NTCP programs include Artist Files/Artist Files Online, a national talent bank; roundtable discussions with industry leaders; a national Information and Consulting Service; and the publications: *New Traditions*, a quarterly newsletter; and *Beyond Tradition*, transcripts of the first national symposium on Non-Traditional Casting. In development is a 3-part series called *Resource Guides on Actors with Disabilities*. Writers of color and/or with disabilities, who are citizens or residents of the U.S. or Canada and have had at least one play given a profession-al production or staged reading should send a resume for inclusion in Artist

Files/Artist Files Online, indicating their cultural identification and, in the case of disabled artists, any accommodation they may use; those interested in contacting listed artists will call them or their agents directly.

NORTHWEST PLAYWRIGHTS GUILD

408 Southwest 2nd Ave, Suite 427; Portland, OR 97204; (503) 222-7010;
    E-mail bjscript@teleport.com;
    Web http://www.teleport.com/~bjscript/nwpg.html
Bill Johnson, *Office Manager*

Northwest Playwrights Guild is an information clearinghouse and support group for playwrights. The guild sponsors public readings, holds workshops and produces regional conferences on theatre that include the full production of original scripts. The guild publishes a quarterly, *Script*, that contains articles on theatre in the Northwest, as well as update newsletters that provide information on current script opportunities. Membership dues are $25 a year.

OLLANTAY CENTER FOR THE ARTS

Box 720636; Jackson Heights, NY 11372-0636; (718) 565-6499,
    FAX 446-7806
Pedro R. Monge-Rafuls, *Executive and Artistic Director*

Founded as a multidisciplinary Hispanic arts center in 1977, OLLANTAY has developed a Hispanic Heritage Center for the arts in America with a view to providing the knowledge and resources needed to pursue research and develop new programs and initiatives in the field. The center maintains a resource bank of video and audio tapes, slides, books, plays and articles, which may be consulted by writing for an appointment. OLLANTAY's Traveling Theater Program tours plays by local writers. Its unique Playwriting Workshop, an annual intensive course of 3–6 weeks, provides an opportunity for playwrights wishing to write in Spanish to work under the direction of major Latin American playwrights who reside outside the U.S. *OLLANTAY Theater Magazine* is a biannual journal in English and Spanish which gives local playwrights, critics and scholars the opportunity to share their knowledge and experience of Hispanic theatre within the framework of American and world drama. The magazine, which publishes at least one play in each issue, is available to subscribers. Annual subscription is $18 for individuals, $25 for organizations.

OPERA AMERICA

1156 15th St NW, Suite 810; Washington, DC 20005-3287; (202) 293-4466,
    FAX 393-0735; E-mail frontdesk@operaam.org
Krista Rimple, *Program Manager, The Next Stage*

Founded in 1970, OPERA America is the not-for-profit service organization for the professional opera field in North America and allied international members. OPERA America provides a variety of informational, technical and financial services to its membership, and serves as a resource to the media, funders, government agencies and the general public.

The Next Stage, a program of OPERA America, is a 3-year pilot program designed to increase the number of North American works in the standard repertory by providing financial, technical and informational assistance to professional opera companies for productions of existing, under-performed works by North American artists.

Application for grants awarded through the program are accepted only from Professional Company Members of OPERA America. Individual artists and other organizations may request information about the program.

PEN AMERICAN CENTER

568 Broadway; New York, NY 10012; (212) 334-1660, FAX 334-2181;
        E-mail pen@echonyc.com
Karen Kennerly, *Executive Director*

PEN is an international association of writers. The American Center is the largest of the 106 centers which comprise International PEN. The 2800 members of PEN American Center are established North American writers and translators, and literary editors. PEN activities include the Freedom-to-Write program; monthly symposiums, readings and other public events; a prison writing program; and a translator-publisher clearinghouse. PEN's publications include *Grants and Awards Available to American Writers*, a biennially updated directory of prizes, grants, fellowships and awards (1996–97 edition $15 postpaid); and *The PEN Prison Writing Information Bulletin*. Among PEN's annual prizes and awards are the Gregory Kolovakos Award, PEN–Book-of-the-Month Club Translation Prize and the Renato Poggioli Award (see Prizes); and Writing Awards for Prisoners, awarded to the authors of the best fiction, nonfiction, drama and poetry received from prisoner-writers in the U.S. The PEN Writers Fund assists writers (see Emergency Funds).

PLAYMARKET

Box 9767; Wellington; New Zealand; 64-4-382-8462, FAX 64-4-382-8461
John McDavitt, *Executive Officer*
Susan Wilson, *Script Advisor*

Playmarket is a service organization for playwrights, established in 1973 as a result of a growing interest in plays by New Zealand writers and a need to find new writers. The organization runs a script advisory and critiquing service, arranges workshop productions of promising scripts, and serves as the country's principal playwrights' agency, preparing and distributing copies of scripts and negotiating and collecting royalties. Playmarket's publications include *The Playmarket Directory of New Zealand Plays and Playwrights*, and a script series *New Zealand Theatrescripts*.

THE PLAYWRIGHTS' CENTER

2301 Franklin Ave East; Minneapolis, MN 55406-1099; (612) 332-7481
Carlo Cuesta, *Executive Director*

The Playwrights' Center is a service organization for playwrights. Its programs include: developmental services (cold readings and workshops using an Equity acting company); fellowships; exchanges with theatres and other developmental programs; a newsletter; the Jones one-act commissioning program; PlayLabs (see Development); Playworks, a professional touring company performing for schools and community organizations; playwriting classes; year-round programs for young writers; and the Many Voices program, designed to provide awards, education and lab services to new and emerging Minnesota playwrights of color. The center awards annually 5 Jerome Playwright-in-Residence Fellowships and 2 McKnight Fellowships, for which competition is open nationally; McKnight Advancement Grants open to Minnesota playwrights; and 3 Many Voices Multicultural Collaboration Grants (see The Playwrights' Center Grant Programs in Fellowships and Grants). The annual Young Playwrights Summer Conference, open to playwrights grades 8–12, offers 2 weeks of workshops and classes for 40 young writers, with daily workshops and readings of students' work; participants, who are selected on the basis of writing samples and recommendations, receive college credit; scholarships are available; applications are available 31 Jan 1997; *deadline:* 22 Apr 1997; *dates:* 15–28 Jul 1997.

A broad-based center membership is available to any playwright or interested person. Benefits of general membership for playwrights include discounts on classes, applications for all center programs, eligibility to apply for one-act commissions and script-development readings, and the center's newsletter. Core (must be MN resident) and Associate Member Playwrights are selected by a review panel each spring, based on script submission. They have primary access to all center programs and services, including developmental workshops and public readings. Write for Membership brochure. Membership applications are available 1 Feb 1997, *deadline:* 1 Apr 1997; *notification:* 1 Jul 1997.

THE PLAYWRIGHTS FOUNDATION

Box 460357; San Francisco, CA 94114; (415) 431-4458, FAX 431-4471
Dyke Garrison, *President*

The Playwrights Foundation provides developmental support to playwrights throughout the U.S., with emphasis on the northern California region. It produces the annual Bay Area Playwrights Festival (see Development). The foundation also sponsors a 10-minute play contest for members only and presents readings of the winning pieces at an annual benefit.

PLAYWRIGHTS HARBOR

160 West 71st St; New York, NY 10023; (212) 787-1945 (c/o M&C Productions)
Stuart Warmflash, *Artistic Director*

Founded in 1994, Playwrights Harbor provides developmental workshops for 15 member theatre writers. Membership is available to playwrights, composers and librettists who have a body of work; are committed to rewrites and developing one project for an entire season; and who seek supportive criticism. The workshop meets every Monday in New York City for 3 hours and provides cold and/or rehearsed readings, followed by a short critique by professional playwrights and the acting company. Dues for the 1995–1996 season were $350. The organization is especially, but not exclusively, seeking minority playwrights.

THE PLAYWRIGHTS' PROJECT

Sammons Center for the Arts, #12; 3630 Harry Hines Blvd; Dallas, TX 75219;
(214) 497-1752
Raphael Parry, *Artistic Director*

The Playwrights' Project was founded in 1990 as a service organization for playwrights from the north Texas area. The project holds biweekly group labs and in-house and public readings, organizes workshops and lecture series, publishes a newsletter and sponsors the annual Robert Bone Memorial Playwriting Award (see Prizes). While the group's resident playwrights pay annual dues of $50, no qualified playwright is excluded for lack of funds. New resident playwrights, who must be from the Dallas area or able to travel to meetings and events in Dallas, are selected annually; applicants should submit 1 full-length play, or 2 one-acts totaling a minimum of 60 minutes, a cover letter containing a brief synopsis of the play(s), a bio, an optional SASE for acknowledgment of receipt and $5 fee; *deadline:* 1 Jun 1997 for residencies starting in the fall of 1997.

PLAYWRIGHTS THEATRE OF NEW JERSEY

33 Green Village Rd; Madison, NJ 07940; (201) 514-1787, FAX 514-2060
John Pietrowski, *Producing Artistic Director*

Founded in 1986, the Playwrights Theatre of New Jersey is both a service organization for playwrights of all ages and a professional developmental theatre. In addition to its New Play Development Program (see Playwrights Theatre of New Jersey in Development), PTNJ sponsors a state-wide playwriting-in-the-schools program; a playwriting-for-teachers project; adult playwriting classes; children's creative dramatics classes; acting classes; and "special needs" playwriting projects which include work in housing projects and with senior citizens, teenage substance abusers, persons with physical disabilities and court-appointed youth, as well as a playwriting-in-prisons initiative. Young playwrights festivals are held in Madison and Newark, in addition to a statewide festival which is part of the New Jersey Young Playwrights Program. Gifted and talented playwriting symposiums, hosted by well-known playwrights, provide intensive 2-day experiences for up to 60 students from various school districts. With the New Jersey State Council on the Arts, PTNJ cosponsors the Writers-in-the-Schools Program, which teaches poetry and prose in schools and community centers statewide.

PLAZA DE LA RAZA

3540 North Mission Rd; Los Angeles, CA 90031; (213) 223-2475,
FAX 223-1804; E-mail plaza@caprica.com
Rose Cano, *Executive Director*

Founded in 1970, Plaza de la Raza is a cultural center for the arts and education, primarily serving the Chicano community of East Los Angeles. Of special interest to playwrights is the center's Nuevo L.A. Chicano TheatreWorks project, designed to discover, develop and present the work of Chicano playwrights. Initiated in 1989 and recurring approximately every 4 years, depending on funding, as part of the Nuevo L.A. Chicano Art Series cycle (Visual Arts, Music, Dance and Theatre), the project develops new one-acts through a 2-week workshop with director and actors, culminating in public readings; some plays are selected for subsequent full production. Latino playwrights who are California residents should contact the center for information on when and how to apply for the next round of the program. In addition to its playwrights' project, Plaza de la Raza conducts classes in drama, dance, music and the visual arts; provides resources for teachers in the community; and sponsors special events, exhibits and performances. Membership in Plaza de la Raza is open to all.

PROFESSIONAL ASSOCIATION OF CANADIAN THEATRES/ PACT COMMUNICATIONS CENTRE
415 Yonge St, 15th Floor; Toronto, Ontario; Canada; M5B 2E7;
(416) 595-6455, FAX 595-6450; E-mail pact@cnetmail.ffa.ucalgary.ca
Pat Bradley, *Executive Director*
Rick Sherman, *Membership and Communications Coordinator*

PACT is the national service and trade association representing professional English-language theatres in Canada. PACT was incorporated in 1976 to work on behalf of its member theatres in the areas of advocacy, labor relations, professional development and communications. The members' newsletter *impact!* is published quarterly. PACT Communications Centre (PCC) was established in 1985 as the charitable wing of PACT in order to improve and expand communications and information services. PCC publishes *The Theatre Listing*, an annual directory of English-language Canadian theatres which also includes valuable information on rehearsal and performance spaces, government agencies and arts service organizations; and *Artsboard*, the monthly bulletin of employment opportunities in the arts in Canada.

PUBLIC BROADCASTING SERVICE
1320 Braddock Pl; Alexandria, VA 22314-1698; (703) 739-5000,
FAX 739-8444, -8458; E-mail www@pbs.org
Corporate Information

The Public Broadcasting Service is a private nonprofit corporation that acquires and distributes programs to its 345 member stations. The PBS Programming Department can advise independent producers about the development of specific projects. Information about the preparation, presentation and funding of projects can be obtained from PBS. Printed materials such as the *PBS Packaging & Technical Guidelines* are also available.

THE PURPLE CIRCUIT
2025 Griffith Park Blvd, Suite 4; Los Angeles, CA 90039; (213) 661-1982
Bill Kaiser, *Coordinator*

The Purple Circuit is a network of gay, lesbian, queer, bisexual and transsexual theatres, producers and performers, and "Kindred Spirits" (theatres which are not exclusively gay or lesbian in orientation but are interested in producing gay or lesbian material on a regular basis). The Purple Circuit publishes news, information and articles of interest to its constituency in its quarterly newsletter,

On the Purple Circuit. The Purple Circuit Directory lists theatres and producers around the world, including "Kindred Spirits," that are interested in presenting gay, lesbian, bisexual and transsexual works. The Purple Circuit Hotline (213) 666-0693 provides information on gay and lesbian shows currently playing in southern California and elsewhere, as well as information for playwrights and for journalists and others interested in promoting gay and lesbian theatre and performance art.

THE SCRIPTWRITERS NETWORK

11684 Ventura Blvd, #508; Studio City, CA 91604; (213) 848-9477
Bettina Moss, *Chair*

Though the Scriptwriters Network, founded in 1989, is predominantly an affiliation of film, television and corporate/industrial writers, playwrights are welcome. Meetings feature guest speakers, developmental feedback on scripts is available, and staged readings may be arranged in conjunction with other groups. The network sponsors members-only contests and publishes a newsletter. Prospective members submit a professionally formatted script and a completed application; membership is not based on the quality of the script. There is a $10 initiation fee, and dues are $60 a year.

THE SONGWRITERS GUILD OF AMERICA

1560 Broadway, Room 1306; New York, NY 10036; (212) 768-7902,
        FAX 768-9048; E-mail songnews@aol.com
George Wurzbach, *National Projects Director*

Head Office:
1500 Harbor Blvd; Weehawken, NJ 07087-6732; (201) 867-7603
Los Angeles Office:
6430 Sunset Blvd; Hollywood, CA 90028; (213) 462-1108
Nashville Office:
1222 16th Ave; Nashville, TN 37212; (615) 329-1782

The Songwriters Guild is a voluntary national association run by and for songwriters; all officers and directors are unpaid. Among its many services to composers and lyricists, the guild provides a standard songwriter's contract and reviews this and other contracts on request; collects writers' royalties from music publishers; maintains a copyright renewal service; conducts songwriting workshops and critique sessions with special rates for members; provides a songwriter collaboration service; issues news bulletins with essential information for writers; and offers a group medical and life insurance plan. Full members of the guild must be published songwriters and pay dues on a graduated scale from $70–400. Unpublished songwriters may become associate members and pay dues of $55 a year. Write for membership application.

S.T.A.G.E. (SOCIETY FOR THEATRICAL ARTISTS' GUIDANCE AND ENHANCEMENT)

Box 214820; Dallas, TX 75221; (214) 630-7722, FAX 630-4468
Marilyn Pyeatt, *Executive Director*

Founded in 1981, S.T.A.G.E. acts as an information clearinghouse for theatre artists and theatre organizations in the north Texas region. The society maintains a library of plays, theatre texts and resource information; offers counseling on agents, unions, personal marketing and other career-related matters; posts listings of miscellaneous job opportunities; and maintains an audition callboard for regional opportunities in theatre and film; sponsors an actor's showcase, Noon Preview; and produces Stages Festival of New Plays, the longest running new play festival in Dallas. Any playwright may submit to the festival, which seeks unproduced one-acts, not more than 20 minutes long, with minimal sets and props and preferably 8 or fewer characters; winning playwrights receive an honorarium and production; send SASE for guidelines; *deadline:* 15 Mar 1997. Members of S.T.A.G.E., who pay annual dues starting at $45 (for volunteers), $65 (for all others), receive a monthly publication, *CENTERSTAGE.*

THEATRE ASSOCIATION OF PENNSYLVANIA (TAP)

1919 North Front St, 3rd Floor; Harrisburg, PA 17102-2284;
(717) 232-9752, FAX (717) 232-9756
Al Franklin, *Executive Director*

Founded in 1968, TAP is Pennsylvania's theatre service organization. Its membership includes theatres of every type, academic institutions, theatre training programs, and artists, educators and other individuals committed to the continuing development of quality theatre and the vital role that theatre plays in the life of the Commonwealth. TAP serves as the central information agency for its membership; sponsors festivals, conferences, workshops and auditions; administers granting programs; acts as a liaison with state and national organizations; and produces a variety of publications, including *TAPLINE, Seasons-at-a-Glance* and *Pennsylvania Theatre Directory.* Membership in TAP is open to all. Annual dues are $30 for individuals, $15 for students, and $45–275 for organizations.

THEATRE BAY AREA

657 Mission St, Suite 402; San Francisco, CA 94105; (415) 957-1557,
FAX 957-1556; E-mail tba@well.com

TBA is a resource organization for San Francisco Bay Area theatre workers whose members include 3200 individuals and more than 240 theatre companies. Its programs include TIX Bay Area, San Francisco's half-price ticket booth; TIX By Mail, a half-price ticket catalog; professional workshops; and communications and networking services. Annual dues of $35 (add $12 for 1st-class postage) include a subscription to *Callboard,* a monthly magazine featuring articles, interviews and essays on the Northern California theatre scene, as well as information on play contests and festivals, and listings of production activity, workshops, classes, auditions, jobs and services. TBA also publishes *Theatre Directory of the Bay Area* (1995–96 edition $18/member, $24/nonmember, postpaid), which includes entries of local theatre companies and listings of rehearsal and performance spaces; *Sources of Publicity* and *Sources of Funding* ($12/member, $14/nonmember); and Management Memo, a monthly newsletter for theatre administrators and artistic directors (free to members only).

THEATRE COMMUNICATIONS GROUP
355 Lexington Ave; New York, NY 10017-0217;
    (212) 697-5230, FAX 983-4847; E-mail: tcg@tcg.org
John Sullivan, *Executive Director*

Founded in 1961, TCG is the national organization for the American theatre. Its mission is to celebrate and inspire excellence in the artistry of theatre in America. To carry out this mission, TCG serves theatre artists and nonprofit professional theatre organizations by recognizing and encouraging artistic diversity; providing a forum for open and critical examination of issues, standards and values; fostering interaction among theatre professionals; collecting, analyzing and disseminating information regarding the profession; and serving as the principal advocate for America's nonprofit professional theatre. With a constituency of more than 300 theatres across America that reach a combined audience of more than 20 million each year, TCG provides centralized services to aid the work of thousands in the field. Its chief programs include grants, fellowships and awards to theatre artists and institutions; conferences, workshops and roundtables; government affairs; surveys and research; and publications. (For more information, see *American Theatre* and *PlaySource* in Publication, and TCG Grant Programs in Fellowships and Grants.)

In addition to *American Theatre* magazine and *PlaySource*, TCG publications of interest to theatre writers include *Theatre Profiles*, a biennial reference guide offering comprehensive statistical, historical and production information on more than 200 nonprofit theatres; *Theatre Directory*, which provides complete contact information for more than 350 theatres and related arts organizations across the U.S.; and *ArtSEARCH*, a biweekly bulletin of job opportunities in the arts. The "Opportunities" column of *American Theatre* supplements information provided in this *Sourcebook*. TCG also publishes plays, translations and anthologies in book form, play texts in *American Theatre*, and books dealing with all aspects of theatre. (For further information, see Useful Publications, and Publications from TCG in the back of this book, or contact TCG for the current Publications catalogue.)

Individual Members receive a free subscription to *American Theatre*, discounts on tickets to performances at more than 150 theatres nationwide, cost-savings on TCG resource materials, and discounts on all books from TCG and other select theatre publishers. Members are also eligible to apply for the TCG credit card, a no-annual fee MasterCard, and receive discounts from Budget Rent A Car, Airborne Express and the Hotel Reservation Network. Individual memberships are available to all theatre professionals, as well as to theatre enthusiasts, for $35 a year. (See membership application in the back of this book.)

THE THEATRE MUSEUM

1E Tavistock St; London WC2E 7PA; England; 441-71-836-7891,
    FAX 441-71-836-5148

The Theatre Museum, a branch of the Victoria & Albert Museum, is Britain's national museum of the performing arts. In addition to its regular displays, which feature 400 years of the history, technology, art and craft of theatre, and its special exhibitions, the museum houses the U.K.'s largest archive of performing arts materials, including play texts, photographic and biographical files, theatre programs and reviews, and books about the theatre. The archive and study room is available by appointment (call during office hours) Tuesday to Friday, 10:30–1:00 p.m. and 2:00–4:30 p.m. The museum's innovative education department runs workshops and study days on theatre practice and set texts for children, students and teachers. The museum also runs a program of celebrity play readings, seminars and events to give visitors insight into current theatre production.

UBU REPERTORY THEATER

15 West 28th St; New York, NY 10001; (212) 679-7540, FAX 679-2033
Françoise Kourilsky, *Artistic Director*

Ubu Repertory Theater, founded in 1982, is a nonprofit theatre center dedicated to introducing translations of contemporary French-language plays to the English-speaking audience (see theatre's entry in Production). In addition to producing several plays a year, Ubu commissions translations and schedules reading programs, photography exhibits, panel discussions and workshops. Ubu publishes a series of contemporary plays by French-speaking playwrights in English translation, distributed nationally by TCG, and houses a French-English reference library of published plays and manuscripts.

VOLUNTEER LAWYERS FOR THE ARTS

1 East 53rd St, 6th Floor; New York, NY 10022;
    (212) 319-2787 (administrative office), 319-2910 (Art Law Hotline),
    FAX 752-6575
Daniel Y. Mayer, *Executive Director*

Volunteer Lawyers for the Arts arranges free legal representation and legal education in the arts community. Individual artists and nonprofit arts organizations unable to afford private counsel are eligible for VLA's services; VLA can be especially useful to playwrights with copyright or contract problems. There is an administrative fee per referral of $30–50 for individuals, $50–100 for nonprofit organizations and $250 for nonprofit incorporation and tax exemption. VLA's education program offers biweekly seminars on nonprofit incorporation and evening seminars held regularly to educate attorneys and artists in specific areas of art law. Publications include *Model Contracts for Independent Contractors: Sample Provisions and Job Descriptions* ($15 plus $4 postage and handling); and the *VLA Guide to Copyright for the Performing Arts* ($5.95 plus $4 postage and handling). For more information about VLA's publications and the 40 VLA affiliates across the country, contact the New York office; referrals can be made to volunteer lawyer organizations nationwide.

WOMEN'S THEATRE ALLIANCE

Box 64446; Chicago, IL 60664-0446; (312) 408-9910
Jennifer Yeo, *President*

W.T.A. is a networking and resource organization for Chicago-area theatre artists including actors, directors, playwrights, producers, stage managers, technicians, designers and educators. Its mission is to advocate women's leadership in the Chicago-area theatre community; to create an empowering resource for women theatre artists to ensure that their voices are heard within that community; and to provide a support network for women theatre artists that will enable them to share their artistic diversity and learn from one another. In pursuit of these goals, W.T.A. holds quarterly meetings; sponsors informal readings, staged readings, play development workshops and an annual actors' showcase and new plays festival; and publishes a monthly newsletter. To join W.T.A., write or call for a Membership/Information Request Form. Membership dues are $30 a year.

THE WOW CAFE

59–61 East 4th St; New York, NY 10003; (212) 460-8067 (service)

The WOW (Women's One World) Cafe is a women's theatre collective whose membership is primarily but not exclusively lesbian. WOW produces the work of women playwrights and performers. It has no permanent staff and its members are encouraged to participate in all aspects of the group's operations. In lieu of dues, members volunteer their services backstage on fellow members' productions in exchange for the opportunity to present their own work. Each show is produced by the member who initiates it. Women interested in becoming members of the WOW Cafe may attend one of the collective's regular meetings, which are scheduled every Tuesday at 6:30 PM.

WRITERS GUILD OF AMERICA, EAST (WGAE)

555 West 57th St; New York, NY 10019-2967; (212) 767-7800
Mona Mangan, *Executive Director*

WGAE is the union for freelance writers in the fields of motion pictures, television and radio who reside east of the Mississippi River. The union negotiates collective bargaining agreements for its members and represents them in grievances and arbitrations under those agreements. It also makes credit determinations for the writing of its members. The guild gives annual awards, and sponsors a foundation which currently teaches film writing to disadvantaged high school students. WGAE participates in reciprocal arrangements with the International Affiliation of Writers Guilds and with its sister union, Writers Guild of America, west. The guild publishes a monthly newsletter, which is available to nonmembers by subscription; and a quarterly journal, *On Writing*. Write for information on WGAE's registration service for registering literary material, or call (212) 757-4360.

WRITERS GUILD OF AMERICA, WEST (WGAW)
7000 West 3rd St; Los Angeles, CA 90048-4329; (213) 951-4000, FAX 782-4800
Brian Walton, *Executive Director*

WGAw is the union for writers in the fields of motion pictures, television, radio and new media who write both entertainment and news programming. It represents its members in collective bargaining and other labor matters. It publishes a monthly magazine, *The Journal.* The Guild registers material, including screen- and teleplays, books, plays, poetry and songs. The library is open to the public Mon–Fri.

YOUNG PLAYWRIGHTS INC.
321 West 44th St, #906; New York, NY 10036; (212) 307-1140, FAX 307-1454
Sheri M. Goldhirsch, *Artistic Director*

Young Playwrights Inc. (YPI), founded in 1981 by Stephen Sondheim and members of the Dramatists Guild, introduces young people to the theatre and encourages self-expression through the art of playwriting. YPI strives to identify, develop and encourage playwrights aged 18 years and younger; to develop new works for the theatre and to aid in the creation of the next generation of professional playwrights through the Young Playwrights Festival (see Prizes), the Young Playwrights Spring Conference, and the Urban Playwriting Retreat; to expose young people to theatre and playwriting through WRITING ON YOUR FEET! in-school playwriting workshops; to train teachers through the TEACHING ON YOUR FEET! Teacher Training Institute; to develop and serve audiences that reflect the complex makeup of our society and to create the next generation of theatregoers through the TAKE A GROWNUP TO THE THEATER! ticket subsidy program, student matinees and a discount voucher program; to bring the vital experience of professional theatre free of charge to neglected inner-city public schools, community organizations and youth centers through the Young Playwrights School Tour; and to serve as an advocate for young writers regardless of ethnicity, physical ability, sexual orientation or economic status, and to ensure that their voices are heard and acknowledged by a diverse community of artists and theatregoers.

Epilogue

- Useful Publications
- Submission Calendar
- Special Interests
- Index

Useful Publications

This is a selective listing of the publications that we think most usefully supplement the information given in the *Sourcebook*. Note that publications of interest to theatre writers are also described throughout this book, particularly in introductions to sections, in Membership and Service Organizations listings, and on the Publications from TCG pages in the back. Before ordering you would be wise to find out if the prices given in all listings still pertain.

We have purposely left out any "how to" books on the art of playwriting because we do not want to promote the concept of "writing-by-recipe." However, we do recommend David Savran's *In Their Own Words: Contemporary American Playwrights* and *The Production Notebooks: Theatre in Process, Volume One*, edited by Mark Bly (see Publications from TCG).

American Theatre
Theatre Communications Group; 355 Lexington Ave;
New York, NY 10017-0217; (212) 697-5230, FAX 983-4847;
E-mail custserv@tcg.org

1-year subscription/TCG membership $35, 2 years $70; single issue $4.95. This monthly magazine includes an "Opportunities" column which updates *Sourcebook* information between editions, announcing new grants and contests. A special

Season Preview issue each October lists schedules for some 200 theatres nationwide and monthly schedules are published in each issue. As part of its comprehensive coverage of all aspects of theatre, *American Theatre* regularly features articles and interviews dealing with theatre writers and their works, and publishes the complete texts of 6 new plays a year.

Back Stage
1515 Broadway, 14th Floor; New York, NY 10036; (212) 764-7300, FAX 536-5318

1-year subscription $75, 2 years $125; single issue $2.25, $3.25 by mail. This performing arts weekly includes industry news; reports from cities across the country; reviews; and columns, including "Playwrights' Corner." Though the primary focus is on casting, theatres and other producers sometimes run ads soliciting scripts; workshops and classes for playwrights are also likely to be advertised here.

A Handbook for Literary Translators
PEN American Center; 568 Broadway; New York, NY 10012;
(212) 334-1660, FAX 334-2181; E-mail pen@echonyc.com

3rd edition, 1995. 35 pp, $2.50 (includes postage and handling) paper. Contents include "A Translator's Model Contract," "Negotiating a Contract," "Selected Resources" and "The Responsibilities of Translation."

Hollywood Scriptwriter
1626 North Wilcox, #385; Hollywood, CA 90028; (805) 495-5447, FAX 495-5447

1-year subscription (12 issues) $44, 6 months $25; discount on renewals. This 12-page newsletter contains a "MARKETS for Your Work" section that includes "Plays Wanted" listings, as well as interviews and articles giving advice that is sometimes useful to playwrights as well as screenwriters. A list of back issues with a summary of the contents of each issue is available; call for information and a free sample.

The Individual's Guide to Grants by Judith B. Margolin
Plenum Press; 233 Spring St; New York, NY 10013;
(212) 620-8051 or toll-free 1-800-221-9369, FAX (212) 647-1898

1983. 314 pp, $19.95 cloth. This comprehensive guide to individual grantseeking, written by a former director of the New York library of the Foundation Center, offers detailed advice on each step of the process.

Into Print: A Guide to the Writing Life
Quality Paperback Book Club; 72 Spring St; New York, NY 10012;
(212) 226-3586, FAX 226-3963; E-mail pwsubs@aol.com

$12.95 paper. Based on practical articles on the business of writing published in *Poets & Writers Magazine* (see below), this book has an all-new introduction and is completely revised and updated. Topics covered include "Contracts and Royalties: Negotiating Your Own," "Cutting the High Cost of Health Care" and "On Cloud Nine: Writers' Colonies, Retreats, Ranches, Residencies and Sanctuaries."

Literary Agents: A Writer's Guide by Adam Begley
Poets & Writers; 72 Spring St; New York, NY 10012; (212) 226-3586,
FAX 226-3963; E-mail pwsubs@aol.com

1993. 196 pp, $10 (plus $3.90 postage and handling plus sales tax where applicable) paper. This book contains several chapters exploring the functions of literary agents and the agent-writer relationship, and includes listings of 196 agencies which will consider unsolicited *queries* plus 37 more agencies which charge fees.

Literary Agents of North America
Author Aid/Research Associates International; 340 East 52nd St;
New York, NY 10022; orders to Box 7263, FDR Station; New York, NY 10150;
(212) 758-4213 or 980-9179

5th edition, 1995. 315 pp, $33 (plus $3.50 postage and handling, $7.50 for priority mail, plus sales tax on NYS orders) paper. Profiles of more than 1000 U.S. and Canadian literary agencies include their areas of interest and policies regarding new writers and unsolicited manuscripts. It also contains 5 comprehensive indexes.

Literary Market Place 1996
R.R. Bowker; 121 Chanlon Rd; New Providence, NJ 07974;
(908) 464-6800 or toll-free 1-800-521-8110, FAX (908) 771-7704

1995. 1942 pp, $169.95 (plus 7% shipping and handling plus sales tax where applicable) paper. This directory of the American book publishing industry gives contact information for book publishers and those in related fields, and includes a "Names & Numbers" index over 500 pages long. The 1997 *LMP* is due out in September 1996.

Market Insight...for Playwrights
Box 4863; Englewood, CO 80155; 1-800-895-4720; E-mail minsight@aol.com

1-year subscription $40 (12 issues), 6 months $25. This monthly newsletter for playwrights provides submission guidelines for theatres, residencies, publishers and contests, as well as updates on personnel changes at theatres, special programs for women writers, and more; call for a free sample.

Music, Dance & Theater Scholarships
Conway Greene Publishing Company; 11000 Cedar Ave; Cleveland, OH 44106;
(216) 721-0077 or toll-free 1-800-977-2665

1995. 512 pp, $20.95 (plus $4.50 shipping and handling) paper. This guide provides information on more than 1800 theatre, music and dance conservatory and undergraduate programs, as well as more than 5000 professional and educational scholarship opportunities. It also includes detailed information on audition requirements, decision processes at individual schools, special scholarship stipulations and student profiles.

The National Playwrights Directory
O'Neill Theater Center; 305 Great Neck Rd; Waterford, CT 06385;
(203) 443-5378, FAX 443-9653

1986. 507 pp, $20 (plus $3.50 postage and handling) cloth. With entries on 495 writers and an index of over 4000 plays, this book is still a useful source of information.

Playhouse America!
Feedback Theatrebooks; 305 Madison Ave, Suite 1146;
New York, NY 10165; (212) 687-4185 or toll-free 1-800-800-8671,
FAX (207) 359-5532

1991. 300 pp, $16.95 (plus $3.00 postage and handling) paper. This directory contains the addresses and phone numbers of more than 3500 theatres across the country; it includes a cross-reference to specialty theatres (e.g., Dinner Theatres & Showboats, Military Theatres).

The Playwright's Companion, Mollie Ann Meserve, ed
Feedback Theatrebooks; 305 Madison Ave, Suite 1146;
New York, NY 10165; (212) 687-4185 or toll-free 1-800-800-8671,
FAX (207) 359-5532

1996. 416 pp, $20.95 (plus $3.00 postage and handling) paper. This annual guide for playwrights publishes submission guidelines for more than 1500 theatres, contests, publishers and special programs. The *Companion* includes useful tips on query letters, synopses, resumes and submission etiquette, as well as a list of state arts councils, agents, and playwriting programs in colleges and universities. The 1997 edition is due out in December 1996.

Poets & Writers Magazine
Poets & Writers; 72 Spring St; New York, NY 10012; (212) 226-3586,
FAX 226-3963; E-mail pwsubs@aol.com

1-year subscription (6 issues) $19.95, 2 years $38; single issue $3.95. Though primarily aimed at writers of poetry and fiction, this newsletter does include some announcements of grants and awards as well as other opportunities open to theatre writers.

Professional Playscript Format Guidelines and Sample

Feedback Theatrebooks; 305 Madison Ave, Suite 1146; New York, NY 10165; (212) 687-4185 or toll-free 1-800-800-8671, FAX (207) 359-5532

1991. 28 pp, $4.95 (plus $1.75 postage and handling) paper. This booklet provides detailed instructions for laying out a script in a professional manner.

Songwriter's Market, Cindy Laufenberg, ed

Writer's Digest Books; 1507 Dana Ave; Cincinnati, OH 45207; (513) 531-2690, FAX 531-7107; E-mail wdigest@aol.com

1995. 523 pp, $22.99 (plus $3 shipping and handling) cloth. This annually updated directory, which lists contact information for more than 2200 song markets, includes a section on musical theatre. It also lists clubs, associations, contests and workshops of interest to songwriters. The 1997 edition is due out in September 1996.

Stage Directions Magazine

SMW Communications; Box 41202; Raleigh, NC 27629; (919) 872-7888,
FAX 872-6888; E-mail stagedin@aol.com;
Web http://www.enews.com/magazines/stage

1-year subscription $26 (10 issues), 2 years $48; single issue $3.50. This magazine provides information on royalty issues, play publishing, new play festivals and workshops/seminars for playwrights. A special Season Planner issue each November/December contains a directory of royalty houses.

Theatre Directory 1996-97

Theatre Communications Group; 355 Lexington Ave; New York, NY 10017-0217; (212) 697-5230, FAX 983-4847; E-mail custserv@tcg.org

1996. 96 pp, $5.95 (plus $3 postage and handling for 1 book, $1 for each additional book) paper. TCG's annually updated directory provides complete contact information for more than 300 nonprofit professional theatres—including new TCG Constituent and Associate theatres that join after this *Sourcebook* is published—and more than 50 arts resource organizations.

Theatre Profiles 12

Theatre Communications Group; 355 Lexington Ave; New York, NY 10017-0217; (212) 697-5230, FAX 983-4847; E-mail custserv@tcg.org

1996. 240 pp, $22.95 (plus $3 postage and handling for 1 book, $1 for each additional book) paper. Useful for finding out about this country's nonprofit professional theatres, the 12th volume of this biennial series contains artistic profiles, production photographs, financial information and repertoire information for the 1993–95 seasons of more than 250 theatres.

U.S. Copyright Office publications
Register of Copyrights; Library of Congress; Washington, DC 20559;
(202) 707-9100 for orders only (machine); 707-3000 for questions and advice

Call and ask for available free circulars, which include No. 1, "Copyright Basics."
If you write for information instead, expect to wait a long time for a response.

The Writer
120 Boylston St; Boston, MA 02116-4615; (617) 423-3157

1-year subscription (12 issues) $28, 2 years $52, 3 years $75. This monthly
magazine announces contests in a "Prize Offers" column, and publishes a special
"Where to Sell Manuscripts" section, which includes lists of play publishers, in
the September issue.

A Writer's Guide to Copyright
Poets & Writers; 72 Spring St; New York, NY 10012; (212) 226-3586,
FAX 226-3963; E-mail pwsubs@aol.com

1990. 63 pp, $10 (plus $3.90 postage and handling plus sales tax where
applicable) paper. This guide contains simply and clearly written information on
copyright laws, authors' rights and the functions of the Copyright Office; it is
illustrated with sample forms.

Writer's Market
Kirsten Holm, ed; Writer's Digest Books; 1507 Dana Ave; Cincinnati, OH 45207;
(513) 531-2690, FAX 531-7107; E-mail wdigest@aol.com

1995. 1008 pp, $26.99 (plus $3 postage and handling plus sales tax where
applicable) cloth. This annually updated directory lists 4000 places to sell what
you write. It includes many opportunities for playwrights and screenwriters. The
1997 edition, which will also be available on CD-ROM is due out in September
1996.

Writers' Resources
Poets & Writers; 72 Spring St; New York, NY 10012; (212) 226-3586,
FAX 226-3963; E-mail pwsubs@aol.com

Series of guides. Each $8 (plus $3.90 postage and handling) paper. These 9
"literary address books" covering the entire U.S. list resources available to the
writer in different areas of the country (Deep South, Mid-Atlantic, Mid-South,
Midwest, New England, Northwest, Southwest, Pacific and Northwest, and Great
Plains). Included are arts councils, bookstores, conferences, grants, literary
agencies, magazines, readings, support groups, typists, workshops and more. For
complete information, call, write or e-mail for Poets & Writers' catalogue.

Submission Calendar

September 1996–August 1997

Included here are all *specified* deadlines contained in Production, Prizes, Publication, Development, Fellowships and Grants, Colonies and Residencies, and Membership and Service Organizations. Please note that suggested submission dates for theatres listed in Production are not included. There are always important deadlines that are not available at press time and so cannot be included here. The "Opportunities" column of *American Theatre* is one place to look for these.

September 1996

1   Cleveland Public Theatre New Plays Festival   *23*
1   Dorland Mountain Arts Colony (1st deadline)   *212*
1   Katherine and Lee Chilcote Award   *102*
1   Lee Korf Awards   *105*
1   Millay Colony for the Arts (1st deadline)   *217*
1   National Hispanic Playwriting Contest   *111*
1   NEH Collaborative Research grant   *191*
1   Villa Montalvo Residency Program (1st deadline)   *221*

1   Waldo and Grace Bonderman Competition for Young
       Audiences   *125*
2   Fund for Artist at International Festivals and Exhibitions (1st
       deadline)   *180*
10 Playwrights Forum (1st deadline)   *162*
15 MacDowell Colony (1st deadline)   *216*
15 New Dramatists membership   *245*
15 New Women Playwright's Contest   *113*
15 Virginia Center residencies (1st deadline)   *221*
16 Jerome Fellowships   *192*
16 Many Voices Multicultural Collaboration Grants   *192*
16 Many Voices Residency Awards   *192*
20 Susan Smith Blackburn Prize   *120*
20 Wordsmiths   *170*
29 TCG Residency Program grants (application)   *194*
30 Dayton Playhouse FutureFest   *94*
30 Hawthornden Castle Retreat for Writers   *213*
30 Lamia Ink! (1st deadline)   *137*
30 Love Creek Short Play Festival   *106*
30 National Play Award   *111*
30 Paul Green Playwrights Prize   *114*
30 Puerto Rican Traveling Theatre Workshop   *164*
30 Theater at Lime Kiln Playwriting Contest   *121*

Contact for exact deadline during this month:
Douglass Center Workshops (1st deadline)   152
New Play Commissions in Jewish Theatre   191

October 1996 _____

1   ASCAP Musical Theatre Workshop   *147*
1   Centrum Residency Program   *211*
1   Hedgebrook (1st deadline)   *214*
1   John Guggenheim Fellowships   *185*
1   Men's Stories Short Play Festival   *7*
1   National Children's Theatre Festival   *111*
1   New York Mills Arts Retreat (1st deadline)   *218*
1   Southern Appalachian Playwrights' Conference   *166*
1   Ucross Foundation Residency Program (1st deadline)   *220*
1   White-Willis Contest   *126*
12 Letras de Oro Competition   *105*
15 Bunting Fellowship Program   *182*

November 1996 ─────────────

December 1996 ─────────────

1   LEND (Lesbian Exchange of New Drama) International
        Lesbian Playwright Exchange Program   *241*
1   National Playwrights Conference   *158*
1   National Ten-Minute Play Contest   *112*
1   Playwrights Week   *164*
1   Red Octopus Theatre Workshop   *164*
6   NEH Humanities Projects in Media   *190*
15   Dorothy Silver Competition   *94*
15   Imagewrighters/New Play Development Program (1st
        deadline)   *19*
15   James Thurber residency   *215*
15   Morton R. Sarett Competition   *109*
15   PlayLabs   *161*
15   Playwrights' Theater of Denton Competition   *116*
15   Sundance Playwrights Laboratory   *167*
15   Tennessee Williams One-Act Competition   *121*
15   Thurber Writer-in-Residence   *215*
20   PEN–Book-of-the-Month Club Translation Prize   *115*
20   Renato Poggioli Award   *116*
20   Wordsmiths   *170*
30   Lamia Ink! (2nd deadline)   *137*
31   Alcazar Scripts in Progress   *147*
31   Alden B. Dow Creativity Center   *209*
31   Apostle Islands National Lakeshore   *210*
31   Artists-in-Berlin Programme   *180*
31   Biennial Promising Playwright Award   *90*
31   Harold Morton Landon Translation Award   *99*
31   PEN Center USA West Awards   *115*
31   Perishable Theatre Women's Playwriting Festival   *115*
31   Robert J. Pickering Award   *117*
31   Warehouse Theatre One-Act Competition   *125*
31   West Coast Ensemble Full-Length Play Competition   *125*
31   Women's Repertory Project   *167*

Contact for exact deadline during this month:
Anna Zornio Children's Theatre Award   *89*

January 1997 ────────────────────

1   Dale Wasserman Drama Award   *93*
1   Kumu Kahua Contest   *104*

1   Midwest Radio Theatre Workshop (scholarships)   *157*
1   Mill Mountain Theatre Competition   *109*
1   Oglebay Institute Towngate Theatre Contest   *114*
10 Playwrights Forum (2nd deadline)   *162*
15 Free Reading Series and Development Workshop   *153*
15 Fund for Artist at International Festivals and Exhibitions (2nd deadline)   *180*
15 Jewel Box Theatre Playwrighting Award   *101*
15 MacDowell Colony (2nd deadline)   *216*
15 Poems & Plays' Tennessee Chapbook Prize   *141*
15 Ragdale Foundation residencies (1st deadline)   *218*
15 Reva Shiner Contest   *116*
15 Source Theatre Competition   *119*
15 Summerfield G. Roberts Award   *120*
15 TADA! Spring Staged Reading Series/New Play Project   *121*
15 Tomorrow's Playwrights   *71*
15 Virginia Center residencies (2nd deadline)   *221*
15 Voice and Vision Retreat for Women   *169*
15 Washington Theatre Festival   *70*
15 Yaddo residencies (1st deadline)   *222*
16 McKnight Fellowships   *193*
17 NYFA Sponsorship Program (2nd deadline)   *159*
24 Dobie-Paisano Fellowship   *183*
27 University of Louisville Award for Music Composition   *123*
31 Baker's Plays High School Contest   *90*
31 David James Ellis Award   *93*
31 Dubuque Fine Arts Players One-Act Contest   *96*
31 Hambidge Center residencies   *213*
31 James D. Phelan Award   *101*
31 LEND (Lesbian Exchange of New Drama) Dyke Drama Award   *241*
31 Margaret Bartle Playwriting Award   *107*
31 McLaren Comedy Playwriting Competition   *108*
31 PlayWorks Festival   *162*
31 Sam Edwards Deaf Playwrights Competition   *117*
31 Short Grain Contest   *118*
31 Texas Playwrights Festival   *166*

Contact for exact deadline during this month:
Arts International Inroads   *180*
Douglass Center Workshops (2nd deadline)   *152*
Scholastic Writing Awards   *117*

February 1997 ⎯⎯⎯⎯⎯⎯⎯⎯⎯⎯⎯⎯

1	Asian Cultural Council Japan-U.S. Program	*181*
1	Asian Cultural Council Residency Program in Asia	*181*
1	Bay Area Playwrights Festival	*148*
1	Blue Mountain Center	*210*
1	Camargo Foundation residencies	*211*
1	Fine Arts Work Center in Provincetown	*213*
1	Lois and Richard Rosenthal Prize	*106*
1	Millay Colony for the Arts (2nd deadline)	*217*
1	Mount Sequoyah New Play Retreat	*157*
1	One World Premiere	*28*
1	Owen Kelly Adopt-a-Playwright Program	*28*
1	Shenandoah International Retreat	*166*
1	TheatreVirginia New Voices for the Theatre	*78*
1	Vermont Playwrights Award	*124*
2	Texas Young Playwrights Festival	*19*
3	McKnight Advancement Grants	*192*
15	Djerassi Resident Artists Program	*212*
15	Drama League New Directors–New Works Series	*151*
15	Isle Royale National Park Artist-in-Residence	*215*
15	Jane Chambers Playwriting Award	*101*
15	Southern Playwrights Competition	*120*
15	Ventana Publications Award	*145*
15	White Bird Contest	*126*
15	Wichita State University Contest	*126*
28	Artist Trust Grants for Artist Projects	*179*
28	FEAT Competition	*97*
28	Little Theatre of Alexandria One-Act Competition	*105*

Contact for exact deadline during this month:
Atlanta Mayor's Fellowships   *181*
Marilyn Bianchi Kids' Playwriting Festival   *28*

March 1997 ⎯⎯⎯⎯⎯⎯⎯⎯⎯⎯⎯⎯⎯

1	Dorland Mountain Arts Colony (2nd deadline)	*212*
1	Nantucket Short Play Competition	*110*
1	National Music Theater Conference	*158*
1	Plays-in-Progress September Festival	*161*

Contact for exact deadline during this month:

April 1997 _____

Contact for exact deadline during this month:
Annual Blank Theatre Company Young Playwrights Festival   *89*
Very Special Arts Young Playwrights Program   *124*

May 1997

31   L. Arnold Weissberger Competition   *104*
31   Writer's Digest Writing Competition   *127*

Contact for exact deadline during this month:
Douglass Center Workshops (3rd deadline)   *152*
NEA Fellowships for Translators   *190*

June 1997

1   Chesterfield Film Company Project   *150*
1   Chicago Dramatists Workshop Resident Playwrights
      Program   *233*
1   George R. Kernodle Contest   *98*
1   HRC's Annual Contest   *100*
1   Jackie White Children's Playwriting Contest   *100*
1   New Christian Plays Award   *112*
1   New England New Play Competition   *112*
1   NPT Screenplay/Playwriting Festival   *113*
1   Playwrights' Project membership   *251*
1   Ragdale Foundation residencies (2nd deadline)   *218*
1   SETC New Play Project   *119*
2   ASF Translation Prize   *90*
14   Meet the Composer Commissioning Grant   *188*
15   Meet the Composer Residencies (application)   *188*
15   Urban Stages Award   *124*
30   Mary Flagler Cary Commissioning Program   *186*
30   West Coast Ensemble Musical Stairs   *125*

Contact for exact deadline during this month:
Headlands Center for the Arts   *214*
Sundance Institute Film Program (2nd deadline)   *167*

July 1997

1   Altos de Chavon residencies   *209*
1   Henrico Theatre Company One-Act Competition   *100*
1   Maxim Mazumdar Competition   *107*
1   Plays-in-Progress May Festival   *161*
15   James H. Wilson Award   *94*

August 1997 ──────────────

Special Interests

Here is a guide to entries which indicate a particular or exclusive interest in certain types of material, or which contain an element of special interest to writers in certain categories. Under Young Audiences and Media, we try to list every entry of interest to writers in these fields. In the case of adaptations, musicals, one-acts, solo pieces and translations, there are numerous theatres willing to consider these types of material; we list here only those theatres and other organizations that give major focus to them. New to this index is a Multicultural category for those organizations expressing general interest in multicultural/multiracial works. Under African-American, Asian-American, Hispanic/Latin-American and Native American Theatre, we have included only those organizations specifically seeking work by or about people from these ethnic groups. Also new to this list is a student category, which refers to college students or students in an affiliated writing program. Young Playwrights is a special interest category only for playwrights 18 or under. We've also added a category for special interest in solo performance, a new category under "types of material."

277

African-American Theatre

Asian-American Theatre

Disabilities: Theatre for, by and about People with Disabilities

Experimental Theatre

Gay and Lesbian Theatre

Hispanic/Latin-American Theatre

Multicultural Theatre

Musical Theatre

Performance Art/Multimedia
(see also Experimental Theatre)

Religious/Spiritual Theatre

Social-Political Theatre

Solo Performance

Student/College Submissions

Young Audiences

Young Playwright Programs

Index

Remember the two alphabetizing principles used throughout the book: First, entries beginning with a person's name are alphabetized by the first name rather than the surname. However, you can find these entries indexed by both names. Hence you will find the Robert Bone Memorial Playwriting Award under R and B, the Jenny McKean Moore Visiting Writer in Washington under J and M and the Helene Wurlitzer Foundation of New Mexico under H and W. Second, regardless of which way "theatre" is spelled in an organization's title, it is alphabetized as if it were spelled "re," not "er."

O

About Theatre Communications Group

Theatre Communications Group is the national organization for the American theatre. Since its founding in 1961, TCG has provided a national forum and communications network for a field that is as aesthetically diverse as it is geographically widespread, developing a unique and comprehensive support system that addresses the concerns of the theatre companies and individual artists that collectively represent our "national theatre."

TCG's mission is to celebrate and inspire excellence in the artistry of theatre in America. To carry out this mission, TCG serves theatre artists and nonprofit professional theatre organizations by: recognizing and encouraging artistic diversity; providing a forum for the open and critical examination of issues, standards and values; fostering interaction among theatre professionals; collecting, analyzing and disseminating information within the profession and to others interested in, and influential to, the health of the field; and serving as the principal advocate for America's nonprofit professional theatre.

TCG's centralized services facilitate the work of thousands of actors, artistic and managing directors, playwrights, literary managers, directors, designers, trustees and administrative personnel, as well as a constituency of more than 300 theatre institutions across the country that present performances to a combined annual attendance of over 20 million people.

Related TCG Publications
Catalogue available upon request

American Theatre
The national, 10-issue-per-year theatre magazine containing news, features and opinion; includes complete texts of 6 plays a year.

Theatre Profiles
The biennial illustrated reference guide to America's nonprofit professional theatres.

Theatre Directory
The annual pocket-sized contact resource of theatres and related organizations.

The Substance of Fire and Other Plays *by Jon Robin Baitz*

Three Hotels: Plays and Monologues *by Jon Robin Baitz*

The Essential Bogosian: Talk Radio, Drinking in America, FunHouse and Men Inside *by Eric Bogosian*

Pounding Nails in the Floor with My Forehead *by Eric Bogosian*

subUrbia *by Eric Bogosian*

The Gospel at Colonus *adapted by Lee Breuer*

Sister Suzie Cinema: Collected Poems and Performances 1976–1986 *by Lee Breuer*

The Open Door *by Peter Brook*

Stories I Ain't Told Nobody Yet *by Jo Carson*

Three Sisters *by Anton Chekhov, translated by Paul Schmidt*

Cloud Nine *by Caryl Churchill*

The Skriker *by Caryl Churchill*

Tales of the Lost Formicans and Other Plays *by Constance Congdon*

The Illusion *by Pierre Corneille, freely adapted by Tony Kushner*

Drinks Before Dinner *by E. L. Doctorow*

Love & Science: Selected Music-Theatre Texts *by Richard Foreman*

Unbalancing Acts *by Richard Foreman*

A Lesson from Aloes *by Athol Fugard*

Blood Knot and Other Plays *by Athol Fugard*

My Children! My Africa! *by Athol Fugard*

The Rug Merchants of Chaos and Other Plays *by Ronald Ribman*

Raised in Captivity *by Nicky Silver*

Company *by Stephen Sondheim and George Furth*

Gypsy *by Stephen Sondheim and Arthur Laurents*

Into the Woods *by Stephen Sondheim and James Lapine*

Pacific Overtures *by Stephen Sondheim and John Weidman*

Passion *by Stephen Sondheim and James Lapine*

Driving Miss Daisy *by Alfred Uhry*

The Baltimore Waltz and Other Plays *by Paula Vogel*

Jelly's Last Jam, *book by George C. Wolfe, lyrics by Susan Birkenhead*

Spunk: Three Tales by Zora Neale Hurston *adapted by George C. Wolfe*

Between Worlds: Contemporary Asian-American Plays
Editor Misha Berson; includes works by Ping Chong, Philip Kan Gotanda, Jessica Hagedorn, David Henry Hwang, Wakako Yamauchi, Laurence Yep.

Coming to Terms: American Plays & the Vietnam War
Includes works by David Rabe, Terrence McNally, Amlin Gray, Tom Cole, Michael Weller, Emily Mann and Stephen Metcalfe. Introduction by James Reston, Jr.

In Their Own Words: Contemporary American Playwrights *interviews by David Savran*

Moon Marked and Touched by Sun: Plays by African-American Women
Editor Sydné Mahone; includes works by Laurie Carlos, Kia Corthron, Thulani Davis, Judith Alexa Jackson, Adrienne Kennedy, Robbie McCauley, Suzan-Lori Parks, Aishah Rahman, Ntozake Shange, Anna Deavere Smith, Danitra Vance.

On New Ground: Contemporary Hispanic-American Plays
Editor M. Elizabeth Osborn; includes works by Lynne Alvarez, Maria Irene Fornes, John Jesurun, Eduardo Machado, José Rivera, Milcha Sanchez-Scott.

Out from Under: Texts by Women Performance Artists
Editor Lenora Champagne; includes works by Laurie Anderson, Laurie Carlos, Lenora Champagne, Karen Finley, Jessica Hagedorn, Holly Hughes, Robbie McCauley, Rachel Rosenthal, Beatrice Roth, Leeny Sack, Fiona Templeton.

Plays of the Holocaust: An International Anthology
Editor Elinor Fuchs; includes works by Nelly Sachs, Peter Barnes, Liliane Atlan, Joshua Sobol, James Schevill, Józef Szajna.

The Way We Live Now: American Plays and the AIDS Crisis
Editor M. Elizabeth Osborn; includes works by William M. Hoffman, Harry Kondoleon, Harvey Fierstein, Susan Sontag, Terrence McNally, Lanford Wilson, David Greenspan, Tony Kushner, Christopher Durang, Paula Vogel. Introduction by Michael Feingold.

TCG Individual Membership

1 s a *Sourcebook* user, you're invited to
come an Individual Member of **Theatre
mmunications Group**—the national orga-
ation for the American theatre and the
blisher of **American Theatre** magazine.
As an Individual Member of TCG, you'll
t inside information about theatre
rformances around the country, as well as
bstantial discounts on tickets to
rformances and publications about the
eatre. Plus, as the primary advocate for
nprofit professional theatre in America,
G will ensure that your voice is heard in
ashington. We invite you to join us today
d receive all of TCG's benefits!

Members Receive These Special Benefits

FREE subscription to *American Theatre*—10 issues...complete playscripts...
rtist profiles...in-depth coverage of contemporary, classical and avant-garde
erformances...4 special issues—including *Season Preview* (October), *Summer
estival Preview* (May) and *Theatre Facts* (April).
iscounts on tickets to performances at more than 230 participating theatres
ationwide.
5% discount on resource materials including *Theatre Profiles, Theatre Directory,
rtSEARCH, PlaySource* and *Dramatists Sourcebook*—all musts for the theatre
rofessional or the serious theatregoer.
FREE catalogue of publications.
% discount on all books from TCG and other select theatre publishers.
ur personalized Charter Membership card.
ustomized TCG Credit Card.
pecial discount for Budget Rent-A-Car and Airborne Express.
p to 60% off regular hotel rate from Hotel Reservations Network.

TCG Individual Membership

As a Member, You Get a FREE Subscription to <u>American Theatre</u> ...

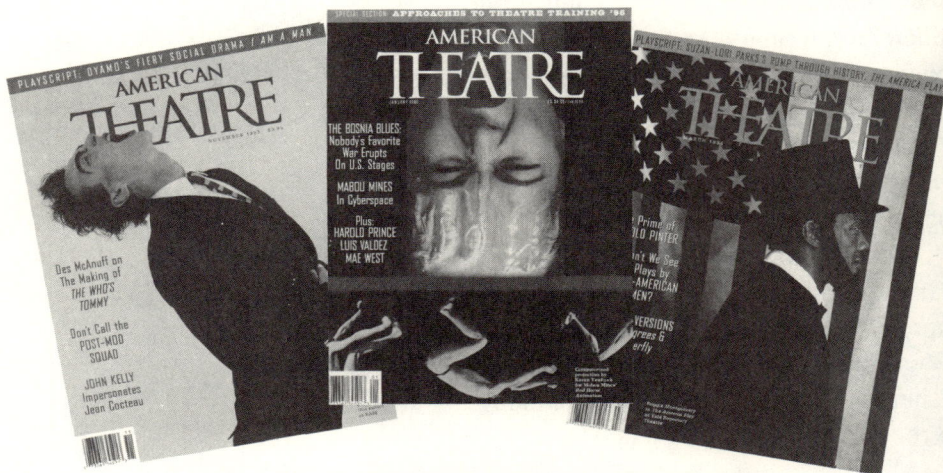

... That's a $49.50 Savings on What You Would Pay at the Newsstand ...

*A*merican Theatre magazine, available 10 issues per year, provides up-to-the-minute coverage of the trends, artists and topics shaping American theatre today. In addition to all the hot articles, you'll also receive six full-length plays – the newest works by prominent playwrights like Edward Albee, Tony Kushner, David Henry Hwang, David Mamet, Maria Irene Fornes and George C. Wolfe. Plus four special issues including "Season Preview" in October, listing the complete performance schedules for more than 200 theatres across the U.S.; "Summer Festival Preview" in May, listing theatre festivals worldwide; "Theatre Facts" in April, providing an invaluable overview of the economic state of the American theatre; and "Approaches to Theatre Training" in January, reporting on the opinions, evolution and theory of theatre education in America.

Join Now and Save

Receive 15% Savings Off
TCG Resources ...

Theatre Profiles provides a historical record of the national theatre movement. Contains comprehensive information on more than 200 theatres nationwide, including production histories.

ArtSEARCH, TCG's twice-monthly national employment bulletin, with more than 6,000 listings of available jobs for the entire spectrum of the arts each year.

- *Dramatists Sourcebook*, the essential annual guide for playwrights, translators, composers, lyricists and librettists, listing hundreds of fellowships, grants and awards, and submission requirements for almost 300 theatres.
- *Theatre Directory*, a handy pocket-sized annual directory providing contact information for more than 300 nonprofit professional theatres and dozens of related organizations.
- *PlaySource*, the national bulletin for new American plays, is published four times a year and contains concise, comprehensive descriptions of hundreds of new plays each year.

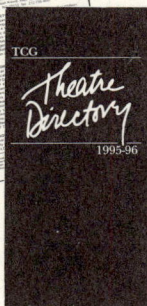

... and 10% Off Other Publications

Save 10% on all TCG publications as well as theatre books published by Nick Hern, Absolute Classics and Ubu Repertory Theater.

Take Advantage Now and Save!
Become a TCG Individual Member and Receive Extraordinary Benefits!

☐ **YES**, I would like a one-year Individual Membership to TCG, which includes a subscription to *American Theatre,* among other extraordinary benefits.

    ☐ Individual Membership ~~$35.00~~ $30.00.

    ☐ Student Membership (enclose copy of ID) $20.

☐ I prefer a two-year membership.

    ☐ Individual Membership ~~$70.00~~ $55.00.

**Not only would I like to become a member,
but I would like to take advantage of my discounts right now!**
(Discount prices are only good if you are a member. If you are not a member,
please use the full price for your order.)

    ☐ Please begin my one-year subscription to *ArtSEARCH.*

Individual   ☐ with E-mail ~~$64.00~~ $54.40   ☐ without E-mail ~~$54.00~~ $45.90

Institutional   ☐ with E-mail ~~$90.00~~ $76.50   ☐ without E-mail ~~$75.00~~ $63.75

    ☐ Please begin my one-year subscription to *PlaySource.*

    ☐ Individual ~~$20.00~~ $17.00

I would like the following resource materials:

☐ *Theatre Profiles 12* ~~$22.95~~ $19.50

☐ *Theatre Directory* ~~$5.95~~ $5.00

    (For the first book purchase, add $3.00 for postage and handling. For every book thereafter, add $1.00.)

☐ **TOTAL ORDER** _____

**To order: Send this form to TCG Order Dept., 355 Lexington Ave., NY, NY
10017-0217 or Call TCG's Order Dept. (212) 697-5230**

☐ Check is enclosed. ☐ Please charge my credit card. ☐ VISA ☐ MC ☐ AMEX

NAME		
ADDRESS		
CITY	STATE	ZIP
* PHONE/FAX/E-MAIL		
CARD #		EXP. DATE:
SIGNATURE		
OCCUPATION/TITLE		

   * all orders must have telephone number

Outside the U.S. add $12 per year (U.S. currency only). Allow 6-8 weeks from receipt of order.